The Essentials of
Technical
Communication

ELIZABETH TEBEAUX
TEXAS A&M UNIVERSITY

SAM DRAGGA
TEXAS TECH UNIVERSITY

New York   Oxford
Oxford University Press
2010

Oxford University Press, Inc., publishes works that further Oxford University's objective of excellence in research, scholarship, and education.

Oxford New York
Auckland Cape Town Dar es Salaam Hong Kong Karachi
Kuala Lumpur Madrid Melbourne Mexico City Nairobi
New Delhi Shanghai Taipei Toronto

With offices in
Argentina Austria Brazil Chile Czech Republic France Greece
Guatemala Hungary Italy Japan Poland Portugal Singapore
South Korea Switzerland Thailand Turkey Ukraine Vietnam

Published by Oxford University Press, Inc.
198 Madison Avenue, New York, New York 10016
http://www.oup.com

Oxford is a registered trademark of Oxford University Press

Library of Congress Cataloging-in-Publication Data

Tebeaux, Elizabeth.
    The essentials of technical communication / Elizabeth Tebeaux, Sam Dragga.
        p. cm.
    Includes index.
    ISBN 978-0-19-538422-2 (pbk.)
    1. Technical writing. 2. Communication of technical information. I.
Dragga, Sam. II. Title.
    T11.T295 2010
    808´.0666—dc22

                                                    2009027607

Printing number: 9 8 7 6 5 4 3

Printed in the United States of America
on acid-free paper

Dedicated to
David H. Stewart
1926–2009

Our first English department head, a scholar fully committed to the teaching of both writing and great literature.

Without his support at the beginning of our careers, neither of us would have enjoyed as productive a life in technical communication as we have had. *The Essentials of Technical Communication* emerges from that support.

Brief **Contents**

Detailed **Contents**

Checklists

Preface

In the workplace, no one wants to read what you write—seriously. Your boss or coworkers may not have the necessary background, the time, or the inclination to wade through your e-mail, memo, or report. We have developed *The Essentials of Technical Communication* with this in mind, as a practical introduction to all aspects of effective professional communication—a handbook to help you get your message across on the job, where time is money and poorly crafted documents can have a host of unwelcome consequences.

As teachers of technical writing with more than 50 years of experience between us, we know that following a few simple guidelines leads to more efficient and effective communications. Our goal in this book is to provide the guidelines you need as you plan, draft, and revise documents. Understanding these guidelines will help you avoid blank-page terror and enable you to write effectively and quickly, both requirements of employees who write for their jobs.

APPROACH

Our rationale is simple: we believe that the effective writer in a work situation must learn and internalize basic concepts of rhetoric and then apply these in developing documents. We've filled this brief book with memorable, concise guidelines. Each chapter in Part One focuses on basic rhetorical principles, and Part Two applies those principles to the planning and writing of particular types of documents.

A brief book has many benefits, but one of the more obvious is that it enables instructors to adapt the book to their own uses. Many teachers want to build on principles by adding their unique approaches, and this book is flexible enough to allow for that possibility.

ORGANIZATION

The book is organized into two parts. Part One (Chapters 1 through 6) lays out essential communication principles:

✦ Chapter 1, Characteristics of Writing at Work, describes technical writing, or writing in the workplace, to show how it differs from academic writing.
✦ Chapter 2, Writing for Your Readers, presents the essential elements of analyzing readers and then choosing content, format, and style as these meet the needs of the intended readers. We embed a discussion of the composing process in this chapter.
✦ Chapter 3, Writing Ethically, discusses the ethics of technical documents. While most professionals have standards of good practice, writers should also follow principles of communication ethics.

+ Chapter 4, Achieving a Readable Style, explains how to write concise, pristine sentences and paragraphs.
+ Chapter 5, Designing Documents, illustrates basic principles for creating accessible and inviting documents. In a world of too much information, readers often miss or ignore important messages not presented in an easy-to-read format.
+ Chapter 6, Creating Illustrations, provides guidelines for developing effective visuals. Graphics software creates practically infinite possibilities for visuals, but effective use requires an understanding of fundamental graphic design principles.

Part Two (Chapters 7 through 12) then applies the principles from Part One to the types of documents most commonly prepared in the workplace:

+ Chapter 7, E-mails, Memoranda, and Letters, presents the basics of correspondence and demonstrates how to ensure that these routine messages are clear, readable, and effective.
+ Chapter 8, Technical Reports, presents the elements of report development along with examples, including an annotated abstract. We provide an annotated formal report in Appendix C and on the book's companion website, **www.oup.com/us/tebeaux.** (We also include links to documentation resources on the website. With the emergence of bibliography and citation software we believe a need no longer exists for extensive instruction in documentation in the text, though we do include a brief guide to the most common documentation systems in Appendix B.)
+ Chapter 9, Proposals and Progress Reports, provides guidelines for developing business proposals and status reports. In this chapter, we use several student examples, as these respond to real situations in a university setting.
+ Chapter 10, Instructions, Procedures, and Policies, describes how to develop clear instructions for a variety of situations.
+ Chapter 11, Oral Reports, provides a short guide to developing and then presenting a concise, effective PowerPoint presentation.
+ Chapter 12, Résumés and Job Applications, describes how to prepare job application documents.

FEATURES

- **Sample Documents:** Although this text is concise, it includes a range of sample documents covering the essential types and styles you're likely to encounter in the workplace. Many of these documents are available for download on the book's companion website, **www.oup.com/us/tebeaux,** along with links to documentation resources.
- **Case Studies:** In Chapters 2, 7, 8, 9, and 10, case studies show how different types of documents function in different situations. These cases contextualize the documents to give you a sense of how and when the techniques we outline can and should be applied.

- **Checklists:** At chapter ends, we have included checklists—lists of questions you can use to ensure that your professional documents achieve your purpose. We hope you find that these are a handy reference tool. They are indexed in the front of the book.
- **Exercises:** Exercises at the end of each chapter guide practice in the techniques outlined in the text. Some of the exercises are designed to be done in class and could be done or discussed in small groups, and others are take-home assignments.
- **Appendices:** Three appendices contain a brief guide to grammar, punctuation, and usage (A), a style sheet for the most commonly used documentation systems (B), and an annotated sample report (C).
- **Companion Website:** The book's companion website at **www.oup.com/us/ tebeaux** offers additional resources for students, including chapter overviews, self-quizzes, downloadable versions of the checklists from the book, helpful links, annotated document pages, and downloadable sample documents, including those from the exercises at chapter ends. The site also includes an Instructor's Manual, featuring downloadable PowerPoint files for use as lecture aids, chapter objectives, teaching strategies, workshop activites, writing projects, worksheets, and discussion questions.
- **Instructor's Manual:** The Instructor's Manual is available in a CD version that includes a Test Bank.

ACKNOWLEDGMENTS

We are grateful to the dedicated book publishers of Oxford University Press for their conscientious efforts to make this book eloquent, elegant, concise, and cogent. We extend our thanks to the reviewers commissioned by Oxford: Susan Aylworth, California State University, Chico; Scott Downing, Kenai Peninsula College, University of Alaska Anchorage; Leslie Fife, Oklahoma State University; Maureen Fitzsimmons, Syracuse University; Elizabeth Holtzinger-Jennings, Pennsylvania State University; Danica Hubbard, College of DuPage; Kevin LaGrandeur, New York Institute of Technology; Lisa McClure, Southern Illinois University, Carbondale; Elizabeth Monske, Northern Michigan University; Brenda Moore, New Jersey Institute of Technology; Marguerite Newcomb, University of Texas at San Antonio; Roxanna Pisiak, Morrisville State College; Liza Potts, Old Dominion University; Denise Stodola, Kettering University; Aaron Toscano, University of North Carolina at Charlotte; and Linda Young, Oregon Institute of Technology.

We also thank the innumerable colleagues and students who have challenged and inspired us in the teaching of technical communication. And, as always, special thanks to Jene and Linda, for their love and support.

PART **ONE**

Principles

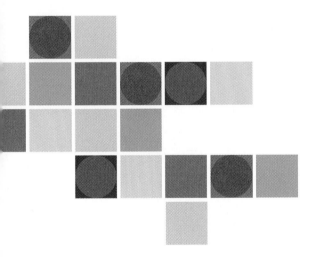

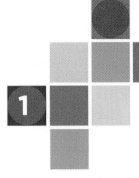

Characteristics of Writing at Work

Technical or business writing describes kinds of writing that occur in a business or work setting. University offices, corporations, research centers, even nonprofit organizations produce large amounts of technical writing, which differs from academic writing in a number of important ways. These differences mean that you cannot write on the job the way you have written in school. Writing in school and writing at work differ because the purposes of each differ. Thus, the products of each contrast sharply.

Technical writing is like any sport: you must first learn the foundational concepts, then understand how these concepts affect the sport before you apply the principles as a participant.

Quick Tips

On the job, keep in mind that **no one wants to read anything you write**. They will read because they need to, not because they want to. They will read because you have information they need to take actions or make decisions. They don't get paid to read: they get paid to take actions and make decisions. The longer it takes them to read your document, the less productive they are. Make sure everything you write is clear, correct, necessary, and polite.

WRITING AT WORK VERSUS WRITING AT SCHOOL

Workplace writing requires that you continue to apply what you have learned about effective paragraph development, correct sentence structure, punctuation, and usage. As an educated adult, your writing should exemplify correctness. Beyond these fundamental principles, business, or technical writing will differ from writing you have done as a student in six ways.

Writing at work:

1. achieves job goals.
2. addresses a variety of readers who have different perspectives.
3. creates excessive paperwork and e-mails that become part of an organization's legal and historical archive.
4. may be read by readers unknown to the writer. Writing can be accessed from an organization's archives over an infinite time.
5. creates legal liability for the writer and the organization.
6. uses a variety of written documents.

Achieving job goals. In school, you write to show your professor that you know the subject matter and to make a good grade. But in the workplace, writing is the major way that people achieve their job goals and document their work. You may talk with people and then record what you have said with writing, such as in a report or an e-mail. You often will write to persuade other employees or clients, to instruct them on how to perform specific tasks, or to inform them about issues important to them. But your main purpose is to help you perform your job within the organization. You can tell people what you have done, but written communications confirm your work. While oral communication lasts only seconds or minutes, written documents have an indefinite life. The writing you do becomes documentation that you have done your work and how you have done it. How well you write will suggest how well you have done your work.

Addressing a variety of readers who have different perspectives. In college, you write your assignments for a single reader, a professor, a specialist in a subject area. But in a work setting, you can expect to write to readers who have varied educational and technical backgrounds, readers who have different roles inside and outside the organization, and readers who may know less about a topic than you do. Your supervisor, for example, may have majored in a field of study very different from yours, or your supervisor's responsibilities may have channeled his or her technical knowledge into other areas. For example, you may report directly to a person whose educational background has been in physical chemistry or electrical engineering but whose responsibilities may now be in personnel management, database administration, quality control, or financial analysis. Many technical people earn MBAs to assist them in management roles.

In a work context, these readers, all of whom have their own job tasks and who come from a variety of educational and cultural backgrounds, will feel no commitment to read what you write unless your messages help them as they do their own work. They will generally not read all documents completely. Each will be interested in how your message affects his/her job goals. What is clear and important to you may not be clear or important to others.

Excessive paperwork and e-mails. In school, you may eventually throw away old completed assignments, but organizations keep both paper and electronic documents on file indefinitely. We live and work in an information age where the quantity of information grows rapidly, where people have more to read than they can ever hope to read. As they see your report or your e-mail subject line, they will immediately ask themselves questions such as "What is this?" "Why should I read it?" "How does it affect me?" "What am I going to have to do?" Without a carefully stated subject line, your readers may delete your message before opening it. If they do open your e-mail, they will want to find the main points and ideas quickly, and they will become impatient if they are unable to find them by glancing at the page. They will not usually read any document completely or bother to respond to it unless, at the beginning, the message indicates that reading your document serves their best interests. How they respond to the first few sentences of your writing will often determine how much more of it they read.

On the job, your readers are not a captive audience, as your teachers have been. They do not have to read what you write. If you want your writing to be read, make your message clear and easy to read; make your message as interesting, relevant, and concise as possible. Because your readers often read selectively, conciseness and clarity are basic ingredients of effective business communication. Mechanical correctness will still be a desirable quality, but correct writing that cannot be read easily and quickly will not be read.

Unknown readers over an infinite time. In school, faculty are your audience. But at work, you will write to a variety of readers, who fall into two main categories: (1) the primary reader(s), to whom the writing is addressed, and (2) the secondary reader(s), who will receive copies of what you write because the information pertains to their job responsibilities. Because e-mail has become a common way of communicating within organizations, you really have no idea who will read what you write, as any message and its attachments may be forwarded. Documents posted online on an organization's website are far from secure from prying eyes and hackers.

Always anticipate unknown readers who may receive copies of your reports or e-mail. Ask yourself this important question: "Does my report or e-mail contain any information that could be misconstrued and affect me or the organization adversely if this communication is read by unknown readers?" While academic writing responds to assignments, applicable only for a specific semester, course, and professor, workplace communications have no specific lifespan. They can be read and then used in ways you never intended or envisioned.

You cannot underestimate the problem that unknown readers present. Nearly everything you write for an organization will remain in the organization's archive indefinitely. Copies of your reports and letters will be placed in files accessible by readers who may not know anything about you or the situation you are writing about. These documents will often be used in assessing your performance and in determining your promotion potential. What you say suggests how well you have done your job. Unknown readers may also use your reports to gain understanding of a work situation they have inherited with a new job assignment. On the job, what you write becomes much more than a knowledge indicator for a grade.

Legal liability for the writer and the organization.   In school, your primary obligation is to avoid plagiarism. But what you write at work can be used against you in lawsuits. Once your sign your name to a report or letter, your signature makes you responsible for the content. Keep in mind that people may use your writing for reasons you never considered, and they make take sentences and even paragraphs out of context for use in situations unrelated to the issue you were addressing in your original document. They can then use what you say to support claims against you and the organization you represent. Because we live in an increasingly litigious society, designing documents that will prevent their misuse should be one of your primary goals.

Using a variety of written documents.   Most academic writing includes essays, essay examinations, research papers, and laboratory reports. All are directed to your teachers. At work, however, employees can expect to write a variety of documents not relevant to academic writing assignments: letters, e-mails, information and procedure memos, proposals, progress reports, project reports, feasibility studies, economic justification reports, policy statements, travel reports, news releases, speeches, training procedures, budget forecasts, employee evaluations, user documentation, and perhaps articles for publication in trade journals. What you write will change with your responsibilities, the kind of job you have, and your position in the organization. How you write each document will depend on the topic being discussed, the situation leading to the document, your readers' needs and perspectives, and your purpose in writing.

The Foundations of Effective Writing at Work

Developing effective documents requires a process involving at least six stages:

1. planning the document
2. determining content
3. arranging ideas
4. drafting
5. revising
6. editing

While each of these stages can be a separate activity, when you write you will more than likely be moving back and forth from one activity to the other, as you develop your document. Following this process will help ensure that content is appropriate as well as correctly and effectively presented.

THE QUALITIES OF GOOD TECHNICAL WRITING

Surveys show that organizations rank writing skills in this order of importance:

1. clarity
2. conciseness
3. readability
4. usability
5. organization
6. correctness—use of standard English

These qualities mean that a document

- makes a good impression when readers first interact with it: document is neat, readable, well-organized, and inviting.
- can be read selectively—for instance, by some users, only the summary; by other users, only the introduction and conclusions; by still other users, the entire report.
- shows a plan that reveals the purpose and value of the document.
- makes sense: ideas appear in a logical sequence immediately evident from document design.
- uses visuals, if necessary, to help readers understand ideas or data.
- conveys an overall impression of authority, thoroughness, soundness, and honest work.
- makes sense to people who were not part of the initial readership.
- makes a positive statement about the writer and the organization.
- enables people who need to use your writing to perform a task to do so.

Beyond all these basic characteristics, good technical writing is free of typographical errors, grammatical slips, and misspelled words. Little flaws distract attention from the writer's main points and call into question the writer's literacy.

As you study, understand, and practice writing for a workplace setting, keep in mind these qualities as well as the differences between the writing you do as an employee and the writing you have done as a student.

EXERCISES

1. Professional associations will often publish articles in their newsletter or magazine or on their official website that describe a day in the life of a prominent individual in the field. Locate such a news article for a professional in your field. How much of this individual's typical day is occupied with speaking and writing? What kinds of letters and reports does this individual compose? How much e-mail does he or she send and receive? Summarize your findings in a one-page memo. Also explain in your memo how your findings compare and contrast with your experience and expectations for this profession.

DEPARTMENT OF HEALTH & HUMAN SERVICES

Food and Drug Administration
Rockville, MD 20857

WARNING LETTER

March 30, 2009

Warren Moseley, Chairman and President
Physicians Total Care, Inc.
5415 S. 125th Avenue
Suite 205
Tulsa, Oklahoma 74146

Products:
  Morphine Sulfate Immediate Release Tablets, 30 mg;
  Hydromorphone Tablets, 2 mg;
  Hydromorphone Hydrochloride Tablets 4 mg

Dear Mr. Moseley:

This letter is written in reference to your firm's marketing of unapproved new drugs in violation
of the Federal Food, Drug, and Cosmetic Act (the Act). Based on the information your firm
submitted to FDA's Drug Registration and Listing System, you distribute the following
prescription drugs:

  • Morphine Sulfate Immediate Release Tablets, 30 mg;
  • Hydromorphone Tablets, 2 mg;
  • Hydromorphone Hydrochloride Tablets 4 mg

As labeled, the above products are drugs within the meaning of section 201(g)(1)(B) and (C) of
the Act [21 U.S.C. §§ 321(g)(1)(B) and (C)] because they are intended for use in the diagnosis,
cure, mitigation, treatment, or prevention of disease and because they are intended to affect the
structure or function of the body. Further, these drug products as distributed by your firm are
"new drugs" within the meaning of section 201(p) of the Act [21 U.S.C. § 321(p)] because they
are not generally recognized as safe and effective for their labeled uses. Under sections 301(d)
and 505(a) of the Act [21 U.S.C. §§ 331(d) and 355(a)], a new drug may not be introduced or
delivered for introduction into interstate commerce unless an application approved by FDA
under either section 505(b) or (j) of the Act [21 U.S.C. § 355(b) or (j)] is in effect for the
product. Based upon our information, there are no FDA-approved applications on file for the
above products. The marketing of these products without an approved application constitutes a
violation of these provisions of the Act.

FIGURE 1-1 Document for Exercise 3

2. Visit the website of a major employer in your field. What kinds of documents do
you find at this site? What do you notice about the writing style or use of illustrations? Do you think you could create documents like these for this employer?
Do you think you could help create better documents? Based on your examination of these documents, what is your impression of this employer?

3. Examine Figure 1-1. If you were the author of this document and were given 15
more minutes to make it better, what changes would you make?

Page 2

Additionally, because the above products are intended for conditions that are not amenable to self-diagnosis and treatment by individuals who are not medical practitioners, adequate directions cannot be written for them so that a layman can use these products safely for their intended uses. Consequently, their labeling fails to bear adequate directions for their intended uses, causing them to be misbranded under section 502(f)(l) of the Act [21 U.S.C. § 352(f)(1)]. Because your products lack required approved applications, they are not exempt under 21 C.F.R. § 201.115 from the requirements of section 502(f)(1) of the Act. The introduction or delivery for introduction into interstate commerce of these products therefore violates sections 301(a) and (d) of the Act [21 U.S.C. §§ 331(a) and (d)].

As described in the guidance entitled "Marketed Unapproved Drugs - Compliance Policy Guide"[1] the Agency may exercise its enforcement discretion and identify a period of time during which the Agency does not intend to initiate an enforcement action against a currently marketed unapproved drug. FDA does not intend to initiate enforcement actions related to the shipment in interstate commerce of your unapproved drug products, Morphine Sulfate Immediate Release Tablets, 30 mg, Hydromorphone Tablets, 2 mg, and Hydromorphone Hydrochloride Tablets, 4 mg, unless they are still being shipped more than 90 days after the date of this letter.

You should be aware that FDA's enforcement discretion will not apply to the following circumstances: (1) if FDA determines that your firm is violating other provisions of the Act; (2) if it appears that your firm, in response to this letter, increases its manufacture or distribution of your unapproved products, Morphine Sulfate Immediate Release Tablets, 30 mg, Hydromorphone Tablets, 2 mg, and Hydromorphone Hydrochloride Tablets, 4 mg, above your usual volume during these periods; or (3) if FDA learns of new information regarding any serious health risk or hazard associated with morphine sulfate, hydromorphone, or hydromorphone hydrochloride drug products.

The violations cited in this letter are not intended to be an all-inclusive statement of violations that exist in connection with your products. You are responsible for investigating and determining the causes of the violations identified above and for preventing their recurrence or the occurrence of other violations. It is your responsibility to assure that your firm complies with all requirements of Federal law and FDA regulations.

You should take prompt action to correct the violations cited in this letter. Failure to promptly correct these violations may result in legal action without further notice, including, without limitation, seizure and injunction. Other Federal agencies may take this Warning Letter into account when considering the award of contracts.

Within fifteen (15) working days of receipt of this letter, please notify this office in writing regarding whether you plan to cease the violative activities described in this letter. If you no longer market the products referenced in this letter, your response should so indicate, including the reasons that, and the date on which, you ceased marketing. Additionally, based on our

---

[1] Marketed Unapproved Drugs—Compliance Policy Guide. Available at
http://www.fda.gov/cder/guidance/6911fnl.pdf

FIGURE 1-1 *continued*

Page 3
_____

information, you do not manufacture the products listed above; therefore, your reply should include the name and address of the manufacturer. If the firm from which you receive these products is not the manufacturer, please include the name of your supplier in addition to the manufacturer.

Your response to this letter should be directed to the attention of Ms. Sakineh Walther, Consumer Safety Officer, at the U.S. Food and Drug Administration, Center for Drug Evaluation and Research, Office of Compliance, WO51 RM 5242, 10903 New Hampshire Avenue, Silver Spring, MD 20993.

Sincerely,

/s/

Deborah M. Autor, Esq.
Director
Office of Compliance
Center for Drug Evaluation and Research
Food and Drug Administration

FIGURE 1-1 *continued*

2

Writing for Your Readers

Before you begin to plan your document, think first about your readers and then your purpose. Every decision you make in developing your document should reflect your audience, their needs, and your purpose.

Avoid becoming absorbed in the ideas and information you plan to include. Never forget that the person or group who will read the document may have a very different view of the content. Your readers cannot climb into your mind and know exactly what you are thinking. When you carefully analyze your readers, you can often design and write your report in a way that helps them understand what's in your mind.

Quick Tips

Remember that in developing any communication, you have three main goals that show the relationship among reader, purpose, and context:

1. You want your readers to understand your meaning exactly in the way you intend.
2. You want your writing to achieve its goal with the designated readers.
3. You want to keep the goodwill of those with whom you communicate.

UNDERSTAND YOUR READERS—
THE HEART OF THE PLANNING PROCESS

To achieve the three goals just listed, you must pursue the following five tasks, both before you begin to write and while you are actually composing your document:

1. Determine as fully as possible who will read what you write.

2. Know what goals you want your writing to achieve.
3. Understand your role in the organization as a writer and how this should be reflected in what you write—the reason you have to write this document.
4. Determine the content by considering your readers' frame of reference and your purpose in writing.
5. Understand the business context in which you are communicating.

In business organizations, particularly large ones, most people have more to read than they can and will read. If you want your letter or report to be read, be sure that important information occurs on the first page of a report and in the first paragraph of an e-mail, memo, or letter and that you answer the following questions your readers will ask:

- What is this?
- Do I have to read it?
- How does it affect me?
- What will I have to do?
- What are the main ideas?

If you answer their questions at the beginning of your document, readers may be willing to read more of your report, e-mail, or letter.

In order to answer these questions in the minds of your readers, you will have to answer three questions yourself about the document you are writing:

- Who will read what I write?
- Who will act on what I write?
- Who else may read what I write?

That is, you will need to know who your readers are and what they will do with your document. Attempt to determine who will act on what you write. In many cases, your primary reader will transmit your document to someone else for action. Perhaps this individual is one of your secondary readers. Or, the person who will be responsible for acting on what you write may be unknown to you.

Determine your readers and their perspectives.   When you consider your readers, determine as much as you can about them.

- How much do your readers know about what you are writing?
- Are your readers experts in this area?

Readers who are technical experts in an area you are writing about have different needs (and often different perspectives) from readers who are not experts.

- Do your readers know anything at all about your topic?
- What are your readers' educational levels?
- What are your readers' cultural backgrounds?

If you work in an organization that does business with readers from other cultures, plan to do background reading on these cultures.

- Will your readers be interested in what you write? If not, how could you present your message to make it appealing?
- What kind of relationship do you have with these readers? What is the readers' attitude toward you, the subject matter you need to communicate, the job you have, and your area within the organization? Do you have credibility with these readers?

When you ask yourself these questions you are trying to determine your readers' perception, which is determined by a host of factors: education, family, geographical and cultural background, job responsibilities, rank in the organization, age, life experiences—just to name a few demographics that define how people see the world. How much your readers know about your topic is critical because it determines what you say and the technical level of your presentation.

- How well do you know your readers?

You may know your readers personally. However, if you know an individual's level in the organization, the responsibilities associated with that level, and the kind of technical expertise your reader has, this information will help you decide what you need to say and how to present your information. Knowing your readers' responsibilities in the organization can be particularly useful in helping you anticipate their attitude—how interested they will be in your subject. Because people tend to read only what is useful to them, try to relate your message to your readers' job. That knowledge can tell you whether the readers will be interested, mildly curious, indifferent, negative, or uninterested. Knowing the readers' attitude toward the topic addressed in your message will help you determine how to present your information.

- Who else is likely to read what you write?

Many times the person to whom you are addressing your report will not be the one to act on it. For that reason, you need to know who else will read your document.

Most reports and letters have distribution lists: the names of those who receive copies. A person on the distribution list may be the person who will ultimately act on what you write. Thus, the needs and perceptions of those who receive copies should be considered.

- Why is each person on the distribution list receiving a copy?
- How much does each person on this list know about your topic?

Sometimes your primary reader may know the situation you are discussing, and the purpose of the report may be to inform others within the organization by going through proper channels.

- What situation led to the need for this document?

Often, you can better understand your reader's perspective if you understand the situation that requires you to write this document. The need for written com-

munications develops from interactions of people involved in a work environment. To be able to select content, level of language (technical or general), and
the amount of explanation needed in a business context, a writer must be careful
to determine the needs of each reader. Closely examining a situation requiring a
written response may even help you determine what you need to tell your readers
and how to present your message.

Determine your purpose.

- Why are you writing?
- What do you want to achieve with your document?

Determining why you are writing—what you want to achieve—is as important
as determining your readers. *Purpose is always related to readers.* And, you may
have more than one purpose. For example, you may be writing to inform readers,
to provide information, to recommend a course of action. In addition, what you
say may serve as documentation—proof of your efforts—to show that you have
provided the information requested. Written messages that document employees'
activities serve a major function in today's business organizations. Without documentation, you may find it difficult to prove that you performed specific tasks.

Understand your role as a writer.

- What is your position in the organization?

As an employee in an organization, you will be hired to perform the duties that
define a particular job. As the individual responsible for performing specific tasks,
you will be communicating with employees above you, below you, and on your
own level in the organization. In writing to individuals in any group, you will communicate, not as you would with a friend or family member, but as the person
responsible for the work associated with that position in the organization. That is,
when you write, you create a personality that should fit the position you hold.

   If you are to have credibility as a writer in an organization, the image that you
project should be appropriate to your position. What you say and how you say it
should reflect your level of responsibility in the organization—the power relationship that exists between you and the reader. The image you project will change,
depending on your readers. You will project the image of a subordinate when you
write to those higher than you in the organization, but you will transmit the image
of the supervisor to those who work directly under you. When you communicate
with others on your own job level, you will convey the image of a colleague. Good
writers have the ability to fit their message to each reader.

Plan the content.

- What ideas should be used to achieve the goals of the message?
- What ideas should be omitted?
- How should your ideas be arranged?

Once you have analyzed your readers and your purpose, you can begin to decide what you want and need to say, then how you will phrase your ideas. Knowing what your readers need to know will help you decide how to arrange your message.

• How do you want your message to sound?

Knowing how your message sounds will always be critical. Note differences in the sound of each message. You should always try to convey a tone that is respectful and commensurate with your position in the organization. How a message is conveyed may often be as important as the content.

Case 2-1 shows how a writer's assessment of audience and purpose change his content and presentation for each reader involved in a routine business situation.

Anticipate the context in which your writing will be received.

• How will your writing be used?

Knowing what will happen to your writing when it is received also helps you know who might read it and what you need to say. For example, once it has reached its primary destination, a document may be quickly skimmed and filed; it may be skimmed and then routed to the person who will be responsible for acting on it; it may be read, copied, and distributed to readers unknown to you; it may be read and used as an agenda item for discussing a particular point; it may be read carefully and later used as a reference. Being able to visualize the context in which it will be read and used can often guide you in deciding not only what to say but also how to organize the information and arrange it on the page.

Case 2-2 shows how consideration of the context helped a writer know how to plan an e-mail.

THE BASIC PARTS OF THE COMPOSING PROCESS

This composing process, integral to your analysis of audience, has six main stages:

1. **analyzing** the situation
2. **choosing/discovering** content
3. **arranging** content
4. **drafting**
5. **revising**
6. **editing** the finished draft

Writing becomes extremely difficult if you try to do all the parts at once. Or (equally difficult) you may try to prepare an outline about the subject or topic first and then try to follow the outline in collecting information. Neither method will produce an effective document. Research has shown that good writers usually follow a standard process—one that will make your writing tasks easier and the results more effective.

Case 2-1: Process Instructions

Bill Ramirez develops and manages training programs for his company. Reading an e-mail from one of the other supervisors, Mark Jaros, Bill finds that a number of employees have been allowed to enroll in a training course for which they do not have qualifications. Unable to talk with Joyce Smith, who enrolls employees for all training programs, Bill sends Joyce the following e-mail. Bill knows that Joyce has been on extended family leave because of one of her children and has just returned to work. Her temporary replacement, Sandra Amaz, was pulled back to her human resources job two weeks before Joyce returned. Bill is polite and concerned but specific in stating his request (Case Document 2-1a).

CASE DOCUMENT 2-1A

Bill's E-mail to Joyce

To: joyce_smith@gyros.net
Sub: Checking Appropriate enrollments for MSW—3

Joyce: Please remove all managers lower than level 2 from the level three managerial skills workshops (MSW—3). We currently have 6-8 people enrolled who don't yet have the service records that qualify them for any of the MSWs. In addition, four people with more than enough time in grade must be enrolled by Friday.

I know you need help in checking lists, as Sandra had to return to HR sooner than we anticipated. But a number of people, not just the four from Jeff's group, have been waiting for this class for months. If we fill existing vacancies from the wait list, we can enroll everybody who needs to be in this session.

Please stop by after lunch today so that we can go over the list of everyone enrolled in all the MSW workshops scheduled to begin in two weeks. Be sure to discuss anyone you are not sure about. I will help you sort this out. A number of department heads are unhappy, but they understand the situation.

Bill then sends an e-mail to Mark Jaron (Case Document 2-1b), who was extrememly unhappy when he found out that his four employees couldn't enroll in the workshop, particularly when he discovered that a number of level 2 employees were enrolled.

CASE DOCUMENT 2-1B

Bill's E-mail to Mark

To: Mark_Jaron@gyros.net
Sub: Checking appropriate enrollments for MSW—3

Thanks for your voice mail. I appreciate your telling me about the problem, and I will have it resolved this afternoon.

Joyce, as you may know, has just returned from extended family leave. She's swamped, as Sandra was pulled back to HR two weeks early because of staff reductions. Joyce and I will be working on the MSW lists this afternoon and will send new enrollment lists to all departments by the end of the day. With our regular team now in place, training schedules/enrollments should be fine.

Bill also decides to send a short e-mail to his supervisor, Marshall Remick, to let him know what has happened (Case Document 2-1c). That way, Bill reasons, Marshall will be prepared if he hears about the problems the training division has had in enrolling people in the wrong classes. Bill wants to protect himself as well as Joyce by explaining the situation to his supervisor.

CASE DOCUMENT 2-1C

Bill's E-mail to Marshall

To: Marshall_Remick@gyros.net
Sub: Checking appropriate enrollments for MSW—3

Marshall: You may hear that we have enrolled the wrong people for some of the MSW workshops. That's true, but the problem will be rectified by the end of today.

Joyce Smith, as you probably recall, has been on extended family leave. Sandra Herzberg, who assumed much of Joyce's job, had to return to HR because of staffing cuts. For two weeks, enrollments were not monitored. Hence the errors.

Joyce and I will be evaluating everyone who has enrolled, and we will (1) notify those who should not have enrolled, and (2) enroll people on the official waiting list. Everyone involved will receive an e-mail. I've already notified Mark.

Case 2-2

Jamie Wheeler, a student assistant in the office of the Graduate Student Council, has been asked by the Dean of Undergraduate Studies to prepare an e-mail to send to all faculty and students. Goal: to announce and encourage faculty and students to participate in student research week. Last year, most people did not even read the e-mail announcement, and participation was abysmal. Read both last year's e-mail (Case Document 2-2a) and Jamie's revision (Case Document 2-2b), keeping in mind that the university's e-mail system limits what she can do with formatting. Can you suggest another revision that will encourage students to read the e-mail and understand what it says?

CASE DOCUMENT 2-2A

Last year's E-mail

To: All students
SUBJ: 11th Annual Student Research Week

Student Research Week is an opportunity for the research community of Texas A&M to join together and showcase the breadth and quality of student research being conducted on our campus. Graduate Student Council (GSC) sponsors the annual event as a way to promote the importance of research in our community.

Registration is now open for the 11th Annual Student Research Week! Register now at http://srw.tamu.edu/. Events take place from March 24, 2008 through March 28, 2008. Competition days will be held on Tuesday, March 25-Thursday, March 27.

Faculty and Staff are encouraged to participate in SRW as a judge. We need a total of 240 in-field and out-of-field judges. To be an in-field judge for graduate sessions, you need a terminal degree in the specific area desired to judge; in-field judges for undergraduate sessions need to have a Master's degree or equivalent in the designated field; to be an out-of-field judge, a Bachelor's degree or higher is required. For more information on judging, visit http://srw.tamu.edu/pages/judging.htm.

Students at both the graduate and undergraduate level are encouraged to present their research. Any student who is the primary author of a research project, class paper or project may submit an abstract to be considered for the oral or poster competition. You can present work previously presented at a conference or for a class or TAMU/non-TAMU summer research project. Abstracts* will be accepted on a first-come, first serve basis until the March 1, 2008 deadline or until registration is full, whichever comes first. Prizes included first, second and third place in each taxonomy group. First place winners will receive a cash prize totaling $300.00. Visit http://srw.tamu.edu/pages/students.htm for more information about the competition and awards.

*Oral presenters will NOT have to upload their entire presentation during registration. In order to submit your registration, please upload the title page of your presentation with the presentation title and presenter's name in PowerPoint 2003. Presentation uploading will be done the week of March 17-21, 2008.

Don't have research to present? Participate in the Research Report Card program (RRCP). RRCP is open to all TAMU undergraduate and graduate students. The RRCP allows students to win prizes for attending events and learning about the research happening on campus during. To register for the RRCP, visit http://srw.tamu.edu and visit http://srw.tamu.edu/pages/RRcard.htm to learn more about the program.

Faculty, Staff, and Graduate Students who would like to offer extra credit or require attendance at an event are supported by the SRW committee to do so. We welcome any participation. Please encourage your students to attend. We offer faculty notification for participation in the Research Report Card program, and will be available at all events to stamp forms for students needing verification of attendance. For a complete list of the 2008 Student Research Week panels and opening & closing sessions visit http://srw.tamu.edu/pages/calendar.htm.

We look forward to connecting with you at the 11th Annual Student Research Week!

SRW 2008 Planning Committee

CASE DOCUMENT 2-2B

Jamie's E-mail

TO: University e-mail-all students
SUBJ: Showcase Your Research & Win Prizes
WHAT: 12th Annual Student Research Week at Texas A&M
WHEN: March 24-28, 2009
WHO: Graduate & Undergraduate Students, Faculty, and Staff
WHY: Present, learn about, and judge student research at TAMU!
WHERE: Rudder Complex
COMPETITION: Register by March 1, 2009 to Present Original Student
Research

*Schedule of events @ http://srw.tamu.edu/pages/calendar.htm

Student Research Week (SRW) is an annual showcase of the breadth and quality of research conducted at Texas A&M University. Graduate Student Council (GSC) sponsors the event and encourages student researchers to present their work, faculty and staff to participate as judges, and all Aggies to come and see the multitude of interesting research being done by fellow Ags!

STUDENTS:
–Graduate & Undergraduate Students
–Research projects, class paper/project, TAMU/non-TAMU summer research
–Oral or poster competition
–Submit ABSTRACT for consideration
–March 1, 2009 DEADLINE
–Cash Prizes!
–More Info @ http://srw.tamu.edu/pages/students.htm

FACULTY & STAFF:
–240 in-field & out-of-field JUDGES NEEDED
–Offer extra credit for attendance with the RESEARCH REPORT CARD
 described below!
–More Info @ http://srw.tamu.edu/pages/judging.htm

COME & WIN!
–ALL TAMU STUDENTS: Register for a RESEARCH REPORT CARD
–Attend presentations to WIN PRIZES!
–Ask your professors about EXTRA CREDIT!
–More Info @ http://srw.tamu.edu/pages/RRcard.htm

We look forward to connecting with you at the 12th Annual Student Research Week!

Analyzing the writing situation—purpose, readers, and context. The first step in composing is the most critical to the success of what you write. In this step, you need to know *why* you are writing: what you are attempting to achieve with your document, what situation or problem has led to the necessity of your writing this document. Then, you need to consider your readers—those who will or may read your document.

Every technical or workplace document responds to a specific situation. Each document has a targeted audience. Writing responds to both—the situation and the readers in that situation. Writing is not simply compiling information about a subject.

Choosing/discovering content. The content you select should always be guided by *why* you are writing, *what* your reader needs, and *how* your reader perceives the subject.

As you search for information, remember your purpose as what you want your reader to know and do with what you write. In the workplace, writing solves problems and enables the organization to operate.

After you have considered your purpose and begun to research your topic, begin to list ideas that you can use to develop your topic. Based on these ideas, ask yourself what additional information you will need to locate. Don't like what you wrote? Delete it. You may want to begin your document by writing your purpose at the beginning to help you stay on track.

Arranging content. As you collect and begin summarizing information and data, you will begin to consider how to arrange the material. In what order should you present your content? Memos, for example, need to begin with the news or essential information they are presenting to ensure that readers at least read what's most important before they start skimming the document or stop reading it altogether. Most reports begin with an introduction, followed by a summary of the report. Alternately, the introduction may be combined with a summary of the report. The discussion section, in which you present the supporting information, follows. Most reports follow some version of this plan. Many business organizations have rules on how reports distributed to clients outside the firm should be written.

A useful way to arrange content is to place material in "stacks" which can be used as a resource when you begin writing. If you know what arrangement you want/are required to use, sort material so that you can easily find it when you begin drafting specific segments of your document. You can also sort material electronically: create folders of information on each segment of your report. Then arrange material within each folder before you begin drafting. This method allows you to track material you use and insert appropriate citations when you use material from a specific source.

If you use electronic articles from your library's database, you can insert these articles into files that can be accessed later when you begin to draft your document.

Drafting. Drafting is a highly individual activity. Probably no two writers do it exactly alike. Most writers work on a document in a start/stop fashion. When you begin your draft, open your file and save it with the name of your report. Then, begin typing ideas or sections. (You may wish to move/paste material you listed, arranged, and then developed in Step 2.) You may wish to type the names of your main segments, boldface those, and insert information beneath the appropriate segment. This method helps you keep track of the information that you are using to develop your draft. Note that some of the ideas in your list of ideas become headings. Some may be combined with other ideas. Note that you can arrange, delete, and add ideas as you need to.

As you continue to draft, you will revise. But during the drafting stage you should revise only for meaning. Try to avoid worrying about sentences that don't sound "quite right." If the sentence you write captures what you want to say, even clumsily, don't stop to revise. You can "clean up" these sentences later. Don't attempt to correct these mechanical problems unless you feel you can do so without slowing your ability to transfer your ideas from your mind to the screen. Focus on presenting your material to your readers: then you can begin a formal revision process once you believe you have your basic ideas on the screen or page.

Revising. During the formal revision process you will want to revise from different perspectives. You may want to revise several times and focus on different issues:

- **Logic.** Does your presentation make sense? Try reading paragraphs aloud that seem to you to be "scrambled." Hearing what you have written often tells you if/where problems in logic are occurring. Is the order in which your material is written appropriate for the purpose and for your readers?
- **Completeness.** Is your presentation complete, in terms of the purpose of your document and your readers' needs and requirements? Is your information correct? Does your document contain all requested information?
- **Style.** Examine each paragraph and each sentence. Are your paragraphs really paragraphs? Do they have topic sentences? Do all the sentences in the paragraph pertain to the meaning you are building in the paragraph? Start each paragraph with a topic sentence. Eliminate or recast sentences that provide little support for the topic sentence. Today's readers usually dislike wordy, dense, complicated sentences. Make your sentences clear, concise, and precise to encourage your readers to follow your ideas. Also watch the length of your paragraphs. Long paragraphs discourage readers and tend to become incoherent.
- **Visuals.** Do you need visuals—photos, graphs, drawings, pictorial illustrations—to help your reader "see" and remember key ideas? Visuals combined with text often provide the best means of communicating with your readers.
- **Document design.** When you began drafting, if you used headings or names of report segments to help you organize your draft, you began at that point to design your document. Document design refers to the way information is arranged and displayed on the page. The importance of how information looks

on the page, cannot be stressed enough. If you want your writing to be read, design the page so that information is inviting and accessible.

Editing. Editing is a critical writing requirement. In complex reports, you will want to perform several "edits": one for mechanics—spelling, usage, punctuation, and sentence structure.

Another edit focuses on citing sources: check your documentation to be sure that you give credit or sources of all information you have used. Be sure that when you use illustrations and ideas from other sources you give credit to the source.

A third edit focuses on the document as a whole. How does it look? How does it sound? Is the important information easy to locate? Is the document complete?

In short, don't try to check for every error at once, in one reading. Editing requires care, objective reading, and diligence.

For an example of how the composing process works when it is applied to a routine business document, read Case 2-3 and track the development of this memorandum. Note how the message looks after Bob's initial revision of his draft.

Case 2-3

Bob Johnson, an engineering project manager with a local civil engineering firm, has been named local arrangement chair of the forthcoming construction engineering conference. Two months before the conference, Bob needs to send a memo to everyone in his group to let them know what responsibilities they will have at the conference. While all employees know about the conference, Bob has informed his group via e-mail that each office group will have responsibilities throughout the conference. Bob wants the memo to inform his group specifically about what they will need to do.

Bob uses the planning stage of developing the memo to decide what topics he wants to present to his group. He will send this memo as an e-mail attachment. As he plans his memo, Bob types the following list of topics:

Location, date, time info of conference
Specific duties of the SE Group
General instructions
Conference schedule
Other information SE Group needs to know

As he develops the memo, he inserts information beneath each heading and then revises. His first draft looks like this (Case Document 2-3a):

CASE DOCUMENT 2-3A

Bob's first draft

Conference Location, Date, time info Time

CE conference—October 28-29—Lancaster Center. Our group's responsibility—serve as greeters, help prevent glitches. Over 150 engineers have already registered, and the cut-off date is still three weeks away. We need to be sure we are organized. Conference may be larger than last year. We want to do our part to ensure the success of the meeting. Help all attendees have a good conference. Be proactive in anticipating problems with people getting where they need to be:

Please be at the Lancaster Center at the following times:

Oct. 28: noon-end of the day
Oct. 29: 7:00-end of the conference. Last session begins at 3:30
Refreshments will be available during break periods. Water in all rooms.

Our Responsibilities
Helping visitors locate the section meetings, answer any questions, deal with any hotel reservation glitches, transportation problems, questions about restaurants. Remain available until after the dinner on Oct. 28. Oct. 29: On site throughout the day.

General Instructions Information
- Number expected to register and attend: 200+.
- Visitors will arrive at the hotel by mid-morning on the 28th. Some will come the evening before. [Contact Ralph to see if we need to be at the hotel on Oct. 27 after 5:00? Check information folder for sponsor letters.]
- Be available no later than noon on 28th. If possible, arrive at the Lancaster Center earlier than that. Dress is business casual.
- If those flying in arrive late, contract Jim or Joanna via their cell phones to ensure that registrations are not cancelled. Jim: 228-3459; Joanna: 322-1875.

Conference Schedule

Oct. 28
Light lunch: noon-1:15
Opening session: 1:30-3:00
Second session: 3:30-5:00 [check sponsors for all sessions. These have to be correct!!!! Check with central planning group.]
Dinner: 6:30—Holcomb Room, 2nd floor of the LC

Oct. 29
Breakfast: Room 104 of the LC, 7:00-8:00 [sponsor? Be sure we have a complete list with all names spelled correctly. Contact info for each.]
Third session: 8:30-10:00 [session sponsor?]
Closing Session: 10:30-noon [sponsor?]
Lunch: noon

Displays
Nine vendors will display software all day the 29th in room 106. Consultants will be on hand to discuss compatibility issues. Be available to help vendors set up.

Conference Materials
Will be available at the check-in desk at the front door
Each folder will contain brochures about new products and a schedule. Add a list of restaurants downtown?

Other
Breakout rooms will be available for the second part of the sessions.
Phone and faxes are available in Room 110 8:00-5:00.

Bob's revision follows (Case Document 2-3b). How could he have improved it with the following goals in mind? He wants his employees to

- report on time,
- know what they should do when they arrive,
- have cell phone numbers for quick contact purposes, and
- know whom to contact throughout the conference.

Does the memo enable Bob's employees to achieve those goals?

CASE DOCUMENT 2-3B

Bob's revision

TO: SE Group   **DATE**: October 1, 2008
FROM: Bob Johnson
SUBJECT: Preparations for the Construction Engineering Conference

Conference Location, Date, Time

The construction engineering conference is scheduled October 28-29 at the Lancaster Center. Our group will serve as greeters. Over 150 engineers have already registered, and the cut-off date is still three weeks away. We need to be sure we are organized to help visitors as they arrive.
Please be at the Lancaster Center at the following times:

Oct. 28:   noon-end of the day
Oct. 29:   7:00-end of the conference. Last session begins at 3:30

SE Group—Specific Duties

We will be responsible for helping visitors locate the section meetings, answer any questions, deal with any hotel reservation and transportation glitches, and remain available until after the dinner on Oct. 28. Oct. 29—We need to be on site throughout the day and help guests who need to leave promptly at the close of the morning session.

General Information

- Number expected to register and attend: 200+
- Visitors will arrive at the hotel by mid-morning on the 28th. Some will come the evening before.
- Be available no later than noon. If possible, arrive at the Lancaster Center earlier than that.
- If those flying in arrive late, contract Jim or Joanna via their cell phones to ensure that registrations are not cancelled. Jim: 228-3459; Joanna: 322-1875.

Conference Schedule

Oct. 28

Noon-1:15	Lite lunch—Mellon Room (Sponsor: KLM Ltd.)
1:30-3:30	Room 105, Opening session
3:30-5:00	Room 105, Second session (Sponsor: Bickle and Lauren)
6:30	Buffet in Holcomb Room, 2nd floor of the LC

Oct. 29

7:00-8:00	Breakfast: Room 104 of the LC
8:30-10:00	Room 105, Third session (Sponsor: MERK Inc.)
10:30-noon	Room 105 Closing Session (Sponsor: Malcolm, Fisher, & Peabody)
Lunch: noon	Mellon Room

Software Displays

Nine vendors will display software all day the 29th in room 106. Consultants will be on hand to discuss compatibility issues. Be available to help vendors with set-up.

Conference Materials
- Available at the check-in desk at the front door
- Registration folder with name tags: will contain brochures about new products and a schedule of activities. List of restaurants in town for those who are staying for the weekend.

Other Information
- Phone and faxes are available in room 110 8:00-5:00.
- Refreshments will be available during break periods. Bottled water in all rooms.

Call me on my cell phone if anything comes up that isn't covered here.

PLANNING AND REVISION CHECKLIST ✔

Analyzing the Situation
☐ What is your subject or topic?
☐ What is the purpose of the document?
☐ Who are your readers, known and potential?
☐ Why are you writing? Why is this document required? What is the situation that led to the need for this document? Who cares?

Selecting Content
☐ What topics do you need to cover? What do your readers need to know? What do you want your readers to do?
☐ What structure do you plan to use? If you have required report sections, what are they?
☐ What information resources do you have available? What resources do you need to locate?
☐ What types of visuals—e.g., graphs, photos, diagrams—are you considering using? Will they help convey the message?

Arranging Content
☐ In what order should the information be placed? What does your reader need to know first?
☐ Have you sorted your material into specific groups?
☐ Can you see a plan for headings that announce the content to your reader?
☐ Is all the material relevant to your purpose?

Drafting
☐ Have you begun to insert information under the headings noted in step 11?
☐ Have you recorded the sources of all information you will use so that you can develop correct citations after you have completed your draft?
☐ Have you noted where you will use graphics? Have you noted the source of each graphic you use from another source?

Revising
☐ Have you stated clearly the purpose of your report?
☐ Does your content support your purpose?
☐ Is your tone appropriate?
☐ Will your readers be able to follow your logic?
☐ Have you included all required items—report sections and required information?
☐ Have your checked all facts and numbers?
☐ Could any material be deleted?

continued

> **PLANNING AND REVISION CHECKLIST** ✔ *continued*
>
> ☐ Is your document easy to read? Are your paragraphs well organized and of a reasonable length?
> ☐ Have you had someone read your draft and suggest improvements?
>
> ### Editing
>
> ☐ Have you checked for misspellings and for other mechanical errors, such as misplaced commas, semi-colons, colons, and quotation marks?
> ☐ Have you checked all points of the completed draft at which your word processing program suggests that you have errors in either sentence structure, mechanics, or spelling?
> ☐ Have you included all the formal elements that your report needs/is required to include?
> ☐ Is your system of documentation complete and accurate (if you are following a style sheet)?
> ☐ Are your pages numbered?
> ☐ Are all graphics placed in the appropriate locations within the text?
> ☐ Is the format consistent—font selected, size, placement of headings?

EXERCISES

1. Interview a professional in your field about his or her writing practices. Who are the different audiences that this individual must write for? How does he or she adjust the message for each audience? What stories of noteworthy success or failure in addressing an audience is this individual willing to share with you? Summarize you findings in a memo, explaining the insights you've gained from this interview about analyzing your audience.
2. Your employer has historically provided free child care to all employees with children ages 3 months to five years. For its fifty years of operation, the company has prided itself on being a family-friendly employer. Tough economic times for the industry and rising costs of operation for the child care center, however, have made it necessary to start charging parents $100 per month per child for the services of the child care center. According to the president of the company, it was either that or freeze wages for all employees or lower the already slim dividend paid to the company's stockholders and risk a loss of investors. The president of the company directs you to write three memos regarding this change: one to parents using the child care center, one to all employees, and one to the stockholders. Note that parents will also receive the memo to employees. Note also that some employees are also stockholders.
3. Find an article in your field or discipline. You may wish to select one from a journal or other publication in your field. Or, you may choose a segment from

a textbook from one of the courses in your major. Revise the article or selection for an audience of readers who have limited understanding of your field. Attach the original to your revision and submit both to your instructor.

4. Examine Figure 2-1. If you were the author of this document and were given 15 more minutes to make it more suitable for its audience, what changes would you make?

FIGURE 2-1 Document for Exercise 4

Writing Ethically

3

Quick Tips

On the job, you typically won't have have time to analyze all the issues or answer all the questions relating to a given ethical dilemma. You might have to make a decision quickly—in minutes or seconds.

In cases like this, think of a person in your company or in your profession you admire for his or her integrity and good judgment (e.g., a colleague, a supervisor, a mentor). Ask yourself, "How would he or she manage this dilemma?" Allow your answer to this question to guide your actions.

YOUR PROFESSIONAL OBLIGATIONS

None of us are isolated individuals, operating entirely separate from the traffic of human society. Your ethical obligations are several, often intersecting, and from time to time competing. Consider, for example, your duties to the following:

- **To yourself:** You will have to make decisions and take actions that allow you to support yourself financially while establishing (and maintaining) your reputation in your field. You can't quit (or lose) your job every time you object to a policy of your boss.
- **To your discipline and profession:** As a member of your profession, you have a responsibility to advance the knowledge and reputation of your field. You must share information with your colleagues that will improve the practices of your profession, clarify understanding, offer new insights, and promote better training of new students of your discipline. You must communicate in a manner that brings credit to your profession and inspires the next generation to want to study and join your profession.
- **To your academic institution:** You have a moral obligation to the institution that trained you for your profession. Your successes or failures will be

indicative of the merits of that institution and its faculty. If you disgrace yourself by illegal or unethical actions, for example, investigating officials and the public might ask why you weren't taught better behavior.

- **To your employer:** Your responsibility as an employee is to serve the interests of your organization, to help it make money, to promote its products and services, and to shield confidential information and intellectual property, especially if doing so offers a competitive advantage.

- **To your colleagues:** You have a duty to your colleagues on the job to do your fair share of the work assigned and to do it with integrity, accuracy, and efficiency. You also have responsibility to use no more than your fair share of the resources allotted and to take no more than your fair share of the credit (or blame) given.

- **To the public:** Your obligation to society is to promote the public good through greater safety, fuller liberty, and a better quality of life. Your decisions and actions on the job could create opportunities for communities to thrive or could make public aspirations the victim of private greed.

In communicating on the job, you will have to juggle your various obligations and determine which has priority. You can't simply do whatever the boss tells you to because you also have important responsibilities to yourself, your profession, your schools and teachers, your colleagues, and the public itself. You will need to make every effort to avoid being either submissive or self-righteous.

Codes of Conduct

Both your professional association and your employing organization are likely to have codes of conduct or ethical guidelines that specify their expectations regarding appropriate behavior on the job. For example, the Society for Technical Communication, a leading international association for technical writers and graphic artists, has composed its guidelines as a list of six principles (Figure 3-1).

Familiarize yourself with the codes of conduct that regulate ethical communication for your company and your profession: from time to time you might have to cite their guidelines to justify your decisons regarding ethical dilemmas on the job. Ordinarily, codes of conduct assert guiding principles that you must interpret and apply to specific situations.

Recognizing Unethical Communication

Also essential to communicating ethically is to recognize the ways in which individuals on the job might be unethical in their communications. Chief among the possibilities are plagiarizing, deliberately using imprecise or ambiguous language, manipulating statistics, using misleading visuals, and promoting prejudice.

STC Ethical Principles for Technical Communicators

As technical communicators, we observe the following ethical principles in our professional activities.

Legality

We observe the laws and regulations governing our profession. We meet the terms of contracts that we undertake. We ensure that all terms are consistent with laws and regulations locally and globally, as applicable, and with STC ethical principles.

Honesty

We seek to promote the public good in our activities. To the best of our ability, we provide truthful and accurate communications. We also dedicate ourselves to conciseness, clarity, coherence, and creativity, striving to meet the needs of those who use our products and services. We alert our clients and employers when we believe that material is ambiguous. Before using another person's work, we obtain permission. We attribute authorship of material and ideas only to those who make an original and substantive contribution. We do not perform work outside our job scope during hours compensated by clients or employers, except with their permission; nor do we use their facilities, equipment, or supplies without their approval. When we advertise our services, we do so truthfully.

Confidentiality

We respect the confidentiality of our clients, employers, and professional organizations. We disclose business-sensitive information only with their consent or when legally required to do so. We obtain releases from clients and employers before including any business-sensitive materials in our portfolios or commercial demonstrations or before using such materials for another client or employer.

Quality

We endeavor to produce excellence in our communication products. We negotiate realistic agreements with clients and employers on schedules, budgets, and deliverables during project planning. Then we strive to fulfill our obligations in a timely, responsible manner.

Fairness

We respect cultural variety and other aspects of diversity in our clients, employers, development teams, and audiences. We serve the business interests of our clients and employers as long as they are consistent with the public good. Whenever possible, we avoid conflicts of interest in fulfilling our professional responsibilities and activities. If we discern a conflict of interest, we disclose it to those concerned and obtain their approval before proceeding.

Professionalism

We evaluate communication products and services constructively and tactfully, and seek definitive assessments of our own professional performance. We advance technical communication through our integrity and excellence in performing each task we undertake. Additionally, we assist other persons in our profession through mentoring, networking, and instruction. We also pursue professional self-improvement, especially through courses and conferences.

Adopted by the STC board of directors
September 1998

FIGURE 3-1 STC Ethical Principles for Technical Communicators
Source: Society for Technical Communication, http://www.stc.org/pFiles/pdf/EthicalPrinciples.pdf.

Plagiarism and theft of intellectual property. On the job, you may be responsible for the security of five kinds of intellectual property:

1. Copyrightable Material: A composition of original material fixed in a tangible medium, such as books, journals, software applications, computer programs, video or audio recordings, illustrations, etc. This includes materials available in digital files, e-mail messages, and World Wide Web pages.

2. Trademark: A display of words or symbols communicated in text, illustrations, or sounds that identify and distinguish the goods and services of a manufacturer or supplier, such as the name or logo of a company.
3. Trade Secret: A design, formula, list, method, pattern, or process that offers a competitive advantage over parties who don't have the same information, such as a special recipe.
4. Invention: A new and unique design, device, method, or process that is subject to patent protection.
5. Tangible Research Property: Tangible items created during research related to copyrightable materials, trademarks, trade secrets, and inventions, such as databases, diagrams, drawings, notes, prototypes, samples, and associated equipment and supplies.

Copyrightable material is unique in that for certain purposes (e.g., criticism, news reporting, research, teaching) you have the right to borrow limited portions for presentation or publication without the explicit permission of the owner. If the borrowing is extensive, however, permission is necessary.

On the job, writers will often recycle the words and images from various documents of their company without identifying the original source. They will readily lift paragraphs from the corporate website, for example, to use in a business letter to a potential client, or they will borrow a table from the annual report to use again in a proposal to a potential funding agency. Such recycling of material is efficient, and it is entirely legal and ethical as long as the participating writers recognize and allow this sharing of effort. In such cases, the company has ownership of the words and images that are being recycled. (If you have doubts about the propriety of such recycling within your company, ask the writer directly for his or her permission.)

If it isn't your company's materials that are being used, however, you must acknowledge the sources of borrowed words, images, and ideas. In the majority of documents you write (such as letters, e-mail messages, and memos), the acknowledgment may be a brief and simple introduction to the borrowed material: for example, "As Dr. Shirley Olson discovered, it's possible to vaccinate mosquitoes to prevent their developing and passing the disease on to human beings."

In formal reports, however, some official system of documentation would be necessary to identify the source of the information and to give full credit to Dr. Olson. Your organization might develop a special style for such source citations or adopt a standard style guide such as *The Chicago Manual of Style* of the University of Chicago Press, the *Publication Manual of the American Psychological Association*, or the *MLA Style Manual* of the Modern Language Association.

To use the words, images, or ideas of others without attribution is plagiarism. It constitutes a theft of intellectual property and is highly unethical and potentially illegal. Your intentions are immaterial: that is, it would be plagiarism if it were deliberate or if it were entirely inadvertent. You must, therefore, be especially cautious to avoid plagiarism: your organization could find itself the subject of a criminal case or a civil suit, and you could lose your job and your reputation.

Note also that material is automatically copyrighted as soon as it is created: it need not carry a copyright notice, and the copyright need not be registered with the United States Copyright Office (copyright.gov), though both actions will help to deter infringement.

If you quote a source (including material from digital files, e-mail messages, or World Wide Web pages), put the borrowed material inside quotation marks (or display it in a separate indented paragraph) and specify the source. If you paraphrase or summarize, you don't need quotation marks but you still must specify the source. Make sure that even your acknowledged paraphrases and summaries differ from the wording and phrasing of the original passage so that you can't be accused of plagiarism.

Here, for example, is the original passage from a source:

> Ethylene oxide has a boiling point of 51°F. It is processed as a liquid through the application of pressure. As the temperature of the ethylene oxide increases, the pressure in the feed line will correspondingly increase. At the time of the explosion, the ambient temperature was around 93°F. The feed line was not insulated or cooled. (from United States Environmental Protection Agency, Office of Solid Waste and Emergency Response. 2000. EPA chemical accident investigation report, Accra Pac Group, Inc. North Plant, Elkhart, Indiana. EPA 550-R-00-001. Washington, DC.)

Here is a summary that would constitute plagiarism even if the source were cited. Note how this passage changes words here and there but essentially duplicates the original passage:

> The boiling point of ethylene oxide is 51°F. Pressure is applied to process it as a liquid. As the temperature of the ethylene oxide rises, so does the pressure in the feed line. The temperature in the vicinity was roughly 93°F at the time of the explosion, and the feed line was neither insulated nor cooled.

Here is a summary that would be considered ethically appropriate. Note how the order of the sentences as well as the words have been substantially changed. Nevertheless, the source of the information must still be identified:

> Ethylene oxide was pressurized as a liquid in a feed line that was neither insulated from external temperatures nor subjected to any kind of special cooling. Ethylene oxide boils at 51°, but the ambient temperature rose to approximately 93°F. Increased pressure from the boiling chemical inside the feed line caused the line to rupture, resulting in the explosion.

If the borrowing is a substantial portion of the original source (e.g., several paragraphs or a single image), you will have two ethical and legal duties:

1) Acknowledge the source.
2) Request permission from the owner of the intellectual property.

The extensive borrowing of copyrighted material will ordinarily be permitted, but often with restrictions and often for a cost. You may contact the copyright owner directly or make your request through a service such as the Copyright Clearance Center (copyright.com). In this case, the borrowed material carries a note indicating both the source and the receipt of permission:

From *Ethics in Technical Communication*, by Paul Dombrowski. Copyright 2000 by Allyn & Bacon. Reprinted by permission.

If you change the original material (e.g., summarizing passages, revising illustrations, pulling still slides from digital video), you would specify the adaptation of the borrowing:

> From Simon, Dan. (2009, March 19). City Offers Free Health Care [Video]. CNN. com. http://www.cnn.com/video/#/video/health/2009/03/19/simon.health.san.francisco.cnn. Adapted by permission.

Permission is not needed for material in the public domain (i.e., intellectual property for which copyright protection has already expired or material created by agencies of the government of the United States), but such sources must always be acknowledged.

Deliberately imprecise or ambiguous language. Ordinarily, unclear and ambiguous language is a result of the writer's negligence, but it could also be a sign of a deliberate effort to mislead or manipulate the reader by hiding or disguising information.

Writers can imply that things are better or worse than they really are through the choice of words. For example, a writer answering an inquiry about her company's voltage generator could reply, "Our voltage generator is designed to operate from the heat of Saudi Arabian deserts to the frozen tundra of Greenland." It may be true that the generator was designed that way, but if it operates effectively only between Atlanta and Cleveland, the writer has made a false implication without telling a straight lie.

Negative assertions are often deceptive. For example, a claim such as "No graphics software does more or costs less than PaintPower" seems to declare that Paint-Power does more and costs less. In order for the claim to be the truth, however, PaintPower doesn't have to be better or cheaper: it could have the same functions as and be the same price as other graphics software. The real claim isn't that it's a better and cheaper product but that it's just as good and just as cheap.

Manipulation of numerical information. A leading way for individuals to be deceived is through the manipulation of statistics. For example, imagine the writer of a feasibility report who wishes to convey the impression that a certain change in company policy is desirable. She surveys all the workers in the company and finds that 51 percent of the 19 percent who returned the survey favor the change. In the report she writes, "A majority of those who completed the survey favored the change." By not revealing that this "majority" is only 51% and that it represents only about 10 percent of the company's workers, she magnifies the thin support for the policy change. She has not exactly lied, but she has likely deceived most readers of the report.

Use of misleading illustrations. Like words, illustrations have the capacity to misrepresent and mislead. For example, a company of one hundred employees has only two who are African Americans. In the recruiting materials it carries to college campuses, the company shows a dozen of its employees doing different jobs, including both of its African Americans. This is unethical communication because it implies that African Americans constitute almost 17% of the employees—a gross distortion of the real situation. Prospective job candidates would be substantially deceived about the diversity of colleagues and the working environment this company offers.

Or consider a line graph such as Figure 3-2 that might be given to prospective investors. Here we see a picture of volatile change followed by a period of relative stability.

If the earlier years are trimmed from the line graph, however, ABC's earlier history of erratic profits vanishes entirely (see Figure 3-3). Viewers of this line graph would be given only the impression of relative stability. Prospective investors would be deceived and would be altogether surprised if a rapid increase or decrease in profits hit the company in later years.

Promotion of prejudice. Writers also communicate unethically by voicing prejudice through their choice of words and illustrations. For example, consider the following passage from a company memo:

> One of the constraints that the company operates under is the need to recruit women candidates for managerial positions. Harriet Smith was clearly ineffective as operations manager.

The unmistakable implication here is that women candidates constitute a negative impact on the business (i.e., "a constraint") and that Harriet Smith is representative of all women. It is unlikely that a man who proved to be inneffective as a manager would be considered representative of all men.

If titles are always used for men in the company but never used for women (e.g., Mr. William Jones, advertising manager, and Harriet Smith, operations

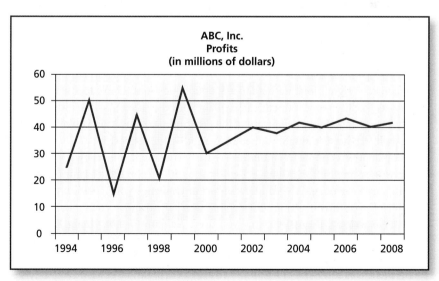

FIGURE 3-2 ABC Profits, 1994–2008

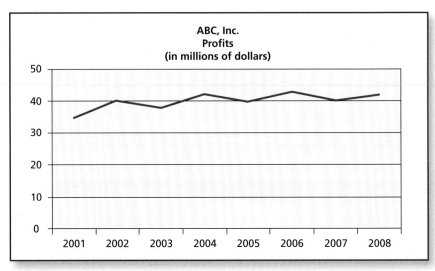

FIGURE 3-3 ABC Profits, 2001–2008

manager), women don't seem as credible and authoritative. If photographs in the company's annual report always show the women sitting at desks staring at computer screens but the men sitting at big conference tables hearing reports and making decisions, the clear message is that men are (or ought to be) important executives while women are suited exclusively for clerical positions.

Your job as a communicator is to make sure that you don't reinforce or inspire prejudice and bigotry. Your ethical obligation is to offer only valid and reliable findings, fair and unbiased analyses, and logically justified conclusions.

Managing Unethical Situations

If you find yourself asked by a boss, colleague, or client to do something that you don't consider right, don't hesitate to ask polite questions. Don't accuse or immediately declare the request unethical. Explain your dilemma. Ask the individual to clarify. He or she might be unaware of the difficult moral position you're being put in by such a request or might immediately modify the request.

If explanations and negotiations don't satisfy you and if time allows, visit with a supervisor or mentor for guidance. Review the code of conduct of your profession or company for passages that might support or challenge your position.

If all of your investigation and deliberation fail to quiet your moral doubts, explain (in writing, if possible) that you don't feel comfortable doing X, but you could do Y. That is, identify both the thing you can't do (the unethical action requested), but also the thing that you could do (the ethical option).

If asked to justify your decision, cite the appropriate passages of your profession's or company's code of conduct. That is, make it clear that it isn't only you who is rejecting the request, but that it is your profession or your company that proscribes this behavior. Again, don't be impolite and don't accuse.

If you see something occurring on the job that you don't think is right, discuss the situation with your supervisor or mentor (in writing, if possible). If your investigation fails to satisfy you that the activity is justified, consider your several ethical obligations, including to your profession and to the public. Always make the decision that you could live with if your decision were made public.

A final piece of advice. Keep in mind that you bring two important credentials to a job: a knowledge of your field and a reputation for integrity. If you don't have a reputation for integrity, your knowledge of your field can't be trusted.

ETHICS DECISION CHECKLIST ✔

- ☐ What is the nature of the ethical dilemma?
- ☐ What are the specific aspects of this dilemma that make you uncomfortable?
- ☐ What are your competing obligations in this dilemma?
- ☐ What advice does a trusted supervisor or mentor offer?
- ☐ Does your company's code of conduct address this issue?
- ☐ Does your professional association's code of conduct address this issue?
- ☐ What are you unwilling to do? What are you willing to do?
- ☐ How will you explain or justify your decision?

EXERCISES

1. Visit the website of two major employers in your field. Locate the code of conduct for each. What are the similarities and differences in the two codes of conduct? What are the values that each employer espouses? What does each employer expect from its employees? From its executives? What additional ethics resources does each employer make available to employees? What can you tell about each employer from the code of conduct? Based on your review of the two codes of conduct, which employer would you prefer to work for? Why? Summarize your findings in a memo and share this memo with your colleagues.

2. You are employed in the corporate offices of a regional chain of athletic equipment stores. Your supervisor asks you to prepare a report for prospective investors about a series of exercise classes that your corporation introduced a week ago at its five biggest stores. Your supervisor hands you a package of materials from a chain of athletic equipment stores operating in Europe: the materials describe the same series of exercise classes with lots of impressive statistics on weight loss and enthusiastic quotations from satisfied clients. Your supervisor

asks you to put the report together as quickly as possible and to "use the stuff in these documents I picked up while on vacation but make it look like it's local customers saying those things." What do you do?

3. Examine Figure 3-4. If you were the author of this document and were given 15 more minutes to make it more ethical, what changes would you make?

NTSB

SAFETY ALERT

National Transportation Safety Board

★ Primary Seat Belt Laws

Tougher enforcement of seat belts laws saves lives

The grim facts

- In 2007, almost 29,000 people died as occupants in auto crashes, 54 percent of whom were unrestrained.
- Lap/shoulder belts, when used, reduce the risk of fatal injury to front seat passenger car occupants by 45 percent and the risk of moderate-to-critical injury by 50 percent.
- When adults are buckled up, 87 percent of children are buckled up, but when adults are not buckled up, only 58 percent of children are buckled up.
- NHTSA estimates that seat belts saved 15,383 lives in 2006. Had all passenger vehicle occupants over age 4 used seat belts, an additional 5,441 lives could have been saved.
- Nearly three-quarters of all crash costs are paid by those not directly involved in crashes. In 2000, those not directly involved in crashes paid over $170 billion.

Effective actions in primary seat belt laws

- Mandate primary enforcement for seat belt laws. According to the 2008 National Occupant Protection Usage Survey, seat belt use in primary enforcement law States was 88 percent, while seat belt use in secondary enforcement law States was only 75 percent.
- Apply seat belt laws to all vehicle seating positions. When used properly, seat belts reduce the risk of fatal injury to front seat passenger vehicle occupants by 45 percent and rear seat passenger vehicle occupants by 44 percent. From 1975 through 2006, seat belts saved more than 226,000 lives nationwide.
- Repeal existing legal provisions that insulate people from the financial consequences of not wearing seat belts.

What can you do to save lives and reduce injuries?

- Make sure seat belts or child restraints are worn by everyone in your vehicle.
- Talk or write to your Sate and local lawmakers and urge them to support NTSB recommendations for State belt use laws.

Need more information?

- Visit the NTSB Web site: www.ntsb.gov

SA-005   October 2008

FIGURE 3-4

Achieving a Readable Style

Style refers to the overall way you express your ideas in a document, from the paragraph level to sentence structure and the words and phrases you choose.

Quick Tips

If you want your report to be read, use a style that is easy for your readers to follow. If your readers can't understand your report as they are reading it, they may just disregard it or toss it out. Unreadable documents usually result from ineffective style.

THE PARAGRAPH

A reminder: the paragraph is a group of sentences that work together to produce a coherent idea. Paragraphs should be a moderate length—long paragraphs discourage readers—and begin with a topic sentence (a central statement) of their content. The supporting sentences build on the idea stated in the topic sentence and should occur in a logical order. In short:

- Begin each paragraph with a topic sentence that summarizes content to come.
- Include only information relevant to the topic sentence.
- Place sentences in a logical order.
- Avoid long paragraphs.

Examples for study. Effective report segments result from effective paragraphs. For example, examine the following introduction to a technical report (Figure 4-1).

Introduction

In 1996, the U.S. Department of Energy (DOE), Office of Fossil Energy, asked Argonne National Laboratory (ANL) to conduct a preliminary technical and legal evaluation of disposing of nonhazardous oil field wastes (NOW) into salt caverns. The conclusions of that study, based on preliminary research, were that disposal of oil field wastes into salt caverns is feasible and legal. If caverns are sited and designed well, operated carefully, closed properly, and monitored routinely, they can be a suitable means for disposing of oil field waste (Veil et al. 1996). Considering these findings and the increased U.S. interest in using salt caverns for nonhazardous oil field waste disposal, the Office of Fossil Energy asked ANL to conduct a preliminary identification and investigation of the risks associated with such disposal.

As Chapter 8 discusses, report introductions must have purpose statements to tell readers what the report will do. Having the purpose statement at the beginning of a paragraph helps readers find the purpose statement.

The purpose of this report is to evaluate the possibility that adverse human health effects (carcinogenic and noncarcinogenic) could result from exposure to contaminants released from the caverns in domal salt formations used for nonhazardous oil field waste disposal. The evaluation assumes normal operations but considers the possibility of leaks in cavern seals and cavern walls during the post-closure phase of operation. It does not consider the risks associated with emissions from surface equipment operating at the site, nor does it consider the risks associated with surface oil leaks or other equipment-related spills or accidents.

The study focuses on possible long-term risks to human health. It does not address potential ecological effects, although such effects could result. Also, risks associated with naturally occurring radioactive materials (NORM) are not addressed. This preliminary assessment estimates risks associated with disposal in a single generic cavern only. No attempt has been made to address the possibly or likelihood that several caverns may be located in relatively close proximity and that more than one cavern could be a source of contamination to a given receptor. Also, no attempt has been made to evaluate the possible impacts of synergistic effects of multiple contaminants on a single receptor.

Because the history of salt cavern use for solid waste disposal is very limited, no readily available data could be accessed for this study. As a result, data from similar operations and professional judgment were used to develop the possible release mechanisms assumed in this hypothetical, generic analysis. The validity of the results would be enhanced if real data could be used. As data are generated on the use and post-closure operations of salt caverns used for solid waste disposal, they should be incorporated to update this study.

Moves from broad to specific in supporting information

In this assessment, several steps were followed to identify possible human health risks. At the broadest level, these steps include identifying a reasonable set of contaminants of possible concern, identifying how humans could be exposed to these contaminants, assessing the toxicities of these contaminants, estimating their intakes, and characterizing their associated human health risks. The risk assessment methodology and techniques used in this report are based in large part on two documents. The first document is a training manual that was developed for a risk assessment workshop sponsored by DOE (DOE 1996). The second is the Risk Assessment Guidance for Superfund (U.S. Environmental Protection Agency [EPA] 1989).

FIGURE 4-1 Effective Introduction to a Technical Report

The remainder of this report consists of nine sections. Section 2 provides background on the development, use, and closure of salt caverns that may be used for disposal of nonhazardous oil field wastes and possible cavern release scenarios. Section 3 identifies contaminants of potential concern that could cause harm to human health. Sections 4, 5, and 6 provide information for assessing potential exposure pathways that the contaminants of concern could take to reach human populations. Specifically, Section 4 describes fate and transport mechanisms of the contaminants of concern; Section 5 describes specific hydrogeologic conditions of locations that are most likely to be used for oil field disposal (Gulf Coast, Texas, and New Mexico); and Section 6 describes potential release modes that could cause contaminants to leak from the cavern and be transported to areas where human populations may be exposed. Section 6 also estimates possible concentrations of the contaminants to which humans could be exposed under various release scenarios. Section 7 describes the toxicity of those contaminants that could come in contact with humans, given the fate and transport mechanisms identified in Section 5 combined with the potential exposure pathways described in Section 6. Section 8 estimates the potential intakes of those contaminants by humans and characterizes the risks to which those humans may be subjected on the basis of the intake of the contaminants (the potential for harm), their toxicities, and the release assumptions. Section 9 addresses the sensitivity of the estimated risks to operating procedures and potential regulatory structures, and Section 10 summarizes the results of the analyses.

> Topic sentence helps readers anticipate presentation of the nine sections. Naming each section allows the writer to show relationships among the sections.

FIGURE 4-1 *continued*

Because each paragraph begins with a topic sentence (highlighted in each example), you can read just the topic sentences and have a clear sense of the content of the introduction. While the final paragraph is the longest of the introduction, its structure allows you to follow easily the development of the paragraph.

This next example paragraph (Figure 4-2) uses a list to draw the reader's eyes to the central idea presented in the paragraph, the criteria for approval. The topic sentence introduces the paragraph and the list.

The listing strategy emphasizes the six items that are front and center in the Lake Ashton project. In this situation, listing highlights the rhetorical immediacy of the problem. A traditional paragraph with linear text would obscure the concerns (Figure 4-3).

Avoid excessive use of any writing technique—too many short paragraphs, too much enumeration (first, second, third, etc.) as well as too many lists. Concise paragraphs that begin with topic sentences and well-structured sentences of moderate length create clear, readable documents. Why is Figure 4-5 easier to read than Figure 4-4?

Note that each paragraph of Figure 4-5 begins with a topic sentence and a clearly stated subheading introduces each segment of the introduction. (Chapter 5 will explain how to design documents, but this revision also exemplifies excellent document design.)

The City of Ashtonville Economic Development Council presented six main concerns to the City Parks and Recreation Department about the proposed Ashton Lake development proposal:

1. Financial feasibility of the project
2. Ability to raise the necessary funds
3. Project maintenance, including long-term
4. Protection/Enhancement of the shoreline
5. Effect of project on changing lake water levels
6. Erosion of project's materials caused by water/sand

The EDC expressed a major concern that the project may not be as family-friendly as needed because it would require extensive funding to develop the recommended recreation facilities. In addition, the concerns stated suggest that the project, if approved, will have to be funded strictly by private donations rather than city or county parks money.

FIGURE 4-2 Effective Use of a List

Basic Principles of Effective Style

Effective writers adjust their style to the needs of their readers: (1) their knowledge of the subject; (2) readers' expectations about style based on the specific kind of writing; (3) readers' probable reading level based on the context in which the document will be read; and (4) the writer's relationship to readers—the professional roles of both writer and readers.

Determine your readers' knowledge of the subject. The reader's familiarity with the subject will determine how many specialized terms you can use. If the reader is thoroughly familiar with the subject, you can use acronyms, specialized nomenclature, and jargon that readers in a specific discipline are comfortable reading and using. If the reader is not thoroughly familiar with the subject, limit the use of specialized vocabulary or perhaps define the terms. Another possibility: substitute phrases or words that will clearly express your meaning.

In a work context, the better you know people who will read your writing, the better you can design your reports, memos, and e-mails. You can also ask people who know your readers to aid you in finding out preferences in organization, style, and length. When you begin a job assignment, ask your supervisor for his/her preferences in both style and organization.

The City of Ashtonville Economic Development Council presented six main concerns to the City Parks and Recreation Department about the proposed Ashton Lake development proposal: financial feasibility of the project; ability to raise the necessary funds; project maintenance, including long-term; protection/enhancement of the shoreline; effect of project on changing lake water levels; and erosion of project's materials caused by water/sand. The EDC expressed a major concern that the project may not be as family-friendly as needed because it would require extensive funding to develop the recommended recreation facilities. In addition, the concerns stated suggest that the project, if approved, will be have to be funded strictly by private donations rather than city or county parks money.

FIGURE 4-3 Ineffective Run-in List

How an MRI Works

Brain perfusion refers to the blood circulation around the brain while exchanging oxygen and nutrients between the blood and the brain tissue. The effectiveness of brain perfusion depends on "blood pressure, blood velocity[...], and diffusion rates of oxygen and nutrients" [1]. An MRI scanner can monitor the perfusion of the brain to determine if a neurological disease is present.

An MRI scan uses a magnetic field to generate enhanced images that show certain parts of the body. The hydrogen atom provides a crucial component in the generation of an MRI scan. The hydrogen atom contains a single proton that interacts with the magnetic field generated by the MRI. The hydrogen atoms in a specific area of the human body will behave differently due to the presence of a magnetic field. The MRI scanner will detect the behavior of these hydrogen atoms to generate an enhanced image of that area.

In many MRI procedures, a contrast agent is used to further enhance the image of the body by increasing the brightness of the tissue being examined. The injection of contrast agents into the body will help the MRI scan retrieve information such as "blood flow [...] and related physiological parameters" [2]. These contrast agents work by altering the local magnetic field in the tissue being examined to generate an illuminated image of that tissue on the MRI scan.

Unfortunately, contrast agents have limited functions when physicians attempt to study the human brain. The brain contains a "membrane structure" known as the blood brain barrier. which protects the brain from foreign chemicals in the blood, while still allowing essential metabolic function [3]. The blood brain barrier filters out any unwanted chemicals that may travel through the brain. Since the blood brain barrier is very effective in its function, the chemicals in the contrast agents will be filtered out by this *membrane structure*. If a neurological disease is present in the brain, it can weaken the blood brain barrier and allow these unwanted chemicals to pass through [3]. The contrast agent would be useful for studying the disease in this situation.

Many methods have been created to penetrate the blood brain barrier. My proposed method will strengthen the interaction between hydrogen atoms with the magnetic field via electrical signals. During an MRI scan, an electrical signal will be emitted around the neck area. This signal will mark the hydrogen atoms that are in the vicinity of the emitted signal. Because no external chemicals are introduced, the blood brain barrier will not detect any foreign chemicals and will let the marked hydrogen atoms into the brain. The hydrogen atoms will travel through the bloodstream around the brain acting as beacons. They will then interact with the magnetic field of the MRI, allowing MRI to enhance the image of the brain, much like contrast agents [4].

FIGURE 4-4 Original Introduction to a Student Research Proposal

Determine whether a particular style will be expected. Use the company style sheet and templates. But remember that you still have to adapt what you say to your intended readers.

Adjust the style to the readers, the purpose, and the context. Most of your business and technical writing should be as concise as possible because of the large quantity of information that most readers confront. Because of the increasing number of messages sent electronically, messages should have concise paragraphs and concise sentences. Even in complex, highly technical reports, readers value conciseness: the longer the report, the less likely that anyone will read all of it.

> **Note:** Conciseness does not equal brevity. When you write concisely, you include all that you need to say without extra words and phrases that contribute little to the main idea. Brevity means that you aim only for economy, rather than completeness of thought.

Introduction

Importance of Brain Perfusion

Brain perfusion refers to the blood circulation around the brain while the circulatory system exchanges oxygen and nutrients between the blood and the brain tissue. Brain perfusion depends on "blood pressure, blood velocity [...], and diffusion (dispersal) rates of oxygen and nutrients" [1]. An MRI scanner can monitor the perfusion of the brain to determine if a neurological disease is present.

How an MRI Works

A magnetic resonance imaging (MRI) scan uses a magnetic field (an attractive force) to show enhanced images of certain parts of the body. A dynamic MRI scan displays a fuller and more detailed result, unlike a conventional MRI. The hydrogen atoms in the human body are very important in an MRI procedure. One hydrogen atom contains a single proton that behaves differently when the MRI emits a magnetic field around that area. The MRI scanner will detect the behavior of these hydrogen atoms to generate an enhanced image of that area.

In many MRI procedures, a contrast agent (a compound fluid) is used to further enhance the image of the body by increasing the brightness of the tissue being examined. The injection of contrast agents into the body will help the MRI scan retrieve information such as blood flow and other related physical characteristics [2].

Limits of the MRI

Unfortunately, contrast agents have limited functions when physicians attempt to study the human brain. The brain contains a "membrane structure" known as the blood brain barrier, which protects the brain from foreign chemicals in the blood, while still allowing essential metabolic function [3]. The blood brain barrier filters out any unwanted chemicals that may travel through the brain. Since the blood brain barrier is very effective in its function, the chemicals in the contrast agents will be filtered out by this *membrane structure*. If a neurological disease is present in the brain, it can weaken the blood brain barrier and allow these unwanted chemicals to pass through [3]. The contrast agent would be useful for studying the disease in this situation.

Value of My Method in Improving the MRI

Many methods have been created to penetrate the blood brain barrier. My proposed method will strengthen the interaction between hydrogen atoms with the magnetic field via electrical signals. During a dynamic MRI scan, an electrical signal will be emitted around the neck area. This signal will mark the hydrogen atoms that are in the vicinity of the emitted signal. Because no external chemicals are introduced, the blood brain barrier will not detect any foreign chemicals and will let the marked hydrogen atoms into the brain. The hydrogen atoms will travel through the bloodstream around the brain acting as beacons. They will then interact with the magnetic field of the MRI, allowing MRI to enhance the image of the brain, much like contrast agents [4].

Subject and Purpose

This research will focus on developing a new method of performing a dynamic MRI scan on the human brain. This new method involves emitting an electrical signal into the body to interact with the hydrogen atoms and performing a dynamic MRI scan. To determine the effectiveness of this new method, I will analyze the MRI scan to determine the rate of perfusion in the brain.

FIGURE 4-5 Revised Introduction to the Student Research Proposal

KEYS TO BUILDING EFFECTIVE SENTENCES

English sentences work more effectively—that is, they are easier to read, understand, and remember—if they follow basic rules of structuring.

Select your level of language; adjust the density of information. Audiences familiar with your subject will expect and tolerate complex information. However, in routine reports and messages that you want readers to digest quickly,

Characteristics of Bad and Good Writing

Bad Writing	Good Writing
few verbs/number of words per sentence	many verbs/number of words per sentence
excessive *is/are* verb forms	concrete verbs
abstract nouns	concrete nouns
many prepositional phrases	few prepositional phrases
few clauses	linked clauses
passive voice	active voice
separation of key words: subject-verb, actor-action	clear actor-action relationship
long, rambling sentences	specific, precise sentences
main idea of sentences is difficult to process	meaning of sentences is easy to find
sentences must be read several times	meaning is clear after one reading

use writing that is less detailed and focuses on the main ideas. For reports, the broader the audience, the more careful you need to be about selecting easy-to-understand language. The audience determines the density of the information and the level of nomenclature.

Watch sentence length. Documents composed of consistently long sentences can become difficult to read. Sentence length should vary, but consider revising sentences that are over 15-20 words. Even legal documents can benefit from shorter sentences and have improved as a result of plain English laws that now govern insurance policies and many other legal documents in various states. Many government entities want their public documents written in concise, easily understood sentences:

Before:
This Appendix contains a brief discussion of certain economic and demographic characteristics of the Area in which the County is located and does not constitute a part of this Official Statement. Information in this Appendix has been obtained from the sources noted, which are believed to be reliable, although no investigation has been made to verify the accuracy of such information.

After:
This Appendix contains a brief discussion of certain economic and demographic characteristics of the Area in which the County is located. The Appendix does not constitute part of this Official Statement. Information in the Appendix has been obtained from the sources noted. They are believed to be reliable. However, the accuracy of the information has not been verified.

Keep subjects and verbs close together. A recipe for sentence clarity: keep the subject of the sentence and the verb close together, and emphasize verbs. The more verbs in a sentence, the sharper and more direct the sentence. We call this verb/word ratio. For example,

> s v   s v
>
> John <u>loves</u> Mary because she <u>inherited</u> money. [verb/word ratio = 2/7]

versus

> s v
>
> Mary's inheritance of money <u>was</u> one of the reasons for John's interest in Mary.
>
> [verb/word ratio = 1/12]

In this simple example, you can see the point: the more verbs, the sharper the sentence.

Let's take this method a step further: lengthy sentences become less distracting to the reader if the writer structures them to enhance clarity and readability. To achieve clarity, build sentences with clauses, using as many verbs and verbals as possible. For example, the sentence,

> When they plan investment portfolios, financial planners recommend a variety of investments because they resist rapid economic changes. (18 words)

develops about three clauses:

> *When they <u>plan</u> investment portfolios*
> *financial planners <u>recommend</u> a variety of investments*
> *because they <u>resist</u> economic change.*

Note that the sentence follows the three guidelines:

> Interlocking clauses [3 in this sentence]
> Specific action verbs: *plan, recommend,* and *resist.*

Subject next to the verb in each clause.

> *they plan*
> *planners recommend*
> *they resist.*

The verb/word ratio in this sentence is 3/17.

Assume that the writer did not follow the guidelines and avoided verbs:

> In plans for investment portfolios, a variety of investments is recommended by financial planners because of their resistance to economic changes.

The verb/word ratio is 1/21. The sentence lacks directness and conciseness. Compare this sentence with the two versions. Can you see the difference? Basically, the more verbs and verbals, the easier the sentence is to read and understand.

For most writing, use conversational language. Write to express, not to impress. Use specific, concrete language:

Instead of:
There is now no effective existing mechanism for introducing into the beginning initiation and development stages requirements on how to guide employees on how to minimize errors in product development efforts.

[verb/word ratio = 3/31]

Use:
The company has no way to guide employees on how to minimize product development errors during the early development stages.

[verb/word ratio = 3/20]

Instead of:
Our lack of pertinent data prevented determination of committee action effectiveness in funding targeting to areas that needed assistance the most.

[Note that the sentence incorporates two clauses and two verbs. Verb/word ratio = 2/21]

Use:
Because we lacked pertinent data, we could not determine whether the committee had targeted funds to areas that needed assistance the most.

[Note the revision of the sentence with four interlocking clauses and four verbs. Verb/word ratio = 4/22]

Or:
We didn't have enough data: We could not decide if the committee had sent funds to areas that needed them most.

When we break the sentence into two sentences, we still have four verbs. In addition, the short sentence, followed by the longer, explanatory sentence makes the meaning clear.

But always be aware of how direct/indirect words affect tone:

(A) We encourage you to anticipate the amount of correspondence you accumulate and suggest you endeavor to answer it promptly.

(B) Please expect large amounts of e-mail and try to answer it quickly.

Note that (B) is easier and quicker to read than (A).

Write squeaky-clean prose. The following excerpt from *DNA: The Secret of Life* is addressed to readers interested in science and possessing a basic understanding of genetics. Note the structure of each sentence, the use of topic sentences, and the development of each paragraph:

> The great size of DNA molecules posed a big problem in the early days of molecular biology. To come to grips with a particular gene—a particular stretch of DNA—we would have to devise some way of isolating it from all the rest of the DNA that sprawled around it in either direction. But it was not only a matter of isolating the gene; we also needed some way of "amplifying" it: obtaining a large enough sample of it to work with. In essence we needed a molecular editing system: a pair of molecular scissors that could cut the DNA text into manageable sections; a kind of molecular glue pot that would allow us to manipulate those pieces; and finally a molecular duplicating machine to amplify the pieces that we had cut out and isolated. We wanted to do the equivalent of what a word processor can now achieve: to cut, paste, and copy DNA.
>
> Developing the basic tools to perform these procedures seemed a tall order even after we cracked the genetic code. A number of discoveries made in the late sixties and early seventies, however, serendipitously came together in 1973 to give us so-called "recombinant DNA" technology—the capacity to edit DNA. This was no ordinary advance in lab techniques. Scientists were suddenly able to tailor DNA molecules, creating ones that had never before been seen in nature. We could "play God" with the molecular underpinning of all of life. This was an unsettling idea to many people. Jeremy Rifkin, an alarmist for whom every new genetic technology has about it the whiff of Dr. Frankenstein's monster, had it right when he remarked that recombinant DNA "rivaled the importance of the discovery of fire itself."
>
> ---
>
> *Source*: Watson, James. *DNA: The Secret of Life* pp. 87–88. Knopf, 2003. Used by permission.

This excerpt uses a variety of sentences of moderate length, close subject-verb patterns, familiar words, and a description of recombinant DNA in terms easily understood by the non-scientific reader—the meaning of *recombinant DNA* is concisely and picturesquely expressed. In short, Watson has focused on simplicity in explaining the story of DNA.

Avoid pompous language; write to express, not impress. The concept of simplicity relates to the concept of naturalness. Writers often believe that they must sound learned and sophisticated to impress readers. The idea that direct writing is not sophisticated frequently derives from writing done in secondary school. Teachers encourage high school students to expand their vocabularies. Academic writing in college reinforces the importance of using jargon-laden language to convince the professor that the student knows the subject and the nomenclature of the discipline. Instructors may reward students for writing ponderous verbiage in research papers. On the job, however, verbose writing may be ignored or misread by readers who are interested in gleaning information relevant to their job needs.

Remember that writing exists for human beings, and few of us enjoy writing that is harder to read than it needs to be. What constitutes "difficult" writing depends on the reader, the topic, and the purpose of the document. But direct, concise writing that uses a conversational style will usually be appreciated by your readers. Using shorter, rather than longer sentences also helps readers follow your thoughts:

> Please give immediate attention to insure that the pages of all documents prepared for distribution are numbered sequentially and in a place of optimum visibility. This is needed to facilitate our ability to refer to items during meetings.

Vs.

> Please correctly number the pages of all documents. Place numbers in the upper right-hand corner. Sequential numbers helps us locate material during meetings.

Or,

> Please number all pages sequentially.

> Three additional examples:

> It has recently been brought to my attention that only a small percentage of the employees in our division are contributors to the citizens' health research fund supported by this firm. This fund is a major source of money for the encouragement of significant discoveries and innovations made in behalf of research relevant to community health.

Vs.

> I have discovered that only a small percentage of employees in our division contribute to the citizens' health research fund. Our firm supports this research because the products of this research improve community health.

> As a result of their expertise, the consulting team is provided with the opportunity to make a reasonable determination of the appropriate direction to proceed regarding their selection of information systems.

Vs.

> The consulting team has the expertise to select the best information systems.

> It is our contention that the necessary modifications should be made to make the system operational because its complete replacement is economically prohibitive.

Vs.

> We believe that the system should be modified to make it operational. Complete replacement costs too much.

Avoid excessive use of is/are verb forms. Choosing specific, concrete verbs for clarity means avoiding forms of the *be* verb, if possible. As the following sentences illustrate, excessive use of *be* verbs often obscures action verbs. Many times, a *be* verb is the best choice (as this sentence exemplifies). However, you can lessen the tendency to use *be* verbs by doing the following:

- Avoid beginning sentences with *there is* or *there are, there was* or *there were.*
- Avoid beginning sentences with phrases such *as it is clear that, it is evident that*, and *it should be noted that.*
- Choose a specific verb rather than *is, are, was*, and *were* verb forms.

Be verbs often create a longer, less direct sentence:

Delegation <u>is</u> a means of lessening the manager's work load.

Vs.

Managers who delegate <u>reduce</u> their work load.

Another example:

My decision <u>is based on the assumption</u> that his statement <u>is erroneous.</u>

Vs.

My decision <u>assumed</u> that his statement <u>is erroneous.</u>

Another example:

Our office <u>has been provided with the authority to make a determination about the selection</u> of a computing system.

Our office was authorized to select a computing system.

The clearest sentences focus on the agent and the action (the verb):

There are two systems presently available for testing job candidates.

Vs.

Two available systems can test job candidates.

There are several national and global organizations dedicated to promoting environmental sustainability for health care facilities.

Vs.

Several national and global organizations promote environmental sustainability for health care facilities.

Use active voice for clarity. The structure of a sentence—the arrangement of words—affects the clarity of the sentence. In active voice, the agent that does the action occurs next to the verb, the agent and the action both appear in the sentence, and the agent is the subject of the sentence.

agent verb
The department teaches the course every spring term.

agent verb
Our office submits all travel vouchers within 24 hours of their completion.

The result? Concise, direct sentences.

Before:
(A) Attempts were made by the division staff to assess the project.

After:
agent verb
(B) The division staff attempted to assess the project.

Sentence (A) uses passive voice. Sentence (B) uses active voice: the agent (staff) occurs as the subject and is located next to the verb (attempted).

Research to determine the most readable sentence structures indicates that active voice sentences may be more readable than passive sentences. Readers often need the agent (the actor) placed near the action (the verb). Placing both the agent/actor and the verb at the beginning of the sentence alerts the reader to the basic meaning of the sentence, as the subject and verb contain the essence of the sentence. The following examples illustrate this concept.

The door is to be locked at 6:00 P.M.

This sentence, which does not specify the agent, could mean either of the following:

The guard (or some designated person) will lock the door at 6:00 P.M.
The last person leaving the building at 6:00 P.M. must lock the door.

As both revisions illustrate, to understand a sentence, readers must know the agent and the action carried out by the agent. When you write, be sure your sentences indicate who or what performs the action.

Passive voice sentences often intentionally do not include the actor or agent doing the action in order to hide responsibility. The result may produce a sentence that is more verbose and less accurate than an active voice version. Passive voice sentences often use "there is" and "there are" constructions. Even in engineering writing, such as articles for academic journals, many editors want active voice sentences because of the increased clarity of the sentences. As in the examples below, the use of active subjects will usually make an explanation easier to read and easier to understand:

Before:
With the growing request of high quality multimedia service, especially in portable systems, efficient algorithms for audio and/or video data processing have been developed. These algorithms have the characteristics of high complexity data-intensive computation. For these applications, there exist two extreme implementations. One is software implementation running on a general purpose processor and the other is hardware implementation

in the form of application-specific integrated circuit (ASIC). In the first case, it is flexible enough to support various applications but may not yield sufficient performance to cope with the complexity of application. In the second case, optimization is better in respect of both power and performance but only for a specific application. A coarse-grained reconfigurable architecture fills the gap between the two approaches, providing higher performance than software implementation and wider applicability than hardware implementation.

After:
(Note: We separate the original passage here so that you can follow the changes in sentence structure.)

To respond to growing requests for high quality multimedia services, especially in portable systems, engineers have developed efficient algorithms for audio and/or video data processing.

These algorithms exemplify high complexity data-intensive computation.

In addition, these applications use two extreme implementations: (1) a *software implementation* running on a general purpose processor and (2) a *hardware implementation*, a application-specific integrated circuit (ASIC). The first (1), is flexible enough to support various applications, but it may not yield sufficient performance to cope with complex applications. In the second (2), we can optimize by power and performance but only for a specific application. A coarse-grained reconfigurable architecture fills the gap between the two approaches. This architecture provides higher performance than software implementation and wide applicability than hardware implementation.

Before:
To ensure dimensional quality of manufactured products, a crucial step is to take coordinate measurements of the geometric features to reconstruct product surface and then to check their compliance with tolerance specifications: my research develops a method to integrate the coordinate measurements from measuring devices of different resolutions for a better reconstruction of the product surface.

After:
To ensure dimensional quality of manufactured products, researchers must take coordinate[d] measurements of the geometric features. The goal: to reconstruct product surface and then check surface compliance with tolerance specifications.

My research develops a method to integrate the coordinate[d] measurements from measuring devices of different resolutions to better reconstruct the product surface.

WORD CHOICE

To write concise sentences, use clear, concise words and phrases. Avoid using longer words when shorter ones will do just as well. (Write to express, not to impress.)

instead of	write	instead of	write
accordingly	so	hence	so
accumulate	gather	implement	carry out
acquire	get	initiate	begin
acquaint	tell	maximum	most
activate	begin	modification	change
aggregate	total	nevertheless	but, however,
assist	help	objective	aim
communicate	write, talk, tell	optimum	best
compensation	pay	personnel	people, staff
consequently	so	procure	get
continue	keep up	purchase	buy
demonstrate	show	terminate	end
discontinue	stop	transmit	send
endeavor	try	utilize	use
facilitate	ease, simplify		

Eliminate dead phrases—words that add nothing to the meaning of the sentence.

to the extent that	in view of
with your permission	inasmuch as
hence	as a matter of fact
with reference to	for the purpose of
in connection with	in order
with respect to	
as already stated	

Avoid words that sound knowledgeable without being specific. Many are technical words that have been overused and poorly adapted to non-technical situations.

parameters	warrants further investigation
logistical interface	broad-based
contact	dynamics

impact
input/output
conceptualize
formalize
multifaceted
systematized
prioritize
time frame
hard date
in-depth study

infrastructure
longitudinal study
matrix
meaningful
monolithic
paradigm
participatory involvement
resource utilization
viability

Avoid redundant phrases.

absolutely complete
absolutely essential
agreeable and satisfactory
anxious and eager
basic fundamentals
complete absence
consensus of opinion
each and every
exactly identical
example to illustrate
few in number
first and foremost
general consensus
green in color

human volunteer
insist and demand
my personal opinion
necessary essentially
past memories
point in time
right and proper
sincere and earnest
small in size
summarize briefly
thought and consideration
true facts
very unique

Avoid business jargon

instead of	write
consideration was given	I considered
prior to the	before
at the present writing	now
effect an improvement	improve
in the neighborhood of	about
beg to advise	tell
cognizant of	know
thanking you in advance	I would appreciate
endeavor	try
viable alternative	possibility
in regard/reference to	about

send under separate cover	send separately
return same to the above	return to us
needless to say	[omit]
it goes without saying	[omit]
in the normal course of procedure	normally
in this day and age	today
in my opinion	I believe
it is our opinion	we think
on a daily basis	daily
on the grounds that	because
pursuant to our agreement	as we agreed
we are not in a position to	we cannot
without further delay	now
please be advised that	[omit]

STYLE CHECKLIST

Planning

☐ How will you adjust your writing style to accommodate your readers' knowledge of the subject?

☐ How will you meet your readers' expectations about style for the specific kind of document you are writing?

☐ What is the appropriate reading level for the context in which the document will be read?

☐ How will you adjust your style so that is appropriate for the professional relationship you have to your readers?

Revision

☐ Do paragraphs start with a topic sentence? Do the following sentences in the paragraph build on the idea in the topic sentence?

☐ Are most sentences twenty words or shorter? Could longer sentences be made shorter?

☐ Are subjects and verbs close together in your sentences?

☐ Have you used specific nouns and concrete verbs?

☐ Have you avoided ponderous and impersonal language?

☐ Have you avoided is/are verb forms whenever possible?

☐ Are most of your sentences written in active voice? Could any sentences with passive voice be changed to active voice?

☐ Have you defined everything that might require defining?

☐ Could any of your sentences be written with equal clarity but fewer words?

EXERCISES

1. Visit the website of two major employers in your field. What kinds of documents do you find at each site? Do the organizations have a style guide for their documents? From looking at a number of the documents at each site (e.g., letter from the president, mission statement, code of conduct) how would you characterize each organization's style? Which organization has the more readable style? How would you make each organization's style more readable?

2. Figure 4-6 is a memo composed by the manager of The Plaza, a relatively new apartment building in Lubbock, Texas. The manager would like to distribute the memo to all residents as soon as possible. As the regional manager of Rite Properties, which operates The Plaza, it is your job to review the official communications coming from managers to residents. What changes would you advise the manager to make to this memo?

3. Examine Figure 4-7. If you were the author of this document and were given 15 more minutes to make it more readable, what changes would you make?

Rite Properties

7001 South Loop 289
Lubbock, Texas 79425
806-555-1327
manager@theplaza.com

September 5, 2009

TO: ALL PLAZA RESIDENTS
FROM: The Management
SUBJECT: towing

Effective today, September 5, 2009, BAILEY CAFETERIA will tow any Plaza residents vehicles or Plaza visitor vehicles that park on the south end of their parking lot on the west side of their building. One visitor vehicle from Plaza was parked directly in front of the cafeteria's back door, blocking the way for a big delivery truck coming in this morning, consequently, no one may park over there any more. Residents, we have been over the parking situation over and over, if you or your guests get towed, don't call me. I've put out several newsletters or spoke with individuals about the parking. It is your responsibility to tell your guests where to park. We have had a good relationship with Bailey's for along time, but when we get in the way, everyone must pay the price. Stop and think where you park, is it going to be in someone's way in the morning? The next time I am called to clear out the cars to avoid being towed because it is blocking a door or driveway at Bailey's, I promise, I will call the tow truck myself.

We have also been changing the filters and checking the smoke alarm batteries this week and there are those of you that are removing or tampering with your smoke alarms!

Repeatedly we have told you not to take the battery out of your smoke alarm. IT IS AGAINST THE LAW. Do you have enough insurance to cover all your home's contents in addition to all the contents of several other homes if a fire breaks out in your apartment and because you have no battery in your smoke alarm, no one was warned before it was too late. When your alarm beeps, it means you need a new battery, we

continued

FIGURE 4-6 Document for Exercise 2

have as I have repeatedly told you have the batteries in the office. Come and get a new battery or call and place a work order. There is absolutely no excuse that can be justified for removing or tampering with any part of the smoke alarm that I will accept. If we didn't have an alarm in your apartment and you had a fire, you would immediately blame us, do we get to blame you when you have removed the battery or tampered with the alarm? Each of you that had removed your alarm battery will be fine $25.00 which is clearly stated and had been explained in several newsletters.

In addition, do not bring rent payments to my home, I do not have a receipt book at my home and I will not return to the office to make one after the office has closed.

This month, several residents put cash in the drop slot of the office, do not do this, for your protection and ours. Get a money order, they can be purchased at any convenience store for $1. When you pay by cash, bring the exact amount of your rent to the office, we do not keep change at the office, if you do not have the correct amount, any amount that is over, will be credited to next month's rent, we will not make change.

Please do not hand me your rent in cash while I am outside in the courtyard, without having a receipt book, this is not a good policy.

Again, it is your responsibility for telling your guests where to park. You know how it feels in and there are no parking spaces because they are filled with guests. I constantly see the same guests parking on the lot, the lot is posted for resident parking with all others towed, I have threatened to tow in the past, but once again, it has gotten out of hand and we are almost full and it takes every space on the lot just so our residents are allowed to park on the lot. Effective today, all non stickered vehicles will be towed with no advance warning. When this happens, perhaps you will want to pay the towing charge to your guest since you did not tell them where to park.

When your guests vehicles get towed, please do not contact me. There will be a sticker telling them exactly where to get in touch with the wrecker service to retrieve their vehicle.

Once again there is trash being left outside apartments overnight and during the day. Please, we take prospective residents thru the courtyard nearly every day and it is very embarrassing to have to pass other people's trash. If you can't carry it out, leave it in your house until you can. It will be greatly appreciated

Finally, please remove all mops that are hanging on balconies and on the pool fence. A good place to put a wet mop is in the water heater closet. It is warm in there and the mop will dry very quickly.

FIGURE 4-6 *continued*

Guidelines for Issuing AMBER Alerts

Every successful AMBER plan contains clearly defined activation criteria. The following guidance is designed to achieve a uniform, interoperable network of plans across the country, and to minimize potentially deadly delays because of confusion among varying jurisdictions. The following are criteria **recommendations**:

Law Enforcement Confirms an Abduction

AMBER plans require law enforcement to confirm an abduction prior to issuing an alert. This is essential when determining the level of risk to the child. Clearly, stranger abductions are the most dangerous for children and thus are primary to the mission of an AMBER Alert. To allow activations in the absence of

continued

FIGURE 4-7 Document for Exercise 3

significant information that an abduction has occurred could lead to abuse of the system and ultimately weaken its effectiveness. At the same time, each case must be appraised on its own merits and a judgment call made quickly. Law enforcement must understand that a "best judgment" approach, based on the evidence, is appropriate and necessary.

Risk of Serious Bodily Injury or Death

Plans require a child be at risk for serious bodily harm or death before an alert can be issued. This element is clearly related to law enforcement's recognition that stranger abductions represent the greatest danger to children. The need for timely, accurate information based on strict and clearly understood criteria is critical, again keeping in mind the "best judgment" approach.

Sufficient Descriptive Information

For an AMBER Alert to be effective in recovering a missing child, the law enforcement agency must have enough information to believe that an immediate broadcast to the public will enhance the efforts of law enforcement to locate the child and apprehend the suspect. This element requires as much descriptive information as possible about the abducted child and the abduction, as well as descriptive information about the suspect and the suspect's vehicle. Issuing alerts in the absence of significant information that an abduction has occurred could lead to abuse of the system and ultimately weaken its effectiveness.

Age of Child

Every state adopt the "17 years of age or younger" standard; or, at a minimum, agree to honor the request of any other state to issue an AMBER Alert, even if the case does not meet the responding state's age criterion, as long as it meets the age criterion of the requesting state. Most AMBER plans call for activation of the alert for children under a certain age. The problem is that age can vary—some plans specify 10, some 12, some 14, 15, and 16. Differences in age requirements create confusion when an activation requires multiple alerts across states and jurisdictions. Overuse of the AMBER Alert system will undermine its effectiveness as a tool for recovering abducted children.

NCIC Data Entry

Immediately enter AMBER Alert data into the National Crime Information Center (NCIC) system. Text information describing the circumstances surrounding the abduction of the child should be entered, and the case flagged as a Child Abduction. Many plans do not mandate entry of the data into NCIC, but this omission undermines the entire mission of the AMBER Alert initiative. The notation on the entry should be sufficient to explain the circumstances of the disappearance of the child. Entry of the alert data into NCIC expands the search for an abducted child from the local, state, or regional level to the national. This is a critical element of any effective AMBER Alert plan.

Summary of Department of Justice Recommended Criteria

- There is reasonable belief by law enforcement that an abduction has occurred.
- The law enforcement agency believes that the child is in imminent danger of serious bodily injury or death.
- There is enough descriptive information about the victim and the abduction for law enforcement to issue an AMBER Alert to assist in the recovery of the child.
- The abduction is of a child aged 17 years or younger.
- The child's name and other critical data elements, including the Child Abduction flag, have been entered into the National Crime Information Center (NCIC) system.

Source: http://www.amberalert.gov/guidelines.htm

FIGURE 4-7 *continued*

5

Designing Documents

Effective writing is more than just putting words on the page or computer screen, more than correct sentences organized in logical paragraphs. To be effective, your document must also be visually intelligible.

With the ever-increasing capabilities of software to change the appearance of text, to integrate illustrations and text, even to include animation and sound with text, you have many choices in how your document will look. This chapter will help you make wise choices for designing both paper and online documents.

Quick Tips

On the job, you will probably write and receive more e-mail messages than any other kind of document. If you design your e-mail messages for quick and easy reading, your recipients will be able to decipher your intended meaning efficiently and respond readily and appropriately to your instructions, questions, and requests. Here are five simple guidelines to follow:

1. **Keep your messages brief.** E-mail is especially effective for brief messages that the recipient will read and reply to quickly. Long, scrolling messages with extensive detail are often better relegated to attachments.

2. **Use short paragraphs.** Short paragraphs separated by white space encourage quick reading and make it easy for your recipient to perceive and retrieve the chief points of your message.

3. **Use the subject line to specify your message.** A clear and specific subject line will preview your message for your recipients, making their reading easier and aiding their understanding. You will also be helping recipients to sort and find your messages later, especially if you write a separate message for each topic you address.

4. **Use headings to identify the sections of your message.** Headings make it easier for your recipient to skim your message for its chief

points and assist in later retrieval of specific information in your message.

5. **Avoid distracting colors and backgrounds.** While mountains and beaches are lovely to view and vivid colors are eye-catching, such decorations are unlikely to clarify or reinforce your message and often make reading more difficult. Text is easiest to read if it is in a dark color (preferably black) and displayed against a light and solid background (preferably white).

UNDERSTANDING THE BASICS OF DOCUMENT DESIGN

Readers judge a document by how it looks as much as by what it contains. In fact, a reader's earliest impression comes from the appearance of the document, not its content. A dense page of long paragraphs will often discourage or annoy a reader even before he or she begins reading. A page designed to help readers locate important information, however, may add to the persuasiveness of your position or convince your readers to put a little more effort into finding what they need and understanding what they find.

These five principles will help you plan your document's visual design:

- Know what decisions are yours to make.
- Choose a design that fits your situation.
- Plan your design from the beginning.
- Reveal your design to your readers.
- Keep your design consistent.

Know what decisions are yours to make.   Many companies have a standard format or template for reports, letters, proposals, e-mail messages, and websites. Before you develop your document, determine the pertinent design requirements. Don't change the format arbitrarily just to be different. If you think the template you are supposed to use isn't appropriate for your audience and your message, find out who makes decisions on such design issues and make a case for the changes that you would like to see.

Keep in mind also that you don't have to use exotic or sophisticated software applications to apply basic principles of document design. The typical word processing program has all the functions you will likey need to create a visually effective document like the one shown in Figure 5-1.

Choose a design that fits your situation.   Don't make your document any more complex than the situation requires. You typically don't need a table of contents or a glossary for reports that are under five pages. Add appendix material only if it is necessary and will be useful for your readers.

Vacation Time Allowed Management Employees

The following schedule describes the new vacation schedule approved by the company. This schedule is effective immediately and will remain in effect until a further update is issued.

Vacation Eligibility
Vacation with pay shall be granted during the calendar year to each management employee who has completed 6 months of service since the date of employment. Employees who have been dismissed for misconduct will not receive vacation with pay.

Net Credited Service and Eligible Weeks
Net Credited Service is determined by the Employee Benefits Committee.

Net Credited Service	Eligible Weeks
• 6–12 months	1
• 12 months–7 years	2
• 7–15 years (or District level with 6 months service)	3
• 15–25 years (or Division level with 6 months service)	4
• 25+ years (or Department head or higher with 6 months service)	5

Guidelines
- If eligibility occurs on or after December 1, vacation may be taken in the next following year if it is taken before April 1.
- If an authorized holiday falls in a vacation week, an additional day of vacation may be taken before April 1 of the following year.

FIGURE 5-1 An Example of Effective Formatting

You'll impress readers most by providing just the information they need in a way that makes it easy for them to find it and understand it. Most people read technical and business documents selectively. They scan the document, looking for sections that are relevant to their needs. They try to grasp the main points quickly because they are busy and have far too much to read. Remember that your readers don't get paid to read documents: they get paid to make decisions and take actions. The more time it takes them to read your document, the less productive they (and their company) are and the less cost-effective you (and your document) are.

Similarly, users working with a computer program are not likely to read the entire user's manual. They go to the manual or to online help when they have a specific problem or need instructions for a specific task. They want to get to the right page or screen immediately. They want the instructions to stand out on the page or screen. Look at Figures 5-2 and 5-3. Notice how the numbered steps make for quick reading and easy understanding relative to the long and confusing paragraph of instructions.

Plan your design from the beginning. Before you start writing, carefully consider how you will organize and display your information. Ask questions like the following:

- How will your readers use the document? Will most people read it from beginning to end? Will they want to skim it and grab the main points without reading more? Will they want to jump to a specific topic? Even if they read the document through once, will they want to come back later and find a specific point quickly?

Drawing Product Help

To draw a box:

Decide where to put one corner of the box and move the mouse so that the cursor is in that position on the screen. Press and hold the left mouse button, sliding the mouse along the diagonal of the box which will appear on the screen as you move the mouse. When the box is the desired size, release the mouse button.

FIGURE 5-2 Instructions in Paragraph Style
This format is difficult to follow, both on screen and on paper.

Drawing Product Help

To draw a box:

1. Decide where to put one corner of the box.

2. Move the mouse so that the cursor is in that position on the screen.

3. Press and hold the left mouse button, sliding the mouse along the diagonal of the box.

   The box appears as you move the mouse.

4. When the box is the size you want, release the mouse button.

FIGURE 5-3 Instructions in List Form
Instructions formatted like this are easier to follow.

- How familiar are your readers with the subject of the document? How much support will they need in understanding and navigating the information you offer?
- How familiar are your readers with the kind of document you are writing? Do they come to the document with certain expectations about how the information will be organized and exhibited?
- Will most of your readers see this document on paper or on a computer screen?

If people will skim a document, for example, a table of contents and headings on every page will help them find information quickly. (The rest of this chapter includes techniques for developing effective designs to help people find what they need.)

If readers don't know much about the subject of the document, a glossary of key words and abbreviations might be necessary. Illustrations might also be important because such readers won't have a store of pictures in their minds on which to call for support.

If readers are unfamiliar with the kind of document, they might benefit from a simple and explicit design that avoids potentially confusing variations. Experienced readers, however, might have rigid design expectations: website users, for example, ordinarily assume that underlined or colored words and phrases are active links and will be annoyed if that isn't the case.

If the document is going to be read on a computer screen, you may have both more constraints and more choices than if the document were printed on paper. We read more slowly from the computer screen than from paper, so limiting the amount of information and leaving blank space between paragraphs or list items is crucial in an online document. Illustrations and color will also be easier and less expensive to include in an online document than in a paper document.

Reveal your design to your readers. Research on how people read and process information shows that readers must see how information is organized in order to make sense of it. That is, as you read, you try to do things at the same time: you try to make sense of the passage you're reading and you try to make sense of how this passage fits with previous passages and what it contributes to the entire document. The more difficult it is to do one or the other, the more difficult the document is to read.

Tables of contents and headings reveal the organization, scope, and direction of your document and give readers a clear overview or map with which to proceed. Using headings (at least one on every page) in a memo will show the structure and logic of the discussion and help readers recognize, remember, and retrieve your major points. Longer reports definitely need headings and a table of contents that lists the headings. In online documents, a contents list links to pages whose titles are like the headings in paper documents.

Keep your design consistent. Consistency in design is essential to easy reading. When you have considered your audiences, the content you have to deliver, and the ways that people will read and use your document, you can develop a page design that will work well for your situation. Once you have decided on the appropriate page design, don't change it for arbitrary reasons. You want your readers to know immediately when they are beginning a new section, and when they are in another part of the same section, because they recognize the differences in the design of the headings at each level.

A good way to achieve this consistency is by identifying the different types of information in your document and using the styles function of your word processing program to duplicate the design.

First, think about all the types of information you will need to display, such as paragraphs, quotations, lists, examples, equations, formulas and various levels of headings. Second, plan a design that always shows the same type of information in the same way throughout your document. The design could include the type size; the typeface, or font; placement of an element on the page; whether the text has a border (also called a line or a rule) over or under it; whether the text or headings are bold or italic; the amount of space that comes before and after a heading; the style of the text that follows each kind of heading; and so forth. Third, use the style

---

Wilson, Wilson, and Fitch
2202 Winding Parkway, Suite 400
Glendale, Arizona 85320

September 14, 2009

Mr. Nick Marshall
Vice President
Multi-Tech Company
34454 Meadows Avenue
Glendale, AZ 85320

SUBJECT: Tax Treatment of Moving Expenses for Employees

Dear Mr. Marshall:

The moving expenses of your employees are regarded as itemized deductions subject to several requirements and limitations. Your employees should have no problem meeting the requirements for deductibility, but they should be informed of the limitations that apply to these expenses.

Conditions for Eligibility

- **Distance Test.** The distance between the old residence and the new residence and the new place of employment must be at least 35 miles farther than the distance between the old residence and the new place of employment. Because your employees will be moving across the country, they will meet this test.

- **Minimum Period of Employment after the Move.** There is a 39-week minimum period of employment following the move. This minimum should have no effect on your employees as long as they continue to work for your company.

Limitations of Expenses

Once the foregoing conditions have been met, the moving expenses qualify as itemized deductions. However, some of these expenses are limited by specific dollar amounts, depending on whether the expense is direct or indirect.

Direct Expenses

Expenses directly associated with moving to the new residence are not limited, except to say that they must be reasonable. Direct expenses include

- Traveling from the old residence to the new residence
- Moving all household goods to the new location.

FIGURE 5-4 Letter That Uses Document Design Principles

function of your word processing program to label and fix the design of each type of information.

Figure 5-4 shows a letter using document design to reveal the content and the relationships among the sections. This example shows how any document, including routine letters and memos, will benefit from the use of a consistent design.

Mr. Nick Marshall
September 14, 2009
Page 2

Indirect Expenses

House hunting and temporary living expenses are limited to a total of $1,500 as a deduction.

1. **House hunting expenses** are all expenses incurred while you are actually looking for a house or dwelling. You must be working for your new company and looking for a house to use these expenses as indirect expenses.

2. **Temporary living expenses** include food and lodging expenses you incur after you move to the area of the new place of employment but before you move into a permanent residence.

   Note: Temporary living expenses will be allowed during a maximum 30-day period only.

3. **Residence expenses** are costs you incur in selling the old residence and/or costs incurred in locating a new one. Examples of these expenses include

   • Closing costs
   • Real estate commissions
   • Expenses necessary in acquiring or settling a lease.

Total deductible expenses in the indirect category, including house hunting costs, temporary living expenses, and residence expenses are limited to $3,000. Any amount incurred in excess of this amount cannot be taken as an itemized deduction.

If you need any further clarification, please call me at 303 444-5609.

Sincerely,

Kelly Jones

Kelly Jones, C.P.A.
Wilson, Wilson, and Fitch

FIGURE 5-4 *continued*

DESIGNING EFFECTIVE PAGES AND SCREENS

Visually effective pages and computer screens are designed on a grid, so readers know where to look for information. They have space inside the text, around the graphics, and in the margins, so they look uncluttered and information is easy to locate. The line length and margins help people read easily. The following suggestions will help you develop visually effective pages and screens:

- Use blank space to frame and group information.
- Set the spacing for easy reading.
- Use a medium line length.
- Use a ragged right margin.

Use blank space to frame and group information. Don't think of blank space as wasted or empty space. Space is a critical element in design for both paper and screens because it makes information easier to find and read. Look at Figures 5-5 and 5-6. Which do you think is easier to read?

You can incorporate blank space into documents in several ways. A critical location for blank space is at the margins. Here, blank space serves to enclose and contain the information and keep the page or screen from looking crowded and chaotic. Clear and generous margins make your information look organized and coherent.

If your document will be read on paper, also think about how it will be bound. If you are putting your work in a binder, be sure to leave room for the binding so that holes don't punch through the text. Similarly, think about whether a reader will want to punch holes in a copy later or put the work in a binder. These guidelines appear proportionately for margins on a standard 8½-by-11-inch page:

top margin	1 inch
bottom margin	1 inch
left margin	1 inch, if material is not being bound
	1½ inches, if material is being bound
right margin	1 inch

If you are going to photocopy on both the front and back of the page, leave space for the binding in the left margin of odd-numbered pages and in the right margin of even-numbered pages. Word processing programs allow you to choose mirror margins so that they alternate for right-hand (odd-numbered) pages and left-hand (even-numbered) pages. If you cannot set alternating margins, set both the right and the left margin at about 1½ inches to allow for binding two-sided copies.

The space in the margins is important, but it's not enough. Graphic designers call margins *passive space* because margins only define the block of the page or screen that readers should look at. Graphic designers know that *active space*—the space inside the text—makes the real difference in designing effective pages or screens. Blank space helps users to find information quickly, keep track of

TO: All Department Heads

SUBJECT: New Copy Procedures

A recent study of our copy center request procedures indicates that we are not fulfilling copy requests as efficiently as possible. A number of problems surfaced in the survey. First, many requests, particularly large orders, are submitted before the copy center opens. Others are submitted after the copy center closes. As a result, the copy center has an enormous backlog of copy orders to fill before it can begin copy orders submitted after 8:30 A.M., when the center officially opens. This backlog may throw the center two or three hours behind schedule. All copy requests throughout the day then require over two hours to complete. By 2:00 P.M., any copy requests submitted may not be filled that day. If large orders arrive unexpectedly even a routine copy request may take two days to complete.

To remedy the situation, we will change to the following copy request procedure beginning Monday, February 7. The copy center will close at 3:00 every afternoon. Two work-study employees will work at the center from 3:00 until 5:00 to complete all orders by 4:00. If you submit copy requests by 3:00, the center will have them ready by 4:00. In short, all requests will be filled the day they are submitted. However, do not leave copy requests after 3:00, as these will not be processed until the following day. However, we guarantee that if you leave your request for copies with us between 8:30 and 3:00, you will have them that day.

Requests for copies of large orders—over 100 copies of one item, single/multiple copies of any document over 25 pages, of front/back photocopying of one item up to 50 copies—will require that a notice be given the copy center one day in advance. That way, the center can prepare for your copy request and be sure to have it ready for you. Copies of the request form are attached. Please complete one of these and send it to Lynda Haynes at the copy center so that she can schedule all big jobs. If you submit a big copy request without having completed the form, your request will be completed after other requests are complete.

Allow plenty of time for routine jobs—at least two hours, and three if possible. Beginning February 7, give all copy requests to the receptionist at your office number. Be sure you attach complete instructions. Give your name, your phone number, and your office number. State the number of copies required and any special instructions. Specify staples or clips, color paper, and collation on multipage copies.

Pick-up procedures also change February 7. All copy jobs, after they are complete, will be placed in each department's mail box. No copies will be left outside the copy center after closing time. No copies will be left with the receptionist. Large orders that will not fit mail boxes will be delivered to your office.

If you have questions about this new procedure, please contact Lynda Haynes at 2257.

FIGURE 5-5 Memo That Violates Format Guidelines

TO: All Department Heads   DATE: January 27, 2009

FROM: Lynda Haynes

SUBJECT: **New Procedures for Ordering Copies from the Copy Center**

EFFECTIVE DATE: MONDAY, FEBRUARY 7, 2009

To handle orders more quickly and efficiently, the Copy Center is changing its procedures. Please inform everyone in your department and ask them to follow these new procedures.

Large Orders and Routine Requests

First, you must decide if you have a large order or a routine request. A large order is

- more than 100 copies of any item
- more than 50 copies of any item to be copied two-sided (front/back)
- single or multiple copies of any document over 25 pages.

Procedures for a Large Order

1. Fill out one of the attached Requests for Copying a Large Order forms.
2. Send the completed form to Lynda Haynes at the Copy Center at least one day in advance of the day you need the copying done.

   That way, Lynda can schedule big jobs, and you will avoid delays in getting your copying completed.

Procedure for a Routine Request

1. Attach complete instructions to your request. Include
   - your name, phone number, and office number
   - the number of copies you need
   - for multiple-page copies: instructions on collating and staples or clips
   - any special instructions, such as paper color
2. Give all copy requests to the Copy Center receptionists.
3. Allow 2 to 3 hours for your order to be filled.

NOTE:

Routine requests left between 8:30 A.M. and 3:00 P.M. will be processed by 4:00 P.M. on the same day.

The Copy Center will close at 3:00 P.M. Orders left after that time will be processed the next day.

Copy Pick Up Procedures

Copies will be delivered to your department's mailbox. If the order is too large for your mailbox, it will be delivered to your office.

If You Have Questions . . .   Contact Lynda Haynes at ext. 2257.

FIGURE 5-6 A Revision of Figure 5-5

the location of information, process the information in identifiable chunks, and retrieve the information later.

Here are three techniques to bring active space to your pages and screens:

- Use headings frequently (and at least once per page or screen). Put them above the text or to the left of the text and put space before them.
- Use bulleted lists for three or more parallel points. Use numbered lists for steps in instructions. Lists are often indented inside the text, and each item may be separated from the others by a blank space.
- Separate paragraphs with an extra blank line, or indent the first line of each paragraph. In online documents, make your paragraphs even shorter than you would in paper documents so that there is space even in a small window. Online, one instruction or one short sentence may make an appropriate paragraph.

Space the lines of text for easy reading. It's customary in paper documents to use single spacing. (For a brief lettter or memo of a single paragraph, double spacing is appropriate.) When you use single spacing, insert an extra line between paragraphs.

Drafts of documents submitted for review and editing are often double-spaced to give writers and editors more room in which to write corrections and notes. When you use double spacing in drafts, you need to have some way to show where new paragraphs begin. Either indent the first line of each paragraph or add an extra line between paragraphs.

For documents that will be read on the computer screen, use single spacing, with an extra line inserted between paragraphs. Double spacing is rarely used for continuous text on the screen because a typical screen holds only about one-third of what a paper page holds.

Set the line length for easy reading. Long lines of text (over 15 words) fatigue readers and make them lose their place in moving from the right margin back to the left margin of the next line. Short lines (under 5 words) are also difficult to read because readers are almost continuously shifting their eyes from the right margin to the left margin of the next line with little time for moving across each line. Figure 5-7 illustrates the problems with both long and short lines of text.

The number of words that fit on a line depends in part on the size and style of type that you are using. If you have one column of text on a page or screen, try to keep the lines of text to about ten to twelve words. In a format with two equal columns, keep each column to about five to seven words.

Use a ragged right margin. The first line of a paragraph of text either starts at the left margin (called *block style*) or is indented two or five spaces (called *indented style*). This book uses indented style for paragraphs. Letters and memos often use block style. In both styles, all the lines after the first one in a paragraph start at the left margin.

Long lines of type are difficult for many people to read. Readers may find it difficult to get back to the correct place at the left margin. The smaller the type, the harder it is for most people to read long lines of type.

Very short lines
look choppy
on a page
and make
comprehension
difficult.

FIGURE 5-7 Line Length

Although text is almost always lined up on the left margin, it is sometimes also aligned on the right margin, creating a tidy rectangle of text. The text of this book, for example, is aligned on both the left and the right margins. Most of the examples in the figures in this chapter, however, are aligned on the left but not on the right. The technique of making all the text align exactly on both the left and the right margin is called *justifying the text*. If the text is aligned on the left but not on the right, it has a *ragged right margin*.

Be careful if you decide to justify type. Think about the purpose and audience for your work. Justified type gives a document a formal tone. Unjustified (ragged right) type gives a document a more friendly, informal feeling. Justified text is often more difficult for readers because every line is the same length, thus eliminating a visual signal that helps readers both to keep their place and to find the next line of text. Online documents almost always have ragged right margins because reading from the screen is more difficult than reading from paper and because writers usually want to make their online documents look friendly and inviting.

HELPING READERS LOCATE INFORMATION

To help your readers find what they need as quickly as possible and make sense of what they find as easily as possible, you have to plan a useful structure for your document, and you have to show that structure to your readers. In the previous sections of this chapter, we showed you how to use page layout and fonts to make your document clear and easy to use. In this section, we show you how to give readers clues to the document's overall structure.

On the job, people usually read technical and business documents selectively. With a print document, readers may glance over the table of contents to see what the document is about and then pick and choose the sections to read by looking for headings that match their needs and interests. They may go straight to the index (or the search function for online documents) to find the location of a specific topic. They may skim through the pages, stopping when a heading or example or illustration strikes them as important. They may go back to the document later to retrieve or verify specific facts.

Following are four ways to help your readers find information easily:

- Use frequent headings
- Write descriptive headings.
- Design distinctive headings.
- Use page numbers and headers or footers.

Use frequent headings. Frequent headings help readers know where they are in a document at all times. In a report, you probably want a heading for every subsection, which might cover two or three paragraphs. In general, in print you want to have clues to the text's arrangement on every page; online you should have a heading on every screen or window. On a website page you want to keep each topic short and give each topic a heading.

Write descriptive headings. Headings are the short titles that you use to label each section and subsection of your document. Even brief documents, such as memos and letters, can benefit from headings. Compare Figures 5-8 and 5-9 to see how useful headings can be, even in a brief memo.

Headings are the road map to your document, identifying the key topics and revealing the direction of thought.

These five suggestions will help you write useful headings:

- Use concrete language.
- Use questions, verb phrases, and sentences instead of nouns alone.
- Use standard keywords if readers expect them.
- Make the headings at a given level parallel.
- Make sure the headings match the table of contents.

Use concrete language. Generic headings such as *Introduction* or *Conclusion* give no indication of the topic you are discussing. Make your headings specific to your document. Make your headings reveal the subject and claims of your document. Readers should be able to read only your headings, without any of the accompanying text, to get a clear sense of your overall message.

Use questions, verb phrases, and sentences instead of nouns alone. The best way to write headings is to put yourself in your readers' place. Will readers come to your document with questions? Then questions will make good headings. Will they come wanting instructions for doing tasks? Then verb phrases that match the actions they need to take will make good headings. Will they come seeking knowledge about a situation? Then statements of fact about that situation will make good headings.

In addition, avoid headings that are individual nouns or strings of nouns: such headings are often perceived as ambiguous. For example, a heading such as "Evaluation Questionnaire Completion" makes it impossible to predict the kind of

TO: David Stewart   DATE: February 18, 2009

FROM: Kathy Hillman

SUBJECT: Short Course Request from Ocean Drilling

Because I will be away on a three-week teaching assignment, I would appreciate your handling the following request, which came in just as I was preparing to leave today.

Randy Allen, director of the offshore drilling research team, would like a short-course in writing offshore safety inspection reports. He would like the short-course taught from 2–4 P.M. <u>Monday–Friday afternoons, beginning week after next.</u> The class must be scheduled then, as the team leaves the following week for their next research cruise.

The drilling research team spends <u>two weeks each month on cruise.</u> After they return, they have one week to complete their reports before briefing begins for the next research expedition. Because of their rigid schedule, <u>they cannot attend our regularly scheduled writing classes.</u>

Allen says that the cultural and educational backgrounds of the team are varied. Five of the ten regular researchers are native Europeans who attended only European universities. Of the remaining five, two have degrees from U.S. institutions, and three attended Canadian universities. <u>As a result of their varied educational backgrounds, their reports lack uniform handling of English and organization.</u> All the researchers have expressed interest in having a short review of standard English usage so that their reports to management will be more uniform.

<u>Sarah Kelley</u> says she can develop a class for the drilling team. We have materials on reports, style, and standard usage in the files. She can work with Ocean Drilling to determine the best report structure and develop a plan. These <u>items can be easily collected and placed in binders.</u> We also have <u>summary sheets</u> on each topic that will be good reference aids when the researchers write their reports following their cruise.

<u>Sarah will contact you Monday morning. If her teaching the class meets with your approval, please give Randy Allen a call, at extension 721, before noon. He has a staff meeting scheduled at 1:30 and would like to announce the short course then. In fact, if the course cannot be scheduled this month, it cannot be taught for seven months because of off-season cruise schedules. Randy wants this course before the team begins a series of four reports during the off-season.</u>

Please arrange a time for Sarah to meet with Randy so they can go over several previous reports. Sarah wants to be sure that what she covers in the course is what they need.

If you need to talk to me about this request, I will be staying at the Hyatt in New Orleans.

FIGURE 5-8 Memorandum That Overuses Underlining and Lacks Headings

TO: David Stewart   DATE: February 18, 2009

FROM: Kathy Hillman

SUBJECT: Request from Offshore Drilling Team for a Special Short Course

ACTION
REQUIRED: Decision from you by Monday, February 21 at noon

Because I will be away on a three-week teaching assignment, I would appreciate your handling the following request, which came in just as I was preparing to leave today.

Offshore Drilling Wants a Special Short Course

Randy Allen, director of the offshore drilling research team, would like a short course in how to write offshore safety inspection reports. He would like the short course taught from 2 to 4 P.M. Monday to Friday afternoons, beginning the week after next. Randy wants this course before they begin a series of four reports during the off-season.

They Cannot Attend Our Regular Writing Classes

The class must be scheduled at the time Randy has requested because the team leaves the following week for their next research cruise. The team spends two weeks each month on cruise. After they return, they have one week to complete their reports before briefing begins for the next research expedition. Because of this rigid schedule, they cannot attend our regularly scheduled writing classes. In fact, **if the course cannot be scheduled this month, it cannot be taught for seven months** because of the off-season cruise schedules.

The Offshore Drilling Team Needs Help with Their Writing

Randy says that the cultural and educational backgrounds of the team are varied. Five of the ten regular researchers are native Europeans who attended only European universities. Of the remaining five, two have degrees from U.S. institutions, and three attended Canadian universities. As a result of their varied educational backgrounds, their reports lack uniform handling of English and report organization. All the researchers have expressed interest in having a short review of standard English usage so that their reports to management will be more uniform.

Sarah Kelley Can Develop the Class

Sarah Kelley says she can develop a class for the offshore drilling team. We have materials on reports, style, and standard usage in the files. She can work with the ocean drilling group to determine the best report structure and develop a plan. These items can be easily collected and put in binders. We also have summary sheets on each topic that will be good reference aids when the researchers write their reports following their cruise.

Please Decide by Monday Noon and Call Randy Allen—Extension 721

Sarah will contact you Monday morning. If you approve of her teaching the class, please call Randy Allen at extension 721, before noon. **He has a staff meeting scheduled for 1:30 and would like to announce the short course then.**

Please arrange a time for Sarah Kelley to meet with Randy Allen so they can go over several previous reports. Sarah wants to be sure that what she covers in the course is what they need.

FIGURE 5-9 Revision of Figure 5-8

information that this section will offer. Much clearer would be a heading such as "How Do I Complete the Evaluation Questionnaire?" or "What Is the Deadline for Completing the Evaluation Questionnaires?" or "Who Must Complete the Evaluation Questionnaire? Figure 5-10 shows how effective it can be to use questions, verb phrases, and statements as headings.

Use standard keywords if readers expect them. You may be working on a document for which readers expect to see a certain set of headings in a certain order, as in a standard proposal format. In that case, organize your material in the order and with the headings that your readers expect. Figure 5-11 shows the headings you might use in a standard proposal format.

Make the headings at a given level parallel. Like list items, headings at any given level in a document should be parallel. Parallelism is a very powerful tool in writing. See for yourself the difference parallelism makes by comparing the two sets of headings in Figure 5-12.

Make sure the headings match the table of contents. To check how well your headings tell your story and to check how well you've maintained parallel structure in headings, use your word processing program to create an outline view or a

---

Questions are useful as headings in a brochure.
  What does the gypsy moth look like?
  How can we protect trees from gypsy moths?
  How often should we spray?

Verb phrases are useful in instruction manuals.
Verb phrases can be gerunds, like these:
  Adding a graphic
  Selecting the data
  Choosing type of graph to use
  Adding a title
Verb phrases can be imperatives, like these:
  Make your attendance policy clear.
  Explain your grading policy.
  Announce your office hours.
  Supply names of texts to be purchased.
  Go over assignments and their due dates.

Short sentences are useful in memos and reports.
  Our workload has doubled in the past year.
  We are also being asked to do new tasks.
  We have logged 560 hours of overtime this year.
  We need three more staff positions.

FIGURE 5-10 Different Structures You Can Use for Effective Headings

Project Summary   Facilities and Equipment
Project Description   Personnel
Rationale and Significance   Budget
Plan of Work

FIGURE 5-11 Keywords as Headings in a Proposal

table of contents for your draft document. Both in print and online, the headings will compose the table of contents. In a print document, readers can use the table of contents to locate a particular section. They know they're in the right place if the heading for that section matches the wording in the table of contents. The same is important online, where readers almost always navigate the document by jumping directly from a heading in the contents to a screen of information. If the heading on the screen they come to doesn't match the heading that they clicked on in the table of contents, they may be unsure of their location. Their confusion will quickly lead to annoyance.

Design Distinctive Headings. Headings do more than outline your document. They also help readers find specific parts quickly, and they show the relationship among the parts. To help readers, headings have to be easily distinguished from the text and each level of heading has to be easily distinguished from all the other levels. Figure 5-13 is a good example of a print document with four levels of headings. You can see how the writer uses boldface to distinguish all headings from the text and then uses type size, capitalization, and position on the page to distinguish each level of heading from the other levels.

These seven suggestions will help you design distinctive headings:

- Limit the number of heading levels.
- Create a pattern for the headings and stick to it.
- Match size to importance.
- Put more space before a heading than after it.

Nonparallel Headings   **Parallel Headings**
Graph Modifications   Modifying a graph
Data selection updating   Changing the data
To add or delete columns   Adding or deleting columns
How to change color or patterns   Changing the color or patterns
Titles and legends can be included   Adding titles and legends

FIGURE 5-12 Nonparallel and Parallel Headings
Headings that use the same sentence structure—parallel headings—are easier for users to follow.

- Keep each heading with the section it covers.
- Use headings frequently.
- Consider using numbers with your headings.

Limit the number of heading levels. Don't make the hierarchy of levels more complicated than it needs to be. Headings are supposed to be an aid to reading, not an obstacle. The more levels of headings you use, the more that readers must do to keep the hierarchy straight in their minds. Paper documents don't need more than four levels of headings. If you have more than four levels, consider dividing the material into two chapters. Online documents don't need more than two levels of headings: readers see much less at one time online than in a paper document and will more easily lose track of the different levels of headings.

Create a pattern for the headings and stick to it. Although your choices depend in part on the technology you are using, you almost certainly have several options for showing levels of headings. Figure 5-13 demonstrates a variety of ways to show different levels of headings. You can combine these to create the pattern for your headings. For example, you can change size, position, *and* capitalization to show the different levels of headings.

Match size to importance. Changing the type size is one way to indicate levels of headings. If you use different type sizes, make sure that you match the size to the level of importance. If the headings are different sizes, readers expect first-level headings to be larger than second-level headings, second-level headings to be larger than third-level headings, and so on, as shown in Figure 5-13. The lower-level headings can be the same size as the text, but no level of heading should be smaller than the text. That would violate readers' expectations. If you use different type sizes for different heading levels, don't make the differences too great.

Put more space before a heading than after it. Headings announce the topic that is coming next in your document. Therefore, you want the heading to lead the

---

Controlling Soil-Borne Pathogens in Tree Nurseries

Types of Soil-Borne Pathogens and Their Effects on Trees
Simply stated, the effects of soil-borne pathogens . . .

Soil-borne fungi
At one time, it was thought that soil-borne fungi . . .

    Basiodiomycetes. The Basiodiomycetes are a class of fungi whose species . . .

    Phycomycetes. The class of Phycomycetes is a highly diversified type of fungus. It is the . . .

Plant parasitic nematodes
Nematodes are small, unsegmented . . .

Treatments and Controls for Soil-Borne Pathogens

FIGURE 5-13 Four Levels of Headings in a Report

reader's eye down the page or screen into the text that follows. One way to do that is to have more space, on the page or screen, before the heading rather than after it. In this way, the heading and its accompanying text constitute a visible chunk of information.

If you are going to use a rule with the heading, consider putting it *above* the heading rather than below it. A rule above the heading creates a "chunk" that includes both the heading and the text that it covers. A rule above the heading also draws the reader's eye down into the text that follows instead of up and away from that text.

Keep each heading with the section it covers. Don't leave a heading at the bottom of a page when the text appears on the next page. Make sure you have at least two lines of the first paragraph on the page with the heading. In some cases, you may want each topic to be on a separate page so that the heading and all the text of a topic appear together. Most word processing programs have functions that help you keep headings from being stranded at the bottom of a page and that allow you to set up your document so that all headings of a certain level start on a new page.

Consider using numbers with your headings. In many companies and agencies, the standard for organizing reports and manuals is to use a numbering system with headings. Figure 5-14 shows two such numbering systems: the alphanumeric system and the decimal system.

```
TITLE
I.  FIRST-LEVEL HEADING                    alphanumeric system
     A. Second-Level Heading
        1. Third-level heading
        2. Third-level heading
     B. Second-Level Heading
II. FIRST-LEVEL HEADING
     A. Second-Level Heading
        1. Third-level heading
           a. Fourth-level heading
           b. Fourth-level heading
        2. Third-level heading
     B. Second-Level Heading


TITLE
1 FIRST-LEVEL HEADING                      decimal system
     1.1 Second-Level Heading
        1.1.1 Third-level heading
        1.1.2 Third-level heading
     1.2 Second-Level Heading
2 FIRST-LEVEL HEADING
     2.1 Second-Level Heading
        2.1.1 Third-level heading
           2.1.1.1. Fourth-level heading
           2.1.1.2. Fourth-level heading
        2.1.2 Third-level heading
     2.2 Second-Level Heading
```

FIGURE 5-14 Two Types of Numbering Systems

A numbering system allows you to refer precisely and concisely to a section of the report by the number of its heading (e.g., Section II.A.3.b or Section 4.3.7). If you add or delete a section later, however, you must be sure to revise the numbering of the report. In addition, a lot of readers find numbering systems confusing and, for example, would fail to recognize immediately that a section numbered 6.8.23 would come after a section numbered 6.8.2.3. If you use a numbering system with your headings, include the numbers before the entries in your table of contents.

Use page numbers and headers or footers. In addition to clearly worded and visually accessible headings, page numbers and running headers and footers are important aids to efficient reading.

Number the pages. Page numbers help readers keep track of where they are and provide easy reference points for talking about a document. Always number the pages of drafts and final documents that people are going to read on paper.

If the document is going to be used online, inserting page numbers could be unnecessary. In websites, for example, readers jump from topic to topic and page to page instead of proceeding in a specified order from start to finish. In addition, word processing programs keep track automatically of the number of pages and typically display this information in the bottom margin of the document window as a reference point for writers and readers. If readers are likely to print your online document, however, they will certainly appreciate your inclusion of page numbers. In slide shows for oral presentations, you will help your audience to track your progress and to stay attentive if you identify the slides with a numbering notation like this:

Slide 1 of 10

Short manuscripts and reports that have little prefatory material almost always use Arabic numerals (1, 2, 3). The common convention is to center the page number below the text at the bottom of the page or to put it in the upper outside corner (upper left corner for left-hand pages, upper right corner for right-hand pages). Always leave at least one double space between the text and the page number. Put the page number in the same place on each page. Page numbers at the bottom of the page often have a hyphen on each side, like this:

-17-

As reports grow longer and more complicated, the page-numbering system also may need to be more complex. If you have a preface or other material that comes before the main part of the report, it is customary to use lowercase Roman numerals (i, ii, iii) for that material and then to change to Arabic numerals for the body of the report.

In a report, the introduction may be part of the prefatory material or the main body. The title page doesn't show the number but is counted as the first page. The page following the title page is number 2 or ii.

You also have to know whether the document will be printed on one side of the paper or two. If both sides will carry printing, you may have to number several otherwise blank pages in word processing files. New chapters or major sections usually start on a right-hand page. The right-hand page always has an odd number. If the last page of your first chapter is page 9, for example, and your document will be printed double-sided, you have to include one otherwise blank page 10 so that the first page of your second chapter will be a right-hand page 11 when the document is printed, copied, and bound.

The body of a report is usually paginated continuously, from page 1 to the last page. For the appendices, you may continue the same series of numbers, or you may change to a letter-plus-number system. In that system, the pages in Appendix A are numbered A-1, A-2, and so on. The pages in Appendix B are numbered B-1, B-2, and so forth. If your report is part of a series, or if your company has a standard report format, you will need to make your page numbering match that of the series or standard format.

Numbering appendices with the letter-plus-number system has several advantages:

- It separates the appendices from the body. Readers can tell how long the body of the report is and how long each appendix is.
- It clearly shows that a page is part of an appendix and which appendix it belongs to. It makes pages in the appendices easier to locate.
- It allows the appendices to be printed separately from the body of the report. Sometimes the appendices are ready before the body of the report has been completed, and being able to print the appendices first may save time and help you meet a deadline.
- It allows the pagination of either an appendix or the body to be changed without requiring changes in the other parts.

Include headers or footers.   In long documents, it helps readers if you give identifying information at the top or bottom of each page. Information at the top of the page is a header; information at the bottom of the page is a footer. Organizations often have standard practices regarding the information to be displayed in headers and footers. A typical header for a report might show the author's name, the title of the report, and the date. It might look like this:

Jane Fernstein   Feasibility Study   June 2009

In this case, the page numbers would likely appear in the footer.

A typical header for a letter might show the name of the person receiving the letter, the page number, and the date. It might look like this:

Dr. Jieru Chen   -2-   June 16, 2009

Or

Dr. Jieru Chen
Page 2
June 16, 2009

Note that headers and footers rarely appear on the first pages of documents because first pages already carry identifying information like the title, author, recipient, and date. Word processing programs allow you to start headers and footers on the second page.

DOCUMENT DESIGN CHECKLIST ✔

- ☐ Is your document clean, organized, and attractive?
- ☐ Is your text easy to read?
- ☐ If your document is supposed to conform to a standard template, does it?
- ☐ Have you left adequate margins? (If necessary, have you left extra room for binding?)
- ☐ Is the spacing between the lines and paragraphs consistent and appropriate?
- ☐ Can the reader tell easily where sections and paragraphs begin?
- ☐ Have you checked the headings? Are the headings informative? Unambiguous? Consistent? Parallel?
- ☐ Will readers get an overall picture of the document by reading the headings?
- ☐ Is the hierarchy of the headings obvious?
- ☐ Can readers tell at a glance what is heading and what is text?
- ☐ If readers want to find a particular section quickly, will the size and placement of the heading help them?
- ☐ Have you checked the page breaks to be sure that you do not have a heading by itself at the bottom of a page?
- ☐ Are the pages of a paper document numbered?
- ☐ Are there appropriate headers or footers?
- ☐ If you are using a numbering system, is it consistent and correct?
- ☐ Did you test representative readers for their ability to locate information easily?

EXERCISES

1. Visit the website of two major employers in your field. What kinds of documents do you find at each site? Do the organizations seem to have a standard template for the design of their documents? From looking at a number of the documents at each site, how would you describe their design? Which organization does a better job of designing documents for its audience and purpose? How would you make the design of each organization's documents more effective?

2. Figure 5-15 is a first draft of the instructions for the GrillWizard.

You are a friend and neighbor of the owner and founder of Fierce Products, a new company in Lubbock that manufactures the GrillWizard. Fierce Products is a family-owned company with 45 employees. The owner (and spouse of the author) has hired you to revise the design of the instructions in order to assure safe and efficient operation of the product as well as to convey a positive impression of the quality of Fierce Products.

After you design this document, you will return it to the company owner for final approval. Fierce Products is ready to release the GrillWizard to market. As soon as the instructions are ready, the product will be boxed and shipped. The sooner you submit your design, the sooner Fierce Products will start making money.

GrillWizard

Fast and efficient frying and cooking with propane gas. Light the burner and instantly you have a hot 100,000 BTU continuous flame.

The **GrillWizard** will help you eliminate fish and other lingering cooking odors from your home.

The **GrillWizard** is used for fast frying of fish potatoes, onion rings, chicken, vegetables, and donuts. Substitute water for oil and it's also great for shrimp, crab, and lobster boils as well as steaming clams.

This cooker is completely portable with all parts easily assembled and disassembled for compact transportation and storage, yet it weighs only 40 lbs.

When the control valve is open, a full 100,000 BTUs of powerful heat prepares cooking oil in 3 minutes for frying. Adjust the heat with a touch of the control valve.

Operating Instructions

Place grill on level ground. Insert tapered end of tubing into the hole in the base of the grill. (CAUTION: Make sure the cooker is level and the burner is facing up.)

Attach grill connector to propane cylinder.

Completely open propane valve.

Slightly open control valve at grill connector and light cooker at top of tube immediately (CAUTION: **DO NOT stand directly over cooker when lighting burner**).

Adjust control valve for desired flame height.

When finished cooking, always close both grill connector valve and propane cylinder valve completely.

The **GrillWizard** works with any size of propane tank cylinder and all will give off the same amount of heat. A 20 pound cylinder will provide approximately 6 hours of cooking time if valves are completely opened.

The intense heat produced by the **GrillWizard** allows you to fast fry all foods. The cooking oils of conventional fryers drop in temperature as food is added, but the **GrillWizard** maintains its temperature with just a quick touch of the control valve.

The **GrillWizard** has been designed for easy care. However, keep all dirt and foreign objects out of connectors, hose, valves, and openings. Failure to do so could cause obstruction of gas and greatly diminish the effectiveness of the **GrillWizard.**

CAUTION: If you suspect leaks **DO NOT** light unit before checking.

For outdoor use only.

After washing pan with soap and water, dry thoroughly and coat the entire pan with cooking oil on paper towel to prevent rusting.

FIGURE 5-15 Document for Exercise 2

3. Examine Figure 5-16. If you were the author of this document and were given 15 more minutes to make it more effectively designed, what changes would you make?

Tuberculosis Facts – Exposure to TB

What is TB?

"TB" is short for a disease called tuberculosis. TB is spread through the air from one person to another. TB germs are passed through the air when someone who is sick with **TB disease** of the lungs or throat coughs, speaks, laughs, sings, or sneezes. Anyone near the sick person can breathe TB germs into their lungs.

TB germs can live in your body without making you sick. This is called **latent TB infection**. This means you have only inactive (sleeping) TB germs in your body. The inactive germs cannot be passed on to anyone else. However, if these germs wake up or become active in your body and multiply, you will get sick with **TB disease**.

When TB germs are active (multiplying in your body), this is called **TB disease**. These germs usually attack the lungs. They can also attack other parts of the body, such as, the kidneys, brain, or spine. **TB disease** will make you sick. People with **TB disease** may spread the germs to people they spend time with every day.

How was I exposed to TB?

You may have been exposed to TB if you spent time near someone with TB disease of the lungs or throat. You can only get infected by breathing in TB germs that person coughs into the air. You cannot get TB from someone's clothes, drinking glass, eating utensils, handshake, toilet, or other surfaces where a TB patient has been.

How do I know if I have been infected with TB germs?

If you have been around someone who has **TB disease**, you should go to your doctor or your local health department for tests.

Skin Test

There are two tests that can be used to help detect TB infection: a skin test or a special TB blood test. The skin test is used most often. A small needle is used to put some testing material, called tuberculin, under the skin. In 2-3 days, you return to the health care worker who will check to see if there is a reaction to the test. In some cases, a special TB blood test is given to test for TB infection. This blood test measures how a person's immune system reacts to the germs that cause TB.

Special TB Blood Test

To tell if someone has **TB disease**, other tests such as chest x-ray and a sample of sputum (phlegm that is coughed up from deep in the lungs) may be needed.

DEPARTMENT OF HEALTH AND HUMAN SERVICES
Centers for Disease Control and Prevention
Division of Tuberculosis Elimination
www.cdc.gov/tb
October 2008

FIGURE 5-16 Document for Exercise 3

6

Designing Illustrations

In communicating technical information, you will often need to use illustrations either in addition to words or instead of words to convey your message. How do you determine whether illustrations are really desirable? Ask yourself two questions:

- What do you want the reader to do or think after reading your document?
- How will illustrations help you to achieve your objective?

Quick Tips

Illustrations are of two types: tables and figures. Tables display numbers and words in columns and rows. Every other kind of illustration is a figure.

If you want to summarize information in order to make it easier to remember or retrieve, use a table.

If you want to emphasize information in order to clarify or reinforce its meaning, use a figure.

CREATING ILLUSTRATIONS

In deciding when and how to use illustrations, remember the following guidelines:

- **Simplify your illustrations.** Keep your illustrations as simple as possible so that your reader has no difficulty understanding your message. Avoid distracting your reader with unnecessary details or decorative flourishes.

- **Use computer applications critically.** Computer graphics software and clip art allow you to include a wide variety of illustrations in your document. To make sure your tables and figures are effective, however, you must evaluate the choices available from the computer. Graphics software, for example, might create artistic but misleading graphs, and clip art might exhibit a pictorial style that isn't quite serious enough or detailed enough to do justice to your subject. It is your job to choose illustrations that display your information clearly and correctly.

- **Consider size and cost.** Calculate the impact of illustrations on the expected length of your document. Illustrations will often increase the size of a document and, if printed, add to the cost of production and distribution.
- **Title your illustrations.** Give each table and figure a title that clearly indicates the message you wish it to convey.
- **Number your illustrations.** If you use several illustrations in your report, number them. Number the tables and figures separately (e.g., Table 1, Table 2, Figure 1, Figure 2). Place the number and title above a table and below a figure.
- **Alert your readers.** Always alert your readers to illustrations by referring to them in the text. Every time you refer to the illustration, use the table or figure number (e.g., see Table 1). Announce the illustration—what it is or shows—then add any verbal explanation your reader will need to fully understand it. Don't lead readers through a complicated explanation and only later refer to the illustration. Point them to the illustration immediately so that they can shift back and forth between the explanation and the illustration as necessary.
- **Position your illustrations strategically.** Place each illustration as close to the passage it explains as possible.
- **Identify your sources.** If you borrow or adapt a table or figure from another source, identify that source (and, if necessary, permission to use it) below the illustration (e.g., SOURCE: *A Legal Primer for the Digital Age,* page 24, by TyAnna K. Herrington. Copyright 2004 by Pearson Education. Reprinted by permission.).

Tables.

- Note that the purpose of a table is to summarize information in specific categories to assist the viewer in accessing and retrieving this information.
- Every column in a table should have a heading that identifies the information below it. In a table of numbers, include the unit of measurement, such as "miles per hour." For large numbers, add a designation such as "in thousands" or "in millions" to the column heading (and delete the corresponding zeros from the numeric data). Headings should be brief. If headings need more explanation, include this information in a footnote below the table. Use lowercase letters, numbers, or symbols (e.g., * or +) to indicate footnoted material.
- If possible, box your table to separate it from surrounding paragraphs.
- Keep tables as simple as possible. Include only data relevant to your purpose.
- Consider omitting lines between rows and columns to avoid giving your table a crowded appearance. If possible, use white space to separate rows and columns.

Figures 6-1 through 6-3 show three ways of presenting tabular data.

Rank	State	Pedestrians Killed	Population (Thousands)	Pedestrian Fatality Rate per 100,000 Population
		Table 22 Ranking of State Pedestrian Fatality Rates from All Crashes in 2001		
1	New Mexico	72	1,829	3.94
2	Arizona	159	5,307	3.00
3	Florida	489	16,397	2.98
4	South Carolina	108	4,063	2.66
5	Hawaii	30	1,224	2.45
6	Louisiana	98	4,465	2.19
7	Nevada	45	2,106	2.14
8	Delaware	17	796	2.14
9	Texas	449	21,325	2.11
10	Mississippi	59	2,858	2.06

FIGURE 6-1

This table is effectively designed with clear headings for the entire table as well as each of the rows. Note how bold type and a light background color work together to differentiate the headings in the table from the data. Note also that words are aligned on the left and numbers on the right (or on the decimal point) to allow the easiest possible reading, navigation, and comparison of information. The only exception is the numbers used to designate the ranking, but misreading here is unlikely.

Source: U.S. Department of Transportation, National Highway Traffic Safety Administration. Pedestrian Roadway Fatalities. DOT HS 809 456. Washington, DC: GPO, 2003. p. 30.

Bar and column graphs.

• Note that the purpose of a bar graph is to compare and contrast two or more subjects at the same point in time, whereas the purpose of a column graph is to reveal change in a subject at regular intervals of time.

• Avoid putting excessive information on a bar or column graph and thereby complicating the reader's ability to decipher it. Consider using a separate graph to communicate each point.

• Be sure to label the x-axis and the y-axis—what each measures and the units in which each is calibrated. Readers can't understand your graph if they don't know what you are measuring or how it is measured.

• For bar graphs, start the x-axis at zero and equally space the intervals on the x-axis to avoid distorting the length of the bars. For column graphs, start the y-axis at zero and equally space the intervals on the y-axis to avoid distorting

Table 5
Large Truck Fatalities by Fatality Type and Day vs. Night
1996-2000

Combination Trucks-Day vs. Night					
Fatality Type	Day	Night	Total	Day(%)	Night(%)
Occupant					
Single-vehicle	1,000	790	1,790	56%	44%
Multiple-vehicle	11,097	5,969	17,066	65%	35%
Total	12,097	6,759	18,856	64%	36%
Non-Occupant	757	674	1,431	53%	47%

Single-unit Trucks-Day vs. Night					
Fatality Type	Day	Night	Total	Day(%)	Night(%)
Occupant					
Single-vehicle	473	169	642	81%	19%
Multiple-vehicle	4,479	917	5,396	83%	17%
Total	4,952	1,086	6,038	82%	18%
Non-Occupant	545	125	670	74%	26%

FIGURE 6-2.

This table is a mess of criscrossing lines of various weights, all of which make reading difficult. Bold type is used for first-level and third-level headings, but second-level headings and numerical data are displayed in the same style of type. It's also a table with excessive information, reporting both the number and percent of day and night accidents involving two different kinds of fatalities and two different kinds of trucks. At least two separate tables would make for easier reading: one for the numbers and one for the percents. As is, the column of totals occurs in the center of the table instead of on the right as we might ordinarily expect it to.

Source: U.S. Department of Transportation, National Highway Traffic Safety Administration. An Analysis of Fatal Large Truck Crashes. DOT HS 809 569. Washington, DC: GPO, 2003. p. 30.

the height of the columns. On a bar graph, neither axis is a measure of time; on a column graph, the *x*-axis is ordinarily a measure of time.

- Color can enhance the effect of a graph, but excessive color can reduce comprehension and distort information. Use the same color for all bars or columns that are representing the same categories of information. Avoid using color as simple decoration.

- Make the graph accurate. Computer graphics allow you to add a range of special effects. However, artistic graphs are not always either effective or accurate. Three-dimensional bars and columns are often deceptive because readers have difficulty visually comparing the relative lengths of the bars and heights of the columns. If you choose three-dimensional bar or column graphs, watch for possible distortion.

- Try to write captions or labels on or near the bars. Avoid legends (or keys) that slow reader comprehension. When bars are divided into too many divisions that cannot be interpreted without consulting a legend, the result can be confusion rather than effective communication. However, placing labels on bars can be difficult if you use colored bars. Even black text will often be difficult to read on any colors but very light ones. For that reason, many graphics software programs offer you the use of legends. In short, legends are fine if you don't have too many segments or bars—more than four—and if the legend is located close to the bars.

- For divided bar and column graphs with extensive divisions, use color or solid shading to distinguish divisions instead of textured patterns that may create distracting optical illusions.

- Avoid crowding the bars or columns within a graph. Such visual clutter makes a graph look difficult to interpret. Using three-dimensional bars or columns will also reduce the number that will fit in a given space. Effective and inviting graphs leave generous space between the bars or columns.

See Figures 6-4 through 6-7 for examples of bar and column graphs.

Circle graphs.

- Note that the purpose of a circle graph (also referred to as a pie chart) is to display the number and relative size of the divisions of a subject.

- Restrict the number of segments in a circle graph to seven or eight. There is a limit to the number of segments into which a circle can be divided before comprehension of the relative sizes is jeopardized. If necessary, combine several smaller segments and create a second circle graph to display the composition of that combined segment.

- Watch for possible distortion when you use three-dimensional circle graphs.

- Clearly label all segments. Whether they are placed inside or outside the circle, labels should be horizontal for easier reading.

TABLE 3. Recommendations for reporting results of testing for antibody to hepatitis C virus (anti-HCV) by type of reflex supplemental testing performed

Anti-HCV screening test results	Supplemental test results	Interpretation	Comments
Screening-test–negative*	Not applicable	Anti-HCV–negative	Not infected with HCV, unless recent infection is suspected or other evidence exists to indicate HCV infection
Screening-test–positive* with high signal-to-cut-off (s/co) ratio	Not done	Anti-HCV–positive	Probably indicates past or present HCV infection; supplemental serologic testing not performed. Samples with high s/co ratios usually ($\geq$95%) confirm positive, but <5 of every 100 might represent false-positives; more specific testing can be requested, if indicated
Screening-test–positive	Recombinant immunoblot assay (RIBA®)-positive	Anti-HCV–positive	Indicates past or present HCV infection
Screening-test–positive	RIBA-negative	Anti-HCV–negative	Not infected with HCV, unless recent infection is suspected or other evidence exists to indicate HCV infection
Screening-test–positive	RIBA-indeterminate	Anti-HCV–indeterminate	HCV antibody and infection status cannot be determined; another sample should be collected for repeat anti-HCV testing (>1 month) or for HCV RNA testing
Screening-test–positive	Nucleic acid test (NAT)-positive	Anti-HCV–positive, HCV RNA-positive	Indicates active HCV infection
Screening-test–positive	NAT-negative RIBA-positive	Anti-HCV–positive, HCV RNA-negative	The presence of anti-HCV indicates past or present HCV infection; a single negative HCV RNA result does not rule out active infection
Screening-test–positive	NAT-negative RIBA-negative	Anti-HCV–negative, HCV RNA-negative	Not infected with HCV
Screening-test–positive	NAT-negative RIBA-indeterminate	Anti-HCV–indeterminate HCV RNA-negative	Screening test anti-HCV result probably a false-positive, which indicates no HCV infection

* Screening immunoassay test results interpreted as negative or positive on the basis of criteria provided by the manufacturer.

FIGURE 6-3. *(see facing page)*
This table is easy to read with effective spacing to separate the cells of information. Nevertheless the table could be more effective. The unnecessary repetition of "Screening-test-positive" in the left column keeps readers from quickly grasping that the table is reporting on only three conditions: positive test, positive test with qualification, and negative test. Thin rules across the table separating the three conditions would also help to make this point immediately clear.
Source: U.S. Centers for Disease Control and Prevention. Guidelines for Laboratory Testing and Result Reporting of Antibody to Hepatitis C Virus. Morbidity and Mortality Weekly Report 52 (No. RR-3): 2003. p. 11.

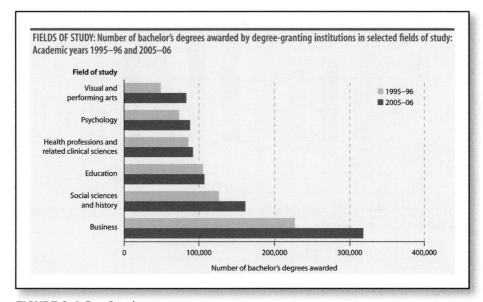

FIGURE 6-4 Bar Graph
This bar graph makes a clear and vivid point: the number of bachelor's degrees awarded in various fields, and especially in business, has risen in the 10-year period from 1995-96 to 2005-06. The dark green bars used for the later academic year seem to jump off the graph, whereas light green bars identify the earlier academic year. The six categories are crisply labeled for easy reading and understanding. The order of the categories is also easily deciphered, with the bars positioned shortest to longest from top to bottom.
Source: U.S. Department of Education, National Center for Education Statistics. *The Condition of Education 2008.* NCES 2008-031. Washington, DC: 2008. p.17.

- As you segment the graph, begin with the largest section in the upper right-hand quadrant. The remaining segments should be arranged clockwise, in descending order. Color the sections clockwise from darker to lighter so that color reinforces size.

See Figure 6-8 for an example of a circle graph.

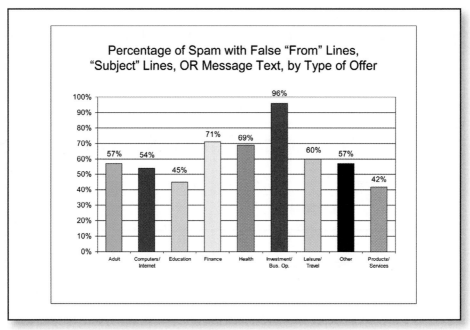

FIGURE 6-5 Column Graph

This column graph would be better designed as a bar graph (i.e., with horizontal bars instead of vertical columns). The series of vertical columns aligned on the x-axis from left to right might be initially perceived as a chronological progression—the same subject displayed at consecutive points in time. In fact, the figure displays different subjects at the same points in time. Displaying the information as a bar graph would avoid any initial misunderstanding and speed the viewer's access to the information. The arbitrary use of color is also distracting, making you pay attention to color instead of quantity . The two-dimensional columns keep the display simple and the labeling of each column is clear and specific, but the ordering of the columns is alphabetical instead of quantitative (from largest to smallest or vice versa.)

Source: U.S. Federal Trade Commission. *False Claims in Spam: A Report by the FTC's Division of Marketing Practices.* Washington, DC: 2003. p.10.

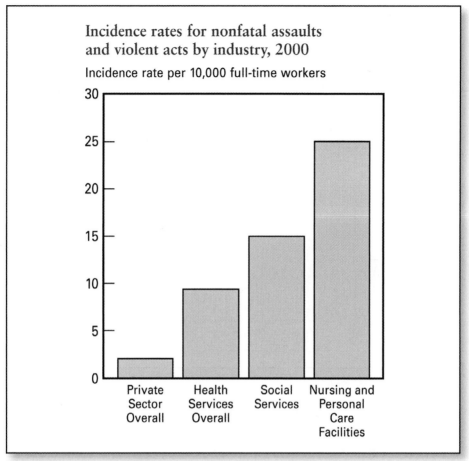

FIGURE 6-6 Column Graph

This column graph is clean and concise. The blue columns are in clear contrast to the white background. The columns also differ enough in size from each other to make the point of the graph easy to decipher (i.e., workers in the health care and social service fields run a substantially higher risk of assault). Numerical labeling of each column or gridlines in the background, as a consequence, are unnecessary.

Source: U.S. Department of Labor, Occupational Safety and Health Administration. *Guidelines for Preventing Workplace Violence for Health-Care and Social-Service Workers.* OSHA 3148. Washington, DC: 2003. p. 1.

Line graphs.

- Note that the purpose of a line graph is to show the degree and direction of change relative to two variables.

- Label each axis clearly. Like bar and column graphs, line graphs must have clearly labeled scales to show the variables you are measuring. Ordinarily, the

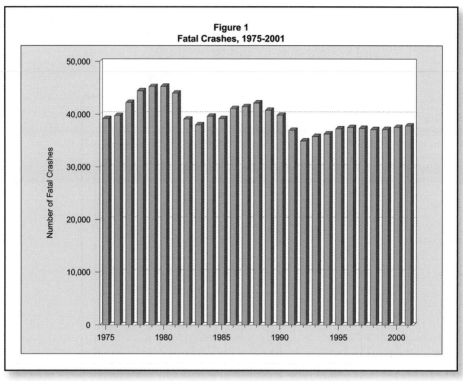

FIGURE 6-7 Column Graph

This graph makes obvious why three-dimensional columns are undesirable. The unnecessary third dimension on each column makes the entire graph look crowded and difficult to decipher. The visual effect is distracting and almost annoying as your eyes continually shift their focus from the light gray and dark gray sides of each column to the narrow and flickering white space between the columns. This effect is only exaggerated by the height of the columns. It would be easier for readers to eliminate the redundant information from 0 to 30,000 and break the y axis (indicating the break with two diagonal slashes through the y axis just above the zero point.) The labeling of each axis is easy to read, but note the inhumanity of the display: only the title implies that we're looking at a representation of a million dead human beings.

Source: U.S. Dept. of Transportation, National Highway Traffic Safety Administration. *Traffic Safety Facts 2001.* DOT HS 809 484. Washington, DC: 2002. p.14.

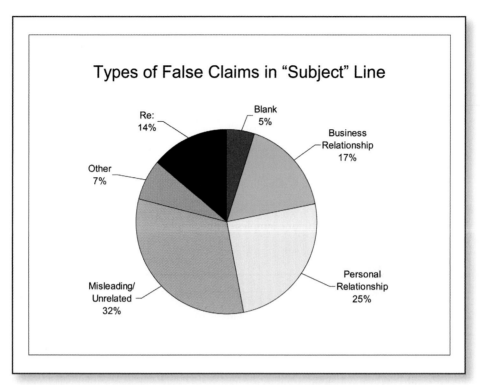

Types of False Claims in "Subject" Line

FIGURE 6-8 Circle Graph

This circle graph uses clear labels for each of its six sections. Note, however, that the sections are arbitrarily ordered and colored. Instead of starting in the upper right quadrant with the biggest piece and progressing clockwise to the smallest piece for easiest reading, the graph fails to puts its information in a logical sequence or use color in a systematic or significant fashion. Here color is only a distracting decoration. Notice, for example, how your eyes go right to the black section of the circle even though that section deserves no special priority on your attention.

Source: U.S. Federal Trade Commission. *False Claims in Spam: A Report by the FTC's Division of Marketing Practices.* Washington, DC: 2003. p. 6.

independent variable is placed on the horizontal *x-axis*, and the dependent variables are placed on the vertical *y-axis* and the diagonal *z-axis* (in a three-dimensional graph).

- Choose the scale of each axis to show the appropriate steepness of the slope of the line. Typically, the scales start at zero, with the intervals equally spaced on each axis.

- The major difficulty in designing line graphs lies in choosing the spacing for each axis so that the steepness (slope) of the line accurately measures the actual trend suggested by the data. Computer graphics will allow you to adjust the intervals on the *x-axis* and the *y-axis,* but your job is to decide whether the slope of the graph accurately depicts your data or gives a distorted impression.

- Avoid using more than three data lines on one graph unless they are spaced apart and do not overlap. Graphs with several intersecting data lines are usually difficult for readers to interpret.

- Keep the data lines on your graph distinctive by using different colors or styles for each line.

- If possible, label each data line. Avoid legends (or keys) that slow reader comprehension.

See Figures 6-9 and 6-10 for examples of line graphs.

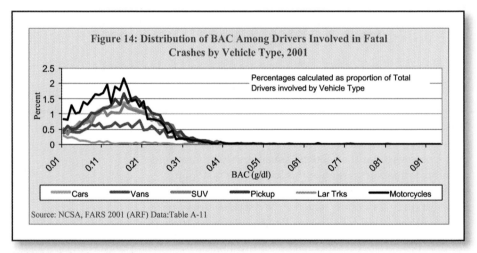

Figure 14: Distribution of BAC Among Drivers Involved in Fatal Crashes by Vehicle Type, 2001

Percentages calculated as proportion of Total Drivers involved by Vehicle Type

BAC (g/dl)

Cars   Vans   SUV   Pickup   Lar Trks   Motorcycles

Source: NCSA, FARS 2001 (ARF) Data:Table A-11

FIGURE 6-9 Line Graph

This line graph uses color coding to differentiate its six data lines. Given that the data lines intersect at multiple points, the color is essential for easy reading. Notice that black—offering the highest contrast and thus greatest visibility—is used to denote the most significant data line. The primary color of blue is used for the data line that is second in importance, but red is used for fifth instead of third. The abbreviation of BAC in the label for the x axis is appropriate, but might be clarified as Blood Alcohol Concentration in the title of the figure, especially for readers who are skimming the report.

Source: U.S. Department of Transportation, National Highway Traffic Safety Administration. *Alcohol Involvement in Fatal Crashes 2001.* DOT HS 809 579. Washington, DC: 2003. p. 9.

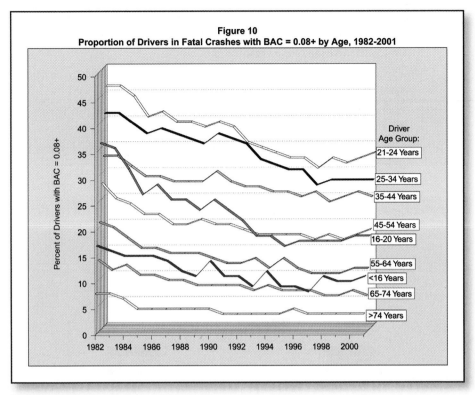

Figure 10
Proportion of Drivers in Fatal Crashes with BAC = 0.08+ by Age, 1982-2001

FIGURE 6-10 Line Graph

This line graph uses a decorative and distracting third dimension that only serves to make reading the graph difficult. Instead of using a complicated legend for its nine different data lines, the graph does include a label for each line, but the labels are located on the right side of the graph instead of the left side. This unusual position requires readers to read each data line from right to left instead of left to right. The labels might be more effective if made smaller and positioned closer to the left side of the graph.

Source: U.S. Dept. of Transportation, National Highway Traffic Safety Administration. *Traffic Safety Facts 2001.* DOT HS 809 484. Washington, DC: 2002. p. 37.

Organization charts.

- Note that the purpose of an organization chart is to to map the various divisions and levels of responsibility within an organization

- Make the chart as simple as the organization itself, with the levels of hierarchy organized highest to lowest and positioned on the chart from top to bottom. The more levels of hierarchy in the organization, the more vertical the chart; the more divisions in the organization, the more horizontal the chart.

- Use the same shape in the same size for all divisions of the organization that are at the same level in the hierarchy.
- Label each division of the organization.
- If space allows, put the labels directly on the division; if not, attach the label to the subject with thin rules (never arrows).
- Position all the labels on the horizontal so that the viewer doesn't have to rotate the page or screen to read the labels.
- Connect each level of the organization to the higher and lower levels with a clear line (never arrows).
- Connect optional, informal, or temporary relationships with a dotted line.

See Figure 6-11 for an example of an organization chart.

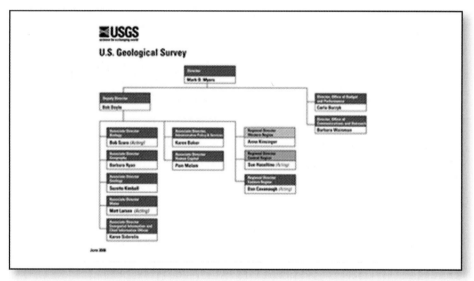

FIGURE 6-11 Organization Chart
This organization chart offers a picture of three levels of authority, with seven Associate Directors and three Regional Directors all reporting to the Deputy Director, who reports to the Director. Also reporting to the Director, is the Director of Budget and the Director of Communications. While color is effectively used to differentiate the three Regional Directors from each other and from the Associate Directors, color might also have been used to differentiate the Associate Directors from the Deputy Director.
Source: U.S. Dept. of the Interior, U.S. Geological Survey. *Organization Chart.*
http://www.usgs.gov/aboutusgs/organized/org_chart.asp.

Flow charts.

- Note that the purpose of a flow chart is to show the sequence of steps in a process or procedure.

- Make the flow chart as simple as the process itself. If a process is simple, design the flow chart so that it progresses in a single direction, usually top to bottom or left to right. Complicated designs that spiral and zigzag imply a more complicated process.

- Use the same shape in the same size for all equivalent steps or phases, but different shapes for steps or phases of a different kind (e.g., circles for the stages in researching a document, squares for the stages of writing, and diamonds for the production stages of printing and binding).

- Label each of the steps or phases.

- If space allows, put the labels directly on the step; if not, attach the label to the step with thin rules (never arrows).

- Position all the labels on the horizontal so that the viewer doesn't have to rotate the page or screen to read the labels.

- Connect each step or phase in the sequence to the next step or phase with a clear directional arrow.

- Connect reversible or interactive steps or phases with double-headed arrows.

- Connect recursive or cyclical steps or phases with circular arrows.

- Connect optional steps or phases with dotted-line arrows.

See Figures 6-12 and 6-13 for examples of flow charts.

Diagrams.

- Note that the purpose of a diagram is to identify the parts of a subject and their spatial or functional relationship.

- Keep the diagram as simple as possible, avoiding unecessary details or distracting decorations and focusing the viewer's attention on the key features or parts of the subject.

- Label each of the pertinent parts of the subject.

- If space allows, put the labels directly on the part; if not, attach the label to the part with thin rules (never arrows).

- Position all the labels on the horizontal so that the viewer doesn't have to rotate the page or screen to read the labels.

See Figure 6-14 for an example of a diagram.

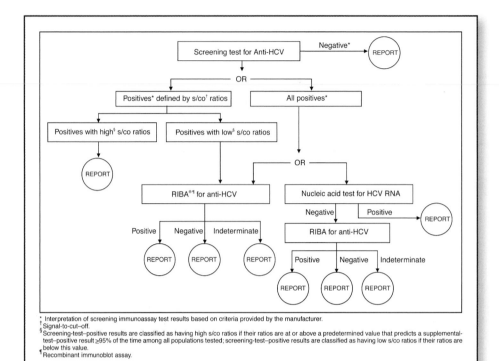

* Interpretation of screening immunoassay test results based on criteria provided by the manufacturer.
† Signal-to-cut–off.
§ Screening-test–positive results are classified as having high s/co ratios if their ratios are at or above a predetermined value that predicts a supplemental-test–positive result ≥95% of the time among all populations tested; screening-test–positive results are classified as having low s/co ratios if their ratios are below this value.
¶ Recombinant immunoblot assay.

FIGURE 6-12 Flow Chart

This flow chart uses rectangles for the testing and circles for the resulting report. Notice also the easy-to-understand top-to-bottom direction of the illustration. Each stage is given a legible label. Upper case letters are appropriately used to highlight the two occurrences of "OR" that identify alternative stages, but the upper case letters are quite unnecessary for labeling the already distinctive circles.
Source: U.S.Centers for Disease Control and Prevention. *Guidelines for Laboratory Testing and Result Reporting of Antibody to Hepatitis C Virus.* Morbidity and Mortality Weekly Report 52 (No. RR-3): 2003. p. 9.

FIGURE 6-13 Flow Chart *(see facing page)*

This flow chart uses diamonds for the questions but two different shapes for the answers: round-corner rectangles and square-corner rectangles. Notice also that the diamonds differ in size, as do the rectangles, giving viewers extra visual variables to decipher and adding unnecessarily to the complexity of the illustration. Also adding to the viewer's difficulty is that all the type is centered, with the exception of the bulleted lists and the footnotes. The clear top-to-bottom direction of the illustration, however, makes the decision process easy to follow.
Source: U.S. Department of Labor, Occupational Safety and Health Administration. *Training Marine Oil Spill Response Workers Under OSHA's Hazardous Waste Operations and Emergency Response Standard.* OSHA 3172. Washington, DC: 2001, p.10.

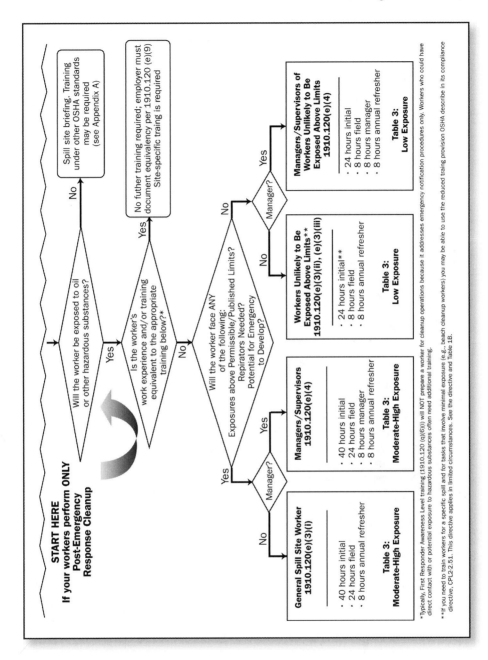

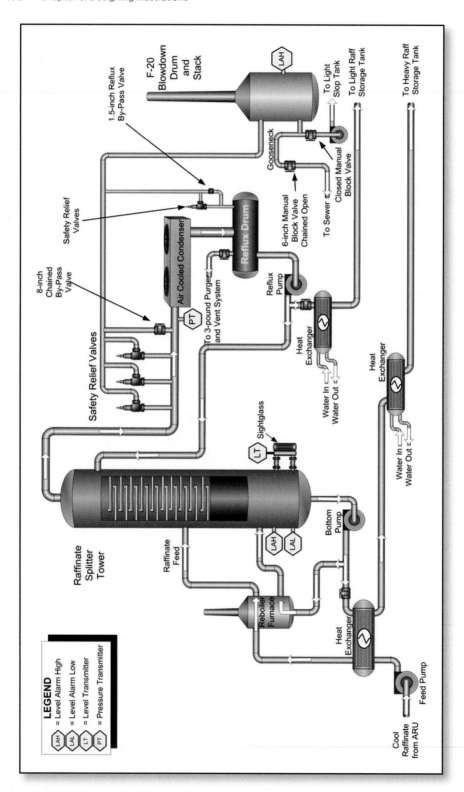

FIGURE 6-14 Diagram *(see facing page)*
This detailed diagram of a section of oil refinery equipment serves to depict its operation and assist investigators in explaining the causes of a catastropic explosion to the public. Notice the clear labeling of all key components as well as the arrows indicating the direction in which liquids passed through the system. The diagram obviously simplifies a complicated technology but suits the audience and purpose.
Source: U.S. Chemical Safety and Hazard Investigation Board. *Final Investigation Report, Refinery Explosion and Fire, BP Texas City, March 23, 2005.* Report No. 2005-06-I-TX. Washington, DC: 2007, p.34.

Photographs.

- Note that the purpose of a photograph is to show what a subject looks like in realistic detail.
- Keep the photograph as simple as possible, focusing the viewer's attention on the key features or parts of the subject.
- Exercise caution in editing or polishing the photograph. Never insert or delete images. Viewers typically expect a photograph to be a representation of reality, and ethical communicators strive to meet that expectation. Cropping a photograph in order to close in on a subject and eliminate distractions in the background is a standard practice, but never insert or delete objects or change the size or color of objects in a photograph.
- If appropriate or necessary for the viewer's understanding, apply labels for each of the pertinent parts of the subject to direct the viewer's attention.
- If space allows, put the label directly on the part; if not, connect the label to the part with a thin rule (never arrows).
- Position all the labels on the horizontal so that the viewer doesn't have to rotate the page or screen to read the labels.

See Figures 6-15 and 6-16 for examples of photographs.

DESIGNING ILLUSTRATIONS ETHICALLY

Displaying information ethically requires that you make careful choices about the design of your illustrations.

For example, the scale of the x- and y-axes on a line graph has a significant impact on the data display. In designing a graph, you ordinarily start the x- and y-axes at 0. Exceptions are possible if beginning at some other point ("suppressing the zero") will not distort information. If several graphs are positioned side-by-side on a page, thus inviting comparison and contrast of the data, it would be unethical to use differing vertical scales because readers would likely come to incorrect conclusions (see Figure 6-17).

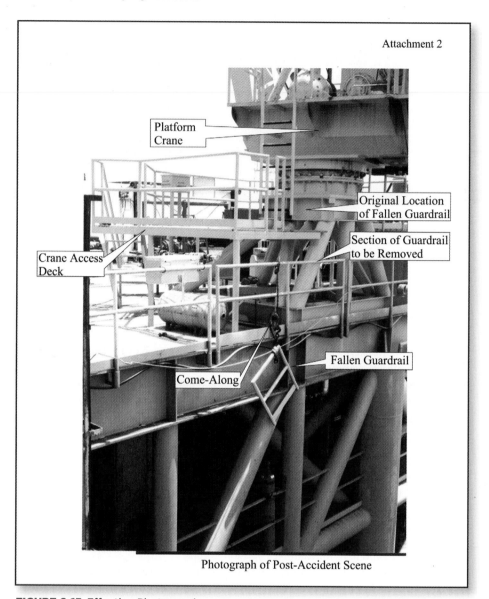

Attachment 2

Platform Crane

Original Location of Fallen Guardrail

Section of Guardrail to be Removed

Crane Access Deck

Fallen Guardrail

Come-Along

Photograph of Post-Accident Scene

FIGURE 6-15 Effective Photograph

This photograph carries clear labels to identify each of the pertinent pieces of equipment at the site of a fatal accident.

Source: United States Department of the Interior, Minerals Management Service. *Investigation of Fall and Fatality, Main Pass Block 140, May 19, 2000.* MMS 2001-042. Washington, DC: 2001. p. 13.

FIGURE 6-16 Ineffective Photograph

This photograph makes viewers look at a lot of distracting detail instead of focusing their attention on essential information. The containment system is nicely centered in the photograph but on the left and right are extraneous shelves and tables loaded with supplies and equipment. In addition, the essential components of the containment system are unlabeled, making it difficult for viewers to notice all the items in the photograph that constitute the containment system. A truly effective photograph would display the containment system in a virtually empty room with either labels or a detailed caption identifying each of the essential components.

Source: U.S. Environmental Protection Agency, Office of Pollution Prevention and Toxics. *Pilot Study to Estimate Asbestos Exposure from Vermiculite Attic Insulation.* Washington, DC: 2003. p. 68.

Using distorted graphs, however, isn't the only error that will result in the creation of unethical illustrations. It is unethical to create a drawing that puts features on a product it doesn't really have. It is unethical to design a flowchart that disguises a procedure's complexity by making things look relatively simple. It is unethical to stage or doctor a photograph to create a positive or negative impression of your subject that isn't fully justified.

In addition, if you illustrate information regarding people, you must strive to be sensitive to their humanity. For example, to use a circle graph to depict the human beings killed in various kinds of automobile accidents (as Figure 6-18 does) or ignore the human beings killed in the map of a gas explosion (as Figure 6-19 does) genuinely diminishes the dignity of the victims, reducing real people to objects.

Figure 7.2 Electricity Net Generation
(Billion Kilowatthours)

Total (All Sectors), Major Sources, 1989-2002

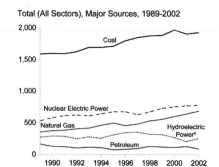

Total (All Sectors), Major Sources, Monthly

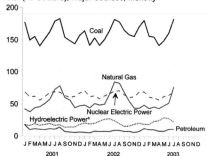

Total (All Sectors), Major Sources, 2002

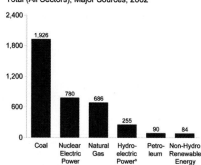

Electric Power Sector, Major Sources, 2002

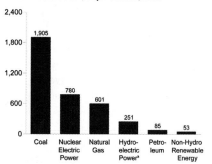

Commercial Sector, Major Sources, 2002

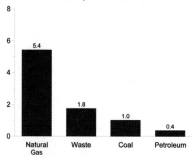

Industrial Sector, Major Sources, 2002

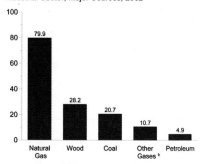

[a]Conventional and pumped storage hydroelectric power.
[b]Blast furnace gas, propane gas, and other manufactured and waste gases derived from fossil fuels.

Note: Because vertical scales differ, graphs should not be compared.
Web Page: http://www.eia.doe.gov/emeu/mer/elect.html.
Sources: Tables 7.2a, 7.2b, and 7.2c.

FIGURE 6-17 Deceptive Series of Graphs *(see facing page)*
This series of graphs could deceive viewers who fail to note
that the vertical scales differ on the top and bottom pair
of graphs, making it impossible to compare and contrast
the information in the graphs despite their side-by-side
positioning. A note on the bottom of the page ("Because
vertical scales differ, graphs should not be compared") is
incorrect in that the middle pair of graphs has the same
vertical scale. This note, however, is likely to be missed in
a quick reading of the page: it requires a more prominent
position and more precise wording to alert viewers to
possible misunderstandings. A better solution would be to
avoid altogether the side-by-side positioning of the graphs if
no comparison of the data is intended.
Source: United States Department of Energy, Energy Information Administration. *Monthly Energy Review.* Washington, DC: October 2003. p. 130.

ILLUSTRATION CHECKLIST

Planning

- ☐ What kinds of illustrations are your audience familiar with?
- ☐ Do you have information that could be more easily or quickly communicated to your audience visually or in a combination of words and graphics?
- ☐ Do you have definitions that could be displayed visually in whole or in part?
- ☐ Do you have any processes or procedures that could be depicted in a flowchart?
- ☐ Do you have information on trends or relationships that could be displayed in tables and graphs?
- ☐ Do you have masses of statistics that could be summarized in tables?
- ☐ Do you need to depict objects? If so, what do you need to display about the objects? Do you need to focus attention on specific aspects of the objects? Do you require the realism of photographs?
- ☐ What are the design conventions of your illustrations?
- ☐ Are there suitable illustrations you could borrow or adapt? Or will you need to create them yourself?

Revising

- ☐ Are your illustrations suited to your purpose and audience?
- ☐ Do your illustrations communicate information ethically?
- ☐ Are your illustrations effectively located and easy to find?

continued

ILLUSTRATION CHECKLIST ✔ *continued*

☐ Are your illustrations numbered and labeled?

☐ Do your verbal and visual elements reinforce each other?

☐ Are your illustrations genuinely informative instead of simply decorative?

☐ When necessary, have you helped your readers to interpret your illustrations with commentary or annotations?

☐ Have you acknowledged the sources for borrowed or adapted tables and figures?

EXERCISES

1. Examine the illustrations used in five journals and magazines in your major field of study. Which types of illustration do you ordinarily find? Which types don't you find? Which occur most often? Which occur least often? What are the conventions for tables and figures in your field. Summarize your findings in a brief oral presentation with slides that display representative illustrations.

2. Aeschylus Corporation, which designs interactive video games, is looking for new employees, especially individuals able to conceive and design state-of-the-art products. It has been a small private corporation for five years and hopes to achieve a major expansion. The president of Aeschylus, Robin Pierce, has asked you to develop recruiting materials for prospective new employees. You've compiled the following information that you believe will be pertinent:

History	Founded in 2005, in Kansas City, Missouri, by Robin Pierce, B.S. in Computer Science, 2002, University of St. Louis; MBA, 2004, Missouri University
Sales	2005: $200,000; 2006: $750,000; 2007: $2 million; 2008: $7 million; 2009: $16 million
Employees	with specialists in design (3), graphics and animation (4), programming (5), video and movie editing (3), production (2), quality assurance (1), documentation (1), sound (1), and music (1)
Products	6 current products, looking to diversify, especially in action–adventure, newest product: Street Maniac (driving game); biggest seller: Trojan War (fantasy role-playing)
Facilities	State-of-the-art equipment, serves both PC and Macintosh systems

Traffic Safety Facts

2006 Data

www.nhtsa.gov

NHTSA

DOT HS 810 813

School Transportation-Related Crashes

A school transportation-related crash is a crash which involves, either directly or indirectly, a school bus body vehicle, or a non-school bus functioning as a school bus, transporting children to or from school or school-related activities.

Since 1996 there have been about 417,705 fatal motor vehicle traffic crashes. Of those, 0.33 percent (1,387) were classified as school transportation-related.

Since 1996, 1,536 people have died in school transportation-related crashes — an average of 140 fatalities per year. Most of the people who lost their lives in those crashes (72%) were occupants of other vehicles involved. Non occupants (pedestrians, bicyclists, etc.) accounted for 20 percent of the deaths, and occupants of school transportation vehicles accounted for 7 percent.

Since 1996, 159 school-age pedestrians (younger than 19) have died in school transportation-related crashes. Over two-thirds (67%) were killed by school buses, 6 percent by vehicles functioning as school buses, and 28 percent by other vehicles involved in the crashes. One-half (50%) of all school-age pedestrians killed in school transportation-related crashes were between the ages of 5 and 7.

"An average of 20 school-age children die in school transportation-related traffic crashes each year — 5 occupants of school transportation vehicles and 14 pedestrians."

Figure 1

Total Occupant and Pedestrian Fatalities in School Transportation-Related Crashes, by Age Group, 1996-2006

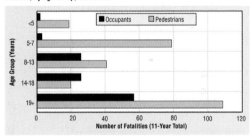

Note: Occupant fatalities shown are for occupants of school buses and non-school buses used as school buses.

NHTSA's National Center for Statistics and Analysis   1200 New Jersey Avenue SE., Washington, DC 20590

FIGURE 6-18 Cruel Bar Graph

Each of the bars on this graph is a tally of human beings killed in tragic school bus accidents, making it a particularly callous display of numerical information. A background or adjacent photograph of a school bus full of boys and girls or of grieving families might give humanity to this illustration.

Source: U.S. Department of Transportation, National Highway Traffic Safety Administration. *Traffic Safety Facts: School Transportation-Related Crashes.* DOT HS 810 813. Washington, DC: GPO 2006. p.1.

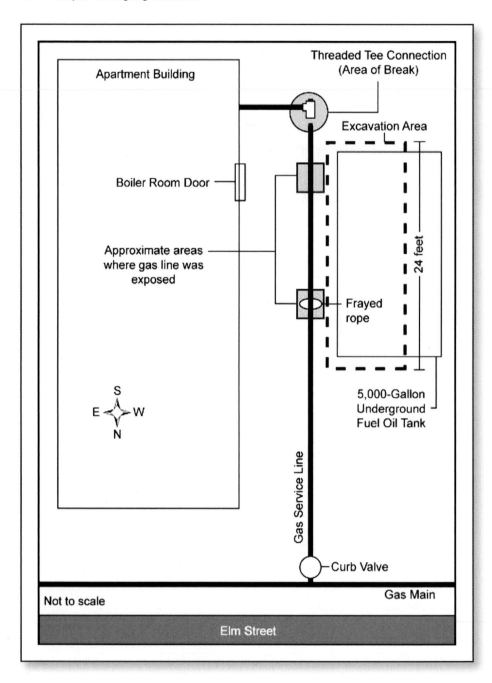

FIGURE 6-19 Unethical Map of Accident Site

(see facing page)

This map depicts the site of a gas explosion caused by a damaged service line. The emphasis here is on the building that was demolished instead of the three people who were killed and the five who were injured. The position of pertinent objects are all clearly specified. A viewer seeing this illustration might be surprised that human beings died in the explosion because none are displayed at the accident location. Ignoring the human consequences of accidents, failures, and negligence, however, is insensitive to the victims and their surviving family and friends.

Source: National Transportation Safety Board. 2007. *Pipeline Accident Brief, Bergenfield, New Jersey, December 13, 2005.* NTSB/PAB-07/01. Washington, DC., p. 3.

Location	1224 Howard Avenue, Kansas City: new building, spacious offices
Salary/benefits	Competitive with industry; excellent medical coverage, 4 weeks vacation each year

Design recruiting materials for Aeschylus Corporation that incorporate as wide a variety of illustrations as possible.

3. In designing your recruiting materials for Aeschylus Corporation, you are surprised by a dilemma. Robin Pierce is willing to hire people with disabilities and would like you to include that information. At this time, Aeschylus has no employees with disabilities, but Jacqueline Brown, a programmer, injured her back in a skiing accident and is temporarily restricted to a wheelchair. Pierce proposes including a photograph of various Aeschylus employees (including Brown in the wheelchair) to indicate to prospective employees that people with disabilities would find a supportive environment at Aeschylus. You mention the idea to staff photographer, Kishor Mitra, but he objects, claiming such a picture would be deceptive. As project leader, you have to decide who is right and compose one of two e-mail messages: either to convince Pierce that such a photograph would be unethical, or to direct Mitra to take the photograph in spite of his objections. How do you proceed?

4. Examine Figure 6-20. If you were the creator of this document and were given 15 more minutes to make it more effective, what changes would you make?

Bureau of Labor Statistics

Crane-Related Occupational Fatalities

Fact Sheet
July 2008
www.bls.gov

FIGURE 6-20 Document for Exercise 4

Source: U.S. Dept. of Labor, Bureau of Labor Statistics. *Crane-Related Occupational Fatalities: Fact Sheet, July 2008*. Washington, DC: 2008, p. 3.

Crane-Related Occupational Fatalities

Crane safety has been in the forefront of the news due to the recent crane accidents in Houston, New York City, Miami, and Las Vegas.

The most recent data are for 2006; in that year, there were 72 crane-related fatal occupational injuries, down from an average of 78 fatalities per year from 2003 to 2005. These include all fatalities where the source of the injury was a crane, the secondary source of the injury was a crane, or where the worker activity was operating a crane[1].

In 2006 there were no multiple fatality incidents involving cranes; however 6 fatalities in 2005 and 8 fatalities in 2004 were the result of multiple fatality incidents involving cranes.

In 2006, 30 crane-related fatalities were caused by being struck by falling objects. Only 9 of these fatalities were due to the crane striking them. The other workers were killed when an object the crane was transporting fell from the crane onto them.

Of the cranes that were specified in the fatality, mobile, truck, and rail mounted cranes, and overhead cranes represented the type of crane involved for the majority of fatalities. Overhead cranes typically have a hook-and-line mechanism on a horizontal beam that runs along two widely separated rails, whereas mobile cranes are usually cranes that are mounted and travel on top of mobile devices such as trucks or rail cars[2]. In 2006, 26 fatalities involved mobile, truck or rail mounted cranes. Nineteen involved overhead cranes.

In 2006, workers employed as construction laborers (10 fatalities); electricians (8); and welders, cutters, solderers, and brazers (6) were the most likely to be killed in crane-related incidents. Crane and tower operators accounted for only 3 fatalities.

Twenty-six workers were killed in crane-related incidents while working in the private construction industry in 2006. Most notably, 6 died working in highway, street, and bridge construction. Manufacturing (17 fatalities) and mining (7) had the next largest number of fatalities in the private sector. Three workers employed by a government entity were killed in crane-related incidents in 2006.

From 2003 to 2006, the most fatal occupational injuries involving cranes occurred in Texas (42). Florida (27), California (25), and Louisiana (17) also had large numbers of crane-related occupational fatalities.

SOURCE: Bureau of Labor Statistics (BLS), July 30, 2008. Fatality data are from the 2006 Census of Fatal Occupational Injuries. This Census is designed to count worker fatalities; therefore, all of the statistics in this fact sheet refer to on-the-job fatalities and do not include other persons who may have

---

[1] The source of injury or illness identifies the object, substance, bodily motion, or exposure which directly produced or inflicted the injury. The secondary source of injury identifies the object, substance, or person that generated the source of injury or that contributed to the event or exposure. The source and secondary source are based on the Occupational Injury and Illness Classification (OIICS) manual. More information on OIICS can be found here: http://www.bls.gov/iif/oshoiics.htm. The worker activity describes what the worker was doing at the time of the fatal injury or exposure. Worker activity is an internal codes used by the Census of Fatal Occupational Injuries (CFOI) program.
[2] Definitions from http://en.wikipedia.org/wiki/Overhead_crane

FIGURE 6-20 *continued*

been killed in crane-related incidents. Fatal injury data for 2007 will be available in the upcoming release scheduled for August 2008.

More information is available from http://www.bls.gov/iif or by calling 202-691-6170.

Crane-related fatal occupational injuries[1], 1997-2006

	1997	1998	1999	2000	2001	2002	2003	2004	2005	2006
Crane-related fatalities	97	93	80	90	72	80	62	87	85	72

[1] Includes fatalities where the source of injury was a crane, where the secondary source of the injury was a crane, or where the worker activity was operating a crane.
SOURCE: U.S. Department of Labor, Bureau of Labor Statistics, in cooperation with State, New York City, District of Columbia, and Federal agencies, Census of Fatal Occupational Injuries.

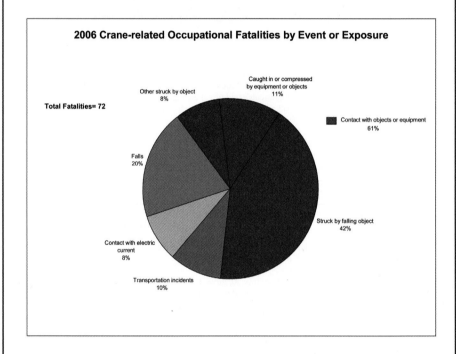

2006 Crane-related Occupational Fatalities by Event or Exposure

Total Fatalities= 72

Other struck by object 8%

Caught in or compressed by equipment or objects 11%

Contact with objects or equipment 61%

Falls 20%

Struck by falling object 42%

Contact with electric current 8%

Transportation incidents 10%

FIGURE 6-20 *continued*

PART **TWO**

Applications

7

E-mails, Memoranda, and Letters

E-mails, memoranda (memos), and letters are among the most frequently written business documents. Because people receive so much correspondence, some items may be overlooked or ignored.

Quick Tips

- Prepare readers for the main information in your message by using a clearly worded subject line.
- Place the main information first.
- Use formatting techniques available through your e-mail system to help readers move rapidly through your message. Format should help readers understand organization and content.
- Always be concise. Keep sentences and paragraphs short. Readers should not have to read your message more than once to grasp your meaning.
- Keep your message to one or two pages or screens.
- If your message is more than one page or screen, use headings to guide your reader through it.

E-MAILS

E-mails are undoubtedly the most common form of workplace communication and may include attachments such as memos or letters. Appropriate e-mail etiquette continues to evolve, but e-mails should be concise and readable. Most people receive too many. If you want your e-mails read, be sure that your main purpose is clear, up front, and easy to see, and be sure to state it in the subject line. Compare the e-mails that follow (Figures 7-1 and 7-2). Which one would you rather read? Why?

Memos and Letters

Memos are short, internal communication documents used within an organization. Memos can be posted on a company's or an individual's portal or sent as e-mail attachments. Because of electronic communication, today few are sent as hard copies through interoffice mail.

Letters differ from memos in that letters are usually written to individuals outside the writer's organization, but they can be used as official documents within an organization. Like memos, letters can be sent via e-mail as attachments. Memos serve as intraorganizational communications only and are not accepted channels for official business with other companies and clients.

SUBJ: Assessment Conference

Dear Colleagues,

As a follow-up to the announcement of the 5th Annual TAMU Assessment Conference being held on February 8th, 2005, the Office of Institutional Assessment and Diversity will be offering scholarships to cover the cost of three registrations from each Academic College and Administrative Division. We would like to request that one of the college representatives be from the newly created College-level QEPC memberships. The Assessment Conference will be held on Tuesday February 8, 2005 beginning at 8:45 a.m. in 201 of the Memorial Student Center. For planning and logistics purposes, please send your nominations of the three faculty or staff members from your unit to Dr. Mark Troy via e-mail at metory@tamu.edu by Tuesday January 25, 2005.

This year's Assessment Conference Theme is "Assessing Research and Learning: What's in it for me?" The conference will help faculty and staff gain a better understanding of how assessment can assist them in their research and in program review. Two "conference tracks" have been designed to better meet faculty and staff's needs. Dr. Arthur B. Ellis, Director of the Division of Chemistry with the National Science Foundation, will lead Track 1, Assessment of Funded Research. Additionally, Dr. Peggy L. Maki, noted Higher Education Assessment Consultant, will be leading Track Two: Assessment of Programs and Courses. Additionally, this conference will help Quality Enhancement Plan Principle Investigators (QEP PIs) develop skills in leading Evidence Based Decision Making processes in their own operational units. Whether faculty and staff are interested in assessing research processes under the guidelines of a grant agency or looking to improve a course, an academic unit, or an administrative program, the Presentations of the 5th Annual Assessment Conference will offer your staff a wealth of knowledge about evidence based decision making and assessment.

I encourage you to take advantage of this opportunity to send three of your faculty and staff to this valuable professional development experience for free. In addition, I encourage you to identify others who would benefit from this day-long workshop. Should you or any of your staff need further information of for registration information, they may go to the Conference website at: http://www.tamu.edu/ode/assessment/. I am attaching 4 copies of the flyer for advertisements in your offices. If you are in need of more copies or have any other questions, please e-mail Dr. Mark Troy with your request.

FIGURE 7-1 E-mail Version 1

SUBJ: Annual Assessment Conference Scheduled For Feb. 8

Dear Colleagues,

Annual Assessment Conference Scheduled For Feb. 8

The conference theme, "What's in it for me?" speaks directly to the benefits of making assessment a fixture of Texas A&M's environment.

PROGRAM

The conference focuses on assessing funded research and assessing student learning in courses and programs. This year's speakers are Arthur B. Ellis of the National Science Foundation, and Peggy L. Maki, a higher education consultant.

WHEN, WHERE, COST

The all-day conference will be held at the MSC, room 201. Registration is $50 until Jan. 31st and $60 thereafter. This fee includes admission to workshops, lunch, parking, and conference materials.

REGISTER and PAY ONLINE

Registration and payment may be made online. More information can be found by visiting http://www .tamu.edu/ode/assessment, by calling Mark Troy at (979) 845-0532, or sending him an e-mail at metroy@ tamu.edu.

FIGURE 7-2 E-mail Version 2

Guidelines for Ensuring Quality

- Watch how you sound when you choose words and structure sentences. Print out memos and letters and reread them carefully before you send them. Plan your e-mail message with even greater care: once you send it, you cannot change what you have said.

- Keep the six Cs in mind as you develop e-mails, letters, and memos: Be **concise, concrete, complete, correct, courteous, and clear**. Be attentive to how what you say can be perceived by your reader. Rephrase anything that you think might be construed in ways you do not intend.

- Be aware of how your message looks. A letter or memo that is poorly word processed or incorrectly formatted makes an unfavorable statement about the writer and the organization. Because e-mail messages may be printed and copies made and distributed, design those with equal care.

- Watch for spelling errors as well as errors in sentence structure and standard English usage. For especially important e-mail messages, consider printing copies before you send them. Editing printed material often reveals errors you may miss as you compose or proofread on your computer. Also use the spell-check tool available on your e-mail system to help you see errors, but keep in mind that spellcheck is no substitute for careful reading.

- Use the following general structure for memos, letters, and e-mail messages:

First Paragraph: states the purpose of the message or the main information the reader needs. If your letter delivers unfavorable news, you may want to "buffer" the bad news with a soft opening. See Figure 7-4.

Middle Paragraphs: provide support for or development of the main topic stated in the first paragraph. Limit each paragraph to one idea.

Final Paragraph: tells the reader what to do or what position to take. The final paragraph also provides appropriate ending comments.

APPROPRIATE TONE IN E-MAILS, LETTERS, AND MEMOS

Be careful how you sound. What you write always carries with it a sound, an attitude toward the reader and the subject. As they absorb your message, readers often vocalize your sentences and phrases. Anticipate the tone that your reader will attach to what you say. Use a respectful, positive tone and avoid words and phrases that sound rude, sarcastic, or peevish. Remember: you want to be clear, but you also want to maintain a favorable relationship with your reader.

Avoid phrases that suggest that the reader is careless or unintelligent:

You neglected to . . .
You failed to . . .
We fail to understand how . . .

Also avoid phrases that imply that the reader is lying:

You claim/state that . . .

Avoid writing that your reader can construe as flattery. Many people are sensitive to insincerity and to any attempt to force them to respond in a certain way:

It is indeed a profound privilege for us to work with you on this project.

We look forward to the opportunity to submit our full proposal. Your firm is known for its commitment to excellence and value, which we are confident we offer.

Attempting to sound objective can often produce impersonal writing:

The changes agreed upon per our conversation are herein included.

Your immediate reply will be greatly appreciated.

Instead, write with a conversational tone that suggests you value your reader as a person:

The changes included here were the ones we discussed during our phone conversations.

Please let us know your decision as soon as you can.

Many times, in an effort to be clear, writers may sound tactless:

If your employees had read the procedures before installing the pump, they would have seen that the installation process requires that the sealant be allowed to set for one hour before beginning Part 2 of the installation. Not following this procedure causes the diagnostic to shut down because the sealant has not dried sufficiently to absorb the test stress. To avoid future installation problems, please see that your employees read the procedures and read them thoroughly.

Thinking about the *emotion* that your writing may convey or provoke will help you to present the same idea in a less caustic way:

Please note in the procedure manual that the second half of the installation process cannot begin until the sealant has set for one hour. This amount of time is necessary for the sealant to dry sufficiently to absorb the test stress. Beginning Part 2 of the installation process before the sealant has dried will cause the diagnostic to shut down.

Examine these additional examples and their revisions:

Regrettably, hotel expense reimbursements are not allowed.

Vs.

The accounting office can reimburse you for travel expense only. Hotel bills belong in a separate category.

We cannot grant your request for a list of company positions and annual salaries, as nobody but company executives are allowed to know this information.

Vs.

The list of positions and salaries you requested is confidential information limited to use by our company personnel only. For your research, however, we can send you related information on industry-wide trends in similar positions.

GUIDELINES FOR DEALING WITH TONE

As a writer, you cannot anticipate every nuance of meaning that your message will have for your reader. But you can be clear and maintain goodwill with your reader if you keep the following guidelines in mind as you compose any letter, memo, or e-mail:

- Allow more time for designing messages that arise from sensitive issues and that may be subject to misreading. Try to avoid sending bad news by e-mail.
- Anticipate the effects of messages that will convey negative or unwelcome news. These can be misinterpreted by readers, who can also misjudge your

attitude toward them and the information you are transmitting. People often take bad news more personally than the business situation warrants.

- Always analyze your reader as carefully as possible, particularly the reader's frame of reference and attitude toward both you and the subject. Always be courteous.

- Read aloud what you have written. When you hear what you have written, you can often detect words and phrases that don't convey the attitude you intend.

- For any difficult message, write the message, print it, and then let it to cool for a while. Then, read the message to check for clarity and goodwill. For e-mail, compose the message, save the draft, let the message "cool," then reread and read aloud what you have typed.

Planning and Writing Common Types of Letters and Memos

The following examples (Cases 7-1 through 7-6) introduce situations in which writers need to respond by memo or letter. In each example, examine the situation and the resulting document.

Review of Principles
As you plan your letters, e-mail, and other routine communications . . .

10 Questions to Ask Yourself

1. How well do I know this person?
2. How much do they know about the topic discussed in the letter?
3. How will they respond to what I will need to say? In what ways can I use this communication to build rapport for the firm?
4. What exactly am I trying to accomplish with this message?
5. What is their level of knowledge about the concepts discussed?
6. What is their attitude toward me and the firm?
7. What previous business dealings have I/we had with them?
8. How much and what kind of information should I include, based on their profile?
9. How technical can I be in presenting my message?
10. What strategies can I use to make this message easy to read and understand?

Case 7-1: Informational memo

Tom Allen, an administrative assistant, needs to write a memo to approximately two dozen people announcing a meeting. Since the meeting will deal with budget cuts, Tom decides to include documents that those attending will need to have read by the meeting. The memo explains the reason for the meeting, the documents attached, and the proposed agenda. As Tom explains, everyone should bring the memo and the attached documents to the meeting.

This memo exemplifies good design (Case Document 7-1). Note the clearly phrased subject line, the action-required statement in boldface type, and the placement of the main information—the meeting and required attendance—in the opening sentence. The meeting agenda appears as a list, and employees are told exactly what they should do with attached materials. The memo is concise, and all information is visually accessible.

CASE DOCUMENT 7-1

HCI Inc.

Memoranda

TO:	Operations Support Staff	DATE:	February 24, 2009
FROM:	Tom Allen (ext. 4901)	EMAIL:	tallen@rosco.hci.com

SUBJECT: Agenda for March 10 Meeting on Proposed Budget Cuts

REF: Vice President of Finance—memo of 10/31/00

ACTION REQUIRED: Prepare New Cost Figures for Your Projects by March 10

All project teams will be required to attend the March 10 meeting to decide how to cut the third and fourth quarter budgets. Please refer to the VP—Finance memo of October 31, 2008, for guidelines on cuts.

Time and Location: 8:30 A.M., Third Floor Conference Room

Please have four copies of your budget prepared. Aim for the 15% cut suggested by the 10/31 memo.

Meeting Agenda

1. Budget presentations and discussion
2. Proposed bid development on the North Shore Power Project (Attachment 1)

continued

3. Revision of Procedures to Meet OSHA guidelines on oxygen tanks (Attachment 2)

4. Cost overrun problem with maintenance contractors on North Shore Project (Attachment 3).

Please review all attached documents and be prepared to discuss viable solutions.

The meeting will probably last until noon. Please reschedule any meetings that will conflict. If you have other commitments, please let me know immediately by phone or email

encls. (3)

pc: File AC—21

   M.L. Selling

Case 7-2: Instructional memo

Like many organizations, Home-Rental provides instructions and instruction memos to their employees. The following one (Case Document 7-2) announces the new rental agreement with a local rental car dealership and provides instructions for arranging to rent cars for both personal use and business use. The writer, Sean Gholson, suggests that readers may want to keep this memo for reference.

CASE DOCUMENT 7-2

MEMORANDUM

TO: HOME-RENTAL INC. EMPLOYEES
FROM: SEAN GHOLSON
SUBJECT: NEW BENEFITS FROM YOU-GO RENT-A-CAR
DATE: 8/7/09

H-R Inc. signed an agreement with You-Go Rent-A-Car offering a 20% discount for personal and business travel. Please retain this memo for your files.

Personal Travel

20% discount on all car rentals

FOR: All Employees with valid **H-R Inc.** business card
         Please use personal payment methods for personal travel rentals.

Business Travel

H-R Inc. company credit cards will be issued by August 30, 2009.

TO: All marketing and management personal, and
         Any personnel requiring significant amounts of travel

Travel Orders can be used until and after the cards are issued
         ⊚ Forms are available from department business administrators
         ⊚ Supervisor signature required

continued

Business Vehicle Guidelines

- 1 or 2 employees traveling: use compact car
  3 or more employees traveling: use sedan or mini van
- Luxurious vehicles for transporting clients or potential clients must be approved by your supervisor.
- Please lease the most economical vehicle available.

Regulations

- Employees are expected to follow all traffic laws
- Employees under 21 cannot drive unless accomplish by fellow employee over 21
- Vehicle can not be used to transport persons or property for hire
- Vehicle can not be used to tow anything
- You-Go and **H-R Inc** are not responsible for loss or theft of personal belongings left unattended in the vehicle

Reservations

To reserve your car for personal or business travel, go online at www.you-go.com or call 1-800-RENT CAR.

- Valid Driver's License needed for reservation
- No deposit required

Online Instructions:

1. Go to http://www.you-go.com
2. Locate the login box for Gold Corporate Customers (GCC)

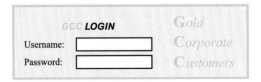

3. Enter the Username: homerental
4. Password: your last name (all lower case)
5. Follow remaining steps as prompted

*For any questions, contact **Susan Jones**, the Office Services Manager, at 757-3478 ext 112.

Case 7-3: Letter requesting information

Alicia Forsythe serves as local arrangement chairperson for ASEE's regional meeting. One of her first responsibilities is to locate a hotel in which the regional meeting can be held. She decides to send a letter to seven hotels near the sports arena so that conferees can enjoy sports events during the evenings of the three-day conference. Alicia writes the same letter to all seven hotels requesting information about their facilities.

When Alicia writes to each of the seven hotels, she has a number of questions she needs answered: if the hotel can host a convention of 500 people on the dates specified; if the hotel has the number of meeting rooms necessary and the necessary audio-visual equipment. Alicia needs each hotel to respond by a specific deadline, and she wants to be sure that every hotel supplies the information she requests. With these answers, she can compare costs and services of hotels that are interested in hosting the convention. She uses a **block letter format**, which has no indention. All letter parts are placed at the left margin.

CASE DOCUMENT 7-3

Caufman University
200 Rosser Hall
Department of Civil Engineering
Glendale, KS 67612

(date)

(name of convention manager)
(name of hotel)
(mailing address)
(city, state, zip)

Dear (   ):

The South Central Chapter of the American Society of Engineering Education will have its annual meeting in Kansas City, March 22-26, 2010. With the convention 15 months away, the local arrangements committee is seeking a hotel that will serve as convention headquarters. Our committee would like to consider your hotel as a possible site because of its location and its reputation

continued

in handling conventions. **By March 1, 2009**, I will need answers to the following questions, if you are interested in hosting our convention. I will contact you by phone no later than April 1, 2009, to arrange an appointment to discuss our needs and your facilities in further detail.

Number of Conferees Expected

Based on registration from past conventions, we expect approximately 500 people to attend. Of that number, approximately 450 will need rooms. Of that number, approximately 250 will require double occupancy rooms.

Conference Accommodations Needed

We need you to provide us answers to the following questions:

1. Can your hotel accommodate 500-600 people, March 22-26, 2010?

2. Since the conference will feature three days of concurrent sessions, do you have available conference rooms in the following configurations:

   - three rooms located in the same general area that will hold 100 people
   - three additional rooms that will hold 50 participants, with six persons per round table.

   We will have three concurrent sessions at each time slot—two in the morning and two in the afternoon

3. Can your hotel provide the following audiovisual equipment for each room?

   - screen
   - overhead projector that can be attached to notebook computers?
   - microphones
   - lectern.

4. Can the seating arrangements be altered in each room between sessions?

5. Can the hotel provide refreshments during the morning break and afternoon break? Can these refreshments be made available at a location that is convenient to the meeting rooms?

continued

Response Deadline

I will need a written response to each question by <u>March 1, 2009</u>. Also, please include in your reply a price list and menu for refreshments available for conferences.

If you have any questions, please contact me at 555-1234 Monday-Friday. If I am away from my desk, just leave a message on my voice mail and a time when I may return your call.

Sincerely,

Alicia Forsythe

Alicia Forsythe
ASEE Convention Arrangements Chair

Case 7-4: Unfavorable news letter

Michele Harmon, an experienced safety engineer, was interviewed by a company for two days. Ms. Harmon was an outstanding candidate. However, after two other candidates were interviewed, the interview team recommended another candidate for the open safety engineering position. Despite Ms. Harmon's qualifications, the second candidate had qualifications that more clearly matched the company's needs. Caren Lafferty, Director of Personnel, has to write Michele to explain that an offer will not be forthcoming.

In this situation, Caren may call Michele to give her the news, but she should also follow the call with a formal letter. Avoid using e-mail to deliver bad news. Note that the letter gives reasons for Michele not being selected, but the news is not explained in a harsh, critical way. It is intended to announce bad news in a positive way. Because Caren was heavily involved with Michele during the application and interview process, she addresses her as "Michele." Do not use first names, unless you know the person to whom you are writing. She uses a **modified block format**, which uses paragraph indentions and shifts the date, closing, and signature line to the right side of the page (Case Document 7-4).

CASE DOCUMENT 7-4

FOSTEC ENGINEERING, INC. ———————— **ESTABLISHED 1954**
 1925 JEROME STREET
 BROOKLYN, NY 11205

(date)

Ms. Michele Harmon
9212 Frost
Glendale, OK

Dear Michele:

All of us enjoyed the two days you spent with us two weeks ago. Your perception of our clients' needs indicates that you have a firm understanding of the role safety engineering plays in the local contracts we win and manage. While your background would be invaluable to us, we have only one position available. For that reason, we have selected an applicant with international project experience.

continued

As we discussed, our range of clients has expanded. We now receive RFP's from countries in Europe, South America, and the Pacific Rim. Developing responses to their needs requires us to expand our team, particularly when we can do so with professionals with international experience.

Thank you for considering us. Everyone was impressed with your professionalism, your analytical skills, and your excellent record as a team player. I was pleased to have the opportunity to meet you.

Sincerely,

Caren Lafferty

Caren Lafferty
Manager, Personnel

Case 7-5: The persuasive letter

Kevin Richardson is the new president of one of the local sports clubs. Because of poor management over the past seven years, membership has dropped. The advisory board recently hired a new management firm. The quality of service, food, maintenance, and customer service has improved dramatically, but the club still needs to regain most of the old members, in addition to new ones, to remain solvent and to be able to afford the services of the new management firm. Kevin writes a letter to all members who once were active in the club and asks them to rejoin.

When Kevin designs the letter he will send to former members of the sports club, he decides to use the **simplified style**, which is similar to the block format but does not use a salutation or a closing (Case Document 7-5). Note that in this style, the phrases "Dear xxxxxx" and "Sincerely yours" are eliminated. This style has not won great acceptance in specific letters that individuals write to other professionals. However, it is a popular style for marketing letters and for broadcast letters, which will be personalized (with mail merge) and sent to a large number of individuals.

Because he does not use a letterhead, but his own stationery, Kevin places the return address before the date.

In this letter, Kevin has a specific goal in mind: to get readers to rejoin the sports club and to return the application form with a check. Thus, he must show readers that the sports club is now worth their money and that management has indeed changed.

CASE DOCUMENT 7-5

KEVIN RICHARDSON
12 Rolling Brook Drive
Glendale, OH 44125

(date)

<name>
<address 1>
<City>,<State> <Zip>

continued

FoxFire Under New Management

You will be pleased to know that Griffin Management, Inc. assumed daily operations of FoxFire as of May 1, 2009. As a result of their leadership, FoxFire now offers the full range of sports activities that it had when it first opened in 1994. The exercise and weight facilities open Monday-Saturday at 6:00 A.M. and remain open until 9:00. All equipment is operational. However, for Fox-Fire to maintain and improve the level of service for which it was designed, your participation is needed.

The club staff is currently offering breakfast for those interested in participating in early morning workouts. However, without a larger membership, adding lunch and supper menus will not be possible. Developing a full summer sports program for teens will require a substantial increase in membership within the next two months. The indoor track will need resurfacing within 18 months. FoxFire has the capability of again sponsoring major weekend sports competitions and can begin doing so if our previous members rejoin. These competitions enhance our community as well as provide weekend sports and recreation activities for all levels of members. Providing competitive summer activities for children, ages 9-17 keeps our young people involved in activities that benefit them socially as well as physically.

To encourage you to again give FoxFire a try, those of us on the advisory board are offering previous members a special discount for purchasing a one-year membership. Family memberships can also be purchased for only an additional $100/person per year.

Please examine the enclosed brochure, which lists all current activities available at FoxFire and the schedules. Then, complete the membership application and return it to us. You will be glad you did!

Kevin Richardson

Kevin Richardson
FoxFire Advisory Board
Enclosures: (2)

Case 7-6: **Letter of reply**

Rick Evans owns an agricultural equipment business. He has just received an order and a check from Mr. Albert Conally, who wants to replace an irrigation pump.

Rick needs to write Mr. Conally and tell him that the pump he has ordered is being discontinued and replaced by two new pumps, both of which are more expensive but are designed to offer better performance. Rick wants to be sure that Mr. Conally doesn't think that Rick is simply trying to sell him a more expensive pump when the current model will do the job.

In designing this letter, Rick wants to be sure that he does not suggest to Mr. Conally that he is the object of a bait and switch. Thus, he opens the letter by telling Mr. Conally that he has the pump and can ship it immediately (Case Document 7-6). However, he wants Mr. Conally to know that several improved models are available and that he may wish to choose one of the new models. Rick then presents all the information he believes Mr. Conally will need to make his decision and then invites Mr. Conally to contact him. Rick could call Mr. Conally and talk to him, but in this case a business letter that expresses concern for Mr. Conally's investment and presents factual information about the alternative pumps makes Mr. Conally's decision easier. Note the block letter format.

CASE DOCUMENT 7-6

--- Evans Irrigation Manufacturing & Supply Co. ---

19963 Valley Mills Drive
Bellmead, TX 77413
817 569-3766

(date)

Mr. Albert Conally
Route 1, Box 616
Crawford, TX 76706

Dear Mr. Conally:

We have received your order and check for $598 as payment for our 15-hp Model XM 21 auxiliary pump. Although we do have several in stock, and we can mail one to you immediately, manufacture of this model has ended. We

continued

are holding your check and order until we hear from you regarding the following alternatives.

Here is the situation. Purchasers of the 15-hpo model have indicated that the low output of this pump is generally insufficient to run the new drip irrigation systems currently being manufactured. This particular pump is not designed to handle extensive operation of these larger systems. As a result, we have discontinued the model. We have reduced the price to $448 due to our inability to warranty the motor for more than one year or supply replacement parts for more than two years.

We now manufacture two larger pumps, a 50-hp model and a 75-hp model. The 50-hp model will power a #70 system. The 75-hp model will power a #90 system. Here is a comparison of these three models.

Hypo Motor	Pumps Model	Rating	Warranty	Price
15hp	21	30	1yr = 2 pts	$448
50hp	31	70	full + 5 yr	$1795*
75hp	41	90		$2350*
*Additional warranty available for $125/yr				

While we believe that you will be happier with the reliability and efficiency of either of the larger pumps, if you choose to purchase the 15-hp model, we will ship it immediately and refund the $150 difference in price. I am sending brochures on both new motors. Please look them over and call me at our 800 number, extension 145 if you have any questions. As soon as we hear from you, we will ship you the motor of your choice within two working days.

Sincerely,

Rick Evans

Rick Evans
Owner

CORRESPONDENCE CHECKLIST ✔

Planning

☐ What is your subject and purpose?

☐ What do you want to have happen as a result of your correspondence? What will you do to achieve your objective?

☐ Who are your primary readers? Secondary readers? Do your primary and secondary readers have different needs? How will you satisfy the different needs of all your readers?

☐ Why will your readers read your correspondence?

☐ What is the attitude of your readers toward you? Toward your subject? Toward your purpose?

☐ If you are addressing international readers, do you understand their cultural practices? What adjustments in your correspondence will their cultural practices require?

☐ Will you write an e-mail, memo, or letter?

☐ Will you choose a direct or indirect style?

Revision

☐ Are your topic and purpose clearly identified?

☐ Have you satisfied your readers' purpose in reading?

☐ Have you adopted a style suitable to your readers' culture?

☐ Have you avoided jargon and clichés?

☐ Is your message clear, concise, complete, and courteous?

EXERCISES

1. Write a memo to colleagues in your organization in which you encourage their participation in a fundraiser for the local public library. In your memo, explain the merits of civic engagement for your organization as well as the mission of the library and its contribution to the community.

2. Civil Engineering Associates of Purvis, Ohio, was established in 2003 by Robert B. Davidson and Walter F. Posey, both graduates of the University of Ohio. Business for the company was good, and CEA took on six additional partners between 2003 and 2009: Alvin T. Bennett, Wayne S. Cook, Frank G. Reynolds, John W. Castrop, George P. Ramirez, and Richard M. Burke—all graduates of the University of Ohio.

   For the last five years, the partners of CEA have met every Friday for a working lunch at Coasters, a local restaurant and bar that features attractive young waitresses wearing provocative swimsuits. The customers are almost exclusively men, and the interaction between customers and waitresses is often flirtatious.

This year CEA hired Elizabeth P. Grider, a Missouri University graduate, as a new partner in the firm. She has attended two of the working lunches at Coasters and is uncomfortable in this environment. She does not feel, however, that she can just skip the events, which are the only regular occasions on which all the partners gather. Projects and work assignments are often discussed and decided at these Friday meetings. In addition, the lunches offer the opportunity to establish a comfortable working relationship with the partners. She realizes that "Friday at Coasters" is a long-standing tradition at the firm, and she is reluctant to upset the status quo, but she really wishes they could find a better place to meet.

As Elizabeth P. Grider, write a memo to the senior partner, Robert B. Davidson, explaining your problem and recommending one or more solutions. You would like to speak to Davidson directly, but you think that writing a memo allows you to organize your thoughts. And after the meeting, you could leave the memo with Davidson as a written record of your position.

3. Examine Figure 7-3. If you were the author of this document and were given 15 more minutes to make it better, what changes would you make?

4. A student at a large university sent an e-mail message to faculty across the university. Goal: to solicit faculty to participate in a survey for her dissertation.

Read the original e-mail (Figure 7-4) and then revise it. Use only the formatting devices available on your university's e-mail system.

Questions to consider: if you were a faculty member who receives several dozen e-mails a day, how would you respond to the survey when you first opened it? What errors in design do you see?

Attach your revision to a memo to your instructor. Explain, in your memo the problems with the original e-mail and the reasons you believe that your revision is better.

EXECUTIVE OFFICE OF THE PRESIDENT
OFFICE OF MANAGEMENT AND BUDGET
WASHINGTON, D.C. 20503

THE DIRECTOR

March 9, 2009

M-09-14

MEMORANDUM FOR THE HEADS OF DEPARTMENTS AND AGENCIES

FROM: Peter R. Orszag
            Director

SUBJECT: Recovery Act Implementation – Improving Grants.gov and Other Critical
            Systems

Effective implementation of the Recovery Act is a critical part of the effort to jumpstart economic activity and a top priority for the Administration. Central to carrying out the provisions of the Recovery Act with unprecedented levels of transparency and accountability is to confirm the capability of current information technology systems to meet the significant increases in financial and programmatic activity that will occur within Federal agencies during the next several months. To this end, OMB has been working closely with Federal agencies to identify system risks that could result in the disruption of effective Recovery Act implementation.

One area of risk that has been identified is in the operation of Grants.gov. As the central portal where citizens may find and apply for competitive grants, Grants.gov has experienced an increasing volume of activity in the past several months. This load has far exceeded the throughput originally anticipated by the system and has at times resulted in noticeably degraded performance. In addition, the Recovery Act is expected to result in an approximate 60 percent additional increase in application volume to Grants.gov, putting the system at a significant risk of failure and thus potentially hampering Recovery Act implementation. After a close and diligent review of system limitations, we have determined this risk to be unacceptably high.

As a result, I am instructing the Department of Health and Human Services, the Federal agency that operates and maintains Grants.gov, and the General Services Administration, which serves as the facilitator of government-wide E-gov solutions, to work together to initiate immediate improvements designed to accommodate this expected volume increase.

I am further instructing Federal grant-making agencies to immediately identify alternative methods for accepting grant applications during the Recovery Act's expected peak period to reduce demand on Grants.gov's limited resources. These alternatives should focus on minimizing any disruption to the grants application processes. Federal agencies should submit recommended alternatives to their counterparts in OMB's Resource Management Offices for review and approval by March 13, 2009.

FIGURE 7-3 Document for Exercise 3

I am pleased that the Grants.gov risk was identified before unnecessary mistakes or disruptions occurred in the application process for competitive grants funded under the Recovery Act. The planned system enhancements will have the added benefit of addressing weaknesses in the Grants.gov system that may also impact grant activity unrelated to the Recovery Act.

The steps being taken to address risks in Grants.gov are an important lesson that can be applied in our ongoing review of other systems. We cannot wait for problems to become crises. Before problems become an impediment to the release of Recovery Act funds, we have an obligation to identify risks, assess options, and implement solutions.

Questions about this memorandum can be addressed to recovery@omb.eop.gov.

Thank you for your cooperation.

FIGURE 7-3 *continued*

Voluntary Survey Opportunity

My name is Xxxxx Xxxxxxxxxxx and I am a Ph.D. student in the Department of Management at the Business School at ABC University. I am currently working on my dissertation which examines the psychological contracts that develop between employees and co-workers. These "contracts" are the underlying and unspoken relationships that exist in an organization and which greatly influence an employee's desire to go "above and beyond" in terms of demonstrating helping behaviors towards coworkers, supervisors and, ultimately, even the organization as a whole. I would like to survey a large number of people from the business and university communities. Specifically, I'd like to ask you to consider participating in my study.

An employee satisfaction survey was recently conducted at ABC by staff by the Office of Employee Services in collaboration with the Mays Business School, Department of Management, to help better understand employee work attitudes and perceptions. That survey included questions about job satisfaction with regard to a wide range of issues about work, life and the community. The outcomes and trends of those findings will be used to help respond to the needs and interests of ABC staff and to assure that ABC University continues to be considered the employer of choice in the region. My survey should not be confused with this on-going collaborative initiative.

If you decide to participate in my study, please know that at least three people will need to participate—an employee, the employee's supervisor and a co-worker of the employee. All information obtained through this survey will remain confidential and no one outside of my research group will have access to the information provided on the surveys. The survey is voluntary; participants may choose to respond to any or all of the questions. The surveys will require less than 20 minutes per person to complete and may be done online or in hard copy—whichever works better for you. Upon completion of the study (late summer 2007) I would be more than happy to provide a summary report of the collective results of the entire study to all participating parties.

As you can imagine, it is important for a doctoral student to have access to a broad base for dissertation research. It is sometimes difficult for students to dip into the "real world" without help. I would greatly appreciate it if you would consider participating in this survey and, possibly, asking others within your organization/university (the more, the better!) to help as well.

If you are willing to participate, please send me an e-mail at X-Xxxx@abc.edu. At that time I will work with you on providing a link to the online survey or towards getting you the hard copy of the survey. This survey structure and content have been reviewed and approved by the Institutional Review Board-Human Subjects in Research at ABC. Again, please consider that if you choose to participate, I would also need the help of your supervisor and a coworker to fill out the other appropriate surveys. If you would like to participate and would prefer that I directly e-mail your supervisor and coworker, I would be more than willing to do so. On the other hand if you are in a supervisory position, I would appreciate it if you could ask two of your employees to participate as well in order to fill the roles of the employee and coworker. If you have any questions please feel free to e-mail me at anytime.

Thank you for your support and for considering this request.

Sincerely,

Xxxxxx Xxxxxxxxxx

FIGURE 7-4 Document for Exercise 4

Technical Reports

8

Reports, like correspondence—e-mails, memos, and letters, discussed in the previous chapter—are among the most commonly written workplace documents. Reports serve a variety of functions: for example, they provide information, instructions, analysis, and recommendations based on analysis.

Given the quantity of information generated and shared in most work environments, getting your report *read* is a critical consideration. In this chapter, we will explain the basics of designing clear and readable reports.

Quick Tips

None of your readers will read your entire report, unless it's a single page. Different readers will read different sections of your report according to their needs. Almost all of your readers will read the summary: make sure this section is especially clear and concise.

If a report doesn't have a summary, readers will flip to the end to find the conclusions. If they can't find those easily, they likely will not read any portion of the report.

KINDS OF REPORTS

Many routine reports provide information, but others go beyond simple reporting. They categorize and then analyze information or data. From the analysis, the writer may evaluate the information, draw conclusions, and perhaps recommend action based on those conclusions. Analytical reports often defy rigid classification, but for the purpose of learning to write analytical reports, we can generally identify the following types:

- If the analysis focuses on a recommendation, the report may be called a **recommendation report**.

- If the analysis emphasizes evaluation of personnel, data, financial options, or possible solutions to problems or avenues for exploration, the report may be called an **evaluation report**.

- A **feasibility report** analyzes a problem, presents possible solutions to the problem, determines criteria for assessing the solutions, assesses the solutions against the criteria, and then shows the best solution(s) based on the reported analysis of the solutions. The recommendation is critical, but the analysis is as critical as the conclusion and recommendation. Available resources discuss methods of determining criteria against which possible solutions may be measured, methods of applying criteria, and analyzing solutions against criteria selected. Many feasibility reports are long, as they represent the way a problem has been defined, studied, and resolved. Results of feasibility studies can lead to major financial expenditures.

- Many reports both inform and analyze: a **progress report** or a **status report**, which will be discussed in Chapter 9, Proposals and Progress Reports, describes and evaluates the work done on a project, the money expended, and problems encountered.

- A **trip report** documents information gathered on a trip, evaluates this information, and may suggest actions based on findings.

- A **personnel report** describes an employee's performance, analyzes effectiveness, suggests methods of improvement, and estimates the employee's potential for promotion.

- An **economic justification report** explains the cost of a project or action and then argues for the cost-effectiveness of the project.

Report Heading

Internal reports use a memorandum heading that may include many of the following items. Organizations have their own specific requirements for internal reports that use a memo heading:

Date:
To:
From:
Subject:
Reference:
Action Required:
Distribution List:

Subject line. The subject line should state clearly—in concise phrasing—the content of the report. The clearer the subject line, the better the odds that your readers will read your report. Your subject line should make your readers want to read your report.

Reference. Many reports respond to previously written reports, to company policies, or to items such as engineering specifications and legal issues. Be sure your readers have what they need and understand how your report links to previous reports.

Action required. If you need your reader(s) to respond to your report by a certain date, then say so here. For example, "Your approval needed by 5/10/2009." (See Case 7-1 on p. 123, which shows a memo with an action-required statement.)

Distribution list. This report segment, which can occur at either the beginning or end of the report, indicates who will receive copies as well as the name of the file in which the report will be stored for later reference. Be sure to include on this list everyone who should receive a copy. Failing to include all readers can create problems for employees, as omitted readers may think that the writer is trying to eliminate that reader from the information delivered.

PARTS OF A TECHNICAL REPORT

Introduction. Reports should begin with an introduction—a section that introduces readers to the content that will be covered. Introductions can be one sentence or several pages, depending on the topic and the needs of readers. For routine reports, attempt to keep your introduction concise but long enough to ensure that readers understand what they are reading and why they are included on the distribution list. Also remember that reports will be kept in files and can be accessed by readers many months and years after you have written the report. The introduction should ensure that all readers understand the report.

Thus, a report introduction should contain the following elements. How much you develop each item will depend on the particular report situation.

Subject. Specific topic.

Purpose. What do you want your report to accomplish? Often, both of these items can be combined into one sentence. If possible, begin the report with a sentence or two that states the subject and purpose. For many routine reports, a subject/purpose statement will be all you need.

Background or rationale. What issues led to the need for this report? Be concise. Place the background or rationale in a separate paragraph. If your main readers don't need to be reminded, then they can skip this paragraph. Readers on the distribution list or future readers will likely be grateful for the information.

Report development. What topics will you cover? Simply state how you will develop the report.

Summary. The summary of the report is the most important element. Many readers who receive copies, simply as information, will read only the introduction and the summary. The summary should tell your readers the essential points and findings in the report.

Introduction + summary. Many reports combine both elements (see Figure 8-1). If your organization or readers like this method, then begin with the summary and include report topic and purpose statement. You can also include conclusions and recommendations.

Conclusion. The report conclusion ties together what you have presented. In long reports, the information in the conclusion should be mirrored or reported in the summary.

Recommendations. If you need to recommend action, then include that here. To improve readability, list and number your recommendations. If you need to discuss them, you can do so following your list.

Attachments. Attachments include any material, provided on hard copy or electronically, that is needed to support your discussion, conclusions, or recommendations. Attachments may be additional data, calculations, or previously written documents on the same subject.

DEVELOPING REPORTS

How reports develop varies, and here we can provide only guidelines and a few examples. In the introduction, you state how you will present your report and the topics that your reader will find. Thus, you can have a main heading for each topic,

---

Congress's Contempt Power: Law, History, Practice, and Procedure

Summary

Congress's contempt power is the means by which Congress responds to certain acts that in its view obstruct the legislative process. Contempt may be used either to coerce compliance (inherent contempt), punish the contemnor (criminal contempt), and/or to remove the obstruction (civil contempt). Although arguably any action that directly obstructs the effort of Congress to exercise its constitutional powers may constitute a contempt, in the last seventy years the contempt power (primarily through the criminal contempt process) has generally been employed only in instances of refusals of witnesses to appear before committees, to respond to questions, or to produce documents.

This report examines the source of the contempt power, reviews the historical development of the early case law, outlines the statutory and common law basis for Congress's contempt power, and analyzes the procedures associated with each of the three different types of contempt proceedings. In addition, the report discusses limitations both nonconstitutional and constitutionally based on the power. Finally, the report discusses the recent investigation by the House Judiciary Committee that has resulted in votes for criminal contempt of Congress and the filing of a civil lawsuit to enforce congressional subpoenas.

FIGURE 8-1 Combined Introduction/Summary
Source: http://www.fas.org/sgp/crs/misc/RL34097.pdf.

and readers who have interest in one or two particular issues can go immediately to those issues. See Case 8-1, which includes an example informal report.

> **Note:** You want to develop a reputation for writing reports that are easy to read as well as informative and accurate. Don't make readers hunt for information—they won't.

The two following reports show different types of purpose and development. Many reports serve only to inform. Figure 8-2, a report prepared by the Tennessee Valley Authority, describes common pollutants that can be found in U.S. homes. Note that the report has been prepared for online distribution and reading. Thus, the report outline, which lists each major report section and topic, allows readers to move to that section by clicking on the heading. The introduction clearly states the report topic, its importance, and the report's purpose. No summary is provided, as the report itself summarizes the issue discussed.

Many reports are prepared to be disseminated on hard copy, even though they may be initially distributed as file attachments to e-mails. The following report, submitted to the Educational Environment Committee of a university, illustrates use of a more formal presentation: title page, table of contents, and summary (Figure 8-3). Any report longer than four or five pages should include a table of contents for accessibility.

Case 8-1

ABC University has invited departments in each college to assess the quality of their undergraduate programs. As part of this assessment effort, the philosophy department asks several dozen students who have completed the undergraduate degree in philosophy to assess their experience with the program. Ariel Chisholm, who graduated with honors, provided the following report, which he addresses to the chair of the undergraduate program assessment committee.

CASE DOCUMENT 8-1

MEMORANDUM

DATE: April 5, 2007

TO: Dr. Scott Austin
            ABC Philosophy Department Undergraduate Advisor

FROM: Ariel Chisholm
            ABC Philosophy Department B.A. Program Graduate

SUBJECT: Curriculum Assessment Report

Attached is my report assessing the ABC Philosophy Department's undergraduate degree plan and course curriculum. I prepared this report at the request of the ABC Philosophy Department faculty, in accordance with ABC's university-wide Quality Enhancement Planning efforts.

This report presents a broad analysis of the Philosophy Department's course curriculum and presents suggestions on how that curriculum might be enhanced. As a recent graduate, my recommendations reflect needs I had in pursuing the curriculum.

I appreciate the opportunity to contribute observations and recommendations to this project and hope the university will continue to assess curriculum.

TO: All ABC Philosophy Department Faculty

FROM: Ariel Chisholm
              ABC Philosophy Department B.A. Program Graduate

SUBJECT: **Requested Student Assessment of the ABC University
              Philosophy Department's Undergraduate Curriculum**

Introduction

As part of ABC's commitment to university-wide Quality Enhancement Planning, The ABC Philosophy Department requested that I draft a memo report assessing the current Philosophy Department degree plan and curriculum, and include suggestions on how the philosophy curriculum might be bettered. This is my resulting report, along with my suggestions for enhancing the curriculum.

I thank the entire Philosophy Department for giving me an opportunity to share my thoughts about this wonderful program. The ABC Philosophy faculty is a committed and passionate group of teachers; and I am in their debt for much of my academic success to date.

With these thoughts in mind, I have focused my report on a set of changes to the Department's curriculum that I think would improve future philosophy students' learning experiences. I believe the department should provide an earlier and more widespread introduction to rudimentary sentential logic and predicate logic theory, in all Philosophy Department courses.

Curricular Recommendations

All of the undergraduate philosophy courses that I have taken from the ABC Philosophy Department each require, to some degree or another, a basic grasp of the idea of formal rules to logical argument. Unfortunately, not many classes cover the most elementary of these rules.

The Philosophy Department has, of course, a rigorous block of logic courses, starting with PHIL 240 Intro to Logic. The problem is that this may not be the first, or even among the first, philosophy courses in which many beginning philosophy students enroll.

As an undergraduate, I myself managed to take five different 3-hour philosophy classes, including two 300-level classes, before taking PHIL 240. Much of the material in the prior classes would have been easier to analyze if I had been armed with a groundwork understanding of some of the basic, rudimentary rules of sentential and predicate logic.

I particularly remember encountering Anselm's ontological proof of the existence of God in my Philosophy of Religion course, and trying to read literary critiques of the proof (already itself a very sophisticated argument) that

continued

utilized sentential and predicate logic formulas and equations. The book material, and the teacher in class, seemed to take it for granted that everyone could follow along with such material, but I clumsily struggled with it until I took PHIL 240, several semesters later.

Student learning in the Department can be improved across the degree plan if efforts are made to enroll students in an introductory logic course earlier in their philosophy studies, and also if efforts are taken to keep students in all Department courses well-familiar with rudimentary sentential and predicate logic theory.

The Philosophy Department Degree Plan

The Department's degree plan is divided into the standard block of courses required by the ABC University College of Liberal Arts (this block of courses will not be discussed in this report), as well as a block of philosophy courses that can be customized to fill in nine areas of departmentally required philosophical study, as diagrammed in this Philosophy Department web chart:

AREA	COURSES	
Logic	One of these courses is required:	240, Introduction to Logic 341, Symbolic Logic 342, Symbolic Logic II
Epistemology/ Philosophy of Science	One of these courses is required:	305, Philosophy of Natural Science 307. Philosophy of Social Science 351, Theory of Knowledge
Metaphysics and Ontology	One of these courses is required:	320, Philosophy of Mind 331, Philosophy of Religion 361, Metaphysics
Value Theory	One of these courses is required:	330, Philosophy of Art 332, Social / Political Philosophy 381, Ethical Theory
The Continental Tradition	One of these courses is required:	414, 19th Century Philosophy 418, Phenomenology / Existentialism 419, Current Continental Philosophy
The Anglo-American Tradition	One of these courses is required:	415, Classical American Philosophy 416, Recent British / American Philosophy 424, Philosophy of Language
History of Classical Philosophy	This course	410, Classical Philosophy
History of Modern Philosophy	This course	413, Modern Philosophy
Philosophy Electives	Any two courses	

PHILOSOPHY COURSES REQUIRED FOR A PHILOSOPHY B.A., ACCORDING TO PHILOSOPHY.ABC.EDU

Among the above-listed courses, only Metaphysics requires PHIL 240 Intro to Logic as a prerequisite (as well it should); but all other classes can be taken without having ever studied even the most elementary rules of premise-conclusion, sentential, and predicate logic. It has occurred to me that this may be a bit like a physics department rarely requiring their students to take math courses commensurate with their physics studies.

Discussion of Specific Courses

Three specific courses currently do not have a logic course prerequisite. I specifically recommend that these courses include some sort of rudimentary logic instruction. These classes are PHIL 331 Philosophy of Religion, PHIL 381 Ethical Theory, and PHIL 424 Philosophy of Language. Each of these courses includes study material far too informed by sentential and predicate logic for a student to fully appreciate the material without an introductory logic class.

Conclusion

The Philosophy Department teaches several courses that could greatly benefit from being taught concurrently with rudimentary sentential and predicate logic material. The department does not now teach these courses concurrently with its introductory logic class, and I think this hinders student comprehension of the material. If the Philosophy Department refines its approach to PHIL 331, 381, and 424 courses to include more basic logic instruction, students could come away from these classes with a much better understanding of the course material.

Indoor Air Quality

Indoor Air Quality: A Serious Health Issue

Introduction

Over the past two decades, outdoor air quality in the United States has improved, while indoor air quality (IAQ) has declined. Indoor air pollution is recognized as one of the top five environmental risks to public health in the United States. Americans spend about 90 percent of their time indoors where concentrations of pollutants are often much higher than those outside. Indoor pollution is associated with many health impacts, including lung cancer and various respiratory health problems. The Asthma and Allergy Foundation of America reports that the number of children with asthma has doubled in the last 15 years.

The origins of IAQ problems date back to the end of World War II when there was great demand for inexpensive housing. Homes began to be built on smaller lots with garages attached to the home, allowing automobile exhaust and evaporative emissions to enter the living space. Home construction costs were reduced by using chipped and laminated wood products and other materials bound by organic resins that emit volatile pollutants. Carpet and other floor coverings requiring adhesives provided more gaseous pollutants, as did cleaning products, personal care items, air fresheners, and pesticides.

Despite the proliferation of these indoor pollutants, IAQ problems were uncommon before the 1970s. Houses, up to this time, were relatively "leaky," and high infiltration rates served to dilute indoor pollutants. The increase in IAQ problems that began in the 1970s can be attributed to changes in home and building design in the years immediately following the oil embargo of 1973, when the public became more concerned with the cost of energy. As houses began to be built more "airtight," IAQ problems have been exacerbated by a combination of more pollutant sources and less dilution of indoor air. This report describes the major pollutants in US homes.

Indoor Air Pollutants and Their Sources

Levels of certain pollutants in indoor air are often much higher than in outside air. The U.S. EPA reports that most Americans will experience their greatest exposure to toxic chemicals indoors. Primary sources of many of these pollutants are consumer products and building materials. Levels of many potentially toxic compounds typically are two to five times greater indoors than outdoors and sometimes as much as hundreds of times greater.

Radon

Radon is a colorless, odorless, and tasteless radioactive gas that cannot be detected without the use of sensitive test equipment. Radon is produced by the breakdown of naturally-occurring uranium in soil, rock, and water. Some radon passes to surrounding air and water and may enter homes through cracks in foundations, openings around sump pumps and drains, crawl spaces, and cracks in basement floors and

FIGURE 8-2 Informational Report

walls. The Surgeon General and the National Academy of Sciences have warned that radon is second only to cigarette smoking as a cause of lung cancer in the United States.

Radon gas is found throughout the world and in every state in America. In the United States, the average level inside homes (1.3 picoCuries per liter [pCi L^{-1}]) is about four times the average level outdoors (0.3 pCi L^{-1}). But restricted air flow and resulting gas accumulations can push indoor levels much higher. When indoor levels reach about three time the average (i.e., 4.0 pCi L^{-1}, the U.S. EPA action level), radon is considered a health threat.

Radon levels generally are highest in areas where soil is underlain by limestone. Evaluations of U.S. county data by EPA and the U.S. Geological Survey indicate that many counties in the Tennessee Valley region have a high potential for radon exposure in the home. Limestone-rich areas of Alabama, Tennessee, and Kentucky are, on average, the most vulnerable to radon, with the Coastal Plain and Delta areas of west Tennessee and Mississippi the least vulnerable. But the variability within all areas is quite high. That is why every home should be tested, regardless of geographic location.

Combustion Pollutants

Water vapor, carbon monoxide (CO), carbon dioxide (CO2), nitrous oxide (NO), nitrogen dioxide (NO2), and fine particles are emitted by combustion sources. Depending on the fuel source, hydrocarbon gases, organic particles, metals, and sulfur oxides also can be emitted.

Unvented combustion sources are a ubiquitous source of NO2 and CO in homes. The NO2 levels in homes with gas ranges are nearly always higher than the NO2 levels in homes with electric ranges. Carbon monoxide emissions from gas ranges typically are ten times higher than NO2 emissions. It is estimated that 45 percent of homes in the United States use natural gas.

Wood stoves and fireplaces emit NO2, CO, and fine particles. Emissions normally are vented outdoors, and only during startup and stoking are emissions likely to contaminate indoor air. Consequently, wood burning increases particulate levels indoors by only a few micrograms per cubic meter (mg/m3). However, the particulate matter from wood smoke has been found to be carcinogenic.

Kerosene heaters, in addition to emitting NO2, CO, and sulfur dioxide (SO2), also emit polycyclic aromatic hydrocarbons that are mutagenic. Approximately 11 percent of the U.S. population is exposed to gas or kerosene space heater emissions. Under certain conditions, exhaust gases from vented combustion appliances can enter the living space. For example, exhaust fans cause combustion emissions to be back-drafted into the living space. Combustion emissions also can leak into homes from roadways or, especially, from nearby attached or sublevel garages.

Tobacco Smoke

Tobacco smoke is probably the most studied indoor air pollutant. Over 50 compounds in tobacco smoke are either known or suspected carcinogens. Studies using electrostatic filters have revealed that, contrary to popular belief, most of the irritation and the odor from tobacco smoke comes from the gaseous pollutants and not the particulates. To place into perspective the issue of human exposure to Environmental Tobacco Smoke (ETS), a comparison was made of exposure to particulates originating from ETS and from coal-fired power plants. According to a 1993 U.S. EPA report, from a human exposure to particulates standpoint, a mere 2 percent reduction in environmental tobacco smoke would be equivalent to closing all coal-fired power plants in the United States.

Particles

Particles, very small solid or liquid substances, can become suspended in air. Particles can be organic or inorganic compounds, or they can be living or dormant organisms. Health effects from particle exposure depend on the types and concentrations of particles present, frequency and duration of exposure, and sensitivity of the individual. Of primary concern are the small respirable particles that can penetrate deep into the lungs and cause acute or chronic health effects. Tobacco smoke and other combustion products, cat dander, bacteria, viruses, asbestos, and outside air are the primary sources of fine particles (< 2 μm). Larger particles, such as mold, pollen, animal dander, and dust allergens do not penetrate as deeply but can cause allergic responses.

FIGURE 8-2 *continued*

Formaldehyde

Formaldehyde is one of the most ubiquitous organic vapors in indoor air. Long before EPA recognized organic vapors as pollutants of indoor air, formaldehyde was known to be a pungent gas that irritated eyes and mucous membranes. It is found in hundreds of products, including medicines, cosmetics, toiletries, and food containers. Its most common use is in resins used to bind together laminated and chipped wood products. Formaldehyde is also used as a carrier for dyes in synthetic carpets. It is an irritant to the eyes, nose, and throat and has been linked to asthmatic symptoms. It also has been listed as a suspected human carcinogen.

Volatile Organic Compounds

Building furnishings, construction materials, consumer products, paints, adhesives, pesticides, and ETS are indoor sources of volatile organic compounds (VOCs). In an EPA study, more than 500 VOCs were identified in the air inside ten public access buildings. Emission rates from construction materials are difficult to predict because they generally decline after construction, having half lives of two to twenty weeks. VOC exposure levels are most influenced by the materials inside the home and the behavior of the occupants. With the exception of benzene, which is a human carcinogen, most prevalent VOCs are not carcinogenic; however, they can cause headaches, irritate the eyes, and reduce productivity of occupants.

Asbestos and Lead

Asbestos and lead from lead-based paints are two pollutants that pose the greatest health risk when they are dispersed in remodeling activities. Stringent control measures are required for renovation activities that involve asbestos. Lead in indoor environments poses the greatest risk to children. Asbestos and lead-based paints are still common in many buildings constructed prior to 1980.

Biological Agents

Biological agents include pollens from trees and plants and microbial cells such as viruses, bacteria, fungal spores, protozoans, algae, animal dander and excreta, and insect excreta and fragments. Mold hidden behind wall coverings and beneath carpet can emit microbial VOCs that can penetrate vapor barriers and enter the living space. Microbial growth most often occurs in bathrooms, damp basements, window casements, air conditioner cooling coils, and condensate drain pans. In general, moisture control in buildings is essential for preventing the growth of bacteria and fungi. Dust mites, a common allergen and cause of asthmatic symptoms among sensitive individuals, also can be controlled by reducing moisture.

Biological contaminants can cause or exacerbate respiratory diseases. Common disorders are hay fever or asthma. A more serious illness that can be caused by biological contaminants is hypersensitivity pneumonitis (farmer's lung disease, humidifier lung, and humidifier fever). Its symptoms are similar to pneumonia; however, the illness is the result of an immune response to an antigen and not an infection. If left untreated, hypersensitivity pneumonitis can cause permanent lung damage.

Indoor Air Pollution Control

Three methods for controlling indoor air pollution are ranked in terms of effectiveness as follows:

1. Eliminate pollutant source
2. Increase ventilation to dilute concentration of contaminant(s)
3. Filter or purify air

Radon, combustion pollutants, ETS, particles, formaldehyde, and VOCs all can be eliminated from indoor air. Radon gas can be vented from beneath slabs or crawl spaces. ETS can be eliminated by prohibiting smoking indoors. Exposure to other combustion emissions can be avoided by proper ventilation. Formaldehyde and VOC pollution in homes can be reduced by selecting building materials and furnishings that do not emit these pollutants and by choosing to use water soluble products in place of solvent-based products. Biological contaminants can be controlled by keeping relative humidity below 60 percent and by removing dust and other particles that can provide nutrients for microbes. Since mold can thrive on air-conditioner cooling

FIGURE 8-2 *continued*

coils and in condensate removal systems, it can be controlled by properly maintaining air-conditioners. Adequate insulation in the outer shell of homes, adequate circulation of air, and the use of storm windows can prevent condensation on windows and walls, eliminating sites for moisture-borne organisms.

Ventilation provides an effective means for diluting the concentration of all indoor air pollutants. Exhaust ventilation can be used to remove moisture from kitchens and bathrooms and ETS from smoking areas. Where VOCs are emitted, ventilation can be used to dilute their concentration. Typically, outside air is pulled into homes when exhaust fans are operated. In homes that are airtight, mechanical ventilation may be required to provide adequate supplies of outside air. To keep bioeffluents and CO2 respired by occupants at acceptable levels, a minimum of 15 ft^3/min of outside air per person is required.

Air filters and air purifiers use one of three types of filters: mechanical, electrostatic, and electronic. While effective in removing large particles, ordinary, flat mechanical filters are less effective in removing small, respirable particles than electrostatic filters or mechanical filters that are either pleated or have extended media. To effectively remove respirable particles in ETS, electronic filters that collect particles on oppositely charged plates are required.

Filters remove only airborne particles. Thus, particles settled on carpet, bedding, drapes and upholstery can be resuspended by occupants and settle out without reaching the filtration system. Filters also are ineffective in removing gases. And some filters that have been specifically designed to remove gases are not effective in removing all the gaseous pollutants typically found in indoor air. Like whole-house filters, air purifiers are only effective in removing ETS if they contain an electronic filter. Air purifiers also are limited by the volume of air they can handle and by how well that air is mixed. Air can be short circuited around the air handler, leaving pockets of air untreated. Ozone generators being sold as air purifiers are not recommended because they can cause indoor ozone levels to exceed the regulated limits for outdoor air.

Conclusions

Public awareness of the hazards associated with indoor air pollution and the high cost of energy required to maintain good indoor air quality have made it important for everyone concerned with construction, maintenance, management, and ownership of buildings to better understand indoor air pollution issues. Consumers can improve their indoor living environment by adopting a few simple IAQ pollution control measures. These measures not only will benefit personal health, but also will improve the integrity of their homes.

FIGURE 8-2 *continued*

Educational Partnerships Committee Report
Texas A&M Chapter of Sigma Xi,
The Scientific Research Society

K-12 Educational Partnerships
at Texas A&M University

FIGURE 8-3 Formal Report

Foreword from Sigma Xi

The Executive Committee of the Texas A&M Chapter of Sigma Xi has created a Committee for Educational Partnerships. This Committee is charged with promoting increased university partnerships with the K-12 school community. We have a special emphasis on promoting student interest and aptitude in science, math, engineering, and technology (STEM) and enhancing the preparedness of students to thrive academically at Texas A&M University.

The initial work of the Committee has led to development of two initiatives: 1) creation of an ongoing seminar series aimed at familiarizing faculty and administrators with K-12 issues and needs, and 2) formulating ideas and specific plans for institutionalizing K-12 partnerships at a university-wide level. This second charge to the committee is the focus of this report.

Committee members include: Don Allen (College of Science), Sarah Bednarz (College of Geosciences), John Fackler (College of Science), Larry Johnson (College of Veterinary Medicine & Biomedical Sciences), Bill Klemm (College of Veterinary Medicine & Biomedical Sciences)(Chairman of the Committee), and Mary Wicksten (College of Science). Any of these members can be contacted for further information and discussion of the contents of this report.

Submitted by: _____   Date: _____

W. R. (Bill) Klemm
Committee Chairman

FIGURE 8-3 *continued*

Summary

Educators in Texas have struggled in recent decades to raise the competence level of pre-college students. The Sigma Xi Committee members are not alone in perceiving that public schools are overwhelmed with the challenges in today's political and cultural environment. Such problems include not only uncertain and insufficient funding, but also a host of cultural influences that are producing students with diminished academic capability compared to students in past decades. These problems are exacerbated by the growing Hispanic and Black populations, which traditionally lag the general population in preparation for college work. We perceive the problems to be especially acute in preparing students for successful college work in science, technology, engineering, and math (STEM) disciplines (See Appendix I).

In the last few years, consistent with Vision 2020 guidelines, some A&M administrative leaders have promoted significant initiatives to move us away from our historical model of leaving support for public schools to the College of Education and Human Development. We need to capitalize on this momentum to make certain that all A&M departments and colleges make the needed impact on preparation of prospective TAMU students.

Our Committee has determined that there are at least 30 different K-12 STEM-related partnerships programs on campus (See Appendix II). These are housed in multiple departments in most of the Colleges at TAMU. These programs generally operate in isolation from each other, often with minimal support from their home departments and colleges. Some of these programs are funded from extramural sources, with amounts involving millions of dollars. We anticipate that many partnership grant opportunities are being lost because potential PIs are not aware of funding opportunities and because there is no structural mechanism to assist partnerships in leveraging the resources of other K-12 outreach programs on campus.

We believe that Texas A&M needs to make structural changes in which K-12 partnerships become institutionalized. This report makes two recommendations:

1. We urge every College to designate K-12 partnering as one of the responsibilities of its academic Associate Dean.

2. We urge creation of a university-wide Office of Educational Partnerships (OEP).We also make specific recommendations on organizing this OEP , its mission, and the specific duties of the Office and its Director.

FIGURE 8-3 *continued*

Current Partnership Practices at Texas A&M

With few exceptions, all existing K-12 partnership programs have been initiated by individual faculty members in various colleges. The STEM-related programs that our Committee is aware of are summarized in Appendix II, which lists each program, its program manager/PI, contact information, and funding sources.

In general, we have identified at least 30 K-12 STEM-related partnerships programs on campus, housed in every College except Architecture, Business, and Liberal Arts. In the Spring of 2006, Sigma Xi hosted a luncheon for the directors of these programs, and it was clear that these directors did not know about all the other programs nor have they been interacting and leveraging their resources and efforts. Six of these programs involve funding in the range of several $million each (Bednarz, L. Johnson, C. D. Johnson, Schielack, Simanek, Stewart). Activity at this level of funding and national recognition provides a critical mass upon which to build a comprehensive, university-wide program of K-12 partnerships. Indeed, we think that this evidence justifies a prediction that Texas A&M could achieve national pre-eminence in this arena if the university would provide leadership and backing.

Sigma Xi is also initiating a university seminar series on K-12 partnerships. The opening presentation, "Why (& How) TAMU Should Be More Engaged in K-12 Education" was delivered on March 28, 2006 (See Appendix I). The thrust of the presentation was to explain why Texas A&M should get more involved in K-12 education policy and practice, and to suggest ways that we could begin institutionalization of partnerships. The second seminar in this series is slated for early September and is to be presented by Dr. Mark Weichold, Dean of Undergraduate Programs and Associate Provost for Academic Services.

FIGURE 8-3 *continued*

Suggested Mission Statement for University K-12 Partnerships

Texas A&M University recognizes the importance to the State of Texas of providing the best possible education for the people of Texas. To help achieve this goal, the resources and academic expertise of the University should be used to assist the K-12 educational community. Moreover, we seek to create and nourish multiple partnerships that are university-wide. University policies, leadership, and reward systems should be mobilized to encourage K-12 partnerships efforts from all departments and colleges.

The partnerships mission statement should be consonant with aims of Vision 2020. Among those aims that are most pertinent here include "Imperative #3—Enhance the undergraduate academic experience." How effective we can be at enriching academic experience depends on the quality of the student body, and that quality in turn depends on the quality of the pool of students in the application pipeline. The Imperative also states that our retention is low compared to peer institutions and that we need to do more to recruit minorities. Both of these needs are profoundly affected by the quality of the applicant pool. Imperative #12 states that "The diverse population of Texas should have access to the best public education in America without having to leave the state." But to achieve this goal, "access" really means that the entering students are fully qualified to thrive in the rigorous academic curricula that the university strives to provide.

We offer as a first consideration the following mission statement:

> Texas A&M University is committed to nurturing the educational enterprise at all levels (K-16), inasmuch as all levels are inextricably interdependent. We seek to create and nurture campus-wide partnerships among our faculty, TAMU administrative entities, and the K-12 educational community. We pledge our support for educational initiatives that will benefit all students in the state, urban and rural, irrespective of their grade level, socio-economic status or ethnicity.

FIGURE 8-3 *continued*

Rationale for Expanded Partnerships

There is an inherent interdependence among those who create knowledge and understanding, those who teach it, and those who learn it. This interdependence pervades all levels of education, K-16. Unfortunately, we believe, this interdependence is not fully appreciated either by the university community or the K-12 community. Education at all levels suffers as a consequence.

There is today a national consensus, especially at the level of the federal government, that U.S. students are not being adequately prepared academically, especially in STEM disciplines. Achievement levels of U.S. students do not compare well those with students in many other countries. Both business and science community leaders are expressing concern over the ability of today's students to compete in the increasingly global economy. The President has announced the "American Competitiveness Initiative," and specifically cited the need for improvement in science education in the recent State of the Union Address.

What is the role of the university in this state of affairs? Can universities sit on the sidelines as if college education is not affected by what goes on in public schools? We believe that Texas A&M should be more active in mobilizing its educational resources to improve educational achievement in the public schools. We believe that Texas A&M should contribute more actively to resolving issues in public education, ranging from helping state agencies and local districts to determine appropriate college-preparation standards, methods of high-stakes testing, and teaching methodology for STEM content .

Members of our Committee have heard faculty state in one form or another that K-12 involvement is not important for them because A&M gets to "skim the cream" of the applicant pool. That specious argument fails on several counts:

1. A&M does not recruit minorities—especially high-achieving minorities—as effectively as it would like. As of Fall, 2006, our enrollment of Hispanics is 10.2% of the student body and of blacks, 2.8%, both far below the average for all state universities.* To increase minority enrollment, we need a larger pool of minorities who can meet A&M admission standards.

2. The "cream" that we do get is not sufficient to give A&M high rankings in nationwide comparisons that emphasize quality of the student body. The average SAT score of A&M students is unimpressive when compared to that of many of the premier universities to which we like to compare ourselves. TAMU ranks 50th among universities*

3. Pre-college preparation today is not what it was a decade or more ago, due to a variety of socio-economic factors over which the university has no direct control. TAMU has adjusted with grade inflation and "watering-down" of many courses. Even so, we, along with other universities, have large numbers of students who take 5 or more years to graduate. At A&M, we have approximately 25% of the student body that has not graduated within six years.*

Moreover, it is increasingly clear from a wide range of sources that today's youth seem less academically capable than in past decades. The problems are reflected in short attention spans, poor work ethic, and declining interest in "hard" subjects such as science and math. Multiple changes in cultural norms contribute to diminished capability of today's students. Unfortunately there is little the university can do about these causes, yet we are increasingly compelled to cope with the consequences. The most direct way to cope is for the university to become more engaged in public education at lower levels.

When professors become engaged with the K-12 community, they become more aware of the nature of today's student and their learning obstacles. Professors then become sensitized to the need for more artful teaching. This will surely improve the quality and effectiveness of professor teaching at the university level.

Some of the data and sources that lead to the conclusions above can be found in the slide show contained in Appendix I. There are also major national initiatives, epitomized by "The Gathering Storm," that

---

*Vision 2020 progress report, 2006: http://www.tamu.edu/vision2020/report.php

FIGURE 8-3 *continued*

will compel universities to become more of a supportive partner in the K-12 world. We would also recommend all interested parties to check landmark publications that raise serious warning flags for universities. Such publications include:

- "The Gathering Storm," National Academies Press, 2006
- "The World is Flat," 2005 by Tom Friedman, Farrar, Straus, and Giroux
- "American Competitiveness Initiative," http://www.whitehouse.gov/stateoftheunion/2006/aci/
- "Teaching The New Basic Skills," 1996 by Murnane & Levy, Simon & Schuster
- "Reality Check 2006," www.publicagenda.org
- "Three Billions New Capitalists," 2005 by Clyde Prestowitz, Basic Books
- "Tapping America's Potential" www.tap2015.org
- "How Long Will America Lead the World," Fareed Zakaria. MSNBC
- "A National At Risk." National Commission on Excellence in Education, 1983. http://www.ed.gov/pubs/NatAtRisk/index.html
- "A National Still At Risk," ERIC Clearinghouse, 1999. http://www.ericdigests.org/1999-4/risk.htm
- "School & College," Section B, Special Report from the Chronicle of Higher Education, vol. LII, no. 27. Spring 2006
- "What Do Our 17-year-olds Know?' 1988, by D. Ravitch and C. E. Finn Jr. Harper and Row
- "Endangered Minds," 1990, 1999 by J. M. Healy. Simon & Schuster
- "The De-Valuing of America," 1995, by W. J. Bennett. Blackstone
- "The Path to National Suicide: An Essay on Immigration and Multiculturalism,"1990, by L. Auster. American Immigrations Control Foundation. Monterey
- "Our Country and Our Children: Improving America's Schools and Affirming the Common Culture ," by W. J. Bennett, Simon & Schuster
- "The Big Test," 1999, by N. Lemann.Farrar. Straus & Giroux
- "The War Against Boys," 2000, by C. H. Sommers. Simon & Schuster
- "The Schools We Need and Why We Don't Have Them, " 1996, by E. D. Hirsch Jr. Doubleday
- "The Bell Curve," 1994, by R. J. Herrnstein and C. Murray. Simon & Schuster
- "Illiterate America," 1986, by J. Kozol, NAL

These and numerous other publications have been sounding alarms that are scarcely heard in the ivory towers of academe. In short, leaving school reform to others is a luxury that universities can no longer afford.

First-tier universities such as A&M have a natural preoccupation with research. We at Sigma Xi, of all people, understand the value of research, inasmuch as promoting research is the purpose Sigma Xi. Yet teaching those who will ultimately become the next generation of scientists is an obvious responsibility of those who know what scientific research is all about. We also see a need for more balance between teaching and research and, moreover, more need for the findings of modern research to inform teaching, both in the university and in K-12.

Increased engagement with the K-12 community should include educational research, for which there are numerous opportunities. Texas A&M has an increasing number of researchers who have an interest in K-12 education, and multiple unexploited opportunities exist for partnership with the College of Education to make this university a national leader in educational research.

FIGURE 8-3 *continued*

Office for Educational Partnerships (OEP)

We urge every College to designate promotion of K-12 partnering as one of the responsibilities of its academic Associate Dean. We also urge the formation of a university-wide Office for Educational Partnerships (OEP). These initiatives would institutionalize and facilitate continuing engagement of the university and K-12 communities.

We believe that OEP should be housed in the office of the Vice President for Research, because this office already has support infrastructure for undergraduate research, graduate studies, and research proposal development. It is also the office that allocates overhead funding and graduate student stipends, both of which are crucial elements of any attempt to increase involvement with K-12. For example, continuing the NSF GK-12 programs when the grants terminate (A&M has three such programs at the moment) requires that the university find a means to support graduate students to serve as STEM consultants to K-12 teachers. The Vice President for Research provides the most obvious way to stimulate, coordinate, and support collaborative educational research partnerships between the College of Education and the rest of the university community.

We recommend that the OEP be provided a secretary and sufficient travel funds to allow its Director to communicate with relevant partners throughout the state and to network effectively at the national level (see below).

The Director should be a tenured Professor, preferably with a full-time salary budgeted from OEP (certainly no less than 50% full time). It is critical that the director should be an established STEM practitioner. This person should have an established record of working with the schools, with teacher professional development, with other STEM disciplines, and the CEHD. The Director should have a demonstrated interest and experience in partnering with K-12 communities, as well as having social skills and political savvy. The most important qualification of all is demonstrable commitment to a vision for nurturing educational partnerships.

FIGURE 8-3 *continued*

Suggested Responsibilities for OEP

The OEP must interact with and promote partnerships among diverse communities: Texas A&M professors engaged in research, university administrators, public school teachers and officials throughout the state, officials in state education agencies, corporate executives, and leaders in federal education agencies.

The OEP needs to develop mechanisms for coordinating the various partnerships that already exist on campus and to stimulate more such activity. This includes developing a Web site for information and resource dissemination and holding periodic meetings, seminars, workshops aimed at leveraging existing resources, talents, and efforts.

The OEP should be a focal point for creating new partnerships among higher education, secondary education, government, and the corporate world and for securing funding and other support for making them successful. The OEP should provide support for forming competitive educational research proposals, and provide specific support for Principal Investigators seeking to satisfy NSF's "broader impacts" requirement and similar requirements that are likely to evolve from other federal research-grant agencies. These efforts should also include seeking funding support from endowments and from university sources for matching or bridging funds for educational research grants. Ideally, the Office should have its own secretary and its own fund raiser.

OEP should recruit faculty to participate in K-12 education and to arrange mentoring and coordination so that they can be optimally effective. OEP should coordinate with leaders in the CEHD and in arranging for their faculty to participate fully in such partnerships. The Office should arrange for training and provide "How To" materials for professors and graduate students who participate in partnerships involving teachers and pubic school districts.

OEP should interact with teachers, directly and through their Associations and the Regional Service Centers. OEP should be engaged with state educational policy makers, particularly the Board of Education and TEA. The Office should participate actively in the dissemination of effective innovative materials and "best practices" ideas.

Efforts should be made to coordinate with other state universities, particularly the University of Texas with the aim of leveraging our activities throughout the state via our respective university Systems.

Finally, OEP should participate in national educational reform efforts, leading where possible, and assuring that Texas A&M and its partners benefit from reforms that take place elsewhere.

The Director should be expected to provide initiative and leadership in all these areas.

FIGURE 8-3 *continued*

Elements of Formal Reports

Long reports should be developed as formal reports. Elements of formal reports should be selected and developed by writers to help readers find their way through the report. The longer the report and the larger the readership, the more elements you will need to help readers find what they need. Each element has a different purpose and often targets the needs of different readers. Remember that reports should be developed with the needs of a variety of readers in mind. Reports are not novels: most reports are not read cover to cover. Any report, but particularly long reports, must be designed so that readers can easily find what they need to read.

In general, reports may include any or all of the following elements. How these elements appear differs widely and depends on the organization preparing the report. We will describe the general characteristics and content of each element and provide several examples.

> Prefatory Elements
> > Letter of Transmittal
> > Title Page
> > Submission Page
> > Table of Contents
> > List of Illustrations
> > Glossary and List of Symbols
> Abstracts and Summaries
> > Informative Abstract
> > Descriptive Abstract
> > Executive Summary
> Discussion, or Body of the Report
> > Parts of the Discussion
> > Collecting and Grouping Information
> > Strategy for Presenting the Discussion
> > Reports with Standard Arrangement Patterns
> > Conclusion
> > Recommendations
> > Appendices

Prefatory elements. Readers initially access a report from the prefatory elements. These show your readers what your report will discuss and how it will approach the topic. Long, complex reports that will likely be read by many readers require prefatory elements. The letter of transmittal, title page, table of contents, abstract, and/or summary are often your reader's first—and only—experience with the report. Each of these elements should be written to help your readers grasp and accept the rhetorical purpose of the report. In no case should prefatory elements be considered routine report "paperwork" needing only perfunctory writing. Instead, each prefatory element should enforce the rhetorical purpose of the report. No matter how well-written and researched the report content, the effectiveness of the report begins with the effectiveness of the elements that contain the content. Many readers will decide to read the body of the report if they find the prefatory elements compelling.

Letter of transmittal. The letter of transmittal is addressed to the individual who will initially receive the report. This person may not be the primary reader but the individual responsible for routing the report to appropriate readers who will digest and use the content. In consulting reports, the CEO of an organization that has solicited the consulting work is usually the person to whom the letter of transmittal is addressed. Or the transmittal letter is addressed to the person who has authorized and requested the information, analysis, work, or recommendations covered in the report.

The letter of transmittal should include the following information at minimum:

- Statement of transmittal + subject and purpose of the report
- Reason for the report

In addition, transmittal letters (or memoranda, for internal reports) may include the following items:

- Background material—the larger issue or problem addressed by the report
- Mention of earlier reports (or additional reports that may be needed)
- Information that may be of special interest or significance to the readers
- Specific conclusions/recommendations that might be of special interest to the person to whom the report is addressed
- Financial implications
- Acknowledgments—list of those who provided help in the project

Case Document 8-1 includes a brief transmittal memo. The sample report in Appendix C also includes a letter of transmittal.

Title page. Title pages perform several functions. Basically, they provide critical identifying matter and may contain a number of identifying items to distinguish the report from others on a similar subject or from reports received in response to specific projects. Many organizations have a standard format for title pages. Whatever items you need—or your organization requires you to include—be sure to make the title page attractive. The following information often appears on title pages:

- Name of the company or individual(s) preparing the report
- Name of the company or course for which the report was prepared
- Title and subtitle of the report
- Date of submission
- Code number of the report
- Contract numbers under which the work was performed
- Company or agency logo
- Proprietary and security notices
- Names of contact/responsible individuals
- Descriptive abstract

Submission page. Reports may use a submission page, which includes the list of contributors to the report and/or the names and signatures of the authorizing officer or project leader. Submission pages emphasize the point we make throughout this book: reports require accountability. Signatures on a submission page indicate that the authors stand behind the content. The submission page usually either precedes the title page or follows it. Or the title page and submission page may be combined.

Table of contents. The table of contents (TOC) performs at least three major functions. First, it indicates the page on which each major topic begins to serve as a locating device for readers who may be searching for specific information. Second, the TOC forecasts the extent and nature of the topical coverage and suggests the logic of the arrangement and the relationship among the report parts. The TOC contains all major headings used in the report. For that reason, major headings, like the title of the report, should reflect the content of the material that follows. Skimming a table of contents should give readers a clear idea of the topics covered, the content presented under each heading, the amount of coverage devoted to that topic, the development of the report, and the progression of information. (See also the table of contents in the report in Appendix C.) While you may wish to use "introduction," "conclusion," and "recommendations," avoid the term "discussion": it tells your reader nothing about how you will present the report content. Third, the TOC should reflect the rhetorical purpose of your report—what you want your readers to know and why your report is important to them.

List of illustrations. If a report contains tables, graphics, drawings, photos—any type of visual—it's customary to use the page heading "Illustrations" or "Exhibits" to list all the visuals. These are usually divided into "tables" and "figures," but specific types may also be listed if you have an array of illustrations: for example, maps, financial statements, photographs, charts, and computer programs.

Glossary and list of symbols. Reports dealing with specialized subject matter often include abbreviations, acronyms, symbols, and terms not known to readers outside a specialized group. Readership should determine if a glossary or list of symbols is needed. Many reports prepared by government agencies for the general public provide glossaries to ensure that any reader can access the report.

Glossaries are sometimes prefatory elements, but they may also be included as an appendix at the end of the report. When you first use a symbol or a term that you will include in the glossary, tell your reader where to find the list or the glossary. You may wish to place an asterisk (*) by a word or symbol that will be covered in the glossary.

Abstracts and summaries. Abstracts and summaries are the most important prefatory items in a report. The title page, table of contents, abstract, and summary may be the only parts of the report many recipients read. Thus, these elements should be carefully planned, as each provides a slightly different perspective. While the title page and table of contents outline the report's content and direction, abstracts and summaries provide the essence of the report: topic, purpose, results, conclusions, and recommendations. Each item can stand alone or be designed in conjunction with other prefatory elements, but the wording of the table of contents should echo throughout an abstract or summary. These elements, when well designed, enable readers to quickly find a specific segment in the body of the report.

Often, the abstract follows or appears on the title page. Summaries may also follow the title page. While abstracts and summaries contain similar information, summaries usually provide more extensive information than abstracts and may be written for decision makers whose needs differ from those of readers who want only the essence of a report.

Abstracts are generally either informative or descriptive. Abstracts, often accompanied by key words, are prepared for use in online indexes and databases. Key words allow your report, if it is stored in a database, to be retrieved. Thus, you should think carefully about the key words that characterize the content of your report. What words will your readers most likely use in a database search? Abstracts with key words may be separated from the report but linked to the full report. Based on the information in the abstract, readers can decide if moving to the full report is needed.

Differences in abstracts are tending to disappear, however, and some abstracts have the characteristics of both traditional informative and descriptive styles. Organizations and journals usually have specific requirements for abstracts and may require, for example, a short descriptive abstract on the title page and an informative abstract after the table of contents.

Because of the increasing quantity of information, well-written abstracts have become critical to report access. The abstract should explain the purpose of the report, the findings, conclusions, and recommendations—anything of significance. Because many readers now use abstract services, they may read only your abstract, or they may decide to retrieve/order your complete report if the abstract clearly shows the relevance of the content and key points.

A good way to plan an abstract is to create a file that contains the names of its main parts:

Purpose
Methods
Findings or Results
Conclusions

Next, insert information under each heading. When you complete your abstract, you can remove the headings. Be sure to check the length of the abstract; publications rarely want abstracts longer than 100 to 150 words. This method allows you to track length easily.

Informative abstract. This type of abstract includes the research objectives, research methods used, and findings, including principal results and conclusions. Recommendations may also be included. Informative abstracts usually range from

50 to 500 words, depending on the length of the report and on the requirements of the disseminating organization and of the abstracting service. Informative abstracts help readers decide if they want or need to access the entire report for more thorough examination. They begin with a statement of the report's purpose, and the remaining sentences give major highlights and conclusions (Figure 8-4).

Descriptive abstract. This type of abstract states what topics the full report contains. Unlike informative abstracts, descriptive abstracts cannot serve as a substitute for the report itself. They begin with the report purpose and then explain content areas or topics covered in the report (Figure 8-5). See also the descriptive abstract on the title page of the sample report in Appendix C.

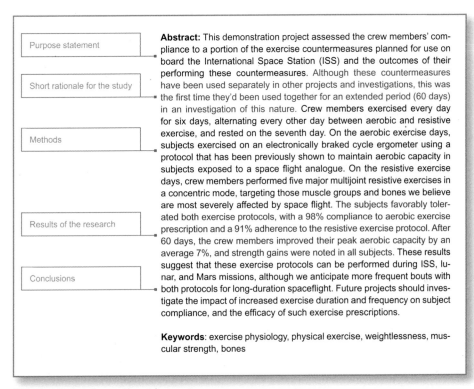

FIGURE 8-4 Informative Abstract
Source: S.M.C. Lee,* M.E. Guilliams,* A.D. Moore, Jr.,* W.J. Williams,* M.C. Greenisen, S.M. Fortney, Exercise Countermeasures Demonstration Project During the Lunar-Mars Life Support Test Project Phase IIA, TM-1998-206537, 1/1/1998, pp. 71, *Krug Life Sciences, Inc. http://ston.jsc.nasa.gov/collections/TRS/_1998-abs .html

1. **Keywords**: motion, motion perception, perception, control, adaptive control

Abstract: The purpose of this report is to identify the essential characteristics of goal-directed whole-body motion. The report is organized into three major sections. Section 2 reviews general themes from ecological psychology and control-systems engineering that are relevant to the perception and control of whole-body motion. These themes provide an organizational framework for analyzing the complex and interrelated phenomena that are the defining characteristics of whole-body motion. Section 3 applies the organizational framework from the first section to the problem of perception and control of aircraft motion. This is a familiar problem in control-systems engineering and ecological psychology. Section 4 examines an essential but generally neglected aspect of vehicular control: coordination of postural control and vehicular control. To facilitate presentation of this new idea, postural control and its coordination with vehicular control are analyzed in terms of conceptual categories that are familiar in the analysis of vehicular control.

FIGURE 8-5 Descriptive Abstract
Source: Gary E. Riccio* and P. Vernon McDonald**, Multimodal Perception and Multicriterion Control of Nested Systems: I. Coordination of Postural Control and Vehicular Control, TP-1998-3703, 1/1/1998, pp. 76, *Nascent Technologies, Ltd. **National Space Biomedical Research Institute. http://ston .jsc.nasa.gov/collections/TRS/_1998-abs.html

Executive summaries. Major reports often include executive summaries, which contain all of the items listed at the beginning of this chapter. However, unlike summaries for routine reports, executive summaries provide extensive development of each information segment to allow decision makers the information they need without having to read or search the full report. An example of an executive summary can be seen in the proposal for Project LEAD (Figure 8-6). Even though you know nothing about this project, the executive summary will provide you with extensive information. In many proposals, the summary often determines whether the proposal itself will be read.

Discussion, or body of the report. The main part of the report—the discussion—takes most of the writer's development time. The information to be reported constitutes the discussion. The discussion will explain in detail—whatever is appropriate to the context, the readers, and the purpose of the report—why the report was done, its objectives, methods, findings, results, analysis of results, conclusions emerging from results, and recommendations for dealing with the results. The discussion is the heart of the report: without it, effective summaries and abstracts could not be written. All conclusions and recommendations derive from the discussion. Stated another way, the presentation of information in the discussion allows the report writer to draw conclusions and perhaps recommendations. In short, the discussion must support all conclusions and recommendations.

The discussion can also stand alone. Because the report discussion begins with an introduction, including an explanation of the approach used in developing the report, the discussion is complete in itself. Many discussions end with a factual summary, which is a concise narrative of the report's findings.

Ironically, however, the main discussion is the report segment read least. While most readers will look at the summary, abstracts, and table of contents, few will actually delve into the discussion. Nevertheless, the discussion becomes the source, foundation, and documentation for every statement written in the abstract and summary. Your conclusions need to evolve from the discussion. Recommendations need to evolve from the discussion and the conclusions. In a sense, then, the discussion is a narrative that comes to a conclusion.

Many readers may need to read parts of the discussion carefully. They will read the introduction, check the table of contents, skip to relevant sections that interest them, and then move to the conclusion or factual summary that pulls together the main results or ideas.

Parts of the discussion. The main body of the report generally begins with an introduction (or introduction + summary) that forecasts what is to follow in the report. It directs the reader's mind to the subject and purpose. It tells the reader how to approach the content by explaining the scope of the report, the plan of development, and any additional information the reader may need. Examine the following introduction from the Virginia Department of Transportation. Note that it presents the topic, the rationale, and the development plan for the report that follows (Figure 8-7). Also examine the introduction to the sample report in Appendix C.

Note that the introduction should always include the report subject, purpose, and plan of development. Some reports place the background and the scope in separate sections that follow the introduction, if these two items are extensive. What you include in the introduction depends on readers. If your readers will expect your report, you can write a short introduction. However, if your report will be archived and read later by people who know little about the report context, you will need to provide a longer, more informative introduction. Avoid long introductions: focus on the subject and purpose in terms that explain the relevance of the report to readers. But do anticipate your readers—who will read this report and when—as you plan the introduction. Without a proper introduction, readers will have difficulty following the main discussion.

Collecting and grouping information. As you gather information, try grouping your material and notes into specific categories. Label these categories, and then begin your report. You may want to develop your report according to major sections—introduction, followed by the topics or categories. Open and name the file and begin. For example:

- Introduction: State the purpose of your report—what you expect to accomplish, what you want your reader(s) to know. You can add additional information later. Stating your purpose at the beginning of the draft helps you stay focused.
- Category/topic 1: phrase describing the issue you want to present
- Category/topic 2: etc.
- Category/topic 3: etc.

Next, begin inserting information under each topic or subject category. Focus initially on inserting information that pertains to the topic heading.

Project LEAD (Leadership Education and Development) for Junior High/Middle Level Preservice and Beginning Teachers

Executive Summary

The College of Education at Texas Tech University proposes to develop a practical project that will address two problems in public education: the teacher shortage caused by beginning teacher attrition and beginning teacher attrition caused by feelings of inadequacy. The present shortage in Texas of 37,000 to 40,000 can be attributed to the attrition of beginning teachers, not the failure of enough new teachers to be certified, according to Ed Fuller, co-director of research at the State (Texas) Board for Educator Certification ("Lawmakers Hear Teacher-Shortage Report," 2002). Since it is the certified beginning teachers, 40 to 50 % nationwide, who are the ones who are unwilling to stay in the classroom, this proposed project will seek to address the problem of new teacher attrition and; therefore, the teacher shortage.

The College of Education at Texas Tech University, along with partners from local school districts, proposes to develop a two-part project—LEAD (Leadership Education and Development) for Junior High/ Middle Level Preservice and Beginning Teachers, which will be built around the theme of leadership and which will consist of two distinct but interrelated programs: a preservice and an induction program. The premise is that if beginning teachers are developed as leaders, they will be retained at a higher rate than those young teachers who do not have their courses, their field experience and their first two years of teaching infused with leadership skills. The LEAD group will be better prepared to do well and to be retained because they will begin teaching with training that will give them a sense of control and support as they begin.

LEAD will be developed by a partnership of beginning teachers, selected junior high/middle level principals and their teachers, and faculty and staff of the College of Education at Texas Tech University. This collaboration will

• Define the term leadership and determine the leadership outcomes that young teachers need;
• Write the mission and philosophy and the goals and objectives of LEAD;
• Determine the type of students to recruit and how to best recruit them;
• Determine how to best implement and evaluate the determined leadership skills in the preservice courses, including student teaching;
• Develop and implement a Leadership Seminar preservice component;
• Plan and implement a two-year induction program that will continue to emphasize leadership skills and will collaborate with district induction programs;

The project will begin with a selected cohort of 30 junior high/middle level preservice teachers in 2004, and by second and third cohorts of 30 in 2005 and 2006. Group one will participate in two years of induction while group two will have one year, and group three will have none, unless additional funding can be secured. Assessment and evaluation of each aspect of the program will be ongoing, and appropriate annual reports will be made to the funding agency.

Need for LEAD

The College of Education and partners from ISD's in Lubbock County propose to initiate a project to develop teacher leaders. The College of Education is interested in developing this project because of the desire to help address the critical issues of the teacher shortage and the attrition rate of beginning teachers in the public schools. The attrition of certified teachers (40-50%) during the first five years of teaching appears to be a major cause of the teacher shortage across the nation and in Texas (35,000 to 40,000 in Texas alone). Addressing these issues requires a systematic approach that cultivates teacher leaders during their preservice training and supports them during the transition into their teaching careers. Project LEAD (Leadership Education and Development) for Junior High/Middle Level Preservice and Beginning Teachers will consist of two distinct but interrelated programs: a two-year preservice teacher program and an induction program designed to address the critical concerns of teacher shortage and beginning teacher attrition by developing teacher leaders.

FIGURE 8-6 Proposal with Executive Summary

Description of LEAD

Three cohorts of students seeking junior high/middle level certification will be recruited to participate in Project LEAD, based on their perceived level of commitment to the teaching profession at the time of their selection. LEAD will tailor the junior high/middle level certification preservice education courses that these students take to stress leadership skills. Once these students are certified and are beginning teachers in local junior high/middle level classrooms, they will be supported by an induction program, which will help them to implement leadership skills in their classrooms. As a result of stressing leadership in the junior high/middle level preservice courses and in the induction program, LEAD teachers will be better prepared to succeed as educators and to be retained in the profession than will other beginning teachers who do not have this training, for this project will enhance the sense of control and support that are critical to the retention of beginning career teachers.

One important strategy for implementing Project LEAD is for the College of Education to collaborate fully with local ISD's to develop the preservice and induction programs of LEAD. The College of Education faculty and staff will enlist the help of junior high/middle level principals, their teachers, and some of their junior high/middle level beginning teachers who had no special leadership preparation during their preservice courses to advise the faculty and staff on what the preservice and induction components of LEAD should be. For example, they, along with faculty and staff from the COE, will

- Specify what the term leadership means for junior high/middle level teachers and schools;
- Determine the leadership outcomes that young teachers need;
- Write the mission and philosophy of LEAD;
- Write the goals and objectives of LEAD;
- Determine the type of students to recruit and how to best recruit them;
- Determine how to best implement and evaluate the determined leadership skills in the preservice courses, including student teaching;
- Develop and implement a Leadership Seminar preservice component;
- Plan and implement a two-year induction program that will continue to emphasize leadership skills and will collaborate with district induction programs;
- Identify Teacher Leaders from the schools who will help with induction;
- Develop and implement an evaluation plan.

Project directors will be especially considerate of the time commitment of ISD participants, being careful not to duplicate programs but to participate in district programming that helps further the goals of both the COE and the district and to provide compensation for students and partners in the ISD's. Mr. Wayne Havens, Interim Superintendent, and Ms. Ann Graves, Assistant Superintendent, of the Lubbock ISD have committed verbally to this project, and we will be receiving a letter of support from them.

The first actual cohort of preservice junior high/middle level teachers will begin in the fall of 2004. This will allow time to develop the partnership with district personnel, to get the items listed above in progress, and to conduct the recruitment of the first cohort. Years 2004-2008 will see three cohorts of 30 each finish their preservice courses and participate in varying times of induction (See Timetable). Assessment and evaluation will be ongoing as will be revisions of the programs given the results of assessment and evaluation.

Timetable

Please see Judy Aycock Simpson for a copy of the timetable.)

Uniqueness of the Project

LEAD will be unique for the following reasons:

- It will be developed as a result of collaboration with Lubbock County ISD's;
- It will target junior high/middle level preservice and beginning teachers;
- It will develop teacher leaders;

FIGURE 8-6 *continued*

• It will enable beginning teachers to be better prepared to succeed because their preservice courses will provide them with the skills to do so;
• It will provide an induction period that will support beginning teachers

Future Plans

If assessment and evaluation efforts reveal that LEAD results in greater success and retention of beginning teachers, the College of Education will seek funding to implement the full induction program for Cohorts 2 and 3 and to implement a secondary preservice component of LEAD.

Proposed Budget Justification

The budget goal is to provide as much incentive as possible for the partners, the preservice teachers, and the beginning teachers. Because faculty and staff believe so strongly in the value of this project, neither the Principal Investigators, the Project Advisor, nor the faculty and staff of Texas Tech working on the project committee will receive any compensation for services, such as being project director or advisor or the like. A total budget of $33,500.00 is sought for redevelopment of the preservice courses, the development of the induction program, and the coordination and implementation of these programs. This amount equals 16% of the $203,800.00 that is necessary to implement this project. Students, principals, and junior high/middle level teacher leaders and beginning teachers will be the recipients of 81% of the funds sought. The College of Education will commit another $129,237.00 of in-kind contributions to make this project a success.
LEAD Budget

Personnel Preparation Costs

Redevelopment of courses $ 7,500.00
Development of Induction $ 7,500.00
Coordination and Implementation of Seminars $ 3,000.00
Coordination and Implementation of Induction Program $ 3,000.00
Evaluation: $2500 for 1 for 5 yrs. $ 12,500.00
Total Personnel Preparation Costs $ 33,500.00

In Kind Personnel Support Cost

Graduate Student Worker: 9 months/20 hrs. week/salary, tuition, fringes, $ 81,737.00
Time of 2 Principal Investigators each year: $2500 each for 5 yrs. $ 25,000.00
Time of Project Advisor/Liaison person: 2500 for 5 yrs. $ 12,500.00
Time for COE Committee: $220 each a yr for 5 yrs. $ 10,000.00
Total Personnel Support Costs $ 129,237.00

Partnership Costs

Teacher Leaders from ISD's: $350 each for 190 of 4 yrs. $ 66,500.00
ISD Advisory Groups: $250 for 40 (8 each yr.) for 5 yrs. $ 10,000.00
Parking and Misc. for Teacher Leaders and Advisory Board for 5 yrs. $ 2,000.00
Total Partnership Costs $ 78,500.00

Student and Beginning Teacher Costs

Seminar Materials: Tapes, recorders, white boards, erasers, etc. $ 2,500.00
Seminar Speakers: $100 each for speakers for 14 a year over 4 yrs. $ 19,600.00
Seminar Texts: $100 each for 200 students over 4 yrs. $ 20,000.00
Professional Materials for seminars: $50 each for 200 students over 4 yrs. $ 10,000.00
Leadership Tapes $ 1,200.00

FIGURE 8-6 *continued*

Food for seminars for 4 yrs/200 students $ 4,000.00
Capstone Materials: Texts and Professional Materials for 200 over 4 yrs. $ 8,000.00
Awards Ceremony: Students, partners, etc. for 250 over 2 yrs. At $15 each $ 4,000.00
Stipends for Summer Induction Institute: $350 each for 50 over 2 summers $ 17,500.00
Total Student and Beginning Teacher Costs $ 86,800.00

General Office Supplies

Paper, pens, copying, phones, mailing, brochures, etc. for 8 over 5 yrs $ 5,000.00
Total General Office Supplies $ 5,000.00

Total Money Sought: $ 203,800.00

In Kind Contribution: $ 129,237.00

FIGURE 8-6 *continued*

This method helps employees who may be trying to work on a report, answer phone calls, answer/send e-mail, and deal with other routine business events throughout the work day. In short, you can arrange, insert material, save what you have, and add other material as time permits. You may also write notes to yourself or use different colors and fonts for text you may want to move, delete, or revise. How you design your report will depend on (1) the kind of report you are writing, (2) your readers' informational needs, and (3) the purpose of your report.

Strategy for presenting the discussion. The discussion should be planned around each topic mentioned in the plan of development. Note that the logic of the discussion should be evident from the headings, as these are repeated in the table of contents.

Each paragraph in the discussion should begin with a topic sentence, followed by supporting sentences, data, and visuals.

Reports with standard arrangement patterns. Some kinds of reports have fairly standard arrangement patterns. Many government funding agencies require that all reports submitted follow a specific plan, and content may be inserted into a template and submitted online. Many organizations also have a standard plan for their policies—what sections must be included and the order in which they appear. Policy and procedure manuals, detailing the rules that apply to the employees of a business entity, usually follow a standard pattern.

Often, however, as in Case 8-1, you will be writing a report in which you, as the writer, must decide how to present your research or the information you need to convey. Generally, you have two basic choices: topical arrangement and chronological arrangement.

Topical arrangement. In topical arrangement, the order in which you present your ideas should be logical and inclusive For example, in a report on disease management of citrus fruit, the writer arranges the report by grouping information about specific citrus diseases. He describes, in parallel arrangement, the main diseases:

- Introduction—Description of treatments for citrus diseases.
- Disease #1—Melanose
  - Description
  - Factors to be considered before the application of fungicides for melanose control
    - Table I. Chemical controls for melanose
- Disease #2—Greasy Spot
  - Description
  - Factors to be considered in the management of greasy spot
    - Table II: Chemical controls for greasy spot
- Disease #3—Foot Rot
  - Description
  - Factors to consider in managing the disease
    - Table III. Chemical controls for foot rot
- Disease #4—Citrus Nematode
  - Description
  - Sampling instructions to determine presence of citrus nematode

Exiting Conditions Report, U.S. Route 29 Corridor Development Study, Combined Phases II and III From the North Carolina State Line to I-64 in Charlottesville, VA

Chapter 1—Introduction

The objective of the Route 29 Corridor Development Study is to evaluate all modes of transportation within the corridor and to develop both short- and long-term recommendations to preserve and enhance the transportation resources in this important corridor. The importance of U.S. Route 29 was recognized in the Intermodal Surface Transportation and Efficiency Act (ISTEA) passed by the United States Congress in 1991. In ISTEA, Congress designated the 240 miles of Route 29 from Greensboro, North Carolina to the District of Columbia as a high priority corridor of national significance and directed that comprehensive transportation studies of the corridor be performed. The designation of these high priority corridors was based upon the findings of Congress that:

❑ The construction of the Interstate Highway System connected the major population centers of the nation and greatly enhanced the economic growth in the United States;

❑ Many regions of the nation are not now adequately served by the Interstate System or comparable highways and require further highway development in order to serve the travel and economic development needs of the region; and,

❑ The development of transportation corridors is the most efficient and effective way of integrating regions and improving efficiency and safety of commerce and travel and further promoting economic development.

More recent legislation, the 1998 Transportation Equity Act for the 21st Century (TEA-21), renewed the commitment to completion of important transportation projects by increasing allocations of federal funds to the states. This national legislation affirmed the long-held recognition of Route 29 by the Virginia Department of Transportation (VDOT) as a vitally important principal arterial highway through central Virginia.

For purposes of study, the Route 29 Corridor in Virginia was divided into four sections. The first section, extending from Warrenton to Interstate 66, was studied as part of transportation needs in the I-66 Corridor. The second section extends from Charlottesville to Warrenton, and was studied in the Route 29 Corridor Development Study (Phase I). This Phase I study was completed in the Fall of 1996. The third and fourth sections extend from Lynchburg to Charlottesville and Danville to Lynchburg, respectively. Both of these sections are included in this current study, which is formally entitled the Route 29 Corridor Development Study (Combined Phases II/III).

The background, methodologies and findings of this study are documented in three separate reports. This report, the first of the three, describes the existing transportation system and its operations, as well as current land uses, socioeconomic conditions, and environmental constraints. The second report, *Route 29 Corridor Development Study (Combined Phases II/III) Technical Report,* describes the development of a statement of purpose and need for transportation improvements, the development of transportation demand forecasts, and the development and refinement of various improvement alternatives. The third report, *Route 29Corridor Development Study (Combined Phases II/III) Recommended Transportation Concept,* describes the final study recommendations for all modes of travel in the corridor.

FIGURE 8-7 Report Introduction

- Table IV: Citrus Nematode counts considered low, medium, or high at specific times during the growing season
- Conclusion: Factors to consider before applying nematicides
  - Table V: Chemical controls for nematodes (summary)

Once the citrus researcher has arranged his information, he can begin inserting information beneath each topic heading.

Chronological arrangement. Some topics can be presented by time. You explain or present information sequentially, in the order in which it occurred. The following outline of a literature review of *Cultural Control of the Boll Weevil—A Four Season Approach—Texas Rolling Plains* illustrates chronological arrangement. This technical report surveys and reviews existing research on how boll weevils can be controlled throughout the agricultural year. Note, too, that the segments use parallel development, and each segment ends with a summary of that segment. This approach allows the reader to choose where to begin and how much to read. For example, the reader may wish to read only the Summary and Introduction and the factual summary for each season:

TABLE OF CONTENTS
- Summary
- Introduction
- Spring Cultural Control
  - Prepare the land for planting
  - Utilize delayed Planting
  - Use uniform planting
  - Summary
- Summer Cultural Control
  - Shorten the growing season
  - Change the microclimate
    - Row direction
    - Bed shape
    - Row Spacing
  - Summary
- Fall Cultural Control
  - Utilize harvest-aid chemicals
  - Role of planting date
  - Terminate irrigations in August
  - Summary
- Winter Cultural Control
  - Eliminate the overwintering habitat
  - Modify the overwintering habitat
  - Avoid the overwintering habitat
  - Summary
- Conclusions
- Acknowledgments
- Supporting Research Studies

Case 8-2

Allan Harper was asked to visit a research facility that his firm has discovered is likely going to be for sale soon. Dick Crandall, the VP for operations, asks Harper to provide a brief overview on the usability of the building as a corporate training facility. Allan visits the building, takes notes on major usability features that he knows will interest Crandall, and writes a brief report for Crandall, known for wanting only important facts and recommendations. Harper begins with a simple report purpose statement, followed by a bulleted list of the facility's features of interest to Crandall. Harper uses notes to himself (in color) as he drafts. He concludes with a brief recommendation of what he believes should be done if Crandall thinks the building should be purchased. The report responds to the information needs and reading (skimming) style of a specific reader, Crandall, who wants "the facts."

CASE DOCUMENT 8-2

TO: Dick Crandall   DATE: October. 9, 2009

FROM: Allan Harper

SUBJECT: Space Assessment of RAMP, 6004 Highway 7

As you requested, I toured the RAMP research facility during my trip to Atlanta October 4–8, 2009. Based on your questions about using the facility for corporate training, I have concluded the following:

Conclusions

- RAMP offers us the space we need and appears to be in excellent condition. Modifications will be necessary, but those required can be done in stages. We can focus on Building 1, then renovate Building 2 and 3 as we want to. The RAMP is composed of two main buildings and one small building (Buildings 1, 2, and 2A on the attached site map).

- Each small office has two internet connections. The main lecture hall has one internet connection and no projection equipment. [Check on price of wireless for the entire building. DC will probably want to know ASAP.]

continued

- The current RAMP buildings are divided into offices for start-up projects. Some of the RAMP income is derived from the space leased by small start-up companies. Cost: $22/sq. foot. [Is this price low/high?] . [Call Dave Redding about laboratory contracts. Cheryl Kempe has his phone number.]

- The debt on RAMP is slightly over $12M with approximately $5M due in April of 2012. (See p. 4 of the Notes to Consolidated Financial Statements.) [Get current balance owed from Fiscal. Perhaps delete for now? Call Debbie in Fiscal.]

- For us to use RAMP for training, instead of research, the entire first floor of Building 1 would need to be redesigned. We could relocate some of the start-up companies to Buildings 2 and 2A, which would preserve the income.

- An attached sketch shows how renovation of the first floor of Building 1 might look. Note:

    Eight office sites for trainers

    Two computer labs

    Five training rooms—two with breakout rooms off the main area.

    One tiered lecture room

Conversion could be made gradually, depending on how many training rooms are needed ASAP. The attached sketch, included along with the original plan, shows one redesign plan.

Assessment of the RAMP Building

- The facility seems to be in good repair. Maintenance seems to be satisfactory. I found no indication of leaks.

- HVAC system needs to be inspected.

- Wireless capability could be easily installed in the main lecture room. ~~The proposed computer laboratories, carved from 12 offices, offer 24 internet connections.~~

- New projection equipment needs to be purchased. [Cost?]

- Main lecture hall could be converted into a tiered lecture room. The two rooms on either side of the lecture hall could be eliminated to further expand the main lecture hall. The kitchen would have to be moved or eliminated—perhaps moved to Building 2.

- Renovation costs will be high, close to $1M (according to rough estimates by Gavin Newberry—see attached email answer to my query) even if only the first floor of Building 1 is refurbished. Current office furniture is usable, but new furniture, IAV equipment, and computers would need to be purchased for training and meeting rooms. Closets/storage would have to be added to all training rooms. Floor coverings would need to be replaced.

- Location—RAMP is easily accessible from three main arteries.

- Estimated remodeling time: 4 months.

Attachments: 3

Persuasive arrangement and development. Many times reports argue for a specific point or position. When you argue, you need to persuade your readers. Understanding what objections you will need to overcome will be critical to planning your report and the presentation of your arguments. Reports that must produce conclusions and recommendations may require writers to develop a report in which the conclusions and recommendations are not what readers will welcome. Or these reports may be prepared for readers who have no preconceived ideas. In each situation, the report can be designed to anticipate the perspective of readers.

Let's assume, for example, in Case 8-2, that Harper believes the RAMP building should be seriously considered, while Crandall has decided to purchase another site. Crandall told Harper to visit RAMP, but he never expected that RAMP would be another site consideration. To respond to this situation, Harper might begin his report as follows:

> As you requested, I toured the RAMP research facility during my trip to Atlanta October 4-8, 2009. Based on my findings, I believe that you should seriously consider the RAMP facility as the site for our CE operation. RAMP offers us what we need in terms of space and location. Renovation costs can be done in stages to reduce cost, and the facility offers us the space and arrangement we need

In short, the reader's perspective often determines how persuasive you need to be if you want your ideas considered.

Conclusion. Reports will end with a statement of the primary issues covered in the discussion. In long reports, a factual summary comes after the discussion and before the conclusions and recommendations. The factual summary does what its name implies: it covers the essential facts but without interpretation. (Interpretation of the factual summary is done in the executive summary.) The longer the discussion, the more useful a factual summary will be to your reader. The conclusions themselves are judgments made about the subject based on the evidence explained in the discussion.

Recommendations. Recommendations, if required or needed, emerge from conclusions. However, many reports end with only a conclusion. The type of ending depends on the type of report. Recommendations are proposed actions to be taken based on the conclusions.

Appendices. Appendices include documents that support or add to information you include in the discussion. While the appendix may not be read, it serves an important role. An appendix may contain tables of supporting data, statistical studies, spreadsheets, or any material that supports the points or arguments you make in your discussion. If you are recommending an action, having letters or e-mails requesting that action in the appendix provides convincing support for your recommendation.

LETTER REPORTS

Reports can be prepared as letters. This example report (Figure 8-8) prepared by a graduate of a school district, assesses the quality of the school's programs. The opening paragraph contains qualities of a summary and an introduction. Note the purpose statement, the plan of the report, in addition to the short summary statement. The effective document design allows the report to be read quickly.

ANNOTATED REPORT FOR STUDY

An annotated report is included in Appendix C.

REPORT CHECKLIST ✔

Planning
- ☐ What is the purpose of your report? Have you stated it in one sentence?
- ☐ What is the scope of your report?
- ☐ Who are your readers? What are your readers' technical levels?
- ☐ What will your readers do with the information?
- ☐ What information will you need to write the report?
- ☐ How long should the report be?
- ☐ What format should you use for the report?

continued

REPORT CHECKLIST ✔ *continued*

☐ What report elements will you need?
☐ What visuals will you need to present information or data?
☐ What elements do you need to include in your introduction?
☐ What arrangement will you use in presenting your report?

Revision

☐ Does your report do the following:
  Introduce the subject and purpose?
  Present enough data in words and visuals to justify any conclusions drawn?
  Discuss and evaluate the data fairly?
  Summarize the data?
  Draw logical conclusions from the data?
  If necessary, present recommendations that are clearly based upon the data and the conclusions?
☐ Are your data accurate?
☐ Do your visuals immediately show what they are designed to show?
☐ Is your format suitable for your content, audience, and purpose?
☐ Have you properly documented all information sources?

EXERCISES

1. Visit the website of a major employer in your field. What kinds of reports do you find at this site? What are the elements and characteristics of these reports? Who are the audiences for these reports? What are the purposes of these reports? What do these reports indicate about this employer? What do these reports indicate about your field?

2. Examine Figure 8-9. If you were the author of this report and were given 15 more minutes to make it better, what changes would you make?

3. Your supervisor asks you to amplify the Figure 8-9 report with detailed explanations and appropriate tables and figures. For this new formal report, identify the major entries in the Table of Contents and the List of Illustrations and compose a 100-word abstract.

4. Figure 8-10 is the Executive Summary from a National Transportation Safety Board Accident Report. This summary is 292 words. How would you cut it to 275 words? Or 250 words? (The full 212-page report is available at http://www.ntsb.gov.)

Laura Anne Ranford

September 30, 2008

Mr. David Russell
Project Director for Quality Enhancement
Jasper Independent School District
128 Park Street
Jasper, TX 75951

Dear Mr. Russell:

I appreciate the opportunity to reflect and then assess on my experience in Jasper High School. While much of my academic program was excellent, several areas do need improvement. My report provides an overall assessment, courses needing improvement, courses effective in preparing for college, recommended changes in college-bound curriculum, extracurricular activities assessment, and general recommendations. These recommendations for improving the quality of a Jasper High School experience are as follows:

- Teach challenging and classic literature.
- Require more writing at all levels.
- Offer more opportunities for motivated students to learn, specifically, more AP courses.
- Refocus health course or add a general nutrition course.
- Emphasize depth over breadth of extracurricular involvement; limit: two to three activities.
- Provide more lab time for science courses.

Overall Assessment of My Jasper High School Experience

My Jasper High School experience has proved to be excellent preparation for my college coursework. I took the most challenging courses offered and participated in extracurricular activities that required learning new skills and getting outside my comfort zone. I was fortunate to have instructors that taught students how to learn on their own, think critically, and apply classroom knowledge to everyday situations. However, there were a few courses that have room for improvement.

Courses Needing Improvement

Health

The Health curriculum focused on the topics of sex, drugs, alcohol, smoking, and sexually-transmitted diseases. This approach was ineffective for two reasons. First, long-term consequences, such as lung cancer or liver failure, do not deter teens from smoking and drinking alcohol because they do not plan that far ahead. Second, most teens make lifestyle decisions based on peer pressure, personal values, or rebelling against an authority, not on what they know about personal and public health. I think a health class promoting proper nutrition, regular exercise and a healthy lifestyle would be more effective in helping teenagers make good decisions.

English I & II

Both freshman and sophomore years, English primarily focused on the TAKS test. The novels read for the courses were adaptations of classics or from the *New York Times'* Bestseller list. As a result, no classic

JHS Evaluation & Recommendations   1

FIGURE 8-8 Letter Report

literature was covered and very little writing instruction was given outside of TAKS writing. Regarding TAKS writing, general characteristics and examples of high-scoring essays were explained. Most writing assignments were given and graded in the TAKS format. Yet, less than 1% of my class grade received a high score on the TAKS writing section sophomore year. Exposure to classic literature and instruction in general composition would improve the quality of underclassman English education.

Courses Effective in Preparing for College

The courses that were most effective in preparing me for college and the key elements each provided are listed below.

Geometry

- Required application of basic concepts. Only general theorems were taught, not specific examples.
- Homework required critical thinking and synthesis of concepts.
- Introduced trigonometry providing a solid foundation for calculus.

AP Chemistry

- Required detailed lab reports demonstrating a grasp of the experiments, chemistry involved, and sources of error.
- Tested over material not covered in class time.
- Expected to synthesize information in problem solving.

Junior English & Dual-Credit English

- Received instruction and constructive feedback on writing.
- Analyzed challenging classic and controversial literature.
- Learned process for writing a research paper.

AP US History

- Expected to prepare for class by reading ahead.
- Taught as a lecture-style course.

AP Calculus

- Created a foundation of theorems, formulas and methods for the Engineering Math courses I have taken at Texas A&M University.

Recommended Changes in College-Bound Curriculum

Offer More Advanced Placement Courses

From my experience, Advanced Placement (AP) courses challenge students to learn on their own, study material before class, come to class prepared to discuss the reading, and express knowledge of subject through writing. The study skills I learned in AP courses have been instrumental to success in college courses. Only Chemistry, US history, and Calculus were offered when I was a student at Jasper High School. For a higher quality college preparatory curriculum, JHS should consider offering additional AP courses such as English, Biology, Spanish, French, and Statistics.

Require Challenging Literature in English I & II

Simply reading well-written literature helps students better understand shorter, less complicated material and literary elements including grammar, sentence structure, punctuation, and style. Exposing students to challenging literature will improve their reading level, writing ability, vocabulary, and standardized test scores.

FIGURE 8-8 *continued*

Designate More Lab Time for Science Courses

More lab time should be designated for science courses. Most scientific knowledge was discovered through experimental observation. Additionally, half of the instructional time in college is spent in a lab setting. Spending more time carrying out experiments will better prepare students for college science courses. Increasing class length or having labs before or after school would provide ample time to include more labs in each science curriculum.

Extracurricular Activities: Pros & Cons and Lessons Learned

Extracurricular activities can be beneficial in moderation. However, over-involvement can be detrimental to a student's academic progress and health. Students should pick two or three activities to be involved in each year.

Pros	Cons
• Working with people teaches teamwork	• Easy to join too many
• Learning information and skills outside the classroom in realistic situations	• Require a lot of after-school hours and weekends
• Developing time management strategies	• Distract from schoolwork
• Competing reveals strengths & weaknesses	• Can be a source of stress
• Serving the school and community	

Extracurricular activities can provide valuable knowledge and skills that cannot be learned in a classroom. A few of my extracurricular activities and the valuable lessons learned through them are listed below.

Cross-Examination Debate

- Evaluated the quality of information found in research—whether current and relevant.
- Developed multiple cases for both sides of a broad topic.
- Spoke persuasively and answered critical questions with confidence.
- Asked questions during cross-examination to reveal opponent's weaknesses.
- Learned to analyze strengths and weaknesses of arguments.
- Developed note-taking skills.

UIL Academic Competition

- Emphasized individual learning.
- Expanded knowledge-base beyond what was required in a given subject.

Sports & One Act Play

- Learned the importance of preparation and teamwork.
- Improvement is always possible.
- Constructive criticism is far more valuable than passive approval or apathy.

Choir

- Practice and repetition facilitate mastering new ideas and techniques.

Lions' Club

- Served community through events and fundraising.
- Organized events in coordination with other clubs.

FIGURE 8-8 *continued*

General Recommendations to Improve the Quality of a Jasper High School Experience

- Teach challenging and classic literature.
- Require more writing at all levels.
- Offer more opportunities for motivated students to learn, specifically, more AP courses.
- Refocus health course or add a general nutrition course.
- Emphasize depth over breadth of extracurricular involvement; limit: two to three activities.
- Provide more lab time for science courses.

Thank you for the opportunity to participate in this project. I enjoyed reminiscing about my high school experience. Evaluating each course and activity renewed my appreciation for several teachers and mentors who invested in my education and development. They challenged, inspired, and prepared me for what lay ahead.

If you have any questions regarding my evaluation or my experiences, please contact me at lar@cumberland.com.

Sincerely,

Laura Anne Ranford

Laura Anne Ranford

FIGURE 8-8 *continued*

National Transportation Safety Board
Washington, D.C. 20594

Safety Recommendation

Date: March 5, 2009

In reply refer to: H-09-3

Mr. Marc Meteyer
President
Compressed Gas Association
4221 Walney Road, 5th Floor
Chantilly, Virginia 20151

The National Transportation Safety Board is an independent Federal agency charged by Congress with investigating transportation accidents, determining their probable cause, and making recommendations to prevent similar accidents from occurring. We are providing the following information to urge your organization to take action on the safety recommendation in this letter. The Safety Board is vitally interested in the recommendation because it is designed to prevent accidents and save lives.

This recommendation addresses the adequacy of fire suppression systems at mobile acetylene trailer loading and unloading facilities. The recommendation is derived from the Safety Board's special investigation of mobile acetylene trailers and is consistent with the evidence we found and the analysis we performed. As a result of this study, the Safety Board has issued three safety recommendations, one of which is addressed to the Compressed Gas Association (CGA). Information supporting this recommendation is discussed below. The Safety Board would appreciate a response from you within 90 days addressing the actions you have taken or intend to take to implement our recommendation.

The Safety Board investigated three accidents that involved highway vehicles transporting bulk quantities of acetylene gas that occurred between July 25 and October 20, 2007, and reviewed reports of a 2008 overturn accident of another vehicle. The vehicles, called mobile acetylene trailers, carried up to 225 cylinders that were connected by a manifold system[1] and filled with acetylene. Two of the accidents occurred as the vehicles overturned on public highways, and two of the accidents occurred while the vehicles were being prepared for unloading, in Dallas, Texas, on July 25, 2007, and in The Woodlands, Texas, on August 7, 2007. In one unloading accident, the fire on the initial trailer spread to cylinders on an adjacent trailer; in the other, the fire spread to cylinders on adjacent trailers and to nearby buildings and vehicles. The failures of the cylinders on these mobile acetylene trailers and the resultant damage raised concerns about the accident protection provided by these vehicles, the adequacy of the minimum safety standards and procedures applicable to unloading these vehicles, and the adequacy of fire suppression systems at loading and unloading facilities. To

---

[1] A *manifold system* collects the acetylene gas from multiple cylinders into one pipe or chamber; when the cylinders are filled, the acetylene gas is dispersed from one pipe to multiple cylinders.

8071

FIGURE 8-9 Document for Exercises 2 and 3

2

address these concerns, the Safety Board conducted a special investigation of mobile acetylene trailers.[2]

The two unloading accidents in the investigation occurred when the mobile acetylene trailers were connected to piping at loading/unloading plants while the operators were preparing the trailers to be unloaded. The trailers in both accidents were operated by Western International Gas & Cylinders, Inc. (Western).

There was no automated water deluge system at either The Woodlands or Dallas. Western installed automated water deluge systems at many of its facilities after the April 10, 2001, mobile acetylene trailer fire at its Bellville, Texas, facility. According to Western, the effectiveness of such systems at controlling the spread of fire to other cylinders on the same trailer and from one trailer to the next was proven at the June 8, 2005, decomposition reaction that also occurred at Bellville. The actuation of the water deluge system limited the spread of the fire to other cylinders on the same trailer. In the Dallas accident, attempts to extinguish the fire using a fire hose were ineffective. Had the unloading facilities at The Woodlands and Dallas had automated water deluge systems, the fires also may have been controlled and the spread of fire between the cylinders and to the nearby mobile acetylene trailers may have been reduced or eliminated. After these accidents, Western completed installation of water deluge systems at all Western-owned and customer unloading sites, including The Woodlands. However, the CGA standards require only conspicuously located and easily accessible fire hoses or fixed spray systems and dry chemical fire extinguishers. Automated water deluge systems, which appear to be effective on acetylene cylinder fires, are not required by the CGA standards.

Therefore, the National Transportation Safety Board makes the following recommendation to the Compressed Gas Association:

Revise the recommended practices in Compressed Gas Association standard G-1.6, section 7, *General Provisions,* to require automated water deluge systems at all mobile acetylene trailer loading and unloading locations to control the spread of fire to other cylinders on a trailer and to nearby mobile acetylene trailers. (H-09-3)

The Safety Board also issued safety recommendations to the Pipeline and Hazardous Materials Safety Administration.

In your response to the recommendation in this letter, please refer to Safety Recommendation H-09-3. If you would like to submit your response electronically rather than in hard copy, you may send it to the following e-mail address: correspondence @ntsb.gov. If your response includes attachments that exceed 5 megabytes, please e-mail us asking for instructions on how to use our Tumbleweed secure mailbox procedures. To avoid confusion, please use only

---

[2] For additional information, see National Transportation Safety Board, *Mobile Acetylene Trailer Accidents: Fire During Unloading in Dallas, Texas, July 25, 2007; Fire During Unloading in The Woodlands, Texas, August 7, 2007; and Overturn and Fire in East New Orleans, Louisiana, October 20, 2007,* Hazardous Materials Special Investigation Report NTSB/SIR-09/01 (Washington, DC: NTSB, 2009), which is available on the Safety Board's website at <http://www.ntsb.gov/publictn/2009/SIR0901.pdf>.

FIGURE 8-9 *continued*

3

one method of submission (that is, do not submit both an electronic copy and a hard copy of the same response letter).

Acting Chairman ROSENKER and Members HERSMAN, HIGGINS, SUMWALT, and CHEALANDER concurred in this recommendation. Member HIGGINS filed a concurring statement, which is attached to the hazardous materials special investigation report.

Original Signed

By: Mark V. Rosenker
      Acting Chairman

FIGURE 8-9 *continued*

On April 12, 2007, about 0043 eastern daylight time, a Bombardier/Canadair Regional Jet (CRJ) CL600-2B19, N8905F, operated as Pinnacle Airlines flight 4712, ran off the departure end of runway 28 after landing at Cherry Capital Airport (TVC), Traverse City, Michigan. There were no injuries among the 49 passengers (including 3 lap-held infants) and 3 crewmembers, and the aircraft was substantially damaged. Weather was reported as snowing. The airplane was being operated under the provisions of 14 *Code of Federal Regulations* Part 121 and had departed from Minneapolis-St. Paul International (Wold-Chamberlain) Airport, Minneapolis, Minnesota, about 2153 central daylight time. Instrument meteorological conditions prevailed at the time of the accident flight, which operated on an instrument flight rules flight plan.

The National Transportation Safety Board determines that the probable cause of this accident was the pilots' decision to land at TVC without performing a landing distance assessment, which was required by company policy because of runway contamination initially reported by TVC ground operations personnel and continuing reports of deteriorating weather and runway conditions during the approach. This poor decision-making likely reflected the effects of fatigue produced by a long, demanding duty day, and, for the captain, the duties associated with check airman functions. Contributing to the accident were 1) the Federal Aviation Administration pilot flight and duty time regulations that permitted the pilots' long, demanding duty day and 2) the TVC operations supervisor's use of ambiguous and unspecific radio phraseology in providing runway braking information.

The safety issues discussed in this report include the pilots' actions and decision-making during the approach, landing, and landing roll; pilot fatigue and line check airman duty time regulations; weather and field condition information and ground operations personnel communications; and criteria for runway closures in snow and ice conditions.

FIGURE 8-10 Document for Exercise 4

Source: NTSB/AAR-08/02, PB2008-910402, *Runway Overrun During Landing, Pinnacle Airlines Flight 4712, Bombardier/Canadair Regional Jet CL600-2B19, N8905F, Traverse City, Michigan, April 12, 2007*, Washington, DC: GPO, 2008, p. ix.

9

Proposals and Progress Reports

Proposals and progress reports are two types of documents that you may either contribute information to or write entirely yourself. Many projects, such as those funded by the National Science Foundation or the National Institutes of Health, begin with proposals and require regular progress reports during the course of the project once it is funded. This chapter explains development strategies for both types of documents. However, any work done by an employee may require a status report be submitted to one's supervisor to explain what has been accomplished. A project may begin with a verbal agreement between supervisor and employees, but the employees may be required to submit a progress report either as an e-mail message or as a short memo report. Progress or status reports serve as a major source of documentation to show that employees have performed their work.

To help you understand how to design and write proposals and progress reports, we first discuss the development of proposals and use a student's research project proposal as an example. We also provide additional annotated examples of progress reports to illustrate how these occur in work settings.

Quick Tips

Keep in mind that proposals and progress reports are persuasive documents. In both cases you write to convince your reader. In a proposal, you write to persuade your reader that you have a good idea, a good method for implementing the idea, and the experience necessary to manage the implementation. In a progress report, you write to persuade the reader either that you are making good progress on your project or that you realize you aren't making good progress but know why and are taking appropriate steps to fix the problem.

The proposal, as its name implies, describes proposed work or research, the reasons it should be done, the methods proposed to accomplish the work, the estimated time required, and often the expected cost.

The progress report, as its name implies, describes and evaluates a project as work is being done. Thus, if an individual or an organization decides to begin a work project or research project, particularly one that requires several months or even several years to complete, the individual or organization will *report the progress* on that project at intervals agreed upon when the proposal is accepted and the resulting agreement or contract is being negotiated.

Employees may also need to report progress on the full range of projects or problems on which they are working. In situations like these, the employee writes a progress report (or status report, as it may be called) to inform supervisors or other individuals about what has been accomplished in completing a job or solving a problem. The progress or status report thus becomes an official and even a legal record of work performed. Many organizations require employees to prepare annual status reports of their work, their accomplishments, and their objectives for the coming year.

Proposals

The starting point of projects is often a proposal. A proposal offers to provide a service or a product to someone in exchange for money. Usually, when the organization—frequently a federal, state, or city government or a business enterprise—decides to have some sort of work or research done, it wants the best job for the best price. To announce its interest, the soliciting organization may advertise the work it wants done and invite interested individuals or organizations to contact the organization. In a university setting, the research and grants office may notify departments that money is available for research projects in a specific area. Faculty members submit project proposals that explain the research they envision; how much time they will need to complete the project; any financial resources required for equipment, salaries, and release time from regular teaching duties; and the goals and benefits of the research to the individual researcher and the university.

When an organization disseminates a description of the work it wants done, this document is usually called a request for proposals (RFP) or a statement of work (SOW). The soliciting organization may send selected companies an RFP/SOW that includes complete specifications of the work desired.

Alternatively, the soliciting organization may first describe the needed work in general terms and invite interested firms to submit their qualifications (Figure 9-1). This type of request is usually called a request for qualifications (RFQ) or a notice of intent and is often published in newspapers and professional journals or newsletters. The United States government posts its RFQs online at http://www.grants.gov/. The responding organizations explain their past accomplishments, giving the names of companies for which they performed work, describing the work they did, and giving references who can substantiate the organizations' claims. Based on the responses it receives, the soliciting organization will send full descriptions of the work (RFPs/SOWs) to the groups it believes are best qualified. The responses submitted to an RFQ or a notice of intent may be called letters of interest or intent (LOIs).

In short, each aspect of the solicitation process, from the RFQ to the RFP/SOW, has an appropriate use, but one or more of them is necessary to initiate action on a project.

Example RFP. The Vice-President for Research at a large university has located funding opportunities for collaborative research grants. These will be available to faculty across various disciplines. He issues an RFP via e-mail to the university's research faculty (see Figure 9-2).

The context of proposal development. Because proposals are time-consuming to write—most require substantial research and analysis on the part of the proposing organization—individuals and organizations wishing to respond to an RFP study it carefully. They do not want to submit a proposal that is unlikely to be accepted. Thus, the proposer—whether a university professor seeking research funds or a highway construction firm seeking to win a contract from a county to upgrade its rural roads—will approach the decision to prepare a proposal carefully.

The individual or the company must first decide whether to respond to the proposal. Can we do the work requested? Can we show that we can do this work, based on what we have already done? Can we do it within the time limit given in the RFP? Businesses responding to RFPs are also interested in economic issues. How

---

-NOTICE OF INTENT-Texas Department of Transportation Notice of Intent— Contract Number 17-8RFP1001. The Bryan District of the Texas Department of Transportation (TxDOT) intends to enter into two (2) contracts with prime providers pursuant to Texas Government Code, Chapter 2254, Subchapter A, and 43 TAC §§9.30-9.43, to provide the following services. The work to be performed shall consist of right of way surveys, aerial photography and digital terrain models for advance planning and PS&E. Work shall include, but is not limited to: on ground surveys, parcel plats, legal descriptions, right of way maps, establishment of horizontal and vertical control for aerial mapping, etc. for various construction projects within the Bryan District. A letter of interest notifying TxDOT of the provider's interest will be accepted by fax at (979)778-9702, or by hand delivery to TxDOT, Bryan District, 1300 North Texas Avenue, Attention: Mr. Chad Bohne, P.E.; or by mail addressed to 1300 North Texas Avenue, Bryan, Texas 77803. **Deadline: Letters of interest will be received until 5:00 p.m. on Wednesday, September 3, 2009.** For more information regarding this notice of intent, please visit the TxDOT Internet Home Page located at www.dot.state.tx.us/business/professionalservices.htm or contact Cecelia McCord at (979) 778-9765. 8-10-08

FIGURE 9-1 Example RFQ from a Newspaper

January 5, 2009

MEMORANDUM

TO: Distribution A

FROM: Dr. Rolfe D. Auston
             Vice President for Research

**SUBJECT: 2009 ABC University-Conacyt: Collaborative Research Grant
             Program**

The Office of the Vice President for Research is pleased to issue a request for proposals for the ABCU-Conacyt: Collaborative Research Grant Program. This program
annually awards one-year grants of up to $24,000 to faculty members to advance
inter-institutional cooperation in science, technology, and scholarly activities that
have a direct application in industry or government through the complementary
efforts of scientists and scholars from ABCU and Mexican institutions.

Two main objectives of the Collaborative Research Grant Program are to provide
seed funding to 1) support the completion of a 12-month inter-institutional project,
and 2) support the development and submission of proposals for external funding
of research from competitive granting agencies both domestic and international
(e.g., NSF, NIH, DOE, World Bank, NATO, UNESCO, etc.) and industry.

ABCU and Conacyt have agreed on several research priority areas as noted in the
request for proposals. The research proposed must be linked to the private sector
and have direct application to solving an industrial or governmental problem. All
proposals must include research that directly improves security for the citizens of
the region or explores issues relating to security challenges facing both countries.

A principal investigator (PI) is required from both Texas ABCU and a Mexican
institution. The PI from ABCU must be a tenured or tenure-track faculty member.
The PI from Mexico must be a scientist or scholar from any Mexican institution
of higher education and research that is registered with Conacyt. Other investigators may include faculty from branch campuses or Mexican faculty, postdoctoral
students, graduate students, or research staff. A letter of intent must be received
by 5:00 p.m. on Friday, March 5, 2009, to be eligible to submit a full proposal. Full
proposals must be submitted, routed electronically for appropriate signatures, and
received by 5:00 p.m. on Friday, April 30, 2009. The request for applications is
available on the Web at http://conacyt.abcu.edu.

Additional information may be obtained by contacting Ms. Catharine J. Restivo
(916-555-555; cjr@abcu.edu).

FIGURE 9-2 E-mail RFP

much will our proposed approach cost? How much money can we make? Who else will be submitting proposals? What price will they be quoting for the same work? Will we be competitive? What other projects are we currently involved in? Could problems arise that would make us unable to complete the job on time and at the price we quote? Do we have personnel qualified to work on this project?

The e-mail RFP in Figure 9-2 would elicit other questions. Is my field applicable to the research opportunity described here? Can I develop a collaborative proposal by the deadline? What types of national security topics would be most likely to attract funding? The university research office often has a person who helps answer these questions.

Many business entities requesting proposals will hold a bidders' conference at which companies interested in submitting a proposal can ask questions about the project or seek clarification of the needs described in the RFP. Most RFPs require that proposals be submitted by a deadline and contain specific information. Proposals that miss the deadline or do not contain the information requested are ordinarily omitted from consideration. Therefore, once an organization decides to submit a proposal, staff members carefully study the RFP and identify the information requirements. Each information requirement is given to an individual or a group who will be responsible for furnishing necessary material and data.

Some proposals, such as university research proposals, may be written by one or two persons. In complex proposals, however, different sections may be written by individuals in different areas of the organization. An editor or proposal writer will then compile the final document. This writer/editor may be assisted by readers who help check the developing proposal to be sure that all requested information is included and that the information is correct. Many proposals have to conform to strict length requirements. Proposals that do not conform will be eliminated from consideration.

Once the proposal has been written and submitted, it becomes a legally binding document. The proposing company or individual is legally committed to do what is described in the proposal, at the cost stated and within the time limit stated. For that reason, the proposing organization carefully checks all information for accuracy.

When a large number of bidders submit proposals in response to an RFP, the soliciting organization may select several finalists and allow each finalist to give an oral version of the proposal. During this oral presentation, the soliciting group asks questions. Representatives of the proposing groups have one more opportunities to argue for the value of what they are proposing, the merits of their organization, and the justification for the cost attached to the proposed work.

Students may be required to submit proposals for semester research projects or for other university programs, such as research opportunities with faculty. These proposals (two appear in this chapter) provide you with good practice in developing proposals you may write in your career. For example, government grants to fund your research, approvals to launch a work-related project, and actual bid proposals to help your business organization win work projects. Explaining to a potential employer during an interview that you have studied and written at least one proposal and a progress report can help you win a job offer.

Effective argument in proposal development. All writing is persuasive, in that it must convince the reader that the writer has credibility and that the writer's ideas have merit. However, the success of a proposal rests totally on the effectiveness of the argument—how convincingly the writer argues for a plan, an idea, a product, or a service to be rendered and how well the writer convinces the reader that the proposing organization is the best one to do the work or research needed. In planning the proposal, the proposer must harmonize the soliciting company's needs with the proposer's capabilities. The writer must be acutely sensitive to what readers will be looking for but not propose action that is outside the capability of the proposing individual or organization. The proposing individual or organization has an ethical responsibility to explain accurately and specifically what work can be done and not done so that there is no possibility of deceiving readers by making promises that cannot be fulfilled.

The following questions are useful in analyzing the effectiveness of the argument, whether in a written or an oral proposal:

- What does the soliciting organization really want?
- What is the problem that needs to be solved?
- What approaches to the solution will be viewed most favorably?
- What approaches will be viewed unfavorably?
- What objections will our plan elicit?
- Can we accomplish the goals we propose?

To answer these questions, the proposer may be required to do research on the organization, its problems, its corporate culture, the perspective and attitudes stemming from its corporate culture, and its current financial status, goals, and problems. As each part of the proposal is developed, the writer should examine it from the intended reader's perspective.

- What are the weaknesses of the plan, as we—the writers—perceive them?
- How can we counter any weaknesses and the reader's potential objections?
- How can we make our plan appealing?
- How can we show that we understand their needs?
- How can we best present our capability to do this project?
- What are our/my strength(s)?
- From our own knowledge of our organization, what are our weaknesses—in personnel and in overall capability to complete this project as proposed?
- Do we need to modify our proposed plan to avoid misleading readers about our ability to perform certain tasks on time, as proposed, and at cost?
- Can we sell our idea without compromising the accuracy of what we can actually do?

As a proposal writer, you should consider each question and determine what evidence you will need to support the merits of your idea and the arguments needed to refute any objections. Every sentence in your proposal should argue for the merits of your plan and your or your organization's ability to complete it. Although the proposal is designed to be a sales document, you are still ethically obligated to present a plan that meets the soliciting organization's needs and requirements. (In considering the ethical issues that confront proposal writers, you will want to review Chapter 3, Writing Ethically.)

Standard sections of proposals. Proposals generally include three main divisions: a summary, a main body, and attachments. The main body focuses on the three main parts of the proposal: the proposal's objectives (technical proposal), methods for achieving objectives (management proposal), and project cost (cost proposal). Proposals vary, but you will see the following segments embedded in some way:

> Project summary
> Project description (technical proposal)
>> Introduction
>> Rationale and significance
>> Plan of the work
>>> • Scope
>>> • Methods
>>> • Task Breakdown
>>> • Problem Analysis
>> Facilities and equipment
> Personnel (management proposal)
> Budget (cost proposal)
> Conclusion
> Appendices

Major business proposals are submitted in complete report format, which requires a letter of transmittal, a title page, a submission page (perhaps), a table of contents, and a summary—all items discussed in Chapter 8. Shorter proposals may be written in a memo or letter format. Many government proposals must be submitted online only. Whatever the format, the main elements will be required, although how they appear will vary with each proposal. In most RFPs, the soliciting organization explains what should be included in the proposal (either specific information to be included or major elements). Often, RFPs indicate the maximum number of pages allowed in a proposal. Writers are well advised to follow these instructions carefully to ensure that the proposal is not rejected during the initial screening process because it fails to follow preparation guidelines stipulated by the RFP.

Summary. The summary is by far the most important section of the proposal. Many proposal consultants believe that a project will be accepted or rejected based solely on the effectiveness of the summary, which is your readers' first introduction to what you are proposing. The summary should concisely describe the project, particularly how your work meets the requirements of the soliciting organization, your plan for doing the work, and your or your company's main qualifications. The summary should be a concise version of the detailed plan, but it should be written to convince readers that you understand what the soliciting firm needs and wants, that what you are proposing can be done as you describe, and that your approach is solid because you have the required knowledge and expertise. After reading the summary, readers should want to read more of your proposal.

Project description (technical proposal). The technical proposal describes what you or your company proposes to do. The description must be as specific as possible. The technical proposal has a number of elements:

Introduction. The proposal introduction should explain what you are proposing, why you are proposing this idea, and what you plan to accomplish. The introduction contains the same elements as any introduction. In short proposals, the summary and introduction can be combined.

Rationale and significance. Much of your success in convincing readers that you should be granted a contract to do the work you propose will rest on your success in convincing them that you understand the project. In the section on rationale and significance, you need to make it clear that you understand readers' needs—as stated in the summary or introduction—and that you have designed your goals by analyzing and defining their needs. Although you will clearly be selling your idea, you should recognize and answer any questions your readers may have as you argue the merits of your project. Convincing your readers that you fully understand what they are looking for is critical in establishing your credibility.

In short,

- You may want to define the problem, to show that you understand it.
- You may want to explain the background of the problem and how it evolved, by providing a historical review of the problem.
- If you are proposing a research project, you may want to explain why your research needs to be done and what results can be expected from your research.
- You may want to describe your solution and the benefits of your proposed solution.

Of greatest importance, however, is the *feasibility* of the work you propose. Is your proposed work doable? Is it suitable, appropriate, economical, and practicable? Have you given your readers an accurate view of what you can and will do?

Plan of the work. The section on the work plan is also critical, particularly to expert readers who will attempt to determine whether you understand the breadth of the work you are proposing. In this section, you will describe how you will go about achieving the goals you have stated. You will specify what you will do in what order, explaining and perhaps justifying your approach as you believe necessary. A realistic approach is crucial in that a knowledgeable reader will sense immediately if your plan omits major steps. A flawed work plan can destroy your credibility as well as the merits of the goals or the solution you are proposing.

Scope. The work plan section may need to describe the scope of the proposed work. What will you do and not do? What topics will your study or your work cover and not cover? What are the limits of what you are proposing? What topics will be outside the scope of your project? As the writer of the proposal, you have both an ethical and a legal obligation to make clear to your readers the limits of your responsibility.

Methods. A work plan may also require a statement of the methods you will use. If you are going to do onsite research, how will you do this research? If you plan to collect data, how will you do so? How will you analyze this data? How will you guarantee the validity of the analysis? If your research includes human subjects, how will you make sure that their participation is voluntary and their privacy is protected? If you are going to conduct surveys or interviews, how will you do so and what questions will you ask? If you plan to do historical research or a literature review of a topic, how will you approach such a review to ensure that your findings are representative of what is currently known about a subject area? What precautions will you take to verify that your reseach is conducted according to applicable ethical and legal standards? A precise, carefully detailed description of your work methods can add to your credibility as one who is competent to perform the proposed work.

Task breakdown. Almost all proposals require you to divide your work into specific tasks and to state the amount of time allotted to each task. This information may be given in a milestone chart, as illustrated in the methods section of the student research proposal (Case 9-1). The task breakdown indicates how much time you plan to devote to each task. A realistic time schedule also becomes an effective argument. It suggests to readers that you understand how much time your project will take and that you are not promising miracles just to win approval of your proposal or business plan.

If a project must be completed by a deadline, the task breakdown and work schedule should indicate exactly how you plan to fit every job into the allotted time. However, do not make time commitments that will be impossible to meet. Readers who sense that your work plan is artificial will immediately question your credibility. Remember, too, that a proposal is a binding commitment. If you cannot do what you propose, what the soliciting organization requires within the required time, you can destroy your professional credibility and leave yourself open to litigation.

Problem analysis. Few projects can be completed without problems. If you have carefully analyzed the problem or work you intend to do, you should anticipate where difficulties could arise. Problems that may be encountered can often be discussed in the rationale section. However, if you discover major obstacles that you believe will occur during the course of the project, you may wish to isolate and discuss these in a separate section. Many organizations that request work or solicit research proposals are aware of problems that may arise. Reviewers in these organizations look carefully at the problem analysis section, wherever it occurs, to see whether the proposer has anticipated these problems and explained the course of action that will be followed in dealing with them. Anticipating and designing solutions to problems can further build your credibility with readers, who will not be impressed if you fail to diagnose points in your work plan that could be troublesome and even hinder your completion of the project as proposed.

Facilities and equipment. The facilities section of the proposal is important if you need to convince the reader that your company has the equipment, plant, and physical capability to do the proposed work. Facilities descriptions are particularly crucial if hardware is to be built at a plant site owned by your organization. Even in research proposals, your readers may want to know what resources you will use. Sometimes existing facilities are not adequate for a particular job and your company must purchase specific equipment. The facilities section enables you to explain this purchase and how it will be included in the cost proposal.

Researchers may need to travel to visit special libraries or research sites. The amount of money needed for this travel will be part of the cost proposal. Thus, the nature of any extra research support, its importance, and its cost to the project should be explained here.

Personnel (management proposal). Any technical proposal or project is only as good as the management strategy that directs it. The management proposal should explain how you plan to manage the project: who will be in charge and what qualifications that person or team has for this kind of work. Management procedures should harmonize with the methods of pursuing the work described in the technical proposal.

Descriptions of your management philosophy and hierarchy should clearly reflect your company's management philosophy and culture. Readers should see the same kind of management applied to the proposed work as to the company and other projects it manages. Any testimony to or evidence of the effectiveness of the management approach will lend credibility to the technical proposal. Proposal reviewers must be convinced that you and your organization have a sound approach supported by good management of that approach.

In research proposals, the researcher who is soliciting funds will want to explain his or her expertise in the subject area proposed. This explanation may focus on educational background, previous projects successfully undertaken, published research on the topic, and general experience.

Budget (cost proposal). The cost proposal is usually the final item in the body of the proposal, even though cost may ultimately be the most crucial factor in industrial proposals. Cost is usually given last and appears as a budget for the length of the proposal period. The technical and management sections of the proposal, with their descriptions of methods, tasks, facilities, required travel, and personnel, should help justify the cost. They should have already explained the rationale for items that will produce the greatest cost. However, any items not previously discussed in the technical and management sections—such as administrative expenses, additional insurance benefits costs, and unexpected legal costs—should be explained. An itemized budget is often submitted as a separate document. It includes items such as the proposing organization's liability for not meeting project deadlines, for cost overruns, and for unforeseen labor strikes and work stoppages. Many budget sections include standard statements such as descriptions of union contracts with labor costs, insurance benefits costs, nonstrike costs, and statements of existing corporate liability for other projects—any existing arrangements that affect the cost of the proposed contract. Clearly, the goal is to explain exactly how much the project will cost and how the cost is determined. How extensive the budget is depends on the magnitude of the project.

Conclusion. The proposal includes a final section that repeats what the proposal offers the potential client or the soliciting agency, why you or your company should be selected to perform the work, and the benefits that the project, when completed, will yield for the client. The conclusion presents the final restatement of your central argument.

Appendices. As in any report, the appendix section includes materials to support information you give in the main body of the proposal—in the technical, management, or cost proposal. For example, the appendix might include résumés of principal investigators, managers, or researchers. These résumés should highlight their qualifications as they pertain to the specific project.

Case 9-1: **Research Proposal**

The undergraduate research office at a university solicits proposals from undergraduate students who wish to pursue research with a faculty member. Case Document 9-1 is a research proposal written by an undergraduate chemical engineering major, Evan Cherry. The proposal includes sections required by the solicitation for these undergraduate research proposals. Readers for this proposal will be faculty from science and engineering. For that reason, the proposal is highly technical and is prepared to meet the strict length requirements given in the RFP.

EVAN CHERRY

Proposal for Undergraduate Research Scholars Program: Effects of Simvastatin and Fluvastatin on Endothelial Invasion

Summary

Millions of people take cholesterol lowering medications. This proposal investigates whether the cholesterol medications simvastatin (Zocor®) and fluvastatin (Lescol®) can additionally alter a key step of wound healing. We will specifically determine whether these medications affect angiogenesis, the formation of new blood vessels from pre-existing structures using a model of endothelial cell invasion. We hypothesize that simvastatin and fluvastatin may have additional effects unrelated to reducing cholesterol. The specific aims are:

1. Determine the effects of simvastatin and fluvastatin on endothelial invasion.

2. Determine whether the effects on invasion are a direct result of altered cholesterol levels or due to inhibition of HMG CoA Reductase activity.

3. Determine the signaling mechanisms affected by simvastatin and fluvastatin.

Introduction

I. Atherosclerosis and Statins

Cholesterol regulation has become one of the primary methods for preventing heart disease. HMG-CoA Reductase inhibitors (statins), the first line of treatment for inhibiting cholesterol synthesis, lower blood cholesterol levels

continued

and significantly reduce both atherosclerosis[1] and the instance of heart disease by 60%.[2]

Atherosclerosis is the buildup of fatty plaques along blood vessel lining. Various stress factors oxidize the cholesterol transport molecule Low density Lipoproteins (LDL). Oxidized LDL adheres to the lining of blood vessels and encourages foam cell accumulation and plaque growth which reduces blood flow and can cause heart attack.[3] Plaque rupture can result in a stroke.

The Agency for Healthcare Research and Quality found that in 2005, 29.7 million people purchased statins for an estimated total of 19.7 billion dollars.[4] Two examples of statins are shown below (Figure 1). Simvastatin is derived from lovastatin, a naturally-occurring compound in the fungus Aspergillus terreus. Fluvastatin, a synthetic statin, has a visibly different structure. (Figure 1)

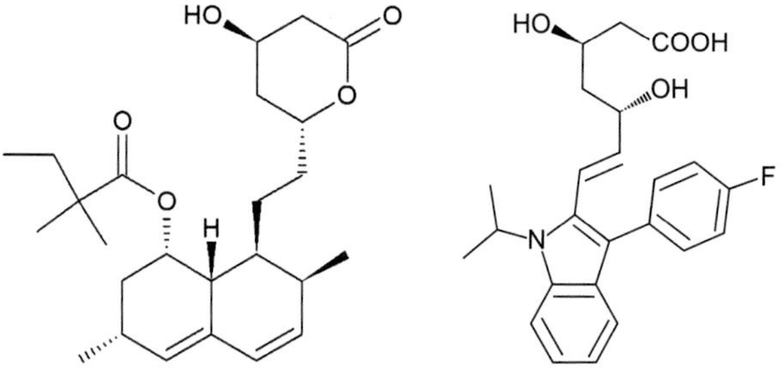

Figure 1: The structures of simvastatin and fluvastatin differ substantially.

II. Angiogenesis

Patients treated with statins exhibit other cardiovascular protective effects, including a lower incidence of cancer.[5] New blood vessel growth, or angiogenesis, is an important part of tumor growth and wound healing. These data have helped form the basis for our hypothesis that statins may affect angiogenesis.

During angiogenesis, endothelial cells lining blood vessels respond to extracellular signals and change into invading structures. (Figure 2) The endothelial cells enter the surrounding matrix form new blood vessel growth. In wound healing, the process relies on platelets, fibroblasts, and neighboring endothelial cells to close the wound. Endothelial cells propagate across the gap until they make contact other endothelial cells and cease multiplying. The simultaneous combination of lipid inducers growth factors is required for endothelial invasion.[6]

For our project, we will investigate if statin therapy changes invasion responses in a model reproducing angiogenesis during wound healing.

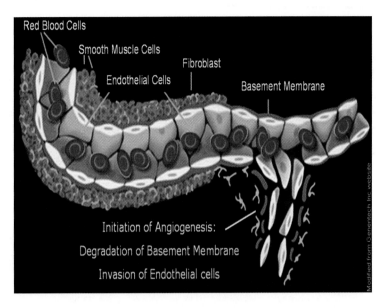

Figure 2. Endothelial invasion begins angiogenesis.

Project Description

We will evaluate the effects of statin therapy on endothelial invasion and whether the effects stem from cholesterol mediation or secondary effects. My project consists of three aims:

1. Determine the effects of statin therapy on endothelial invasion.

We will conduct invasion experiments using statin pre-treated endothelial cells and quantify both the number of cells invading and invasion depth.

2. Determine whether the effects on invasion are a direct result of altered cholesterol levels or HMG CoA Reductase.

We will analyze cholesterol levels in the cells using a commercially available kit and decrease cholesterol levels.

3. Determine how simvastatin and fluvastatin alter signaling.

Preliminary data indicate that several proteins mediate invasion responses. We will analyze levels of activated proteins at various time points of invasion.

Methodology and Timeline

Dr. Bayless' lab implements an artificial angiogenesis model using three-dimensional collagen that mimics the extracellular matrix. We place collagen

continued

solution containing nutritive media and sphingosine-1-phosphate (S1P). S1P is a lipid that signals the endothelial cells to invade the collagen matrix.[7] We add human endothelial cells to the top surface of the collagen. The cells form a single layer and attach to the gel. We then add additional nutritive media and growth factors.

After the cells incubate 18-24 hours, we preserve the cells with formaldehyde before staining with 4′,6-diamidino-2-phenylindole (DAPI), a molecule that causes nuclei to fluoresce under ultraviolet light. This allows us to count the number of invading cells before we stain them with toluidine blue and cut cross-sectional slices. Photographs show invading cells and photography software measures the depth of the invading cells. (Figure 3)

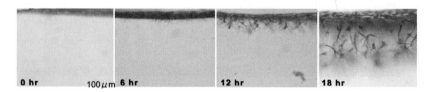

0 hr   100μm 6 hr   12 hr   18 hr

Figure 3. Endothelial cells invade the 3-dimensional matrix.

To complete *Aim 1* I will place cells pre-treated with simvastatin or fluvastatin in assays as shown in figure 3. The invasion density and depth will be counted. All experiments will be confirmed three times. (n=3)

To complete *Aim 2* we will measure cellular cholesterol levels by using a commercially available kit and measure any differences in cholesterol synthesis between fluvastatin and simvastatin. The cholesterol profile will tell us whether the two compounds comparably inhibit cholesterol.

If we observe any differences in cholesterol levels or invasion, we will assume that these effects are due to decreased HMG CoA Reductase activity. To confirm this we will knockdown HMG CoA Reductase by delivering a small hairpin RNA (shRNA) sequence to the endothelial cells using lentiviruses produced in the Bayless lab. We will check gene knockdown by western blot and analyze the behavior of these cells in our invasion model.

If fluvastatin or simvastatin affect invasion responses, we will assume they are altering signaling events that control invasion. Two of these events are phosphorylation of Akt and p42/44 MAP Kinase (Figure 4). To complete *Aim 3* we will treat cells with simvastatin or fluvastatin and extract proteins over time. For the western blot, we will line up the treated and control extracts on an acrylamide gel and separate them by electrophoresis.

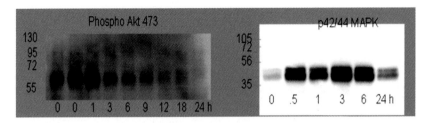

Figure 4. Western blots show Akt and p42/44 levels vary with invasion time.

We will specifically look for differences in activation of Akt and ERK p42/p44. While we do not know all the proteins involved in the invasion response, we do know that these proteins occur early in the process.

The possibility exists that simvastatin and fluvastatin have no effect on these designated proteins; we can then conclude that effects may occur further down the pathway and continue from there.

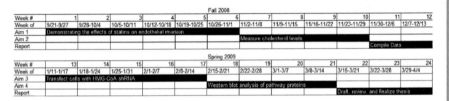

Table 1. The proposed process spans 24 weeks and finishes early April 2009.

Qualifications

I am a junior chemical engineering major with an interest in medicine and healthcare. I have been employed as a pharmacy clerk and am a phlebotomist. Following graduation, I plan to enter an MD/PhD program. This past summer I worked with Dr. Bayless on the statin project during the Summer Undergraduate Research Program at the Health Science Center and gained experience performing invasion experiments.

I have completed the following elective courses in addition to my major while maintaining a GPA of 3.9.

- Cell & Molecular Biology (BIOL 213)
- Biochemistry (BICH 303)
- Genetics (GENE 301)

continued

References

[1] S. Nissen, S. Nicholls, et al. *Effect of Very High-Intensity Statin Therapy on Regression of Coronary Atherosclerosis*, Journal of the American Medical Association Volume 295 No. 13 pp. 1556–1565 (2006)

[2] M. Law, N. Wald, A. Rudnicka. *Quantifying effect of statins on low density lipoprotein cholesterol, ischaemic heart disease, and stroke: systematic review and meta-analysis.* The British Medical Journal Volume 326 (2003)

[3] P. Libby, M. Aikawa, U. Schonbeck. *Cholesterol and atherosclerosis.* Biochimica et Biophysica Vol. 1529 Issues 1–3. pp.299–309 (2000)

[4] Marie N. Stagnitti, *Statistical Brief #205: Trends in Statins Utilization and Expenditures for the U.S. Civilian Noninstitutionalized Population, 2000 and 2005.* Medical Expenditure Panel Survey (2008)

[5] M. Demierre, P. Higgins, S. Gruber, E. Hawk, S. Lippman. *Statins and Cancer Prevention.* Nature Reviews Cancer 5, pp. 930–942 (2005)

[6] G. Davis, K. Bayless, A. Mavila. *Molecular basis of endothelial cell morphogenesis in three-dimensional extracellular matrices.* The Anatomical Record Vol. 268 Issue 3, pp. 252–275 (2002)

[7] K. Bayless, G. Davis. Sphingosine-1-phosphate markedly induces matrix metalloproteinase and integrin-dependent human endothelial cell invasion and lumen formation in three-dimensional collagen and fibrin matrices. Biochemical and Biophysical Research Communications. Vol. 312 Issue 4 pp.903–913 (2003)

Case 9-2: **Project Proposal**

The pre-medical honor society at Texas A&M University has invited students to propose and then write, if the proposal is accepted, a discussion of issues important to future physicians. Kendra Wheeler proposes a report that discusses the medical malpractice issue. This proposal includes a summary, a list of topics, methods to be used in developing the topic, a tentative report outline, and an initial list of sources. Since it deals with a non-technical topic, the level of language needs no technical detail. The audience for the report will be other pre-medical students and perhaps faculty who work with the pre-medical society.

CASE DOCUMENT 9-2

TO:	Phillip Anderson	**DATE:** March 6, 2007
CC:	Elizabeth Tebeaux	
FROM:	Kendra Wheeler	
SUBJECT:	Proposal topic for an AED meeting: Inefficiencies Contributing to the Rising Cost of Medical Care	

For presentation at April 19th AED meeting

Summary:

This report I propose will describe to students hoping to go into the medical field some of the big contributors to the rising cost of medical care. Specifically, the report will focus on current inefficiencies that could be resolved but are instead currently driving up costs. Because of the increasing concerns surrounding malpractice, AED students need to understand the basic issues surrounding malpractice: malpractice insurance, defensive medicine, and medical insurance. The report will survey each of these three topics and provide conclusions about the status of medicine, as a field, in dealing with malpractice.

Plan for Selected Topics:

1. Defensive Medicine
    a. New technologies increase the cost of medical care.
    b. A balance must be maintained between using these innovations to improve diagnosis of illness and ordering unnecessary and costly testing.
    c. Doctors are becoming more and more inclined to order unnecessary testing in order to defend themselves against malpractice suits.

continued

2. Malpractice Insurance
    a. Along with improving diagnosis, new technology provides lawyers with a means to prove that a doctor has made a mistake. Failure to prescribe a potentially life saving test can also leave a doctor vulnerable to malpractice suits.
    b. These mistakes can result in costly settlements forcing doctors to invest in malpractice insurance.
    c. The cost of this insurance is then transferred to the patient.
3. Medical Insurance
    a. When a patient receives medical care, they pay for their tests, the doctor's insurance, and the doctor's time and expenses.
    b. The cost for receiving this care is constantly rising. This makes it necessary for patients to invest in medical insurance in order to pay for care.
4. Most students think of the medical profession as a means to improve the health of patients while making money at something they enjoy.
    a. It is important, however, that they are aware of these other unpleasant financial issues and the impact their choices will have on their future patients.

Method to be Used to Develop the Report:

1. Create a rough outline of some of the main factors in the following issues: malpractice suits, defensive medicine, and medical insurance.
2. Research these issues to further develop the topics
    a. Talk to a librarian
    b. Use on-line databases/indexes
        i EX: LexisNexis, medline, etc
    c. Use on-line periodicals
    d. Find current statistics on who is insured, who is not, what organizations or persons pay for health care through the census bureau.
3. Fill in the outline with complete information on each topic
4. Do any final research needed to complete the discussion
5. Transfer the outlined information into the report format
6. Edit, revise, repeat
7. Ask a friend to edit
8. Make final revisions and make sure format is satisfactory
9. Submit report

Tentative Outline of the Report:

1. Introduction
2. Defensive Medicine
    a. Common tests that doctors ask for and what they cost
    b. Tests that doctors most often order when they are not really necessary
    c. Why doctors order tests that are not necessary
    d. Court cases as examples
    e. Are patients turned away who have problems that are too complicated or who need procedures with too high of a risk?
        i. Restriction of practice- physician limiting the types of patients that they will treat
        ii. Referral of patients to other specialists for consultation
    f. Other ways doctors can guard themselves against malpractice suits besides excessively ordering unnecessary tests or avoiding difficult cases
3. Malpractice Insurance
    a. Example court cases: why the patients were awarded money, and how much
    b. What is tort pleading?
    c. Propose definitions of when a settlement is justified and when it is frivolous.
        i. Example court cases of each.
    d. Other systems that have been suggested to handle cases where mistakes are made by doctors other than the current process of suing the doctor.
4. Medical Insurance
    a. Why does it cost so much to go to the doctor?
    b. Common forms of medical insurance
    a. Outline who is insured, who isn't, and who pays for it.
    b. Outline the problems
        i. Cost for those who pay for insurance
            1. Companies, the government, and private insurance
            2. The "free money" mentality—the thought that, "my insurance will cover it so why not get the extra test?"
        ii. How those without insurance get health care (or not)

continued

    c. Filing with health insurance organizations

    d. Differences between private providers and government paid insurance

    e. Alternate systems to pay for medical care

5. Conclusion: Summarize the three discussed sources of inefficiencies that contribute to the high cost of health care.

    a. Why they cost.

    b. What some alternatives are.

Initial List of Resources:

"Best Health Plans 2006." U.S. News and World Report 2007. 5 Mar. 2007 http://www.usnews.com/usnews/health/best-health-insurance/topplans.htm.

Collins, Sara R., Michelle M. Doty, Karen Davis, Kathy Schoen, Alyssa L. Holmgren, and Alice Ho. The Affordability Crisis in US Health Care: Findings From the Commonwealth Fund Biennial Health Insurance Survey. The Commonwealth Fund. 2004. 1-38. 5 Mar. 2007 http://scholar.google.com/scholar?hl=en&lr=&client=firefox-a&q=cache:cLSZAEzxEksJ:www.cmwf.org/programs/insurance/collins_biennial2003_723.pdf+.

Gianakos, Dean. "Litigation: Not Easy to Do in 2004 Preventing Medical Errors, Avoiding." Chest 126 (2004): 1408-1409. 5 Mar. 2007 http://www.chestjournal.org/cgi/content/full/126/5/1408.

Ginsburg, Paul B. "Controlling Health Care Costs." The New England Journal of Medicine 351.16 (2004): 1591-1593. 5 Mar. 2007 http://content.nejm.org/cgi/content/full/351/16/1591.

Health Insurance Coverage: 2005. U.S. Census Bureau. 2006. 5 Mar. 2007 http://www.census.gov/hhes/www/hlthins/hlthin05/hlth05asc.html.

Kessler, Daniel, and Mark McClellan. "Do Doctors Practice Defensive Medicine?" The Quarterly Journal of Economics 111.2 (1996): 353-390. 5 Mar. 2007 http://links.jstor.org/sici?sici=0033-5533(199605)111%3A2%3C353%3ADDPDM%3E2.0.CO%3B2-0.

Liebowitz, Stan. Why Health Care Costs Too Much. Cato Institute. 1994. 5 Mar. 2007 http://www.cato.org/pubs/pas/pa211.html.

Mohr, James C. "American Medical Malpractice Litigation in Historical Perspective." Journal of the American Medical Association 283.13 (2000): 1731-1737. 5 Mar. 2007 http://jama.ama-assn.org/cgi/content/abstract/283/13/1731.

Studdert, David M., William P. Sage, Catherine M. Desroches, Jordon Peugh, Kinga Zapert, Troyen A. Brennan, and Michelle M. Mello. "Defensive Medicine Among High-Risk Specialist Physicians in a Volatile Malpractice Environment." Journal of the American Medical Association 293.21 (2005): 2609-2617. 5 Mar. 2007 http://jama.ama-assn.org/cgi/content/short/293/21/2609.

PROGRESS REPORTS

When a soliciting organization requests a proposal, it often states that a specific number of progress reports will be required, particularly if the project covers a long time period. As their name suggests, progress reports, sometimes known as status reports, tell readers how work is progressing on a project. Their immediate purpose is to inform the authorizing person of the activities completed on a project, but their long-range purpose should be to show the proposing organization's or the individual's competence in pursuing a task and completing it.

Status reports may also be prepared in paper format and submitted to supervisors. These progress reports help you or your work group provide evidence or documentation of your activities. They generally have three goals:

- To explain to the reader what has been accomplished and by whom, the status of the work performed, and problems that may have arisen that need attention.
- To explain to your client how time and money have been spent, what work remains to be done, and how any problems encountered are being handled.
- To enable the organization or individual doing the work to assess the work and plan future work.

Structure of progress reports. Any work project, such as transportation or construction projects, requires regular progress reports. While these differ, they incorporate the same basic segments: goal of the project, work accomplished (for a given period), work remaining/planned (for the next period), problems encountered, and financial expenditure.

Structure by work performed. This is the standard structure for progress reports.

Beginning
- Introduction/project description
- Summary

Middle
- Work completed   or   • Task 1
  Task 1   Work completed
  Task 2, etc.   Work remaining
- Work remaining   • Task 2
  Task 3   Work completed
  Task 4   Work remaining
- Cost   • Cost

End
- Overall appraisal of progress to date
- Conclusion and recommendations

In this general plan, you emphasize what has been done and what remains to be done and supply enough introduction to be sure that the reader knows what project is being discussed.

For progress reports that cover more than one period, the basic design can be expanded as follows:

Beginning
- Introduction
- Project description
- Summary of work to date
- Summary of work in this period

Middle
- Work accomplished by tasks (this period)
- Work remaining on specific tasks
- Work planned for the next reporting period
- Work planned for periods thereafter
- Cost to date
- Cost in this period

End
- Overall appraisal of work to date
- Conclusions and recommendations concerning problems

Structure by chronological order. If your project or research is broken into time periods, your progress report can be structured to emphasize the periods.

Beginning
- Introduction/project description
- Summary of work completed

Middle
- Work completed
  Period 1 (beginning and ending dates)
    Description
    Cost
  Period 2 (beginning and ending dates)
    Description
    Cost
- Work remaining
  Period 3 (or remaining periods)
    Description of work to be done
    Expected cost

End
- Evaluation of work in this period
- Conclusions and recommendations

Structure by main project goals.   Many research projects are pursued by group-ing specific tasks into major groups. Then the writer describes progress according to work done in each major group and perhaps the amount of time spent on that group of tasks. Alternatively, a researcher may decide to present a project by re-search goals—what will be accomplished during the project. Thus, progress re-ports will explain activities performed to achieve those goals. In the middle of the plans below, the left-hand column is organized by work completed and remaining, and the right-hand column by goals.

Beginning
- Introduction/project description
- Summary of progress to date

Middle

• Work completed	or	• Goal 1
Goal 1		Work completed
Goal 2		Work remaining
Goal 3, etc.		Cost
• Work remaining		• Goal 2
Goal 1		Work completed
Goal 2		Work remaining
Goal 3, etc.		Cost
• Cost		

End
- Evaluation of work to date
- Conclusions and recommendations

Case 9-3

Recipients of research funds from the pre-medical honor society are expected to submit a progress report. Kendra submits her report several weeks before the research reports will be completed and submitted.

CASE DOCUMENT 9-3

TO: Elizabeth Tebeaux   **DATE:**   April 22, 2007
             Filo Maldonado
FROM: Kendra Wheeler
SUBJECT: Progress on Medical Malpractice Report

This report communicates the status of my major project to be addressed to students in AED, an honors premedical society. Work is proceeding well. The report will be ready for the April meeting.

Work Completed

Preliminary research

• I conducted preliminary research on major issues in the medical profession using Google. Based on this effort, I selected malpractice insurance, defensive medicine, and medical insurance as the topics for my major project.

Writing center

• My next step was to go to the writing center for advice on how to improve my internet research technique.
  ◦ Because I was looking for advice to aid my initial search and because my schedule is complicated, I was unable to make an appointment to speak with an advisor prior to the time that I expected to have already completed my research.
  ◦ Instead, the writing center provided me with several hand outs that made suggestions on how to use different on-line databases. Some of them were the ones that had been given out when the writing center representative spoke to our class, others I had not seen before.

Major research

• Using this information, I began my major research.
  ◦ I first used Google to do a broad search. I found a few sources, but the majority of the sites that came up were special interest groups so I was concerned about their objectivity.

- ○ Lexis-Nexis was the first database that I tried. I found a few articles, but it was difficult to narrow my search.
- ○ The most useful database that I found was the Academic Search Premier, especially the visual search option. It gave me subtopics to choose from and the option of narrowing the publication dates of the articles.
- With over 20 selected sources I then began to read through each article more thoroughly and narrow the sources to those that explicitly applied to the scope of my paper.
  - ○ So far nine of the articles either are redundant to more applicable articles or did not contain information pertinent to the project.
  - ○ I found one legal article analyzing medical malpractice claims in Texas, and another legal article defining and discussing defensive medicine. These seemed to be highly applicable to my topics.
  - ○ The remaining articles that I read more closely contain good supporting information.

Work Remaining

Research

- I have 4 articles left to read discussing medical insurance
- I may need to gather more information on medical insurance, and I have not yet explored the census bureau for information. It may be more applicable to find state department of insurance websites for additional information.

Project construction

- When my research is completed, I will select subtopics and create an outline containing the information I would like to use from the articles.
- Using this outline, I will then write the discussion of the major project.
- With the discussion written, I will then be able to complete the remaining sections of the major project.

Editing and revision

- With the rough draft complete, I will edit and revise several times.
- I will also try to get a peer to edit it before submission.

Assessment of progress to date

- Research has gone smoothly, although reading through the articles has taken longer than expected.
- I highlighted major points and visuals that I would like to address in my project, so I expect time spent on research should be recovered during the construction of the discussion.
- I believe I am on schedule to have the rough draft completed by Monday night, in time to thoroughly edit.

Case 9-4

In business, progress reports are standard. COSMIX (Colorado State Metro Interstate Expansion) posts its progress on road projects on the Internet so that the public can track progress with text and pictures. This transportation progress report provides a list of tasks completed by month throughout a three-year period. This type of online progress report provides transparency and allows the public to see how COSMIX spends highway expansion dollars.

CASE DOCUMENT 9-4

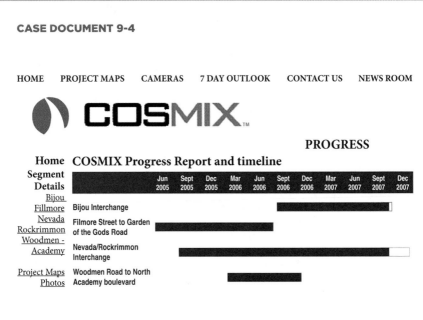

October 2007
October marked a significant milestone on the COSMIX project, when the Bijou bridge reopened to traffic. In addition, COSMIX crews began the final piece of work in the North Nevada/Rockrimmon segment when the Rockrimmon/Mark Dabling intersection was closed for reconstruction. Other progress on the project included:

- Continued placement of architectural railings on the Bijou bridge
- Landscaping and streetscape was completed on and near the Bijou bridge
- Completed asphalt paving between South Nevada/Tejon and Cimarron Street
- Utilities and drainage on the Spruce St. cul de sac was completed
- Northbound bridge structure over Colorado Ave. was completed

September 2007

This month, crews worked around the clock to prepare for the opening of the Bijou bridge on October 1. Progress became visible to the traveling public throughout the corridor when three lanes of I-25 became available between North Academy Boulevard and Bijou Street. In addition, crews made progress on the following:

- Completed landscaping behind the Pulpit Rock noise wall.
- Opened three lanes north and southbound between Bijou and Uintah Streets, allowing three lanes throughout the project between North Academy Boulevard and Bijou Street.
- Continued placing decorative railing and light fixtures on the Bijou bridge.
- Continued construction on the landscaping on the northwest corner of Bijou Street and the I-25 interchange, and underneath the Bijou bridge over Monument Creek.
- Continued construction on the I-25 bridges over Colorado Avenue.
- Reopened the Pikes Peak Greenway Trail under the Bijou bridge.
- Prepared for opening of the Bijou bridge.
- Completed paving one-half mile south of North Academy Boulevard, and between the Martin Luther King bypass and Circle Drive.

August 2007

Good weather in August allowed the COSMIX Crews to make quite a bit of progress. Some of the significant COSMIX work in August included:

- Poured concrete on the new I-25 southbound bridge over Colorado Avenue
- Replaced road panels and bridge expansion joints on I-25 southbound between Fontanero and Uintah streets
- Eliminated "the dip" on northbound I-25 at Nevada Avenue with a process known as "mud-jacking"
- Opened the Nevada/Corporate Drive intersection
- Began placing decorative railing on the Bijou bridge
- Installed light fixtures on the Bijou bridge
- Began construction on the aesthetic upgrades on the northwest corner of Bijou Street and the I-25 interchange
- Began landscaping underneath the Bijou bridge over Monument Creek

July 2007

The month of July began with a COSMIX gift to Colorado Springs. Before the July 4th holiday, construction crews opened up the new third lane on north and southbound I-25 between Woodmen Road and Garden of the Gods Road, giving the traveling public three lanes all the way from North Academy Boulevard to Fillmore Street. *continued*

In addition, crews also worked on the following:

- Switched traffic onto the new northbound I-25 bridge over Colorado Avenue and began construction of the new southbound I-25 bridge over Colorado Avenue, including caisson drilling and retaining wall construction.
- Continued work on the Corporate Centre Drive/Nevada Avenue connection.
- Completed the new North Nevada Avenue alignment.
- Finished placing panels and staining noise walls at Uintah Street and Pulpit Rock.
- Completed final striping between Woodmen Road and North Academy Boulevard.
- Continued construction to repair concrete panels and bridge joints between Fontanero and Uintah Streets.
- Continued work on the Bijou bridge including:
- Completed paving of the northbound on and off-ramps
- Completed placement of the bridge deck over Monument Creek and the Union Pacific Railroad
- Completed 75 percent of the sidewalk and median concrete work
- Completed the concrete staining of the abutments and pier columns
- Began architectural stone veneer installation and painting of the decorative railings

June 2007

June 30 marked the two-year anniversary for construction on the COSMIX project. With two years of construction behind us and only six months left on the project, crews made some very visible progress in June, to include:

- Completed concrete staining on most of the North Nevada/Rockrimmon interchange.
- Completed the Pulpit Rock noise wall.
- Opened the third lane southbound between Nevada Avenue and Fillmore Street.
- Poured the concrete median and sidewalks for the Bijou bridge over I-25.
- Poured two of the four deck sections of the Bijou bridge over Monument Creek and the Union Pacific Railroad.
- Re-opened the southbound I-25 off-ramp at Bijou Street.
- Paved the northbound on and off-ramps for the Bijou interchange.
- Completed the reinstallation and rehabilitation of the Works Progress Administration (WPA) wall along Monument Creek near Downtown.
- Shifted traffic onto the new portions of the I-25 bridges over Colorado Avenue and the Midland Trail.
- Completed roadway work on the west side of the Bijou bridge.

May 2007

Several major milestones were completed in May, most notably, both north and southbound I -25 were taken off the frontage roads and put back onto the elevated interstate lanes in the Nevada/Rockrimmon area. It took just less than a year to complete the 2.5 miles of new interstate lanes, eight new bridges, and 1.8 miles of retaining walls associated with the interstate in this area. Some of the significant COSMIX work in May included:

- Shifted southbound onto the new interstate in the Nevada/Rockrimmon area on May 4.
- With the southbound traffic shift, the outdated left-hand interstate exit to North Nevada Avenue was permanently eliminated and replaced with a right hand exit.
- Demolished the old northbound I-25 bridge over the former southbound exit to North Nevada Avenue.
- Shifted northbound I-25 traffic onto the new northbound interstate in the Nevada/Rockrimmon area on May 24.
- Poured the remaining two bridge monuments on the east side of the Bijou bridge.
- Paved northbound I-25 over the Monument Creek and the Works Progress Administration (WPA) Wall.
- Reconstructed and reopened the entry to the parking lot of the Bijou Street Denny's in less than two weeks.
- Began placing noise wall panels for the Pulpit Rock neighborhood sound barrier.

April 2007

Throughout April crews worked to complete the southbound mainline in the North Nevada/Rockrimmon segment in anticipation of shifting traffic off the frontage road and onto the new interstate lanes in early May. Other significant COSMIX work in April included:

- Poured the last of twelve bridge decks in the North Nevada/Rockrimmon segment on April 6.
- Placed the remaining Bijou bridge girders over Monument Creek and the Union Pacific Railroad.
- Poured two of the four Bijou bridge monuments.
- Poured the northbound I-25 bridge deck over Colorado Avenue.
- Closed Bijou Street from I-25 to Spruce Street to begin raising the grade for the Bijou bridge.
- Began the rehabilitation of the northbound Midland Bridge deck.
- Demolished the remainder of the old northbound I-25 bridge over Monument Creek in the North Nevada/Rockrimmon segment.

continued

- Completed pouring the southbound mainline between the bridges in the North Nevada/Rockrimmon segment.

March 2007
Progress has begun to visibly accelerate in the Colorado Avenue to Bijou Street segment with dramatic changes to the corridor's appearance. Some of the significant COSMIX work in March included:

- Placed the girders for the Bijou Street bridge over I-25 and poured the bridge deck.
- Constructed the north and southbound I-25 lanes under the Bijou Street bridge.
- Shifted northbound I-25 traffic under the new Bijou Street bridge.
- Began the demolition of the south half of the Cimarron Street bridge over Conejos Street and the UPRR.
- Finished pouring piers for the Bijou bridge over Monument Creek and the UPRR.
- Placed girders for the northbound I-25 bridge over Colorado Avenue.
- Placed caissons and columns for the Pulpit Rock noise wall
- Poured the northbound bridge deck over Monument Creek in the Nevada / Rockrimmon area.

COSMIX construction crews reached 40 percent completion on the Bijou Street Interchange last week, when traffic on north and southbound Interstate 25 was shifted onto the new concrete lanes under the Bijou Street bridge. The shift marked the second major milestone in the Bijou segment. The first milestone was accomplished earlier in March, when crews set girders for the Bijou Street bridge over I-25.

February 2007
Construction crews received a reprieve from the unusual amounts of snow in January and February as temperatures began to warm up. Although the snow and cold temperatures returned mid-February, workers made significant progress in the Colorado Avenue to Bijou Street segment and the Nevada/Rockrimmon segment. Some of the significant COSMIX work in February included:

- Shifted northbound I-25 traffic over the Midland bridge to the west to allow for the northbound deck rehabilitation.
- Began placing the northbound retaining wall between Colorado Avenue and Bijou Street.
- Continued with the demolition of the Bijou bridge over Monument Creek and the Union Pacific Rail Road.
- Poured the center piers and placed the abutment panels for the Bijou bridge over I-25.

- Opened the southbound I-25 off-ramp to Garden of the Gods road in its final configuration.
- Re-striped north and southbound I-25 from North Nevada Avenue to Woodmen Road to accommodate the opening of the southbound auxiliary lane from Woodmen Road to Corporate Centre Drive.
- Opened the southbound off-ramp to Corporate Centre Drive.
- Poured the I-25 bridge decks over the Rockrimmon Boulevard extension.
- Poured the southbound I-25 bridge deck over Monument Creek in the Nevada/Rockrimmon area.
- Refreshed the striping throughout the corridor several times after the last few winter storms began to deteriorate the pavement markings.

January 2007
January marked the start of construction on the Bijou bridge. Despite the snow and cold temperatures, crews moved ahead on the demolition of the bridge over I-25 and over Monument Creek and the Union Pacific Rail Road.

Highlighted below are some of the other areas where crews made progress:

- Continued work on the north and southbound I-25 bridges over Monument Creek, Nevada Avenue, Rockrimmon Boulevard, Mark Dabling Boulevard and the Union Pacific Rail Road.
- Continued construction on northbound I-25 over Colorado Avenue.
- Completed rehabilitation work on the southbound bridge over the Midland Trail.
- Completed demolition of the Bijou bridge over I-25.
- Began demolition of the Bijou bridge over Monument Creek and the Union Pacific Rail Road (40 percent complete).
- Continued work on the caissons for the Monument Valley Park Noise Walls.
- Began placing precast columns for the Monument Valley Park Noise Walls.

<u>**COSMIX Progress for 2006**</u>

<u>**COSMIX Progress for 2005**</u>

Click on button below
for previous I-25 Web site.

<u>Statewide Weather and Travel Information</u>

Contact Webmaster
Last Modified: Mon, Jan, 07, 2008

Get
ADOBE® READER®

STYLE AND TONE OF PROPOSALS AND PROGRESS REPORTS

The proposal and its related report documents are, in effect, sales documents, but writers have an ethical commitment to present information about a project in a clear and accurate manner. Proposals, once accepted, become legally binding documents. Because contracts are based on proposals, organizations must be prepared to stand behind their proposals. Thus, the style should be authoritative, vigorous, and positive, suggesting the competence of the proposer. Generalizations must be bolstered by detailed factual accomplishments. Problems should be discussed honestly, but positive solutions to problems should be stressed. Neither the proposal nor the progress report should resort to vague, obfuscatory language.

CHECKLIST FOR DEVELOPING PROPOSALS AND PROGRESS REPORTS ✔

Proposals

Planning

☐ Have you made a list of all requirements given in the RFP?

☐ Who are your readers? Do they have technical competence in the field of the proposal? Is it a mixed audience, some technically educated, some not? To whom could the proposal be distributed?

☐ What problem is the proposed work designed to remedy? What is the immediate background and history of the problem? Why does the problem need to be solved?

☐ What is your proposed solution to the problem? What benefits will come from the solution? Is the solution feasible (both practical and applicable)?

☐ How will you carry out the work proposed? Scope? Methods to be used? Task breakdown? Time and work schedule?

☐ Do you want to make statements concerning the likelihood of success or failure and the products of the project? Who else has tried this solution? What was their success?

☐ What facilities and equipment will you need to carry out the project?

☐ Who will do the work? What are their qualifications for doing the work? Can you obtain references for past work accomplished?

☐ How much will the work cost (e.g., materials, labor, test equipment, travel, administrative expenses, and fees)? Who will pay for what? What will be the return on the investment?

☐ Will you need to include an appendix? Consider including biographical sketches, descriptions of earlier projects, and employment practices.

continued

CHECKLIST FOR DEVELOPING PROPOSALS AND PROGRESS REPORTS ✔ *continued*

☐ Will the proposal be better presented in a report format or in a letter or memo format?

Revising

☐ Does your proposal have a well-planned design and layout? Does its appearance suggest the high quality of the work you propose to do? Do your readings both promote and inform?

☐ Does the project summary succinctly state the objectives and plan of the proposed work? Does it show how the proposed work is relevant to the readers' interest?

☐ Does the introduction make the subject and the purpose of the work clear? Does it briefly point out the importance of the proposed work?

☐ Have you defined the problem thoroughly?

☐ Is your solution well described? Have you made its benefits and feasibility clear?

☐ Will your readers be able to follow your plan of work easily? Have you protected yourself by making clear what you will do and what you will not do? Have you been careful not to promise more results than you can deliver?

☐ Have you carefully considered all the facilities and equipment you will need?

☐ Have you presented the qualifications of project personnel in an attractive but honest way? Have you asked permission from everyone you plan to use as a reference?

☐ Is your budget realistic? Will it be easy for the readers to follow and understand?

☐ Do all the items in the appendix lend credibility to the proposal?

☐ Have you included a few sentences that urge the readers to accept the proposal?

☐ Have you satisfied the needs of your readers? Will they be able to comprehend your proposal? Do they have all the information they need to make a decision?

Progress Reports

Planning

☐ Do you have a clear description of your project available, perhaps in your proposal?

continued

CHECKLIST FOR DEVELOPING PROPOSALS AND PROGRESS REPORTS ✔ *continued*

☐ Do you have all the project tasks clearly defined? Do all the tasks run in sequence, or do some run concurrently? In general, are the tasks going well or badly?

☐ What items need to be highlighted in your summary and appraisal?

☐ Are there any problems to be discussed?

☐ Can you suggest solutions for the problems?

☐ Is your work ahead of schedule, right on schedule, or behind schedule?

☐ Are costs running as expected?

☐ Do you have some unexpected good news you can report?

Revising

☐ Does your report have an attractive appearance?

☐ Does the plan you have chosen show off your progress to its best advantage?

☐ Is your tone authoritative, with an accent on the positive?

☐ Have you supported your generalizations with facts?

☐ Does your approach seem fresh or tired?

☐ Do you have a good balance between work accomplished and work to be done?

☐ Can your summary and appraisal stand alone? Would they satisfy an executive reader?

EXERCISES

1. Write a proposal to a charitable trust or private foundation for funds in support of your favorite local non-profit organization. Interview a representative from the non-profit to assist you in identifying appropriate trusts or foundations to apply to as well as the specific projects to which the non-profit would apply the funds.

2. Write a progress report that details your research and writing efforts on your funding proposal for the non-profit organization. List the activities you have completed, the activities in progress, the activities remaining as well as mistakes made, problems encountered, and solutions discovered and implemented.

3. Examine the following proposal (Figure 9-3). If you were the author of this proposal and were given 15 more minutes to make it more persuasive, what changes would you make?

To:	Chief Walter Posey
From:	Officer Rick Dominguez
Subject:	International Police Mountain Bike Association Conference
Date:	February 11, 2009

I recently received an invitation from the International Police Mountain Bike Association (IPMBA) in reference to a conference being held by the association June 3rd through the 11th, 2009. This conference is a comprehensive training program designed to thoroughly train officers in all aspects of bicycle patrol. The conference is a requirement for the IPMBA instructors school, which is recognized worldwide. Instructors at the conference consist of officers from all over the world and the U.S.

I am respectfully requesting travel funds to attend the conference in order to represent our department. There are workshops at the conference that deal with the establishment of bicycle patrols by police departments. There are two pre-conference courses that are being conducted. These are the IPMBA Police Cyclist Certification Course, June 3–6, and the IPMBA Maintenance Officer Certification Course, June 7–9. The remaining workshops and training sessions are held June 9–11. The workshops are as follows:

- Community Oriented Policing
- Uniform /Equipment Selection
- Legal Issues
- Maintenance
- Defensive/Pursuit Tactics
- Suspect Apprehension
- Handling Urban Obstacles
- Officer Survival
- Night Operation
- Non-Urban Bike Patrol
- Nutrition and Fitness
- Fundraising for Bike Units

When we have the ability to staff a bike unit, it will be necessary for the department to obtain all of the facts regarding bike patrol, and to examine what other departments have done to implement and operate their bike units.

Attached to this memo is a copy of the letter I received from IPMBA. In this letter are the details for registration, travel, and accommodations for officers attending the conference.

If you have any questions regarding the conference or outfitting, please feel free to contact me at any time.

FIGURE 9-3 Document for Exercise 3

10

Instructions, Procedures, and Policies

INSTRUCTIONS VERSUS PROCEDURES

Procedures provide general guidelines for performing a task, while instructions provide specific, detailed steps. Procedures—or general guidelines—will be appropriate for some situations, while instructions may be necessary for readers who need detailed directions to perform a job task or process.

Instructions and procedures can appear in several formats: in letters and memoranda (see Chapter 7 for an example instructional memo), in reports, in technical papers or notes, in stand-alone documents to accompany mechanisms or processes, or in complete manuals. Complex procedures and instructions usually appear as manuals which use many of the report elements described in Appendix C. E-mail is not a suitable method of sending instructions/procedures, unless you send these as an e-mail attachment (in a standard rtf, doc, docx, or pdf file) that can be printed or read on the receiver's computer screen. Differences in e-mail applications can produce text that is awkwardly formatted and difficult to read.

Quick Tips

Many people resist reading instructions. They try to figure out for themselves how to operate a product or perform a task and will turn to the instructions only if all their efforts fail. When they do read the instructions, they want to understand everything immediately without having to read anything twice. A simple design, plain wording, and clear illustrations will be critical to encouraging readers to pay attention to your instructions or procedures:

1. Use concise headings and subheadings to describe and highlight each section.
2. Leave plenty of white space around headings.
3. Use numbers for every step in a chronological process; use bullets for lists of conditions, materials, and equipment.
4. Use white space to make items in lists easy to find and read.
5. Highlight safety information and warnings.
6. Keep illustrations as simple as possible.
7. Locate illustrations at the point where the reader needs them. Don't expect readers to locate an illustration that is several pages away from the instruction to which it pertains.
9. Label every illustration, and at the appropriate point in the related text, write "See Figure X."
10. Do not begin an instruction at the bottom of one page and complete it at the top of the next page. Insert a "page break" and move the entire instruction to the next page.

Planning Instructions and Procedures

Instructions and procedures should enable those who need them to perform the tasks covered. Successful instructions and procedures can be easily read, easily understood, and correctly followed by the intended users with minimal difficulty. Understanding your target readers and, in some cases, the context in which the documents will be used, is paramount. If readers are confused or misled by statements, they can hold the company liable for injury or financial damage suffered because of poorly written instructions or procedures. Instructions, particularly those that involve processes that could be hazardous, should explain the knowledge level required of the target audience.

Who are the readers? What do your readers know about the subject? These questions will determine how much information you provide and the type of language you use. The audience for instructions should be specified, especially if readers not conforming to that audience should not attempt to follow the instructions. For general instructions, remember that many people resist reading instructions. They tend to avoid reading them, if possible, and attempt to perform the task without them. When they do read the instructions, they want to understand them immediately without having to reread them. Design features (layout), format, choice of language, and use of visuals can be critical to encouraging readers to focus on the instructions or procedures.

What is your purpose? Successful instructions/procedures require that both you and your readers know your purpose. What should your readers know and be able to do after they read these instructions/procedures? Any information that isn't applicable should be omitted.

What is the context in which the instructions/procedures will be used? Knowing how documents will be read can help you design effective documents. Readers may be focusing on them while they are sitting at their desks. They may need to read the entire document before trying to perform the task, or they may perform the task as they go.

Do your readers need to read the instructions/procedures before they begin? Your telling them how to read the instructions may be necessary. For example, you can include detailed instructions for first-time readers, and then have a summary of steps for readers to use once they are familiar with the longer instructions. Context-sensitive instructions can be found in numerous settings:

- Some sailboards have instructions for how to right the sailboard—if it turns over in the water—on the bottom of the boat where riders can see the instructions if the boat turns over.
- "Quick Start" instructions for many hand-held devices can be found inside the top or lid of the device.
- Instructions used in machine shops on manufacturing floors are often printed in large type on eye-saver yellow or green paper and laminated to resist grease. These instructions may be in metal loose-leaf notebooks so strong that pages cannot be torn out.
- Basic operation instructions and trouble-shooting information for large clocks can be found inside the clock mechanism access compartment. These are designed to accompany the booklet that contains detailed instructions.

Will the instructions be available online or in paper? If instructions will be available online, focus on readability of the material. Avoid instructions that are "text heavy" and lengthy. Partition your instructions into distinct sections that are hyperlinked in a logical way. Or, you may want to tell your readers immediately that they should print a copy of the instructions if they are too long and complex for online reading.

Planning is particularly critical for writing instructions or procedures. Remembering or even using the document analysis checksheet at the end of this chapter will help you determine whether you need instructions or procedures, the delivery medium (online or paper), the content you will include, and any design strategies that could help you produce an effective document. Effective instructions require sensitive attention to readers information needs, their current knowledge of the topic, and what you want them to know as a result of reading the instructions.

STRUCTURE AND ORGANIZATION

First, analyze the audience, purpose, and context; then, begin to structure your procedures/instructions. Examine the following general guide for what elements to include, but remember that what you decide to include will depend on your topic, your audience, your purpose, and the reader's context. Comprehensive instruction/procedure manuals will usually contain most of these elements, while shorter instructions/procedures may require fewer. To illustrate instructions, we will focus on three examples.

Introduction. The introduction should familiarize readers with the task to be performed: specifically, what the instructions will allow readers to do and what skill level the person should have to perform the task successfully.

Theory governing the procedure or instruction. For some types of procedures, readers will perform tasks better if they have a general overview of the process. Knowledge of the process may help them understand when they have made an error and how to avoid errors. If you are going to give instructions for operating a mechanism, some explanation of the value and purpose of the mechanism can prepare readers for the process.

Warnings, cautions, hazards, and notes regarding safety or quality. Given the wide variety of technologically complicated and potentially dangerous products available today, you really cannot "over-warn" readers. And a failure to warn could have costly legal implications for your organization. Any level of hazard needs to be described—what will happen and why—if a particular action is performed. Identify the hazard, followed by the reason or the result, and be sure that all warnings, cautions, and notes are clearly visible. Warnings may also be repeated if they are associated with a particular step or direction. Warnings given at the beginning alert readers to possible problems they may encounter. Be sure that warnings stand out so that readers' eyes are drawn to them. The American National Standards Institute (www.ansi.org) articulates standards for hazard statements. A review of research on hazard messages is available from the United States Occupational Safety and Health Administration (www.osha.gov).

Conditions under which the task is to be performed. Some instructions, particularly laboratory instructions, may require you to describe the physical conditions required to perform a task: room size, temperature, time required for the entire process and for individual steps, specific safety processes. If time is a constraint, readers need to know how much time will be needed before they begin the task.

Name of each step. For each step, give the following: purpose of this step, warnings, cautions, and notes, any conditions necessary for performing the step, time required to perform the step, and the list of materials needed for this step.

- Place instructions in chronological order.
- Number each step.
- Limit each instruction to one action.
- After you have written the instruction, state in a separate sentence the reason for the instruction, but only if you believe that the reader may not follow the instruction without an explanation. Include warnings whenever necessary. And be sure to explain all warnings if you believe that people will not understand the reason for the warning.

Case 10-1: **Process Instructions**

Stefi Lee, a graduate student who supervises a biochemistry lab, decides that the laboratory instructions for recrystallization are too confusing and decides to revise these before assigning the lab. The original instructions appear in Case Document 10-1a. She will expect students to read the original instructions but also to have the revision available when they actually begin the experiment. Her first step in revising is to do a pre-writing analysis:

Pre-writing Analysis for Revising Recrystallization Instructions

1. Who is/are your reader(s)?
My readers are students new to Organic Chemistry lab. Those enrolled in this course will be required to recrystallize and perform certain tasks in lab they have never done before.

2. What is your reader profile? Background, attitude toward following instructions?
These students have not been previously exposed to Organic Chemistry Lab experiments. They know only basic knowledge from General Chemistry Lab, which does not teach the techniques and methods required in Organic Chemistry Lab. They will have no idea what equipment they will be using nor what each piece of equipment will look like. The only equipment they will have a general idea of are beaker, Erlenmeyer flask, and spatula. They will be totally reliant on the instructions through the entire experiment and won't be able to perform the experiment by memory until they repeat it with the instructions several times. The students want the instructions to be simple and easy to learn, so they understand the general purpose and procedures of the experiment.

3. How much do your readers know about the subject?
The readers don't know anything about this subject because lab experiments in Organic Chemistry Lab are much more advanced and different from General Chemistry Lab.

4. Will you have to define any terms that your readers may not understand?
Yes, some equipment and chemical terms will need to be defined.

5. What do you want your readers to be able to do after reading the instructions or procedures?
I want my readers to fully understand the experiment and be able to learn the steps by memory after following the procedures a few times. After learning to perform the experiment correctly, my readers should know the purpose and intent of the experiment.

continued

6. What is the situation that led to the need for these instructions?

In my first semester of Organic Chemistry lab, I was very confused in lab. The lab manual did not provide very clear instructions on how to set up the equipment. Thus, I performed the experiment very inefficiently and didn't obtain the correct results in the end. The instructions were condensed in long paragraphs, and often times I would lose my place in the procedures. After I finished the experiment, I had no idea what I had done and the purpose of the lab.

7. How will your readers use these instructions? Will they need to read every time, or will they be used only for reference?

My readers will follow these instructions carefully the first few times. They will need to use them several more times until they are able to commit every step of the experiment to memory. Thereafter, they will be able to perform the experiment themselves.

8. What kinds of pictorials will you use?

Graphics of the equipment used and results of the experiment will be provided.

9. What kinds of formatting and page design strategies will you use to make the instructions easy to read?

I will bold headings, provide bullet points, use white space to make the steps easy to see and follow, and underline important steps.

10. What content segments will you include?

I will include descriptive segments for equipments used, personal safety wear for self-protection, experiment procedures, and clean-up procedures.

CASE DOCUMENT 10-1A

Recrystallization

Purpose: To demonstrate the use of recrystallization to purify an impure sample of a solid compound.

Reading: *Techniques:* Recrystallization
Techniques: Melting Points

INTRODUCTION

Organic chemistry tends to be an almost endless adventure into isolation, identification, and/or synthesis of new compounds. Unfortunately, organic compounds have a unique sense of humor and reactions tend never to go to completion. Even if all the starting material has been used, it is a very good bet that more than one product has been formed. Recrystallization is one of four major techniques used to separate and purify organic compounds. Unlike the other techniques, recrystallization requires that the material to be purified be solid.

EXPERIMENTAL PROCEDURE

As soon as you arrive in the laboratory, begin heating 75 mL of water in a 250-mL beaker.

Dissolving the Compound. Weigh approximately 1.5 g of the impure acetanilide into a 125-mL Erlenmeyer flask. Break up the larger lumps with a stirring rod and add a boiling chip to the flask. Add about 25 mL of hot water to the flask containing the impure acetanilide. Heat this mixture on the steam bath. Swirl the flask occasionally (using crucible tongs) to aid in dissolving the solid and to prevent bumping. When recrystallizing an impure solid, it is desirable to use the minimum amount of hot solvent to dissolve the solid (30 mL of hot water are required to dissolve 1.5 g of pure acetanilide). Add small portions of hot water, 1 to 2 mL, until all the acetanilide dissolves. Be careful not to add too much hot water. The impure acetanilide contains water insoluble impurities. If no more material dissolves after you add more hot water, the material left is the insoluble impurity. If the acetanilide forms an oil rather than dissolving, more hot water should be added to dissolve the oil. Be careful not to add too much water.

Filtering Insoluble Impurities. While you are dissolving the acetanilide in hot water, set up a filter flask and a Büchner funnel for a hot vacuum filtration. (The steps required are outlined in *Techniques: Recrystallization*) Then conduct a hot vacuum filtration to remove insoluble impurities.

continued

Recrystallizing the Acetanilide. After completion of the hot vacuum filtration, allow the hot solution to cool slowly. If the solution is cooled too rapidly, small impure crystals form. Notice if an oil forms as the solution cools. If oil droplets are observed, heat the solution until the oil dissolves, add about 5 mL of water, and allow the solution to again cool slowly. After crystallization seems complete (the flask will have cooled to the point that you can comfortably hold it), place the solution in an ice-water bath for about ten minutes to increase the recovery of acetanilide.

Isolating and Drying the Pure Acetanilide. Vacuum filter the ice-cold solution to collect the crystals of acetanilide. Be sure the Büchner funnel is clean if it was used in the hot filtration. Wash the crystals with about 5 mL of ice cold water. The crystals in the funnel will still be quite wet. They should be dried thoroughly before weighing or taking a melting point. Some water may be removed by pressing on the crystals with a spatula while air is being drawn through the funnel by the aspirator. After the crystals have been dried, remove the filter paper and crystals from the Büchner funnel. Place another piece of filter paper on top of the crystals and wrap well in a piece of 15-cm filter paper. Tape with a piece of colored tape as a label. Label the sample with your name, section and course number, and experiment number. Store the sample in your section's storage drawer until the next laboratory period.

The sample of pure acetanilide will be thoroughly dry by the next laboratory period. Weigh the recovered acetanilide and determine its melting point. Compare this weight to the amount of impure acetanilide and determine the percent recovery. Compare the melting point range to the melting point of pure acetanilide reported in the literature.

CLEAN-UP PROCEDURES

The filtrate in the filter flask at the end of the experiment should be poured into the appropriately labeled waste container in the hood. Dispose of the used filter paper in the waste container labeled for this purpose in the hood. Rinse the used equipment with acetone, collect and dispose of the first rinse in the container labeled for this purpose in the hood.

Second Week Lab Period Clean-up Procedures. After you have weighed and determined the melting point of your acetanilide sample, dispose of the acetanilide in the container marked "waste acetanilide." You will also put the filter paper used to store the crystals in this same container. The used melting point capillary tubes should be disposed of in the box designated for broken glass.

SAFETY

Acetanilide is an irritant, avoid getting this on your hands. Wash your hands immediately following contact. You will be using *HOT* water. Use clamps to secure your filter flask to avoid tipping and unnecessary exposure to hot liquids or the acetanilide. Clamps may also be necessary to prevent your flask from tipping over while it is being chilled in the ice-water bath.

Following her analysis of the original lab instructions, Stefi revises the original instructions (see Case Document 10-1b).

CASE DOCUMENT 10-1B

Recrystallization

Step-by-step instructions for carefully and correctly performing Recrystallization.

Recrystallization is a technique used to separate and purify organic[1] compounds from liquid to solid matter.

Before starting this experiment, think safety! These chemicals could be hazardous to your skin and eyes.

For Safety:
- Keep your safety goggles on *at all times*.
- Tie back long hair.
- Wear closed-toe shoes.
- Wear gloves if needed.
- Do not consume any food, drinks, or chemicals during lab.
- Do not wear loose clothing.

Equipment Required:
Check off items ☑ as you collect these before you begin.

☐ 250-mL Beaker	☐ Crucible Tongs
☐ 125-mL Erlenmeyer Flask	☐ Filter Flask
☐ Stirring Rod	☐ Buchner Funnel
☐ Boiling Chip	☐ Black Tube
☐ Steam Bath	☐ Filter Paper
☐ Clamp	☐ Watch Glass
☐ Rubber FilterVac	

Chemicals used:

☐ Water
☐ Acetanilide[2]

---

[1] Organic—relating to chemical compounds containing carbon, especially hydrocarbons.
[2] Acetanilide—a white, crystalline, odorless, organic powder, C_8H_9NO, produced by the action of glacial acetic acid on aniline, used chiefly in organic synthesis and formerly in the treatment of fever and headache.

continued

Conducting the Experiment

This experiment requires five steps:

1. Dissolving the compound,
2. Using the balance,
3. Setting up the hot vacuum filtration apparatus,
4. Recrystallizing the acetanilide, and,
5. Cleaning up following the procedure

1. Dissolving the compound

1. Using a graduated cylinder, measure 75 mL of water and add it to a 250 mL beaker.
2. Set the beaker on the cylindrical steam bath on your laboratory desk and turn the **red** knob at the side of your desk to begin heating.
3. While your water is heating, use the balance to weigh approximately 1.5 g of impure acetanilide (Impure acetanilide can be found in a bottle at the front counter). Use a watch glass to accurately weigh the impure acetanilide.

2. Using the balance

1. Obtain a watch glass from your instructor and set it on the balance. Figure 1 is an example of a watch glass.

2. Tare[3] the balance by pushing the "tare" button so that the watch glass has a mass of 0.0 grams.

Figure 1-Watch Glass

3. Then using a spatula, carefully add impure acetanilide onto the watch glass until the balance reads approximately 1.5 grams. Then add the impure acetanilide to the 125-mL Erlenmeyer flask.

4. Break up the clumps of acetanilide with a stirring rod and add a black boiling chip (found at the front counter) to the flask.

5. Add approximately 25 mL of the heated water from the beaker into the flask containing the impure acetanilide.

6. Using crucible[4] tongs, swirl the flask occasionally to prevent clumping. Crucible tongs will protect you from burning your hands. Never pick up hot objects with your hands.

---

[3] Tare—to obtain the weight of a container or wrapper that is deducted from the gross weight to obtain net weight.

[4] Crucible—metal or refractory material employed for heating substances to high temperatures.

7. If all the acetanilide has not dissolved by this step, add 1-2 mL portions of hot water until it dissolves.

8. While the acetanilide is dissolving, set up the hot vacuum filtration apparatus.

3. Setting up the hot vacuum filtration apparatus

1. Obtain a Buchner funnel and a filter flask from your instructor. Figure 2 is an example of how your funnel may look, and Figure 3 is an example of a filter flask.

Figure 2-Buchner funnel

2. Obtain a clamp from your lab drawer and securely clamp the filter flask to the metal frame connected to your desk.

3. Obtain a rubber FilterVac from your lab drawer and place it on top of your Filter flask. Figure 4 is an example of what your FilterVac may look like. Then place the Buchner funnel on top of the FilterVac.

4. Obtain a black long tube from your lower lab drawer. Attach one side of the heavy-walled tube to the side-arm of your flask and the other side to the water aspirator. Figure 5 is a representation of how your entire set-up should look.

Figure 3-Filter flask

5. Obtain a small filter paper and neatly fit it into the Buchner funnel so that it covers all the holes at the bottom of the funnel. Wet the filter paper with 1-2 drops of distilled water. Then turn the water aspirator (green knob) on full blast by turning it all the way to the left. The suction pressure from the water aspirator should suck the filter paper to the bottom of the funnel.

Figure 4-FilterVac

6. At this time, slowly cool the hot solution in the flask by turning down the red knob every few minutes.

7. If oil droplets form, turn up the red knob and heat the solution until the oil dissolves. Then, add about 5 mL of water and allow the solution to cool again slowly. If oil droplets appear again, repeat this step.

Figure 5-Hot Vacuum Filtration Set-up

continued

8. When white clumps begin forming in the flask (sign of crystallization), the solution is ready to be filtered through the Buchner funnel.

4. Recrystallizing the acetanilide

1. With the water aspirator on full blast, vacuum filter the solution by slowing pouring the contents of the flask into the Buchner funnel.

2. Once all your contents are poured, rinse the flask with hot water and pour it into the funnel again. This filtration should produce white crystals that look similar to baby powder.

3. Pour 5 mL of ice cold water into the funnel to wash the crystals formed.

4. Use a spatula to remove the boiling chip and press on the crystals to remove water.

Note: Do NOT turn off the water aspirator until you are ready for to clean up!!!

5. After the crystals have dried, carefully dump and wrap the crystals in a 15-cm filter paper. Tape and label the filter paper with your name and section number. Store it in your lab section drawer for next week. By this time, the crystals will be fully dry.

5. Cleaning up following the procedure

1. Do not turn off the water aspirator until the black tube is disconnected from the sidearm of the flask. If water is turned off before the tube is disconnected, water may back up into the freshly cleaned solution and you will have to start over.

2. Pour the filtrate[5] in the filter flask into the waste bottle in the hood at the end of the experiment.

3. Dispose of the small filter paper that was used to filter the solution into the waste container.

4. Carefully take apart the vacuum filtration set-up and wash the equipment thoroughly with acetone in the sink. Return all equipment used to your instructor.

---

[5] Filtrate—liquid that has been passed through a filter.

Case 10-2: Instructional Report

Texas A&M University hosts a camp for first-year students during the summer prior to the beginning of the fall term. Students who work for "Fish Camp" each have responsibilities. One of the student leaders prepares a two-page set of instructions for workers who will be developing the discussion group folders. These folders will be given to each student during Fish Camp.

   This instructional report (see Case Document 10-2) is designed to be read quickly and for reference before and during the preparation of the folders. Document design is critical to ensure that all material is included.

CASE DOCUMENT 10-2

Fish Camp Mission Statement

Fish Camp believes all members of the organization, through their actions, shoulder the responsibility to aid in the freshmen's transition from high school to Texas A&M in an unconditionally accepting environment. To that end we strive to welcome freshmen into the Aggie Family by creating a support system that allows them to build relationships and share in the Aggie Spirit.

Purpose

Creating discussion group (DG) folders fulfills the Fish Camp Mission Statement above. All the 10 to 15 freshmen within each DG will be provided a folder of information to serve as valuable reference material as they begin their first semester at A&M.

IMPORTANT NOTES

1. These folders must be ENTIRELY finished before you come to College Station two days before camp. They will be turned into your co-chairs for inspection on the first day of your two days before camp. Session dates are as follows:

      Session A: August 3-6 (Two days before, starts August 1)
      Session B: August 6-9 (Two days before, starts August 4)
      Session C: August 9-12 (Two days before, starts August 7)
      Session D: August 12-15 (Two days before, starts August 10)
      Session E: August 15-18 (Two days before, starts August 13)
      Session F: August 18-21 (Two days before, starts August 16)

2. OVERPLAN, OVERPLAN, OVERPLAN!!! Though a DG is usually made up of 10-15 freshmen, you DO NOT want to risk running short on folders. Make 15-20 plus one for you and your partner so that you will be able to go through it with them during the final DG time.

continued

Steps for Creating Folders

1. Purchase 15-20 folders in your camp color (green, blue, red, aqua, yellow, or purple). Make sure the folders have
   - Pockets (front and back)
   - Brads

2. From your Fish Camp Binder, remove each of the required folder pages located behind the *DG Folder Templates* tab:
   - Aggie Terminology (2 pages)
   - "Before I came to college, I wish I had known . . ." (1 page)
   - What Should I Do the First Week of School? (1 page)
   - College is . . . (1 page)
   - Famous last words (1 page)
   - Got a Lil Story for Ya Ags (4 pages)
   - Silver Taps Letter (1 page)
   - Fightin' Texas Aggie Songs (1 page)
   - Fightin' Texas Aggie Yells (1 page)
   - "The Last Corps Trip" (1 page)
   - Local Restaurants (1 page)
   - Friends in my Major (1 page)
   - Roll Call for the Absent (1 page)
   - Study Suggestions (1 page)
   - Useful Phone Numbers (1 page)
   - Good Ag Consulting (1 page)
   - Fish Camp Friends (1 page)

3. Personalize! You will want to add other pages to be put into the folder with those above. You and your partner can decide on any additions you want to create. Options include, but are not limited to, the following:
   - Letter to your freshmen from you and your partner*
   - Information page about both you and your partner. The information on this page can include basics like hometown, birthday, and contact information (cell phone, email, etc.) and other facts like favorites, major, and class year.*
   - All Fish Camp Hump It
   - Your Individual Camp Hump It
   - Aggie Traditions*
   - Interesting Facts about A&M*

- Contact information for all counselors in your camp
- Future Events and Important Camp Dates*
- Anything you can think up that would help your fish!!!

4. Go to the Texas A&M website, www.tamu.edu, and print off the most recent bus routes and campus map.

5. Make 15-20 copies of each of the pages you plan to include in your folders, the required pages and those that you add beyond them. Make sure to have the copy machine punch holes in all of these so you won't have to do it by hand!

6. Separate out the pages into the individual folders so that each folder has one copy of each page.

7. Place the pages in any order you find to be most logical and effective for your freshmen.

8. Put all of the pages into the brads of the folders.

9. Decorate the front of each folder. You can decorate them to correspond to A&M, your DG, your camp, etc.

10. At camp, save these to give to your freshmen until the last DG time (DG #10). Go through the folders page by page with them so they understand everything inside and will be able to use them when they get back to campus.

* See examples of these pages following the instructions.

Case 10-3: Instructional Letter

Jonathan Varner, president of a professional organization, writes the incoming VP to explain how elections for new officers should be conducted.

The letter can be used as a reference by Dr. Dawson as she plans and executes the elections (see Case Document 10-3).

CASE DOCUMENT 10-3

May 12, 2009

Dr. Gabrielle Dawson
Department of Geography
San Diego State University
San Diego, CA

Dear Gabrielle,

As we discussed at AAGG in April, the VP of AAGG is responsible for conducting elections. From my experience in conducting the last election, I recommend that you begin this process immediately. The more persistent you are, the more efficient the process. Do as much as you can before faculty leave campus for the summer.

Time Table

In general, the election process begins during the late spring early summer. Ballots are developed and mailed by mid-September. Ballots should be returned and tabulated by mid-January and the results reported to the vice president. As vice president, you will inform me and then inform each person whose name appeared on the ballot about the results of the election.

Election Procedures

The following procedures should help you conduct the elections. Ultimately, when the AAGG procedures manual is complete, these will appear in the manual. Until that time, however, each president will be responsible for informing the vice-president of election procedures.

Materials Needed

- Election File—contains ballots of previous elections and names of nominating committees
- AAGG Directory—names, phone numbers, and email addresses of all members

Gabrielle Lawson   -2-   May 20, 2009

- Annual Meeting Agendas—protocols for announcing newly-elected officers

Step 1: Creating a Nominating Committee

1. At the annual meeting in April, the president asks the general membership to consider individuals who should be asked to run for the office of Vice-President and Members-At-Large. Members are invited to send the names of individuals to the President.

2. The president also organizes a nominating committee. At AAGG, I asked three individuals—Steve Jones, Pam Souther, and Casey Morgan—to serve as the nominating committee. All agreed to serve. Casey Morgan agreed to chair the committee.

   Note: Former officers of the organization are good choices for the nominating committee. They know what is involved in executing the duties of each office. I attempted to select a nominating committee of individuals from different regions in the US. With that point in mind, you could select four members of the committee, but more than four makes the committee unwieldy.

3. The nominating committee must recommend a minimum of six nominees for three member-at-large positions. Eight nominees will be fine, too. Three Vice-President nominees should be chosen. The chair of the nominating committee should ask each candidate for a one-paragraph (150-word) biographical profile.

Step 2: Selecting Nominees for Offices

1. In selecting candidates, you will want to consider several factors:

   - Interest in AAGG and its Activities. Look for people who have shown interest in the organization: attendance at regional and national meetings, people who engage in conversation on the listserv, people who make solid suggestions.

   - Interest in Geography and/or Geoscience. AAGG needs individuals who are effective spokespersons for both as fields of teaching and research: i.e., individuals who are effective and prolific researchers; people who are in charge of programs; people who are regular presenters at meetings.

   - Record of Dependability. VERY IMPORTANT! Try to determine how reliable an individual is. Stay in touch with the nominating committee.

continued

Gabrielle Lawson   -3-   May 20, 2009

> Once you get a list of individuals you are considering, please post the list on the Executive Committee listserv. If any of the potential nominees has a track record of non-performance, this is the time to determine that! Many people are "all talk," but slow on performance.

Note: Choose the VP very carefully. Sherry, this is the person who will succeed you as president of AAGG. Because the president and vice-president have so much responsibility and because they will need to work as a team, be sure you choose someone with whom you can work and someone who will continue to strengthen the organization. AAGG has very strong individuals in its thirty-year history. Each group of officers must be committed to developing AAGG further.

Step 3: Developing the Ballot

1. Be sure to let Casey Morgan know when you want the final list of names. I would suggest that you ask for the list by the second week in September.

2. Contact each individual whose name was submitted by the nominating committee. Be sure that each person has agreed to be nominated and understands what is involved.

3. Develop the ballot and a letter that will be sent along with the ballot.

4. Send the ballot and the letter to Dan Jameson. He will make copies. Try to get this material sent to Dan no later than the third week in September.

Step 4: Monitoring the Election Process

1. Once he has the materials, Dan will duplicate and mail the ballots to the membership. He knows the procedure: each ballot has a self-addressed, stamped return envelope to ensure better response.

2. Dan will want all ballots returned by early January. He will count the ballots and report the results to you. As soon as you have the results, please call—rather than email—each candidate and report the results.

Step 5: Preparing for the Annual Meeting

1. Plan to introduce each of the officers at the meeting. After my farewell speech, I will hand the reins of the organization to you.

2. To help prepare for the meeting, discuss your agenda as president with the incoming VP. I would also suggest that you plan an informal gathering of the all the new officers BEFORE the Executive Committee meeting. At the EC, as you are aware, we always have several hours of business to conduct. Meeting with the incoming officers will give you planning time with them.

Gabrielle Lawson   -4-   May 20, 2009

3. Be prepared to tell the general membership at the annual meeting your goals for the next two years. The newly-elected VP and members-at-large should be allotted time to express their concerns. Usually we allot fifteen minutes for this segment of the annual meeting.

Final Thoughts

The election process has been developed to attempt to involve a variety of individuals in the election process. The nominating committee should seek involvement of members in the organization who want to become more involved in AAGG. In no sense does the election process seek to exclude individuals other than those who are not interested in Geography and/or Geoscience and the development of AAGG as an organization.

As you work with the elections, keep notes on ways that the EC can improve the election process. Then add these to the agenda for the 2010 meeting.

As always, if you have any questions, please call me.

Sincerely,

Jonathan

ONLINE INSTRUCTIONS

Online instructions need to follow the same readability considerations as those used in letters, reports, and stand-alone instructions. Otherwise, the instructions will create confusion for many users.

Case 10-4

A university explained how to download class rosters from the faculty e-mail system and insert these into an Excel spreadsheet (see Case Document 10-4a). Note how the application of principles discussed in this chapter improves the instructions (see Case Document 10-4b). The revision supplanted the original, which diminished the number of calls to the computing help desk from faculty who were confused by the original instructions:

CASE DOCUMENT 10-4A

Original Online Instructions

○ **How exactly do I get my roster from NEO, put it into an Excel spreadsheet and make a comma separated value (csv) file for uploading?**

1. Log into your neo account, go to the **Class Roster** tool and go to the appropriate semester. Click on **Download Class Roster** and you'll see your class roster as a comma separated value (csv) file. Copy and paste this file into a blank excel spreadsheet and save. There's no way right now to actually download it.

2. To get rid of the quotes, go to **Edit**, then **Replace**. You want to find every " and replace it with a blank, so in the **Find what** box, type ", and put nothing into the **Replace with** box. Click on **Replace All**, and the quotes disappear.

3. Under **File**, select **Save As** option, and save the file as **Formatted Text (space delimited)(*.prn)**. Choose **OK** and **Yes** to the questions that pop up. Close the file and answer **no** to the popup box. You don't want to save the changes.

4. Open the **.prn** file. The **Text Import Wizard** will pop up. Leave the file type as **delimited** and click next. Change the delimiter from **tab** to **comma** and click **next**. Holding the ctrl key down, click on the last four columns, and choose **Do not import column (skip)**, then choose **Finish**.

5. Under **File**, select the **Save As** option. Change the file name to something that does not include the .prn, and save the file as **CSV (Comma delimited) (.csv)**. Always answer **yes** to the question, "Do you want to keep the workbook in this format?" and when you close the file, answer **no** to "Do you want to save the changes?". Voila! This is the file the administrator needs.

6. To upload your students into your course, you only need the UIN numbers as a csv file. So, just delete the name columns and any rows above your data, and save. Always answer **yes** to the question, "Do you want to

keep the workbook in this format?" and when you close the file, answer
no to "Do you want to save the changes?". Upload your file according to
the directions in CPR. [top]

CASE DOCUMENT 10-4B

Revised Online Instructions

How to Download Your Roster

1. Click on **download class roster**. Note that your class roster now appears as a comma separated value (CSV) file.

2. Without closing the roster on Neo, create an Excel spreadsheet.

3. Go back to your roster. Copy the names.

4. Paste the roster into the Excel spreadsheet just as you copied it.

Get rid of the quotes (" ").

1. Go to **Edit** on the toolbar, then to **Replace**.
   You want to find every " " and replace it with a blank.

2. In the **Find what** box, type " " , and put nothing into the **Replace with** box.

3. Click on **Replace All**, and the quotes disappear.

Prepare to Format the Information in the Excel Spreadsheet.

1. Under **File**, select **Save As** option, and save the file as **Formatted Text (space delimited) (*prn)**.

2. Choose **OK** and then **Yes** to the questions that pop up.

3. Close the file and answer **no** to the popup box.

4. Open the .prn file. The **Text Import Wizard** will pop up.

Select the Correct Boxes on the Wizard.

1. Leave the file type as **delimited**. Then click **next**.

2. Change the delimiter from **tab** to **comma**. Then click **next**. You will see the opening rows of your roster appear in neat columns.

3. Under **File**, select the **Save As** option.

4. Save the file as an Excel file. Be sure to save with a name descriptive of the contents.

With your file in an Excel spreadsheet, you can now create a grade or attendance sheet.

Reflections on Developing Effective Instructions

Case 10-5

Writing instructions for a process familiar to you presents the greatest challenge, because you often have difficulty looking at the process from the perspective of a person who does not know how to perform it. Assume that you serve as a community volunteer with your university's student center. Your task: you have to explain to a group of senior citizens how to use MySpace. Write a set of instructions for them. What specific considerations in format will these readers require?

As you think about that task, examine the following instructions for Facebook (Case Document 10-5). Do you think they are effective? How could you improve them? What ideas could be replicated for your instructions for using MySpace (or a similar social networking site)?

Your instructions will be printed in paper copies and made available to every senior citizen at the local community center who wants a copy.

Pre-writing Questions for Facebook Instructions

This is a first draft of instructions for using the Facebook website. It shows the basic steps in signing up for a Facebook page and accessing the basic features. It is tailored for an adult audience, which ordinarily has had trouble with the website in the past.

• **Who are your readers?**
Middle-aged or senior citizens would be my target audience. Younger users generally learn how to use websites such as Facebook and MySpace naturally.

• **What is your reader profile? Background, attitude toward following instructions?**
Keeping in touch with younger generations encourages adults to use websites such as Facebook. However, technology can sometimes become a hassle to maintain or to operate. The instructions have to be clear, specific, and inviting to be successful.

• **How much do your readers know about the subject?**
The older readers will know less about the subject because the subject is relatively new. Hopefully, the instructions will help reduce the uncertainty.

• **Will you have to define any terms that your readers may not understand?**
There could possibly be some technical terms that need defining. Also, slang terms that are incorporated into the everyday use of the website.

• **What do you want your readers to be able to do after reading the instructions or procedures?**

The ultimate goal is to have the readers operating and using Facebook without having to ask fundamental questions on how to operate the personalized site.

• **What is the situation that led to the need for these instructions?**

A technology gap between generations makes it sometimes difficult for an adult user to keep in touch with their relatives. Facebook allows users of all ages to gather in a social network. These instructions will make it possible for adults to communicate with their younger relatives through the Internet.

• **How will your readers use these instructions? Will they need to be read every time, or will they be used only for reference?**

These instructions should be seldom read if the reader frequently uses the website. Most of the difficult things when first getting started eventually become habits.

• **What kinds of pictorials—if needed—will you use?**

Screen shots could be used. Diagrams for buttons or options will help the reader "see what's going on".

• **What kinds of formatting and page design strategies will you use to make the instructions easy to read?**

Bullets will be used to mark lists of important information. Notes or tips can be used during important sections.

• **What content segments will you include?**

The instructions will include segments on signing up, navigation, visiting other people's pages, and options and uses.

CASE DOCUMENT 10-5

Obtaining and Using a Facebook Account

Signing up

The first step to becoming a Facebook user is signing up for an account. Signing up for an account requires personal information, an email account, and a password. Have these things prepared before starting.

Steps:

1. Get on a web browser and visit www.Facebook.com.
2. Locate the section under the label "Sign Up", and enter your personal information. This will include your name, email, password, gender, and birthday. These are required for proper identification and access to the site.

continued

3. Click the sign up button.
4. From this point, a security check will be done to filter out hackers trying to make fake accounts. All that is required is to type in scrambled letters to confirm you are a normal user. Then proceed to the next page.
5. An email will be sent to your email account. Check your email account and click the link provided in an email labeled "Facebook Registration Confirmation". This makes your account active.
6. You will now be required to login every time you want to browse Facebook.

To log in, just key in your email and password.

7. Logging in prevents unwanted users from accessing the website. It also helps keep track of your activities and interests while you are online.

Navigating

Navigating Facebook can be broken into two sections. Browsing your own page often lets you change or modify your options, pictures, or other information. The second part of navigating Facebook is browsing friends' pages, which can be an enjoyable experience. This allows friends to communicate without actually being in contact with each other.

Browsing your own page
After logging into Facebook successfully, you will arrive at your unique home page. At the top of the homepage is the navigation bar.

This bar is useful for navigating Facebook. At any time, it is possible to return to the home page by clicking "home" on the toolbar. This will return to the same page you start on when logging in. The home page is useful for viewing activities friends have recently done to you. It also alerts you to new messages or notifications.

The profile tab allows you to see how your Facebook is presented to your friends. If you click on the profile tab a page will load with the following:

• A wall where others can post comments
• A profile picture, or a space to upload a profile picture

- Information
- Links to friends (Note: it is necessary to add friends first for this to show up.)
- Photos
- A status bar
- Advertisements

Most of these attributes will show up blank when a profile is first created. All of these attributes can be changed or hidden.

Visiting Other People's Pages
To visit a friend's page, you generally have to find and add a friend. To find a friend do the following:

1. Type the name of the friend you want to add in the search box. Then click the magnifying glass button to the side.

This will generate a list of people you may be looking for.

2. Find the appropriate one and click "add friend" by their name. This will give them the option of accepting the add or not.

Once a friend has been added, you can visit their profile. This is done by clicking on their name when it appears on your profile or homepage. It can also be done by typing their name in the search box and clicking on the appropriate profile.

Options and Uses

Facebook has many uses. Some of these are as follows:

- Adding applications
- Joining groups
- Uploading pictures
- Messaging

Adding applications and joining groups are done in a similar manner to finding friends. These add flavor to your Facebook page and are often very entertaining. Uploading pictures allows you to have the equivalent of a public album for all your friends to see. You can also be selective of which friends see which album. Messaging is similar to emailing your friends. Messages are accessed through the browsing toolbar at the top of every page.

CHECKLIST FOR DEVELOPING INSTRUCTIONS/PROCEDURES ☑

Because instructions require careful analysis of readers from many perspectives—the context in which the instructions will be read and used—following a checklist can be helpful in ensuring that you have considered critical issues needed for the instructions:

☐ Who are your readers? Describe them in terms of their knowledge of the subject: educational level, technical level, responsibilities in the organization.

☐ What do you want them to be able to do as a result of these instructions/procedures?

☐ What is the situation that has led to the need for these instructions/procedures to be written?

☐ How will these instructions/procedures be used? Will readers need to read all of them before they begin the task? In what context will readers be using these instructions?

☐ What problems could readers encounter in attempting to use these instructions/procedures?

☐ What types of problems in safety and/or quality control do you need to emphasize? What warnings or notes will you need to include?

☐ What topics do you want to be sure to include/exclude?

☐ What format will you use? Online, online to be printed, paper, manual, poster?

☐ Given the context in which the instructions/procedures will be read, what formatting strategies do you need to use to enhance accessibility?

☐ What types of visuals will you need to include?

☐ What is the basic outline of your instructions? Does this outline meet the needs of your readers? Will it achieve your purpose?

EXERCISES

1. Compile a list of the kinds of instructions a professional in your major field of study might have to write. Who would be your audiences? What would be the challenges involved in writing each kind of instructions? What cautions and warnings would be required? What kinds of illustrations would be necessary?
2. You are employed by a small manufacturer of all-organic ready-to-eat breakfast cereals. The company would like to develop its sales overseas, especially in Africa. Because ready-to-eat cereals would be relatively new to the majority of the population in Africa, your package will include instructions on how to prepare and eat a serving of cereal. Compose step-by-step instructions, including rough illustrations, to fit on the side of the package.
3. Examine the following real instructions (Figure 10-1). If you were the author and were given 15 more minutes to make the instructions more effective, what changes would you make?
4. Find a set of instructions you have attempted to use: for example, instructions for a lab experiment, a product you have bought and had to assemble and then use, or instructions for performing some online task, such as registering a product or determining if your product is still under warranty. Write a memo to your instructor explaining the deficiencies in the original instructions. Then, revise the instructions to remove the deficiencies you perceive. Be prepared to show both the original set of instructions and your revision to your class.

WHAT TO DO IN CASE OF FIRE

The interior local alarm system installed in this building is **NOT** connected with the Municipal Fire De - partment. It is for evacuation purposes only.   **IN CASE OF FIRE** pull the interior local alarm station, following the instructions on the face of the alarm box; then, pro - ceed at once to call the Fire Department. Familiarize yourself with the location of the Municipal Fire Alarm Box **NOW**   The nearest Municipal Fire Alarm Box is located at   or telephone   **911**

Remember this interior Alarm System   **DOES NOT** call the Municipal Fire Department.

FIGURE 10-1 Document for Exercise 3

Oral Reports

Your ability to present oral presentations and oral reports can be as critical to your success as your ability to write reports. In today's work environment, knowing how to speak effectively and use presentation slides is a valuable asset, whether you are in an academic or in a non-academic work environment. In applying for a job or admission to a graduate program, you may be asked to give an oral presentation on a specific topic or perhaps on a research project you have conducted. You may be asked to prepare a written document of an oral presentation you have given. Or, you may be asked to make an oral presentation of a written document. Whatever the venue, you will benefit from knowing and then practicing basic strategies of developing effective oral presentations.

Quick Tips

- In the introduction, interest the audience in the subject, establish your authority to speak on the subject, and enumerate the key points you will cover (e.g., "I will cover the following five points.").
- In the discussion section, make it easy for your audience to pay attention and keep track of where you are in your presentation by numbering each point as you cover it (e.g., "Now let's proceed to my second point.").
- In the conclusion, signal to the audience that you are about to conclude so that they will pay extra attention. Audiences know that you will now summarize what you've said, and they can thus catch anything they missed earlier. Once you've said "in conclusion," you have about a minute before you must stop talking. Audiences grow hostile to speakers who promise to stop but then don't. In the remaining minute of your presentation, fix in the audience's mind the one or two things that you want them to remember or take away from your presentation.
- Keep your presentation as short as possible. Nobody wants to listen to a long presentation.

Understanding the Speaking-Writing Relationship

Effective oral and written presentations share the following requirements:

- Analyze your audience.
- Understand and articulate your purpose clearly.
- Develop sufficient and appropriate supporting material.
- Understand the context in which your presentation will be received.
- Organize the material so that it is easy for the audience to follow.
- Choose a speaking style—level of language, approach to the subject, and tone—suitable to your role as well as your audience and purpose.
- Select the presentation format that will enhance your audience's understanding of your message.

Analyzing the Audience

Analyzing your listening audience follows the same principles discussed in Chapter 2:

- How much does my audience know about the subject?
- How much do they know about me?
- What do they expect from me?
- How interested will they be in what I say?
- What is their attitude toward me?
- What is their attitude toward my subject?
- What is their age group?
- What positions do they occupy in the organization?
- What is their educational background?
- What is their cultural/ethnic background?
- What is their economic background?
- What are their political and religious views?
- What kinds of biases will they likely have toward me and my topic?

To be an effective speaker, you must know your audience, establish an effective relationship between you and them by being sincere and knowledgeable about the subject, and then conform to their expectations about dress, demeanor, choice of language, and attitude toward them and the topic. When you speak to people from other countries, you should plan to do research on the culture of that country. Be aware that hand gestures you use routinely may have different meanings in other cultures. Also, the clothing you choose to wear should be selected with the culture of the audience in mind: you want your audience to pay attention to what you are saying instead of what you are wearing.

DETERMINING THE GOAL OF YOUR PRESENTATION

Oral presentations, like written presentations, must be designed for a specific purpose. By knowing what they will be hearing from the beginning of the presentation, audiences can understand the reason for the content. State your goal in one sentence, as you begin to plan. Announce your purpose early in the presentation to prepare your audience for the main ideas to come.

Remember that oral presentations, like written presentations, can enhance your reputation within an organization. Therefore, consider every speaking opportunity an opportunity to sell not only your ideas but also your competence and your value to the organization.

CHOOSING AND SHAPING CONTENT

Preparing the oral presentation often requires careful research.

- Determine what information you will need.
- Choose information that will appeal to your audience—particularly their attitudes, interests, and dispositions toward the topic.
- Consider a variety of information types: statistics, testimony, cases, illustrations, history, and particularly narratives that help convey the goal you have for your presentation. Be sure that every item you include pertains to the goal of your presentation.

ANALYZING THE CONTEXT

Analysis of context is often difficult to separate from analysis of audience: In analyzing context, know why your presentation is required.

- What is the broader concern underlying the need for the presentation?
- What primary issues underlie the presentation?
- How does your presentation relate to these issues?
- What will be happening in the organization when you make your presentation?
- How does your presentation fit into the organizational situation?
- If you are one of several speakers, what kinds of presentations will the other speakers be making?
- In what surroundings will you be making the presentation?

CHOOSING THE ORGANIZATION

Like written communications, oral presentations must be organized with your audience's needs and perspective in mind.

- Is your audience interested in what you will say?

- What are the main ideas you want to convey?
- Based on your purpose and the needs and expectations of the audience, in what order should you present these ideas?

Answers to these questions will help you decide how to go about organizing your presentation. Generally, however, like the written presentation, oral presentations have distinct parts—an introduction, a main body, and a conclusion. The introduction should clearly tell the audience what the presentation will cover so that the audience is prepared for what is to come. The body should develop each point stated in the introduction, and the conclusion should reiterate the ideas presented and reinforce the purpose of the presentation.

While you are doing your research and collecting content for your presentation, begin organizing your information. Divide your content into main categories of ideas:

I. Idea 1
II. Idea 2
III. Idea 3, etc.

Once you have the main content "chunks" or divisions, begin to subdivide each main idea. Order the subdivisions so that the information moves in a logical sequence:

I. Idea 1
    A, B, C . . .
II. Idea 2
    A, B, C . . .
III. Idea 3
    A, B, C . . .

Introduction: Be sure that you state your goal near the beginning. Even if you use some type of opening statement to interest your audience, state the goal of your presentation next. Then, state how you will proceed in your presentation: what main issues you will discuss. The main ideas should be announced and enumerated here.

Main Body: Here you must explain each of your key ideas in order. Also try to include at least one example or anecdote for each point in order to make your ideas more vivid and memorable. The easier you make it for your listeners to pay attention to you, the more they (and you) will profit from your presentation.

Conclusion: At a minimum, restate the main issues you want your audience to remember, but be concise. Nothing is worse than a conclusion that drags on and doesn't conclude. Tell your audience exactly what you want them to remember from your presentation. Try to find a concluding narrative or statement that will have an impact on your audience. The conclusion should leave the audience with a positive feeling about you and your ideas.

Choosing an Appropriate Speaking Style

How you sound when you speak is crucial. You may have effective content, ideas, accurate, and supporting statistics. However, how you speak your ideas can "make or break" the effectiveness of what you say. Avoid sounding patronizing, rude, overly solicitous, gushing, and insincere. Use a conversational style: short sentences, concrete language, speech that suggests to your audience that you are really talking with them. Remember that tone and degree of formality will be dictated by your organizational role and your relationship to your audience.

- Do they know you?
- Is your rank in the organization above or below them?
- Are you speaking to an audience of individuals from all levels within the organization?
- What demeanor, approach, and level of formality does the organization usually expect from those giving oral presentation?
- Is the audience composed of people who understand American English? How well do they understand American English?

If you are speaking before a group composed largely of people from another country, determine beforehand how fluent they are in American English. If they are not comfortable with American English, speak more slowly; avoid idiomatic expressions; choose concrete words; and speak in relatively short sentences. Limit each sentence to one idea.

Choosing Visuals to Enhance Your Purpose and Your Meaning

Because we live in a time when communication is visual and verbal, illustrations can make your ideas more persuasive and more professional. Many of the guidelines for using visuals in oral presentations mirror those for written documents: they need to fit the needs of the audience, they must be simple, and they must be clear and easy to understand.

Formal presentations should use PowerPoint or similar presentation software to help your listeners follow your ideas. PowerPoint allows you to give your listeners the outline of your presentation and insert pictures, graphs, tables, drawings, photographs, diagrams, and flow charts as well as sound and video. But because these will be seen while the audience is listening to you, be sure that all visuals are as simple and as easy to read as possible:

- Limit the information on any single slide (as in Figure 11-1).
- Use boldface type in a font size that can be easily read (as in Figure 11-2b or c).
- Avoid backgrounds as in Figure 11-2a that distract from the slide content.
- Limit the fonts you use to two per visual (as in Figure 11-2b).

- Avoid all caps.

- Use a type—size and font—that contrasts distinctly with the background (as in Figure 11-2b).

- Avoid visuals as in Figures 11-3 and 11-4 that are "busy" or complex.

- Avoid making your audience study your slides. Figure 11-4, for example, will require your audience to study the data. If they are busy trying to decipher your slides, they will not be listening to you. Bar graphs, circle graphs, simple diagrams, and pictures, are standard types of visuals. Whatever visual you decide to use, limit the aid to the concept, data, or point you are trying to make.

- Do not read your slides to your audience. Let them read each slide as you make it available, then begin to comment.

- Be sure that what the visual says is immediately evident, a requirement that Figures 11-3 and 11-4 fail to meet.

As shown in the example slides, PowerPoint allows you almost unrestricted use of color, but it's easy to use too much color or a slide background that is entirely too ornate. If you are preparing slides or transparencies for video conferencing, use the plain background and a color—such as yellow or light green—and black text. Color can enhance a visual, but it can also reduce the effectiveness of the message.

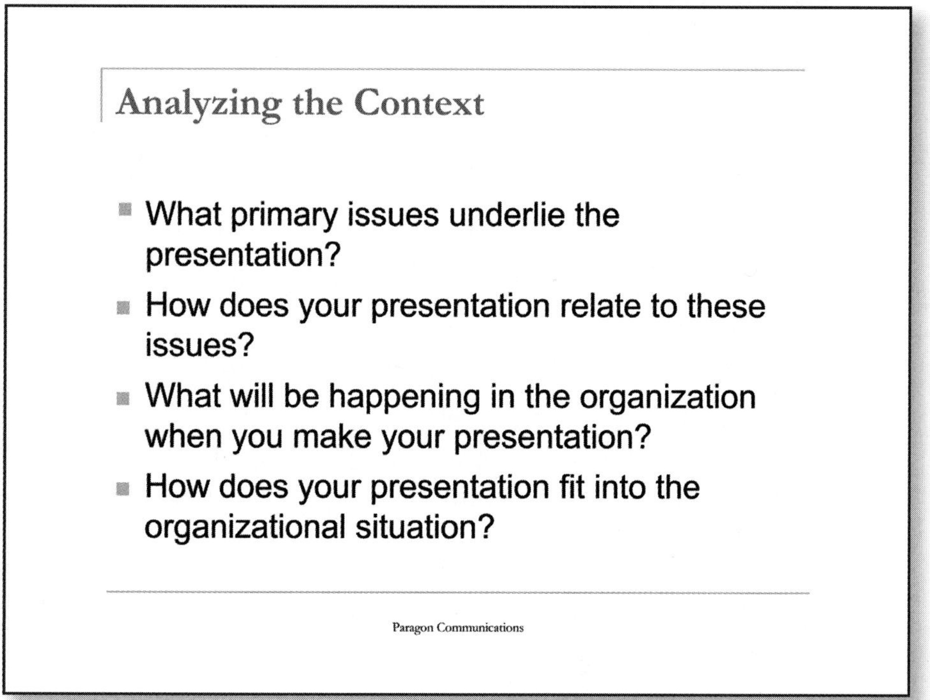

Analyzing the Context

- What primary issues underlie the presentation?
- How does your presentation relate to these issues?
- What will be happening in the organization when you make your presentation?
- How does your presentation fit into the organizational situation?

Paragon Communications

FIGURE 11-1a

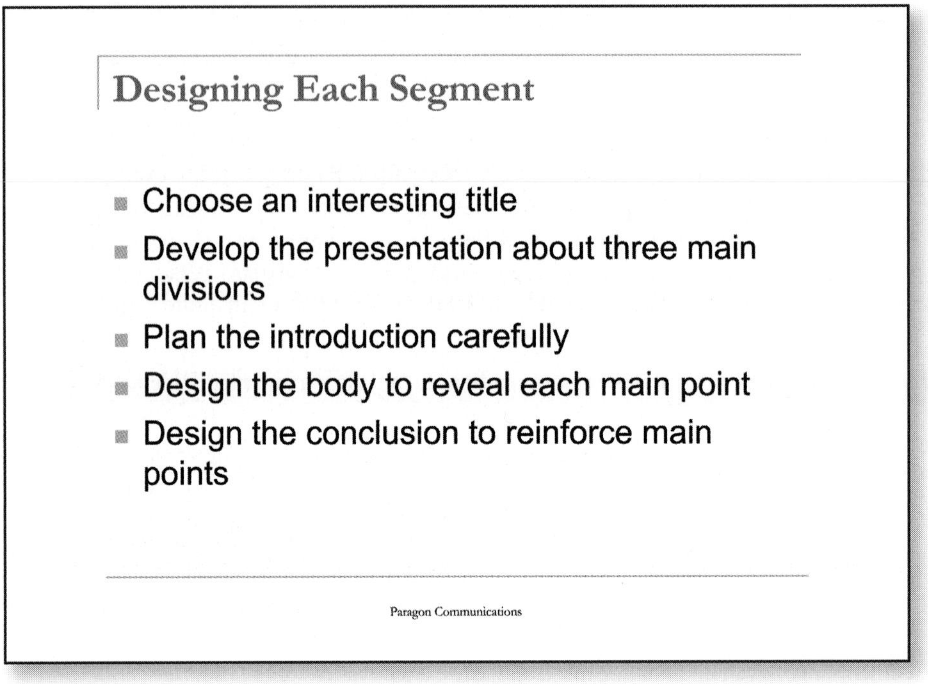

Designing Each Segment

- Choose an interesting title
- Develop the presentation about three main divisions
- Plan the introduction carefully
- Design the body to reveal each main point
- Design the conclusion to reinforce main points

Paragon Communications

FIGURE 11-1b

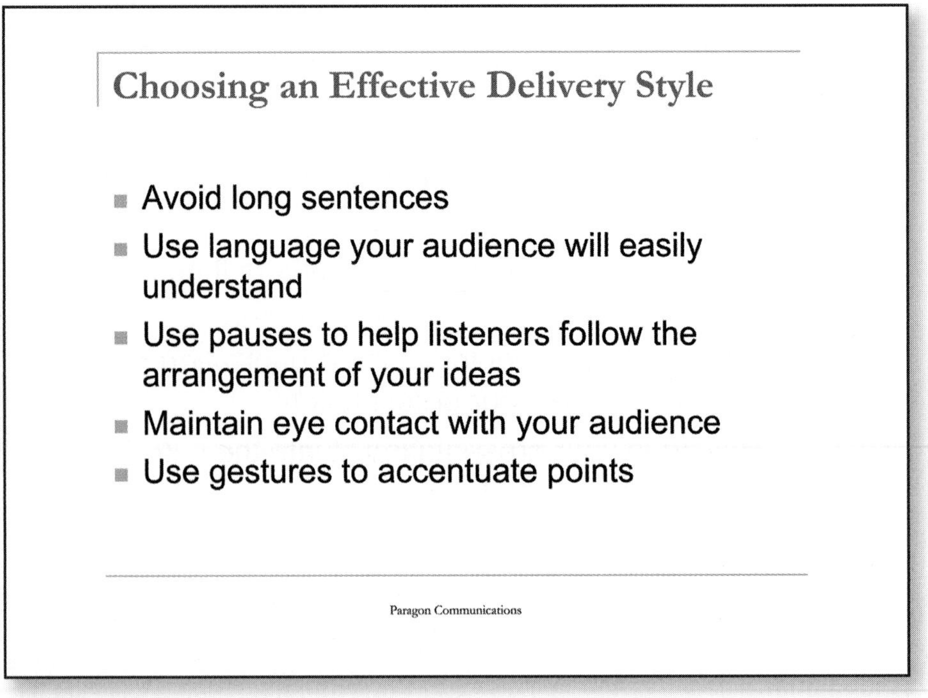

Choosing an Effective Delivery Style

- Avoid long sentences
- Use language your audience will easily understand
- Use pauses to help listeners follow the arrangement of your ideas
- Maintain eye contact with your audience
- Use gestures to accentuate points

Paragon Communications

FIGURE 11-1c

FIGURE 11-2a
Background is "busy," and type is not as sharp as that in 11-2c.

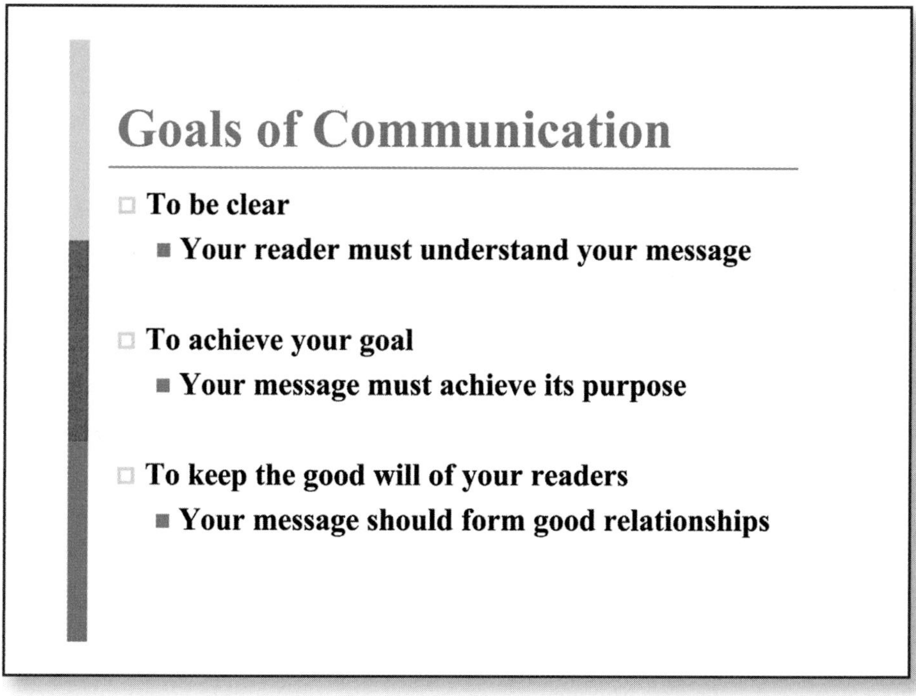

FIGURE 11-2b
Background makes content easy to read, but type could be changed to improve the sharpness of the image.

FIGURE 11-2c
Background is "busy," but the type is sharp and easy to read.

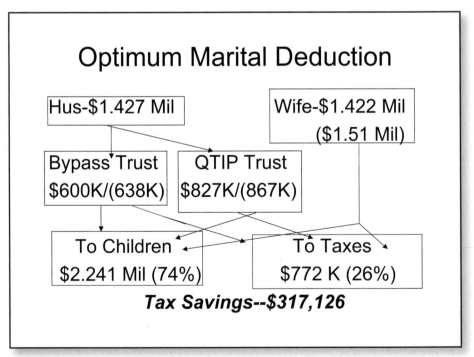

FIGURE 11-3
Slide with excessive content that is hard to follow.

HHSC LAR Summary Request

	GOAL	FY 2004-2005 Expend/Budgeted	FY 2006-2007 Base Request	FY 2006-2007 Exceptional Items	FY 2006-2007 Total Request
Goal A	HHS Enterprise Oversight and Policy	1,156,491,420	1,125,138,046	42,468,432	1,167,606,478
Goal B	Medicaid	23,471,668,180	23,332,396,442	8,422,660,942	31,755,057,384
Goal C	CHIP Services	992,065,427	928,111,026	497,720,007	1,425,831,033
Goal D	Encourage Self Sufficiency	934,980,796	916,383,704	14,941,490	931,325,194
Goal E	Program Support	80,253,130	76,907,054	3,806,910	80,713,964
Goal F	Information Technology Projects	143,844,506	60,721,687	73,692	60,795,379
	Total, Agency Request	$ 26,779,303,459	$ 26,439,657,959	$ 8,981,671,473	$ 35,421,329,432
Method of Financing:					
	General Revenue	$ 9,362,087,538	$ 9,758,885,600	$ 3,636,164,845	$ 13,395,050,445
	General Revenue - Dedicated	66,328,051	33,559,464	10,921,685	44,481,149
	Earned Federal Funds	7,278,695	6,956,612	264,586	7,221,198
	Federal Funds	16,601,429,277	15,945,771,302	5,331,446,091	21,277,217,393
	Other Funds	742,179,898	694,484,981	2,874,266	697,359,247
	Total, Method of Financing	$ 26,779,303,459	$ 26,439,657,959	$ 8,981,671,473	$ 35,421,329,432

Page 11

FIGURE 11-4

Table with excessive information.

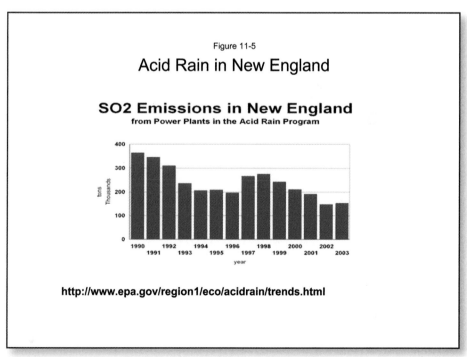

Figure 11-5

Acid Rain in New England

SO2 Emissions in New England
from Power Plants in the Acid Rain Program

http://www.epa.gov/region1/eco/acidrain/trends.html

FIGURE 11-5

Graph that has been copied and pasted from a website. Background and type produce a readable slide.

Figure 11-6
Fall Beauty in New England Depends on Control of Acid Rain

Source: http://www.epa.gov/region1/eco/acidrain/trends.html

FIGURE 11-6
Slide with a photo copied and pasted into a slide. Background and type produce a slide that is easy to read.

Figure 11-5 was generated with Excel and transported into PowerPoint. Note that both graphics use color effectively. Yet, they are simple, and the message each conveys is immediately accessible. The graph is clearly labeled: it has a title and the x- and y-axes are labeled, as are the quantities measured by the bars. The source of the graphic is also given. Figure 11-6 illustrates how you can select and paste photos into PowerPoint and include the source. Remember: any time you use any verbal, visual, or multimedia material that you did not create yourself, you must identify the source of the material.

Planning Your Presentation— Questions You Need to Ask

Analyze each point listed above by answering the following questions, just as you did in planning your written communication.

Audience.

- Who is my audience?
- What do I know about my audience—background, knowledge, position in the organization, attitudes toward me and my subject?

Purpose.

- What is my purpose in giving this oral presentation?
- Is there (should there be) a long-range purpose?
- What is the situation that led to this presentation?
- Given my audience's background and attitudes, do I need to reshape my purpose to make my presentation more acceptable to my audience?

Context.

- Where will I be speaking?
- What events will be transpiring in the organization (theirs or mine) that may affect how my audience perceives what I say?

Content.

- What ideas do I want to include and not include?
- Based on the audience and the context, what difficulties do I need to anticipate in choosing content?
- Can any ideas be misconstrued and prove harmful to me or my organization?

Graphics.

- What kinds of visuals will I need to enhance the ideas I will present?
- Where should I use these visuals in my presentation?

Style.

- What kind of tone do I want to use in addressing my audience?
- What kind of image—of myself and my organization—do I want to project?
- What level of language do I need to use, based on my audience's background and knowledge of my subject?
- What approach will my audience expect from me?
- How formal should I be?

SPEAKING TO MULTICULTURAL AUDIENCES

As organizations become more international, you may find that you need to give presentations to groups in other countries. Because you will want any audience to respond positively to your presentation, you will need to do research to understand how people from other cultures will likely interpret what you say, how you say it, how you dress, and how you act in your dealings with them. The visuals you use may also have to be changed, as symbols in one culture may have an entirely different meaning in another culture.

In your library and online, you will find a list of resources and books that can help you understand the perspectives of international audiences. As you consider your audience and the content you want to present to this audience, remember that your understanding of the cultural profile of your listeners is perhaps as important as your correctly discerning their knowledge of your topic and their interest level.

Designing Each Segment

The structure of the oral presentation is crucial for one main reason: once you have said something, the audience cannot "rehear" what you said. In reading, when you do not understand a sentence or paragraph, you can stop and reread the passage as many times as necessary. To help your audience follow what you say, you must design your presentation with your audience, particularly their listening limitations, in mind.

Audiences generally do not enjoy long presentations. Listening is difficult, and audiences will tire even when a presentation is utterly fascinating. For that reason, look for ways to keep your message as concise as possible. Don't omit information your audience needs, but look for ways to eliminate non-essential material. Again, without carefully analyzing your audience—their attitude toward the subject, their background knowledge of the topic, their perspective toward you—you cannot decide either content or arrangement of content.

Choose an interesting title. A good way to grab your audience's attention is to develop a title that, at the very least, reflects the content of your presentation but does so in an interesting way. The title of an oral presentation should prepare your audience for the content you will present.

Develop your presentation about three main divisions. Helping your audience follow your message requires that you build into your structure a certain amount of redundancy. That means that you reiterate main points. In the introduction, you "tell them what you are going to tell them"; in the main body, you "tell them"; and in the conclusion, you "tell them what you told them." This kind of deliberate repetition helps your audience follow and remember the main points you are making. (Again, readers can "reread" text, but listeners cannot "rehear" oral remarks.) To design your presentation with planned repetition, you must clearly know your purpose and what you want your audience to know.

Plan the introduction carefully. During the introduction you focus your audience's attention on your theme and the way you plan to present the theme. Unless the introduction is effective and interests the audience, you will have difficulty keeping your audience's attention. The effective introduction thus tells your audience how to listen, what to expect, and the path you will follow in presenting your message. You may also wish to introduce your topic with an attention-getting device: a startling fact, a relevant anecdote, a rhetorical question, or a statement designed to arouse your audience's interest. Again, the device you choose will depend on the audience, the occasion, the purpose of the presentation.

Or, if your audience is unreceptive or unfamiliar with the subject, you may want to include background material to help them grasp and process your main points:

1. Acknowledge that you perceive the problem that your audience has with you or your topic.

2. Establish a common ground with the audience—your points of agreement.

3. Attempt to refute (if you can do so efficiently) erroneous assumptions that you believe the audience may have about you or the subject.

4. Ask the audience to allow you the opportunity to present your information as objectively as possible.

Design the body. In the introduction you state the main issues or topics you plan to present. Thus, in designing the body of the presentation, you develop what you want to say about each of these main points or ideas. You may want to present your ideas in a chronological sequence, a logical sequence, or a simple topical sequence. This method will help your audience follow your ideas if you are giving an informative speech, an analytical speech, or a persuasive speech. The important point, however, is that you need to demarcate and announce each point in the body as you come to it so that your audience knows when you have completed one point and begun another.

Design the conclusion. The conclusion reinforces the main ideas you wish your audience to retain. How you design the conclusion will depend on your initial purpose. A strong conclusion is nearly as important as a strong introduction, as both the beginning and the end will be the parts most likely remembered.

CHOOSE AN EFFECTIVE DELIVERY STYLE

Avoid speaking in a "written" style. Use phrases, and use a variety of sentence lengths. Avoid excessively long, complex sentences, as listeners may have difficulty following your ideas. In general, keep your sentences short. If you concentrate on getting your point across by having a conversation with the audience, you will likely use a natural, conversational style. Many suggestions for clarity in writing also apply to clarity in speaking:

• Avoid long, cumbersome sentences. Long sentences can be as hard to hear as they are to read.

• Avoid abstract, polysyllabic words. Instead, use concrete language that your audience can visualize.

• Avoid jargon, unless you are sure that your audience will be readily familiar with all specialized terms.

• Use short, active voice sentences.

TECHNIQUES TO ENHANCE AUDIENCE COMPREHENSION

Because your audience cannot "rehear" ideas, once you have stated them, look for ways to help your audience easily follow your ideas:

1. Be sure you clearly demarcate the beginning and end of each point and segment of your presentation:
   - Announce each main topic as you come to it so that your audience knows when you have completed one topic and are beginning the next one.
   - Allow a slight pause to occur after you have completed your introduction, then announce your first topic.
   - After completing your final topic in the main body of your presentation, allow a slight pause before you begin your conclusion.

2. Speak slowly, vigorously, and enthusiastically. Be sure you pronounce your words carefully, particularly if you are addressing a large group or a multicultural group.

3. Use gestures to accentuate points. Move your body deliberately to aid you in announcing major transition points. In short, avoid standing transfixed before your audience.

4. Maintain eye contact with your audience. Doing so helps you keep your listeners involved in what you are saying. If you look at the ceiling, the floor, or the corners of the room, your audience may sense a lack of self-confidence. Lack of eye contact also tends to lessen your credibility. In contrast, consistent eye contact enhances the importance of the message. By looking at your audience, you can often sense their reaction to what you are saying and make adjustments in your presentation if necessary.

5. Do not memorize your presentation. You don't want it to sound like something you are reciting to your listeners. You want it to seem like your turn in a conversation you are having with your listeners.

6. Do not read your slides to your audience. Allow them to see the information on your slide before you begin discussing the material or points on each slide.

7. Rehearse your presentation until you are comfortable. Try walking around, speaking each segment and then speaking aloud the entire presentation. Rephrase ideas that are difficult for you to say—these will likely be hard for your audience to follow. Be sure to time your presentation so that it does not exceed the time limit. Keep your presentation as short as possible.

8. If possible, record your speech. Listen to what you have said as objectively as possible. As you listen, consider the main issues of audience, purpose, organization, context, content, and style.

9. Listen for tone, attitude, and clarity. Is the tone you project appropriate for your audience and your purpose? Is each sentence easy to understand? Are

you speaking too rapidly? Are the major divisions in your presentation easy to hear? Are any sentences difficult to understand?

10. Try not to provide the audience handout material before you begin. To do so encourages your audience to read rather than listen. If you must provide written material, be sure the material is coordinated with your presentation so that you keep your audience's attention on what you are saying as you are saying it.

11. When you use slides, tell the audience what they will see, show them the slide; give them time to digest what they are seeing; then comment on the slide. Do not begin talking about another topic while a slide depicting a past topic is still showing. Remember: people cannot see and listen at the same time. Avoid using too many slides.

12. When you are planning your presentation, determine how you will handle questions. Prepare for questions your audience may ask and decide how you will answer each one. Again, unless you have analyzed your audience and the reason for your presentation, you will not be able to anticipate questions that will likely arise.

13. Keep the question and answer time moving briskly. Answer each question as concisely as possible, then move to the next questions. If you are faced with a difficult question, reword the question or break the question into several parts. Then answer each part. Be sure to restate questions if listeners in the back of the room are unable to hear questions asked by those near the front.

DESIGNING AND PRESENTING THE WRITTEN PAPER

Papers presented at professional meetings are frequently read from written manuscripts if the material to be delivered is complex. These papers may then be published in the official proceedings of the professional society.

However, presentations may need to be read for other reasons:

1. A presentation that discusses company policy, a sensitive issue, or a topic that must be approved by someone in the organization before the presentation. In situations like these, the presentation is carefully written and read from the approved, written manuscript to ensure accuracy.

2. A presentation that will be circulated or filed as documentation. In a situation like this one, a spokesperson may read a carefully prepared statement, particularly if a possibility exists that material may be misconstrued by those in the audience.

3. Inexperienced speakers who must deal with a difficult problem may be more comfortable reading from a prepared manuscript. With the manuscript in front of you on the lectern, you don't have to worry about losing your train of thought or forgetting important details.

Written presentations can be effective if the speaker plans and writes the presentation carefully and then utilizes a number of delivery techniques to enhance the effectiveness of the oral reading.

Structuring the written speech. The structure of the written speech is the same as the extemporaneous speech. The speech has three main parts: the introduction, the main body, and the conclusion. Each section should be structured like the extemporaneous speech. However, you will need to write each section completely. If you know that the speech will be published, you may wish to write it like an article for publication or a report and use headings and subheadings to reveal the content and organization of the speech.

Writing the speech. After you have designed the content of your paper and made final revisions in your ideas, you will need to give close attention to your sentences and paragraphs, since you will be reading these directly from the page.

1. Be sure that each section is clearly demarcated from other sections. This means that each section should have an overview that clearly announces that the section is beginning. Each paragraph should also begin with a topic sentence that summarizes the content of the paragraph. In short, in writing a speech to be read, you are making a concerted effort to accentuate every device for revealing organization, since your audience cannot stop and rehear what you have just said.

2. Limit each section and each paragraph within sections to one idea. Watch length so that your audience will not lose track of the main idea you are presenting.

3. Avoid excessive detail.

4. Use enumeration to help your audience follow your main points and to know when one point has ended and the next point is beginning.

5. Avoid long sentences. Long sentences are as difficult (or more difficult) to hear and follow as they are to read.

6. Prune every sentence to make it as clear and concise as possible.

7. Use active voice whenever possible so that your sentences will preserve the natural quality of spoken language.

8. Type your presentation in a large type—pica (12 point type) or larger. Triple space and leave wide margins on each side of the page.

9. With a marker, draw a "break" line after the introduction, between each main point in the body, and before the conclusion.

10. Underline or highlight important phrases or sentences throughout the presentation.

11. Consider using visuals, even though these may not be published separately.

Again, choose visuals that will clarify any difficult or important points.

Practicing the presentation.

1. Read each sentence aloud. Rewrite sentences that are difficult for you to say.

2. As you practice reading the presentation, try to look directly at your audience and speak important phrases or sentences to the audience.

3. Use overviews and topic sentences to announce each major topic as you come to it. To further alert your audience to the beginning of a new point, pause briefly; look at your audience; then read your overview statement or topic sentence. If possible, try to speak these to your audience instead of reading them.

4. As you practice reading your presentation, continue to listen for any sentences or words that are difficult to articulate. Recast sentences and paragraphs that do not sound organized, logical, and clear. If possible, replace difficult words with others that are easier to speak.

5. As you read, speak slowly and enunciate clearly and distinctly.

6. Once you can read each sentence with ease and without haste, time your presentation to be sure that it does not exceed a time limit if you have been given one.

7. Read your speech into a recorder. Allow some time between recording and listening so that you can gain some objectivity. As you listen, check for sentences that are hard to follow. Listen for breaks between major sections and major points.

CHECKLIST FOR PREPARING ORAL REPORTS ✔

Audience

☐ Who is your audience?

☐ What do you know about your audience—background, knowledge, position in the organization, attitudes toward you and your and your subject?

☐ What is the relationship between you and your audience?

☐ What is the attitude of your audience toward you and your presentation likely to be?

☐ Is your audience from a culture markedly different from yours? What adjustments to your presentation will any such differences require?

continued

CHECKLIST FOR PREPARING ORAL REPORTS ✔ *continued*

Purpose

☐ What is your purpose in giving this oral presentation?

☐ Is there (should there be) a long-range purpose?

☐ What is the situation that led to this presentation?

☐ Given your audience's background and attitudes, do you need to adjust your purpose to make your presentation more suitable for your audience?

Context

☐ Where and when will you be speaking?

☐ What events will be transpiring in the organization (theirs or yours) that may affect how your audience perceives what you say?

☐ What equipment, applications, and materials are available to you?

Slideware?

Audio?

Video?

Internet connection?

Chalkboard?

Flipchart and easel?

Handouts?

Content

☐ What ideas do you want to include and exclude?

☐ Based on the audience and the context, what difficulties do you need to anticipate in choosing content?

☐ Can any ideas be misconstrued and prove harmful to you or your organization?

☐ Do you have a good opening that will interest your audience and create a friendly atmosphere?

☐ Have you limited your major points to fit within your allotted time?

☐ Does your talk contain sufficient examples, analogies, narratives, and data to support your generalizations? Have you repeated key points?

☐ Can you relate your subject matter to some vital interest of your audience?

Graphics

☐ What kinds of visuals will you need to clarify or reinforce the ideas you will discuss?

☐ Where should you use these in your presentation?

continued

CHECKLIST FOR
PREPARING ORAL REPORTS ✔ *continued*

☐ Are these visuals immediately readable and understandable?
☐ Do they successfully focus the listeners' attention and augment and clarify your message?
☐ Do they meet the four criteria that govern good graphics?
    Visibility
    Clarity
    Simplicity
    Controllability

Style

☐ What kind of tone do you want to use in addressing your audience?
☐ What kind of image—of yourself and your organization—do you want to project?
☐ What level of language do you need to use, based on your audience's background and knowledge of your subject?
☐ What approach will your audience expect from you?
☐ How formal should you be?
☐ Which delivery technique will be more appropriate? Extemporaneous? Manuscript?
☐ If you are speaking extemporaneously, have you prepared a speech outline to guide you?
☐ If you will be reading from a manuscript, have you introduced a conversational tone into your talk? Is your typed manuscript easy to read from?
☐ Do you have a good ending ready, perhaps a summary of key points or an anecdote that supports your purpose? If you began with a story, do you want to go back to it now?
☐ Have you rehearsed your talk several times?

EXERCISES

1. Choose one of the chapters in this book and adapt the material as a series of slides to accompany your 15-minute oral presentation on the subject of technical communication for professionals in your field.
2. In adapting the following document (Figure 11-7) for a slide presentation, which pieces of information are especially important to display? How will you display this information to make it easy to read and easy to remember?
3. Prepare a five-minute/eight-slide PowerPoint presentation for the proposal you write for your technical writing class.
4. Prepare a PowerPoint presentation of your major semester project, including a paper copy of your slides to distribute to your audience.
5. Examine the following real slide presentation (Figure 11-8). If you were the author and were given 15 more minutes to make the slide presentation more effective, what changes would you make?

Department of Veterans Affairs

Strategic Goals

Goal 1 -- Restore the capability of veterans with disabilities to the greatest extent possible, and improve the quality of their lives and that of their families.

Goal 2 -- Ensure a smooth transition for veterans from active military service to civilian life.

Goal 3 -- Honor and serve veterans in life, and memorialize them in death for their sacrifices on behalf of the Nation.

Goal 4 -- Contribute to the public health, emergency management, socioeconomic well-being, and history of the Nation.

Enabling Goal -- Deliver world-class service to veterans and their families through effective communication and management of people, technology, business processes, and financial resources.

February 2008

VA Leadership

Secretary of Veterans Affairs -- James B. Peake, MD

Deputy Secretary -- Gordon H. Mansfield

Under Secretary for Benefits -- Daniel L. Cooper

Under Secretary for Health -- Michael J. Kussman, MD

Under Secretary for Memorial Affairs -- William F. Tuerk

Assistant Secretary for Management -- Robert J. Henke

Assistant Secretary for Information & Technology -- Robert T. Howard

Assistant Secretary for Policy & Planning -- Patrick W. Dunne

Assistant Secretary for Operations, Security & Preparedness -- Charles L. Hopkins III

Assistant Secretary for Human Resources & Administration -- Michael W. Hager

Assistant Secretary for Public & Intergovernmental Affairs -- Lisette M. Mondello

Assistant Secretary for Congressional & Legislative Affairs -- Christine Hill (Acting)

Helpful Information

Benefits	1-800-827-1000
Education & Training	1-888-442-4551
Life Insurance	1-800-669-8477
Special Issues	1-800-749-8387
Health Care	1-877-222-VETS (8387)
Headstones/Markers	1-800-697-6947
VA Inspector General	1-800-488-8244
Suicide Prevention Hot line	1-800-273-TALK (8255)
TDD	1-800-829-4833

http://www.va.gov

Produced by the National Center for Veterans Analysis and Statistics (NCVAS).

OEF/OIF Initiatives

- In 2007 prioritized claim processing for OEF/OIF veterans, finalizing claims received in an average of 110 days.
- Hired 100 new outreach coordinators to provide services to returning OEF/OIF veterans.
- Created an Advisory Committee on OIF/OEF Veterans and Families to advise the Secretary.
- Coordinated 8,236 transfers of OEF/OIF service members and veterans from a military treatment facility to a VA medical facility.
- Received 39,000 referrals from the Post Deployment Health Reassessment (PDHRA) initiative.
- Participated in 805 PDHRA On-Site and 247 Call Center events since November 2005. A total of 32,321 referrals were made to VAMC and 15,842 to Vet Centers.
- Contacted 91% of severely-injured or ill OEF/OIF service members/veterans, by a VA case manager, within 7 days of notification of transfer to the VA health care system.

OEF/OIF veterans' statistics:

- 48% are Active Duty, 52% are Reserve/National Guard
- 88% are men, 12% are women
- 65% Army; 12% Air Force; 12% Navy; 12% Marine
- 34% were deployed multiple times
- 52%, largest age group, is 20-29 years old
- 69% of those who filed disability claims received service-connected disability compensation award

Veteran Population

There are about 23.8 million living veterans, 7.5% of whom are women. There are about 37 million dependents (spouses and dependent children) of living veterans and survivors of deceased veterans. Together they represent 20% of the US population.

Most veterans living today served during times of war. The Vietnam Era veteran, about 7.9 million, is the largest segment of the veteran population.

In 2007, the median age of all living veterans was 60 years old, 61 for men and 47 for women. Median ages by period of service: Gulf War, 37 years old; Vietnam War, 60; Korean War, 76; and WW II 84.

Sixty percent (60%) of the nation's veterans live in urban areas. States with the largest veteran population are CA, FL, TX, PA, NY and OH, respectively. These six states account for about 36% of the total veteran population.

FIGURE 11-7

Benefits

More than half of Department of Veterans Affairs' (VA's) budget (nearly $86 billion in obligations in 2007) is paid directly to veterans in the form of statutory benefits.

Over 3.7 million veterans and beneficiaries receive compensation or pension benefits from VA. In 2007, VA processed nearly 825,000 claims for disability benefits and added almost 250,000 new beneficiaries to the compensation and pension rolls.

Approximately 523,000 students received education benefits in 2007; 20 percent of them are first time recipients of VA education benefits.

VA guarantees an average of 11,109 loans a month for veterans realizing the American dream of home ownership. VA currently guarantees 2.2 million active home loans to veterans. Those loans total $243 billion.

Over half of VA's home loan guarantees went to first-time home buyers. Approximately 90% of the loans use the "no down payment" feature that makes the VA loan guaranty so effective.

VA will pay 1.2 million veterans insurance policy holders $969 million in dividends this year. VA will also pay $2.5 billion in life insurance beneficiary claims to 105,000 survivors of veterans and service members.

Approximately 200 children and widows of Spanish-American War veterans still receive VA survivor benefits. There are three survivors of Civil War veterans still receiving VA benefits.

There are 4 million veterans or service members insured under VA-administered life insurance programs. The average basic insurance amount is $240,000. All policies have a total face value of $1 trillion, an amount higher than the gross domestic product of most countries.

Average annual amounts paid to veterans or survivors under various benefits programs: disability compensation, $9,811; pension, $8,509; Dependency and Indemnity Compensation, $13,612; and death pension, $3,829.

As of September 2007, 223,564 Operation Enduring Freedom/Operation Iraqi Freedom (OEF/OIF) veterans filed for disability claims, 89% received claims decisions and 11% are waiting for claims decisions.

Health Care

VA's healthcare mission covers the continuum of care providing inpatient and outpatient care; and a wide range of services, such as pharmacy, prosthetics, and mental health; long-term care in both institutional and non-institutional settings; and other health care programs such as CHAMPVA and Readjustment Counseling. The Veterans Health Administration (VHA) healthcare and research budget ($37.3 billion in obligations) constituted 43% of the VA's total obligations in fiscal year 2007.

VHA delivers health care through 21 Veterans Integrated Service Networks (VISNs) that manage 153 medical centers, 731 community-based outpatient clinics, 135 nursing homes, 209 readjustment counseling centers (Vet Centers) and 47 domiciliaries.

In 2007, VHA provided healthcare services to approximately 5.5 million unique patients, up from 3.8 million in 2000. VHA staff is treating more outpatients than ever before, increasing from 53.4 million outpatient visits in 2006 to 55.7 million in 2007. VHA has also enrolled over 100,000 new patients with resources by over $500 million in FY 2007 to meet the influx of veterans of all service eras with mental and emotional health care needs.

The most recent American Customer Satisfaction Index survey gave VA patient satisfaction scores of 84 and 82 out of 100 for inpatient and outpatient care, respectively. VA scores are 5 points and 4 points higher than the corresponding private sector scores.

VA led the way in care for traumatic brain injury (TBI) veterans by developing a mandatory TBI training course for select VA health care professionals. Additionally, VA instituted a program to screen all patients who served in the combat theaters of Afghanistan or Iraq for TBI.

VA hired suicide prevention counselors at each of its 153 medical centers to help support the national suicide prevention hot line. The hot line puts veterans in touch with trained, caring professionals who can help them cope with emotional crises. The hot line is available 365 days a year, 24 hours a day.

VA established 100 new patient advocate positions to help severely injured veterans and their families navigate VA's systems for health care and financial benefits, providing a smooth transition to VA health care facilities.

Memorial Affairs

The National Cemetery Administration (NCA) honors veterans with final resting places in national shrines and with lasting tributes that commemorate their service to our Nation.

NCA maintains more than 2.8 million gravesites at 125 cemeteries in 39 states and Puerto Rico, as well as in 33 soldier's lots and monument sites.

The nation's 125th national cemetery, South Florida VA National Cemetery, began operation in April 2007. VA is planning six additional cemeteries to serve the areas of Bakersfield, CA; Birmingham, AL; Columbia, SC; Jacksonville, FL; Sarasota, FL; and Southeastern PA.

Of the 125 national cemeteries in operation, 65 are open to all interments; 21 can accommodate cremated remains and family members of those already interred; and 39 are closed to new interments but accommodate family members in occupied gravesites.

Annual interments in VA national cemeteries have increased from 36,400 in 1973, when VA took responsibility for national cemeteries, to 101,200 in 2007, including dependents. More than 67,500 veterans were laid to rest in a VA national cemetery in 2007.

Since 1973, NCA has provided nearly 9.9 million headstones and markers. In 2007, NCA furnished more than 361,000 headstones and markers.

In 2007, NCA provided more than 423,000 Presidential Memorial Certificates to the loved ones of deceased veterans.

Since 1980, the State Cemetery Grants Program has obligated more than $312 million to 36 states, plus Guam and Saipan, for the establishment, expansion or improvement of 69 state veterans cemeteries. In fiscal year 2007, VA supported state veterans cemeteries by providing more than 22,000 interments.

VA estimates that more than 686,000 veterans died in 2007. About 13 percent of veterans choose to be buried in VA national and state cemeteries.

In 2007, volunteers donated approximately 366,000 hours at national cemeteries and more than 8.1 million people visited them.

FIGURE 11-7 *continued*

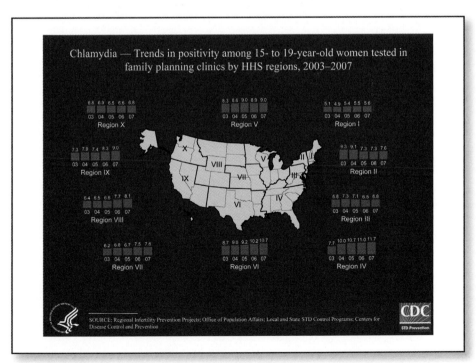

FIGURE 11-8a

FIGURE 11-8b

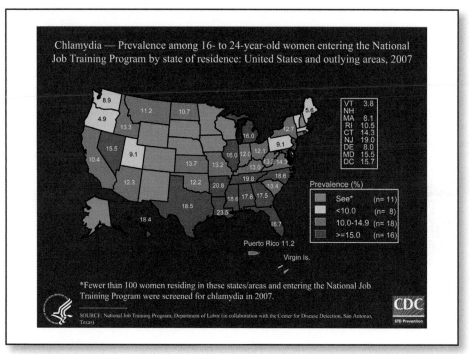

FIGURE 11-8c

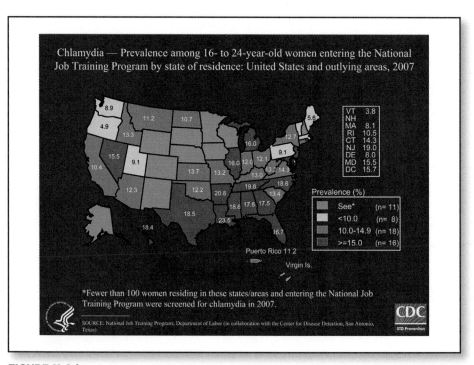

FIGURE 11-8d

FIGURE 11-8e

FIGURE 11-8f

Résumés and Job Applications

Quick Tips

Finding a job is itself a job. Information and advice are available, but you can't be timid or passive. You have to search actively and assertively for support and opportunities.

You will likely experience both excitement and disappointment in your search. It will be exciting to imagine yourself working for different companies and living your life in different cities. It will also be disappointing if you don't immediately get your dream job. The search process is often a roller coaster of emotions—highs and lows.

Keep in mind that a variety of factors entirely aside from your credentials are involved in every hiring decision. If you aren't offered a job for which you applied, don't take it personally and don't be discouraged. The key to finding a satisfying job is perseverance.

THE CORRESPONDENCE OF THE JOB SEARCH

A persuasive letter of application, sometimes called a *cover letter,* and a clear and organized résumé won't guarantee that you get a job, but ineffective ones will usually guarantee that you don't.

Letter of application. Plan the mechanics of your letter of application carefully. Buy the best quality white bond paper. This is no time to skimp. Use a standard typeface. Don't use italics or bold. Make sure your letter is mechanically perfect and free of grammatical errors. Be brief, but not telegraphic. Keep the letter to a single page unless you have extensive pertinent experience to emphasize and explain. Don't send a letter that has been duplicated: each copy of your letter must be individually addressed, printed, and signed. Accompany each letter with a résumé. We discuss résumés later.

Pay attention to the style of the letter and the résumé that accompanies it. The tone you want in your letter is one of self-confidence. You must avoid both arrogance and timidity. You must sound interested and eager, but not obsequious or desperate. Don't give the impression that you *must* have the job, but, on the other hand, don't seem indifferent about getting it.

When describing your accomplishments in the letter and résumé, use action verbs. They make your writing concise and specific, and they make you seem dynamic and energetic. For example, instead of reporting that you worked as a sales clerk, explain that you maintained inventories, promoted merchandise, prepared displays, implemented new procedures, and supervised and trained new clerks. Here's a sampling of such action verbs:

administer	edit	oversee
analyze	evaluate	plan
conduct	exhibit	produce
create	expand	reduce costs
cut	improve	reorganize
design	manage	support
develop	operate	promote
direct	organize	write

You cannot avoid the use of *I* in a letter of application, but take the you-attitude as much as you can. Emphasize what you can do for the prospective employer—how your getting this job will benefit the company. The letter of application is not the place to be worried about salary and benefits. Above all, be mature and dignified. Avoid tricky and flashy approaches. Write a well-organized, informative letter that highlights the skills you have that the company desires in its employees.

The beginning. Start by explaining that you are applying for a job and by identifying the specific job for which you applying. Don't be aggressive or inventive here. A beginning such as "WANTED: An alert, aggressive employer who will recognize an alert, aggressive young programmer" will usually direct your letter to the reject pile. If you can do so legitimately, a bit of name dropping is a good beginning. Use this beginning only if you have permission and if the name you drop will mean something to the prospective employer. If you qualify on both counts, begin with an opening sentence such as this:

Dear Mr. Dominguez:

Professor Theresa Ricco of Nebraska State University's Department of Biochemistry has suggested that I apply for a research position in the virology division of your company. In June I will receive my Bachelor of Science degree in Biochemsitry from NSU. I have also worked as a research assistant in Dr. Ricco's lab for two years.

Remember that you are trying to arouse immediate interest about yourself in the potential employer.

Sometimes the best approach is a simple statement about the job you seek, accompanied by a description of something in your experience that fits you for the job, as in this example:

> Your opening for a researcher in the virology division has come to my attention. In June of this year, I will graduate from Nebraska State University with a Bachelor of Science degree in Biochemistry. I have also worked part-time for two years in a cell and molecular research laboratory at NSU. I believe that both my education and my work experience qualify me for this position.

Be specific about the job you want. Quite often, if the job you want is not open, the employer may offer you an alternative one. But employers are not impressed with general statements such as, "I'm willing and able to work at any job you may have open in research, production, or sales." Instead of indicating flexibility, such a claim usually implies that your skills and interests are unfocused—that you would be adequate at several things but truly exceptional at nothing.

In addition, make it clear in this opening that you know something about the company—its history, its achievements, its special projects, its reputation in the industry—anything that will demonstrate that you did your research and picked this company to apply to because something about it was impressive, something about it made you think you could make a key contribution to its success.

The body. In the body of your letter you highlight selected items from your education and experience that show your qualifications for the job you seek. Remember always that you are trying to show the employer how well you will fit into the job and the organization.

In selecting your items, it pays to know what things employers value the most. In evaluating recent college graduates, employers look closely at the major, academic performance, work experience, awards and honors, and extracurricular activities. They also consider recommendations, standardized test scores, military experience, and community service.

Try to include information that employers typically consider important, but emphasize those areas in which you are especially noteworthy. For example, if your grades are good, mention them prominently: otherwise, maintain a discreet silence about your academic record. Speak to the employer's interests, and at the same time highlight your own accomplishments. Show how it would be to the employer's advantage to hire you. The following paragraph, an excellent example of the you-attitude in action, does all these things:

> The advertisement for this position indicated that extensive interaction with international colleagues, especially from South America, would be expected. I would like to note that I studied Spanish and Portugese in college and have a high fluency in both languages. I also visited Argentina and Brazil two years ago for a six-week intensive

summer session. I am familiar with the major cities as well as the history and key traditions. I would thus be a confident and articulate representative of the company.

Be specific about your accomplishments: otherwise, it will sound like bragging. It is much better to write, "I was president of my senior class" instead of "I am a natural leader." "I was president" is a piece of evidence; "I am a natural leader" is a conclusion. Your job is to give employers the evidence that will lead them to the right conclusions about you.

One tip about job experience: the best experience relates to the job you seek, but mention any job experience, even if it does not relate to the job you seek. Employers believe that a student who has worked is more apt to be mature than one who has not. If you have worked at a job, you are more likely to have effective work habits and a real work ethic. If you have worked at a job, it indicates that another employer once judged you worthy of hiring.

Don't forget hobbies that relate to the job. You're trying to establish that you are interested in, as well as qualified for, the job.

Don't mention salary unless you're answering an advertisement that specifically requests you to. Keep the you-attitude. Don't worry about insurance benefits, vacations, and holidays at this point in the process. Keep the prospective employer's interests in the foreground. Your self-interest is taken for granted. If are offered the job, that's the time to inquire about such details if they are not readily provided to you.

If you are already working, you will emphasize your work experience more than your college experience. Identify your responsibilities and achievements on the job. Do not complain about your present employer. Such complaints will lead the prospective employer to mistrust you.

In the last paragraph of the body, refer the employer to your enclosed résumé. Mention your willingness to supply additional information such as references, letters concerning your work, research reports, and college transcripts.

The ending. The goal of the letter of application is to get you an interview with the prospective employer. In your final paragraph, you request this interview. Your request should be neither apologetic nor aggressive. Simply indicate that you are available for an interview at the employer's convenience, and give any special instructions needed for reaching you. If the prospective employer is in a distant city, indicate (if possible) a convenient time and location that you might meet with a representative of the company, such as the upcoming convention of a professional association. If the employer is really interested, you may be invited to visit the company as its expense.

The complete letter. Figure 12-1 shows a complete letter of application. The beginning of the letter shows that the writer has been interested enough in the company to investigate it. The desired job is specifically mentioned. The middle portion highlights the writer's course work and work experience that relate directly to the job she is seeking. The ending makes an interview convenient for the employer to arrange.

Letter of application

635 Shuflin Road
Watertown, CA 90233
March 23, 2009

Mr. Morell R. Solem
Director of Communications
Price Industries, Inc.
2163 Airport Drive
St. Louis, MO 63136

Dear. Mr. Solem:

Identifies specific job and demonstrates knowledge of company	I am writing to apply for the position of technical editor advertised in the March issue of *Technical Communication Today*. Price Industries has a growing reputation for innovative publications, and I believe my education and experience would contribute to your efforts.
Highlights education	I am graduating in May of this year from Texas University with a bachelor's degree in Technical Communication. I have completed courses in technical editing, document design, usability testing, publication management, website design, and interactive website design, and developed proficiency in all pertinent Adobe applications.
Highlights work experience	In addition, I have a year of experience as a document designer and editor at a consulting company. I know how to take a project from the initial meeting with a client, through the publication process, to delivery and billing. I have also worked in computer support, developing both my technical skills and my ability to interact courteously and effectively with customers.
Refers to résumé	You will find more detailed information about my education and work experience in the résumé enclosed with this letter. I could also supply descriptions of the courses I have taken, copies of the projects completed in those courses, and a complete list of my job duties at each place of employment.
Requests interview	In April, I will attend the regional meeting of the Society for Technical Communication in St. Louis. Would it be possible for me to visit with a representative of Price Industries at that time?

Sincerely yours,

Ty Williams

Ty Williams

FIGURE 12-1 Letter of Application

Keep in mind that a personnel officer skims your letter and résumé in about thirty seconds. If you have not grabbed his or her interest in that time, you are probably finished with that organization.

The résumé. A résumé provides your prospective employer with a convenient summary of your education and experience. As in the letter of application, good grammar, correct spelling, neatness, and brevity—ideally, only one page—are of major importance in your résumé. Although the traditional paper résumé is still commonplace, more and more organizations are using electronic media for screening their job candidates. Therefore, it's important to have versions of your résumé available in the following formats:

- Traditional paper
- Scannable format
- E-mail format
- Online format

Because résumés of different kinds are similar in content and organization regardless of format, we discuss those aspects first.

Content and organization. The three most widely used résumés are chronological, functional, and targeted résumés. All have advantages and disadvantages.

Chronological résumés. The advantages of a chronological résumé (Figure 12-2) are that it's traditional and acceptable. If your education and experience show a steady progression toward the career you seek, the chronological résumé portrays that progression well. Its major disadvantage is that your special capabilities or accomplishments may sometimes get lost in the chronological detail. Also, if you have holes in your employment or educational history, they show up clearly.

Put your address at the top. Include your e-mail address and your telephone number (including the area code). If you have a fax number, include it.

For most students, educational information should be placed before work experience. People with extensive work experience, however, may choose to put it before their educational information.

List the colleges or universities you have attended in reverse chronological order—in other words, list the school you attended most recently first; the one before, second; and so on. Do not list your high school. Give your major and date, or expected date, of graduation. Do not list courses, but list anything that is out of the ordinary, such as honors, special projects, and emphases in addition to the major. Extracurricular activities also go here if they are pertinent to the job you seek.

As you did with your educational experience, put your work experience in reverse chronological order. To save space and to avoid the repetition of *I* throughout the résumé, use phrases rather than complete sentences. The style of the sample résumés makes this technique clear. As in the letter of application, emphasize the experiences that show you in the best light for the job you seek. Use nouns and active verbs in your descriptions. Do not neglect less important jobs of the sort you may have had in high school, but use even more of a summary approach for them. You would probably put college internships and work–study programs here, though you might choose to put them under education. If you have military experience, put it here. Give the highest rank you held, list service schools you attended, and describe your duties. Make a special effort to show how your military experience relates to the civilian work you seek.

You may wish to provide personal information. Personal information can be a subtle way to point out your desirable qualities. Recent travels indicate a broadening

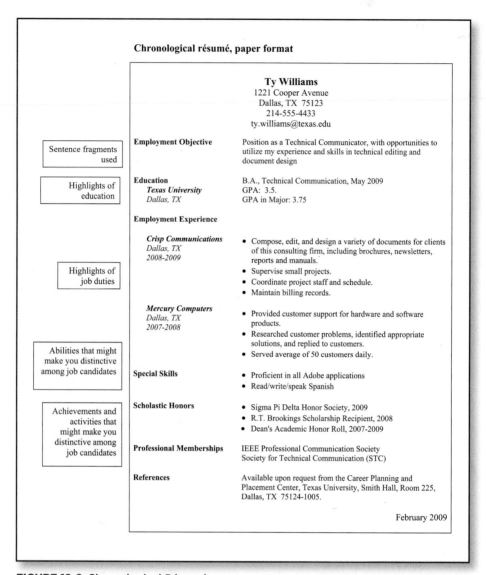

Chronological résumé, paper format

Ty Williams
1221 Cooper Avenue
Dallas, TX 75123
214-555-4433
ty.williams@texas.edu

Sentence fragments used	**Employment Objective** — Position as a Technical Communicator, with opportunities to utilize my experience and skills in technical editing and document design
Highlights of education	**Education** — B.A., Technical Communication, May 2009
	Texas University — GPA: 3.5.
	Dallas, TX — GPA in Major: 3.75

Employment Experience

Crisp Communications
Dallas, TX
2008-2009

- Compose, edit, and design a variety of documents for clients of this consulting firm, including brochures, newsletters, reports and manuals.
- Supervise small projects.
- Coordinate project staff and schedule.
- Maintain billing records.

Highlights of job duties

Mercury Computers
Dallas, TX
2007-2008

- Provided customer support for hardware and software products.
- Researched customer problems, identified appropriate solutions, and replied to customers.
- Served average of 50 customers daily.

Abilities that might make you distinctive among job candidates

Special Skills

- Proficient in all Adobe applications
- Read/write/speak Spanish

Scholastic Honors

- Sigma Pi Delta Honor Society, 2009
- R.T. Brookings Scholarship Recipient, 2008
- Dean's Academic Honor Roll, 2007-2009

Achievements and activities that might make you distinctive among job candidates

Professional Memberships

IEEE Professional Communication Society
Society for Technical Communication (STC)

References

Available upon request from the Career Planning and Placement Center, Texas University, Smith Hall, Room 225, Dallas, TX 75124-1005.

February 2009

FIGURE 12-2 Chronological Résumé

of knowledge and probably a willingness to travel. Hobbies listed may relate to the work sought. Participation in sports, drama, or community activities indicates that you enjoy working with people. Cultural activities indicate you are not a person of narrow interests. If you are proficient in a language aside from English, mention this: more and more organizations are looking for employees with the potential to support international business activity.

If you choose to indicate that you are married or have a family, you might also emphasize that you are willing to relocate. Don't discuss your health unless it is to describe it as excellent.

You have a choice with references. You can list several references with addresses and phone numbers or simply put in a line that says "References available upon request." Both methods have an advantage and a disadvantage. If you provide references, a potential employer can contact them immediately, but you use up precious space that might be better used for more information about yourself. Conversely, if you don't provide the reference information, you save the space but put an additional step between potential employers and information they may want. It's a judgment call, but your first goal is to interest the potential employer in you. If that happens, then it will not be difficult to provide the reference information at a later time. If, however, one of your references is a prestigious individual in the discipline or industry, be sure to list your references on the résumé.

In any case, do have at least three references available. Choose from among your college teachers and past employers—people who know you well and will say positive things about you. Get their permission, of course. Also, it's a smart idea to send them a copy of your résumé. If you can't call on them personally, send them a letter that requests permission to use them as a reference, reminds them of their association with you, and sets a time for their reply.

Dear Ms. Zamora:

In May of this year, I'll graduate from Watertown Polytechnic Institute with a B.S. in metallurgical engineering. I'm getting ready to look for a full-time job. If you believe that you know enough about my abilities to give me a good recommendation, I would like your permission to use you as a reference.

As a reminder, during the summers of 2007 and 2008, I worked as a laboratory technician in your testing facility at Watertown. They were highly instructive summers for me and reinforced my college studies.

I want to start sending my résumé out to some potential employers by March 1 and would be grateful for your reply by that time. I've enclosed a copy of my résumé so that you can see in detail what I've been doing.

Thanks for all your help in the past.

Best regards,

At the bottom of the traditional paper résumé, place a dateline—the month and year in which you completed the résumé. Place the date in the heading of scannable and e-mail résumés.

Functional résumés. A main advantage of the functional résumé (Figure 12-3) is that it allows you to highlight the experiences that show you to your best advantage. Extracurricular experiences show up particularly well in a functional résumé. The major disadvantage of this format is the difficulty, for the first-time reader, of discerning a steady progression of work and education.

The address portion of the functional résumé is the same as that of the chronological. After the address, you may include a job objective line if you like. A job

Functional résumé, paper format

Ty Williams
1221 Cooper Avenue
Dallas, TX 75123
214-555-4433
ty.williams@texas.edu

Employment Objective	Position as a Technical Communicator specializing in technical editing and document design
Education	Texas University Dallas, TX B.A., Technical Communication, May 2009
Communication Skills	• Compose, edit, and design a variety of documents, including brochures, newsletters, reports and manuals. • Create projects using all Adobe applications • Provide customer support for hardware and software products • Research customer problems, identify appropriate solutions, and reply to customers by telephone or e-mail message. • Read/write/speak Spanish • Graduating with Honors: GPA: 3.5; GPA in Major: 3.75
Project Management	• Supervise small document design projects from initial meeting with client through publication and delivery • Coordinate project staff and schedule. • Maintain billing records.
Professional Involvement	• Sigma Pi Delta Honor Society • Association for Computing Machinery (ACM) • IEEE Professional Communication Society • Society for Technical Communication (STC)
Work Experience	• Crisp Communications Dallas, TX, 2008-2009, document design • Mercury Computers, Dallas, TX, 2007-2008, customer support
References	Available upon request from the Career Planning and Placement Center, Texas University, Smith Hall, Room 225, Dallas, TX 75124-1005.

February 2009

Academic and work experience categorized by categories

Summary of work experience in reverse chronological order

FIGURE 12-3 Functional Résumé

objective entry specifies the kind of work you want to do and sometimes the industry or service area in which you want to do it, like this:

Work in food service management.

or like this:

Work in food service management in a metropolitan hospital.

Place the job objective entry immediately after the address and align it with the rest of the entries (as shown in Figure 12-3).

For education, simply give the school from which you received your degree, your major, and your date of graduation. The body of the résumé is essentially a classification. You sort your experiences—educational, business, extracurricular—into categories that reveal capabilities related to the jobs you seek. Remember that in addition to professional skills, employers want good communication skills and good interpersonal skills. Possible categories are *technical, professional, team building, communication, research, sales, production, administration,* and *consulting.*

The best way to prepare a functional résumé is to brainstorm it. Begin by listing some categories that you think might display your experiences well. Brainstorm further by listing your experiences in those categories. When you have good listings, select the categories and experiences that show you in the best light. Remember, you don't have to display everything you've ever done, just those things that might strike a potential employer as valuable. Finish off the functional résumé with a brief reverse chronological work history and a date line, as in the chronological résumé.

Targeted résumés. The main advantage of the targeted résumé (Figure 12-4) is also its main disadvantage: You zero in on one goal. If you can achieve that goal, fine—but the narrowness of the approach may block you out of other possibilities. The targeted résumé displays your capabilities and achievements well, but, like the functional résumé, it's a format that may not have complete acceptance among all employers.

The address and education portions of the targeted résumé are the same as those in the functional résumé. The whole point of a targeted résumé is that you are aiming at a specific job objective. Therefore, you express your job objective as precisely as you can.

Next you list your capabilities that match the job objective. Obviously, you have to understand the job you are seeking to make the proper match. Capabilities are things you could do if called upon to do so. To be credible, they must be supported by achievements or accomplishments, which are listed next in your résumé. You finish off the targeted résumé with a reverse chronological work history and a date line, as in the functional résumé.

As with the functional résumé, brainstorming is a good way to discover the material you need for your targeted résumé. Under the headings Capabilities and Achievements, make as many statements about yourself as you can. When you are finished, select those statements that best relate to the job you are seeking.

Paper résumés. As Figures 12-2, 12-3, and 12-4 illustrate, in a paper résumé you use variations in type and spacing to emphasize and organize information. Make the résumé look easy to read—leave generous margins and white space. Use distinctive headings and subheadings. The use of a two-column spread is common, as is the use of boldface in headings. You might use a 12-point type like Arial for headings and a 10-point type like Times for the text. Be sparing, however, with the typographical variation: you want to organize the page of information visually without pulling the reader's attention away from your abilties.

If you are printing your resume, use a high-quality bond paper in a standard color such as white or off-white. Ideally, your letter and résumé are on matching paper. If you are attaching the resume as an electronic file to an e-mail message or uploading it to a job site, make sure you submit it in one or more widely used

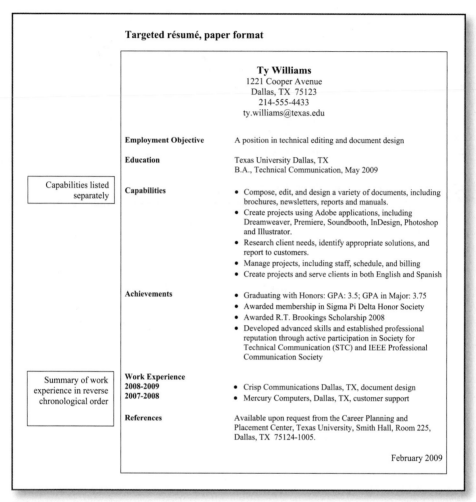

Targeted résumé, paper format

Ty Williams
1221 Cooper Avenue
Dallas, TX 75123
214-555-4433
ty.williams@texas.edu

Employment Objective	A position in technical editing and document design
Education	Texas University Dallas, TX B.A., Technical Communication, May 2009
Capabilities	• Compose, edit, and design a variety of documents, including brochures, newsletters, reports and manuals. • Create projects using Adobe applications, including Dreamweaver, Premiere, Soundbooth, InDesign, Photoshop and Illustrator. • Research client needs, identify appropriate solutions, and report to customers. • Manage projects, including staff, schedule, and billing • Create projects and serve clients in both English and Spanish
Achievements	• Graduating with Honors: GPA: 3.5; GPA in Major: 3.75 • Awarded membership in Sigma Pi Delta Honor Society • Awarded R.T. Brookings Scholarship 2008 • Developed advanced skills and established professional reputation through active participation in Society for Technical Communication (STC) and IEEE Professional Communication Society
Work Experience **2008-2009** **2007-2008**	• Crisp Communications Dallas, TX, document design • Mercury Computers, Dallas, TX, customer support
References	Available upon request from the Career Planning and Placement Center, Texas University, Smith Hall, Room 225, Dallas, TX 75124-1005.

February 2009

Capabilities listed separately

Summary of work experience in reverse chronological order

FIGURE 12-4 Targeted Résumé

formats (e.g., as a doc file, docx.file, pdf file, or rtf file) so that it might be easily accessed by the recipient. Make the file read-only so that nothing will be later inserted or deleted.

Who is the recipient for your letters and résumés? When answering an advertisement, you should follow whatever instructions are given there. You might be directed, for example, to a company-wide job site to submit your application electronically. Otherwise, direct the materials, if at all possible, to the person in the organization who directly supervises the position for which you are applying. This person often has the power to hire for the position. Your research into the company may turn up the name you need. If not, don't be afraid of calling the company switchboard and asking directly for a name and title. If need be, write to human resources directors. Whatever you do, write to *a specific individual* by name.

Sometimes, of course, you may gain an interview without having submitted a letter of application—for example, when recruiters come to your campus. Bring a résumé with you and give it to the interviewer at the start of the interview. The résumé gives the interviewer a starting point for questions and often helps to focus the interview on your qualifications for the job.

Scannable résumés. A scannable résumé is a paper résumé that has been modified so that it can be electronically scanned. Many organizations now scan the paper résumés they receive and enter the information into a special database for quick retrieval by keywords (see Figure 12-5.) For example, if the company needs an environmental specialist, the hiring manager scours the database for words such as *environment* and *ecology*. Only job candidates with the keywords on their résumé will be considered. In a scannable résumé, therefore, you must make sure that the keywords of your occupation, often nouns, are present in abundance. You must get through the computer to be considered by a human reader.

For your résumé to be scannable, you must also modify its format. Ordinarily, a scanner reads résumés from left to right and often makes mistakes if it encounters such features as italics, underlining, changes of typeface, and small sizes of type. In designing your scannable résumé, therefore, adopt the following guidelines:

- Display all information in a single column.
- Align all information on the left margin.
- Use spaces instead of tabs to separate headings from text, or place headings on a separate line.
- Use a single typeface.
- Use all capital letters for your name and major headings.
- Use 12-point type.
- Do not use italics and underlining.
- Do not use rules and borders.
- Submit a clean and crisp copy.
- Do not fold or staple the résumé.

Online résumés. Many companies allow you to submit résumés and cover letters online, either as uploaded files (doc, docx, pdf, or rtf) or as documents generated electronically by filling in the fields on a series of pages at the site. The fields solicit the details of your address, credentials, and objectives and allow you to identify the job or jobs for which you are applying. This information is automatically compiled in a standardized format for access by hiring managers. Because you can't organize the information yourself to emphasize your knowledge and experience, using keywords to highlight your suitability for the job will be critical.

Functional résumé, scannable format

TY WILLIAMS
1221 Cooper Avenue
Dallas, TX 75123
214-555-4433
ty.williams@texas.edu
February 2009

EMPLOYMENT OBJECTIVE
Position as a Technical Communicator specializing in document design and technical editing.

EDUCATION
Texas University Dallas, TX
B.A., Technical Communication, May 2009

COMMUNICATION SKILLS
Compose, edit, and design a variety of documents, including brochures, newsletters, reports and manuals.
Create projects in all Adobe applications.
Provide customer support for hardware and software products.
Research customer problems, identify appropriate solutions, and report to customers by telephone or e-mail message.
Read/write/speak Spanish.
Graduating with Honors, GPA: 3.5; GPA in Major: 3.75

PROJECT MANAGEMENT
Supervise small document design projects from initial meeting with client through publication and delivery.
Coordinate project staff and schedule.
Maintain billing records.

PROFESSIONAL INVOLVEMENT
Sigma Pi Delta Honor Society
Association for Computing Machinery (ACM)
IEEE Professional Communication Society
Society for Technical Communication (STC)

WORK EXPERIENCE
Crisp Communications Dallas, TX, 2008-2009, document design
Mercury Computers, Dallas, TX, 2007-2008, customer support

REFERENCES
Available upon request from the Career Planning and Placement Center, Texas University, Smith Hall, Room 225, Dallas, TX 75124-1005.

FIGURE 12-5 Functional Résumé in Scannable Format

Follow-up letters. Write *follow-up letters* (1) if after two weeks you have received no answer to your letter of application; (2) after an interview; (3) if a company fails to offer you a job; and (4) to accept or refuse a job.

No answer. If a company doesn't acknowledge receipt of your original letter of application within two weeks, write again with a gracious inquiry such as the following:

Dear Mr. Petrosian:

On 12 April I applied for a position with your company. I have not heard from you, so perhaps my original letter and résumé have been misplaced. I enclose copies of them.

If you have already reached a decision regarding my application or if there has been a delay in filling the position, please let me know at your earliest opportunity.

I look forward to hearing from you.

Sincerely yours,

After an interview. Within a day's time, follow up your interview with a letter. Such a letter draws favorable attention to yourself as a person who understands business courtesy and good communication practice. Express your appreciation for the interview. Emphasize any of your qualifications that seemed to be especially important to the interviewer. Express your willingness to live with any special conditions of employment, such as relocation. Make clear that you want the job and feel qualified to do it. If you include a specific question in your letter, it may hasten a reply. Your letter might look like this one:

Dear Ms. Kuriyama:

Thank you for speaking with me last Tuesday about the food supervisor position you have open.

Working in a hospital food service relates well to my experience and interests. The job you have available is one I am qualified to do. A research report I am working on for one of my courses examines the efficiency with which hospital food services provide varied diets to people with specific dietary requirements. May I send you a copy next week when it is completed?

I understand that the position would include working alternating weekends. This requirement presents no difficulty for me.

I look forward to hearing from you soon.

Sincerely yours,

After being refused a job. When a company refuses you a job, good tactics dictate that you acknowledge the refusal. Express thanks for the time spent with you and state your regret that no opening exists at the present time. If you like, express the hope of being considered in the future. You never know; it might happen. In any case, you want to maintain a good reputation with this employer and its representatives. These are people working in the same industry as you: you may encounter them at professional conferences or meetings of the local chapter of your professional association. They may later come to work at your same company as your colleague, your supervisor, or your subordinate. The few minutes you devote now to a courteous reply will create a lasting impression on them of your extraordinary professionalism.

Accepting or refusing a job. Writing an acceptance letter presents few problems. Be brief. Thank the employer for the job offer, and accept the job. Determine the day and time you will report for work, and express pleasure at the prospect of joining the organization and working with your new colleagues. A good letter of acceptance might read as follows:

Dear Mr. Gafaiti:

Thank you for offering me a job as research assistant with your firm. I happily accept. I will report to work on 1 July as you have requested.

I look forward to working with Price Industries and particularly to the opportunity of doing research with Dr. Ertas.

Sincerely yours,

Writing a letter of refusal can be difficult. Be as gracious as possible. Be brief but not so brief as to suggest rudeness or indifference. Make it clear that you appreciate the offer. If you can, give a reason for your refusal. The employer who has spent time and money in interviewing you and corresponding with you deserves these courtesies. And, of course, your own self-interest is involved. Some day you may wish to reapply to an organization that for the moment you must turn down. A good letter of refusal might look like this one:

Dear Ms. White:

I enjoyed my visit to the research department of your company. I would very much have liked to work with the people I met there. I thank you for offering me the opportunity to do so.

After much serious thought, I have decided that the research opportunities offered me in another job are closer to the interests I developed at Nebraska State University. Therefore, I have accepted that job and regret that I cannot accept yours.

I appreciate the great courtesy and thoughtfulness that you and your associates extended to me during the application and interview process. The individual you do hire will be blessed with exceptional colleagues.

Sincerely yours,

INTERVIEWING

The immediate goal of all your preparation and letter and résumé writing is an interview with a potential employer.

The interview. If you have prepared properly, you should show up at the interview knowing almost everything about the organization, including its basic history, chief locations, key products and services, financial situation, and mission.

You should have the following with you: your résumé, in both regular and scannable formats; a portfolio of your work, if appropriate; pen and notebook; a list of your references; and your business card.

The interviewer will probably start with a bit of social conversation to put you at ease before proceeding to questions aimed at assessing your skills and interests and how you might be of value to the organization. You might anticipate questions such as the following:

- What can you tell me about yourself?
- What are you strengths and weaknesses?
- What do you want to be doing five years from now?
- Why would you want to work for us?
- Why should we hire you?
- What accomplishment are you most proud of?
- What is the biggest problem you've encountered and how did you solve it?

To the question, "What can you tell me about yourself?" the interviewer really doesn't expect an extended life history. This question provides you the opportunity to talk about your work and educational experiences and your skills. Try to relate your skills and experience to the needs of the organization. Don't overlook the people and communication skills essential to nearly every professional job.

In your answer to this and other questions, be specific in your examples. If you say something like "I have good managerial skills," immediately back it up with an occasion or experience that supports your statement. Focus on offering the specific evidence that will lead the interviewer to the right conclusions about you. Such specifics are more memorable than unsupported claims and will help you stick in the interviewer's mind.

In answering questions about your strengths and weaknesses, be honest, but don't betray weaknesses that could eliminate you from consideration. Admit to weaknesses that would have no impact on the specific job for which you are interviewing: for example, if the job has no managerial duties, it would be okay to acknowledge that your managerial skills are undeveloped.

To the question, "What do you want to be doing five years from now?" a good answer would identify a job with greater responsibilities at the same company.

The question "Why do you want to work for us?" allows you to display what you have learned about the organization. In answering this question, you should again show that what you have to offer fits with what the company needs.

In the final portion of the interview you will typically be given a chance to ask some questions of your own. It's a good time to get more details about the job or the working environnment. Ask about the organization's goals. "What is the company most proud of?" is a good question. Or "What are you looking for in the candidate for this position?" What will you want him or her to accomplish in the first year on the job?" Don't ask naive questions—questions you ought to know the answers to already from your research—like the size of the company or the number of employees. Don't ask questions just to ask questions. The interview is a good time for you to find out if you really want to work for this organization. Not every organization is going to be a good fit for what you have to offer and what you want to do. Avoid questions about salary and benefits unless the interviewer has raised this subject.

If you really want to go to work for the organization, make that clear before the interview ends. But don't allow your willingness to appear as desperation. Companies don't hire desperate people. At some point in the interview, be sure to get the interviewer's name (spelled correctly!), title, address, phone number, e-mail address, and fax number. You'll need them for later correspondence. When the interviewer thanks you for coming, thank him or her for seeing you and leave. Don't drag the interview out when it's clearly over or linger at the door.

Negotiation. Interviewers rarely raise the subject of salary and benefits until they either see you as a good prospect or are sure they want to hire you. If they offer you the job, the negotiation is sometimes done in a separate interview. For example, your future boss may offer you the job and then send you to negotiate with the human resources staff.

Sometimes, the negotiator may offer you a salary. At other times, you may be asked to name a salary. Now is the time to put to good use the information you may have received through your networking activities. Or check the online job finding services or specialized services such as Salary.Com (www.salary.com) for their estimates of earnings for different positions in different industries.

Your research in these sources will give you not a specific salary but a salary range. If asked to name a salary, do not ask for the bottom of the range. Ask for as near the top as you believe is reasonable given your education and experience. The negotiator will respect you the more for knowing what you are worth. However, balance the compensation package—vacations, pension plans, health care, educational opportunities, and so forth—against the salary. Some compensation packages are worth a good deal of money and may allow you to accept a lower salary.

The location of the job is also a critical factor to consider. Online services such as Salary.Com (www.salary.com) offer cost-of-living calculators that determine the comparative worth of salaries by location. For example, $50,000 in New York City could be the equivalent of $35,000 in Chicago, $29,000 in Houston, or $42,000 in Los Angeles.

Before and after the interview. If you have not participated in job interviews before, you would be wise to practice with several friends. Using the information that we have given you and that you have gathered for yourself, practice several interviews, with two of you as interviewer and interviewee and the remainder as observers. Ask the observers to look for strengths and weaknesses in your answers, diction, grammar, and body language and to give you a candid appraisal. Practice until you feel comfortable with the process.

After you finish each interview, write down your impressions as soon as possible. How did your clothes compare to the interviewer's? Were there unexpected questions? How good were your answers? What did you learn about the organization? What did you learn about a specific job or jobs? Did anything make you uncomfortable about the organization? Do you think you would fit in there? By the next day, get a thank-you note (letter, e-mail, or fax) off to the interviewer.

JOB SEARCH CHECKLIST

The Letter and Résumé

Planning

☐ Your letter of application:
   What position are you applying for?
   How did you learn about this position?
   Why are you qualified for this position?
   What interests you about this company?
   What will you do for the organization?
   How will the employer reach you?

☐ Your résumé:
   Do you have all the necessary details about your education and experience (e.g., dates, job descriptions, schools, majors, degrees, extracurricular activities)?
   Which résumé format will suit your experience and abilities? Chronological? Functional? Targeted?
   Do you need to prepare your résumé in a scannable format? If so, which keywords will you use?
   Do you have permission to use the names of at least three people as references?

Revising

☐ Your letter of application:
   Do you seem self-confident but not arrogant or boastful?
   Does your letter show how you could be valuable to the employer?
   Does your letter reflect interest in a specific job?
   Have you emphasized the education and experience that suit you for this job?
   Have you made it clear you would like to be interviewed? Have you made it easy for the employer to arrange the interview?
   Is your letter completely free of grammatical and spelling errors? Is it designed for easy reading and skimming?

continued

JOB SEARCH CHECKLIST ✔ *continued*

☐ Your résumé:

Have you picked the résumé type that suits your experiences and qualifications?

Have you listed your education and job experience in reverse chronological order?

Have you used active verbs and appropriate keywords to describe your education and experience?

Is your résumé completely free of grammatical and spelling errors? Is it designed for easy reading and skimming?

The Interview

Planning

☐ Have you completed your research about the organization? Are you familiar with its history, goals, products, locations, and reputation in the industry and region?

☐ Have you practiced your answers to likely questions?

☐ Do you have good questions to ask the interviewer?

Reviewing

☐ Did you answer all the questions effectively? Which questions could you have answered better?

☐ Were you asked questions that you didn't expect?

☐ How did the interviewer answer your questions? Did he or she seem to think you asked good questions?

☐ Do you think you will be offered the job? Why or why not?

☐ Do you think you are a good fit for this organization? Why or why not?

EXERCISES

1. Investigate a potential employer of majors in your field. Locate information available from the employer's website as well as online job-finding services. Are all the profiles of this employer basically similar? Do you notice important differences? Locate additional information available in newspapers, magazines, and government documents about this employer. What is the public perception of this employer? What is its reputation in the industry? Interview employees or managers for their perspectives on the advantages and disadvantages of working for this employer. Compile the findings of your research in a slide presentation for majors in your field.

2. Given the findings of your investigation of a major employer in your field, list the characteristics of this employer's ideal job candidate. What would be the ideal job candidate's education and experience? What would be his or her special skills, dispositions, and achievements? How are you similar to this ideal job candidate? How do you differ?

3. Given the findings of your investigation of a major employer in your field and your inventory of the ideal job candidate, tailor your typical letter of job application and résumé to the needs and interests of this employer. What changes will you make in your usual version of each document? How will these changes increase the likelihood of your being interviewed for a job?

4. If a friend of yours were applying for a position as a lab assistant, which of the following two résumés (see Figure 12-6) would you advise he include with the letter of application? If you were given 15 more minutes to make this résumé more effective, what changes would you make?

George Castillo
gcastillo@texas.edu

Local Address   307 Spruce Street, Dallas, TX 75270, 214-555-1603
Permanent Address   2292 Governor Avenue, Katy, TX 77450, 281-555-0096

EDUCATION	**Texas University, Dallas TX**
	Bachelor of Science Degree
	Double Major: Biomedical Science and Entomology
	Graduated: December 2008
	GPR: 3.15/4.0
EXPERIENCE	**Texas University, Dallas TX**
	The History of Medicine Study Abroad, Germany, Summer 2007

- Shadowed and Observed a triple bypass surgery, North Rhine Westfalia Heart and Diabetes Center
- Visited German veterinary cloning facilities in Bayer Healthcare Target Research Facilities, Chemical Research Facilities, and fermentation facilities

St. Joseph's Hospital, Bryan TX
Day Surgery Tower Volunteer, August 2006—present

- Assisted patients and their families while at the hospital.
- Aided doctors, nurses, and staff in various duties.

International Student Volunteers (ISV) Conservation Project

- Traveled to Australia to work with a team on trail building in national forests, planting over 1,000 trees, sages, and grasses, and removing invasive species from devastated swamp lands.

ACTIVITIES   **Sigma Nu National Fraternity**

- Executive Council
  - Candidate Marshall—Fall 2008
  - Lieutenant Commander (Vice President) Spring 2007—Spring 2008
  - Sentinel and Risk Reduction Fall 2006—Spring 2007
- Head of Philanthropy Committee 2007-2008, Recruitment Committee, Academic Chair—Spring 2007, Social Chair—Fall 2005, House Manager—Spring 2005, Candidate Class Social Chair—Fall 2004

Biomedical Science Association (BSA) Fall 2004—present
Texas Pre-Med Society Fall 2006

AWARDS   **Sigma Nu Fraternity**

- Commander's Award 2007—Spring 2008
- Man of the Year Fall 2007—Spring 2008
- Scholar of the Year Fall 2006—Spring 2007
- Big Brother of the Year Fall 2006—Spring 2007

Study Abroad Fellowship and International Education Fee Scholarship
National Scholar's Honor Society—inducted Fall 2007

FIGURE 12-6a Document for Exercise 4

GEORGE CASTILLO
gcastillo@texas.edu

Local Address   **Permanent Address**
307 Spruce Street   2292 Governor Avenue
Dallas, TX 75270   Katy, TX, 77450
(214) 555–1603   (281) 555–0096

EDUCATION   **Texas University, Dallas TX**
                     Bachelor of Science Degree
                     Double Major: Biomedical Science and Entomology
                     Graduated: December 2008,   GPR: 3.15/4.0

LABORATORY QUALIFICATIONS

Collegiate Science Coursework

- General Chemistry w/ lab I & II
- General Biology w/ lab I & II
- Physics w/ lab I & II
- Organic Chemistry w/ lab I & II
- Biochemistry
- Microbiology w/ lab
- Basic knowledge of diseases

Collegiate Entomology

- Identifying Species of Insects
- Collection of Insects
- Forensic Entomology
- Medical Entomology w/ lab
- Veterinary Entomology w/ lab
- General Entomology w/ lab
- Insect Morphology w/ lab

Other Skills

- Microsoft Office—Word, Excel, PowerPoint, and Access

EXPERIENCE

The History of Medicine Study Abroad, Germany, Summer 2007

continued

FIGURE 12-6b

- Shadowed and Observed a triple bypass surgery, North Rhine Westfalia Heart and Diabetes Center
- Visited German veterinary cloning facilities in Bayer Healthcare Target Research Facilities, Chemical Research Facilities, and fermentation facilities

St. Joseph's Hospital, Bryan TX

Day Surgery Tower Volunteer, August 2006—present

- Assisted patients and their families while at the hospital.
- Aided doctors, nurses, and staff in various duties.

International Student Volunteers (ISV) Conservation Project

- Traveled to Australia to work with a team on trail building in national forests, planting over 1,000 trees, sages, and grasses, and removing invasive species from devastated swamp lands.

ACTIVITIES   Sigma Nu National Fraternity
                      Coastal Conservation Association
                      Biomedical Science Association (BSA) Fall 2004—present
                      Texas A&M Pre-Med Society Fall 2006

AWARDS

Sigma Nu Fraternity

- Commander's Award, Fall 2007—Spring 2008 The chapter president recognizes one exceptional individual within the chapter.

- Man of the Year, Fall 2007—Spring 2008. The Fraternity recognizes the individual who has demonstrated excellence in the area of Leadership.

- Scholar of the Year, Fall 2006—Spring 2007. The Fraternity recognizes the individual who has demonstrated excellence in the area of scholarship.

- Big Brother of the Year, Fall 2006—Spring 2007. The Fraternity recognizes an exceptional Big Brother in the chapter.

Study Abroad Fellowship and International Education Fee Scholarship

National Scholar's Honor Society—inducted Fall 2007

REFERENCES FURNISHED UPON REQUEST

FIGURE 12-6b *continued*

Appendix A

▬▬ ▬ ▬▬▬▬▬ ▬▬ ▬▬ ▬▬

A Brief Guide to Grammar, Punctuation, and Usage

ab ▶ ABBREVIATIONS

Every field uses standard and specialized terms that may be abbreviated for convenience and conciseness.

First, decide whether your audience is familiar enough with the unabbreviated term to allow you to use it without defining it. Second, decide whether your audience is familiar enough with the abbreviation for you to use it without spelling it out.

If you decide that an abbreviation is appropriate and must be explained, place the abbreviation in parentheses following your first use of the unabbreviated term. Thereafter use the abbreviation by itself. If necessary, after the parentheses, provide a definition of the term. Make the definition as detailed as necessary for your purpose and audience:

> Fluid catalytic cracking (FCC) changes crude oil to gasoline by breaking the long-chain molecules that are characteristic of hydrocarbon liquids. The process involves exposing the oil to a special chemical agent under high temperature and pressure. FCC is the key conversion process at oil refineries.

Use Latin abbreviations like *i.e.* (that is), and *e.g.* (for example) in parenthetical explanations, or in tables and figures if space is limited.

Avoid starting sentences with abbreviations: spell out the abbreviation or revise the sentence to shift the abbreviation to a later position in the sentence.

Check the appropriate style guide or publication manual in your field for specific guidelines on abbreviations.

apos ▶ APOSTROPHES

Use apostrophes to indicate the possessive case of nouns (e.g., singular: manager's; plural: managers') and the missing letters in contractions (could've: could have).

With coordinated nouns, use apostrophes to make all possessive in order to indicate individual ownership. To indicate joint ownership, make only the final noun possessive.

- Maria's and David's reports are late. (i.e., The reports written by Maria and the reports written by David are late.)

- Maria and David's reports are late. (i.e., The reports written together by Maria and David are late.)

Also use apostrophes to indicate the possessive case of indefinite pronouns ending in *–one* or *–body* as well as *either, neither, another* or *other*:

- Everyone's paycheck is incorrect because of a computer error.
- The change must have raised somebody's profits this quarter.
- I asked both managers and either's approval is enough to proceed.
- I asked both managers but neither's approval was forthcoming.
- We preferred each other's answer.
- She preferred another's answer.

acro ▶ ACRONYMS

Acronyms are names for objects or entities formed from a combination of the initial letters of the words in a title or phrase. Unlike abbreviations, acronyms are pronounced as words: for example UN (United Nations) versus UNICEF (United Nations International Children's Emergency Fund).

First decide whether your audience is familiar enough with the acronym to allow you to use it without showing the phrase from which it is derived. Second decide whether the phrase from which it is derived is itself a sufficient definition or explanation of the acronym.

If you decide that an acronym is appropriate, place the phrase from which it is derived in parentheses following your first use of the acronym. If necessary, supply additional explanation immediately following. Thereafter use the acronym by itself:

The mysterious illness was identified as SARS (Severe Acute Respiratory Syndrome), a disease similar to pneumonia but viral in nature and thus impervious to antibiotics. SARS killed 299 people in Hong Kong in a 2003 epidemic.

brackets ▶ BRACKETS

Use brackets inside quotations or parentheses to insert a clarifying note or comment:

- "This is the highest level of membership in the organization [8.1% of 375,000] and indicates exceptional professional achievement."
- If you would like more information about this policy, please call my office (M-F 8-5 [EDT], 866-555-7243).

cap ▶ CAPITALIZATION

Capitalize months but not seasons (e.g., January was unusually mild this winter.)

Capitalize *geographic areas* but not directions (e.g., The stores were all originally in the Southeast, but soon spread not so much north as west.)

Capitalize titles preceding names but not following or in isolation:

- President Juanita Solis Ybarra arrived early to the meeting.
- Juanita Solis Ybarra, president of the company, arrived early to the meeting.
- The president of the company is Juanita Solis Ybarra.

colon ▶ COLON

Use a colon to introduce quotations, lists, or supporting statements:

- Dr. Smith's testimony was unequivocal: "This test has no predictive value and should not be promoted as though it does."
- The company has five locations: Atlanta, Chicago, Dallas, Los Angeles, and New York.
- The book explains the maieutic method: that is, the practice of teaching by asking questions that stimulate thinking and elicit new ideas.

Never use a colon immediately following a verb or a preposition:

WRONG: The five stores are located in: Atlanta, Chicago, Dallas, Los Angeles, and New York.
WRONG: The locations of the five stores are: Atlanta, Chicago, Dallas, Los Angeles, and New York.
RIGHT: The stores are in five locations: Atlanta, Chicago, Dallas, Los Angeles, and New York.
RIGHT: The stores are located in the following cities: Atlanta, Chicago, Dallas, Los Angeles, and New York.

Use a colon to separate two independent clauses if the second clause explains or amplifies the first:

- Analytical skills are necessary but insufficient: we must also develop the ability to synthesize information.
- The new facility uses icons to identify its various services: for example, a picture of a glowing question mark identifies the information booth.

Use a colon following the salutation of a business letter.

Dear Mr. Ramirez:

c ▶ COMMA

Use a comma before a coordinating conjunction (*and, but, or, nor, for, yet*) that joins two independent clauses:

- The engineers arrived at their recommendation almost immediately, and the supervisor supported their judgment.
- The engineers arrived at their recommendation almost immediately, but the supervisor questioned their judgment.

Use a comma after an introductory word, phrase, or clause:

- Unfortunately, the company must declare bankruptcy.
- In appreciation of their efforts on the project, the president awarded each of the scientists a $500 bonus.
- After you have completed the usability testing, the engineers will modify their design of the product.

Use commas to separate nonrestrictive modifiers from the remainder of the sentence.

> RESTRICTIVE: Cotton farming that is conducted without artificial irrigation lowers the cost of production but raises the risk of a poor crop.
> NONRESTRICTIVE: Cotton farming, which typically involves the use of defoliants as well as herbicides and pesticides, has high costs for the environment.

A restrictive modifier is necessary to the meaning of the sentence. The writer has thus *restricted* the subject of cotton farming to that which is conducted without artificial irrigation. The writer here is making a single claim: cotton farming without artificial irrigation has lower costs but higher risks.

A nonrestrictive modifier supplies additional information about the subject without restricting it. The writer here is making two claims: cotton farming usually has high costs for the environment, and cotton farming usually involves defoliants, pesticides, and herbicides.

Use commas to separate items in a series of words, phrases, or clauses.

- This unit of the facility produces ethylene oxide, ethylene dichloride, and polyethylene.
- Ethylene contributes to the ripening of fruit, the opening of flowers, and the shedding of leaves.
- Florists complain about the impact of ethylene exposure on the life of their flowers, grocers worry about high-ethylene products like bananas, and shippers focus their efforts on good temperature controls to minimize the chemical's release.

Use commas to separate dates, geographical locations, and titles:

- On Wednesday, June 18; 2008, the case was closed.
- The marble sculpture was shipped from Palermo, Sicily, by boat to Galveston, Texas, and transported from there by truck to Albuquerque, New Mexico.
- The new members of the citizen review board are Ritu Raju, Ph.D., and Pamela Brewer, J.D.

dm ▶ DANGLING MODIFIER

A dangling modifier occurs whenever a modifying word or phrase is used without a suitable noun for it to modify:

WRONG: Assuming the contamination was widespread, the eggs were discarded.
RIGHT: Assuming the contamination was widespread, the manager discarded the eggs.

dash   ▶   DASH

The dash serves the same function as parentheses (i.e., separating a tangential or explanatory comment from the remainder of the sentence), but the dash does so with greater emphasis—like a shout instead of whisper.

ell   ▶   ELLIPSIS

Use three spaced periods to indicate that words have been omitted from a quotation. If the quotation is at the end of a sentence, use four periods (i.e., three spaced periods for the ellipsis and a period for the sentence).

- "In a work context, these readers . . . will feel no commitment to read what you write unless your messages are useful to them as they do their own work."
- "In a work context, these readers, all of whom come from a variety of educational and cultural backgrounds, will feel no commitment to read what you write unless your messages are useful to them. . . ."

If the quotation is obviously incomplete, skip the ellipsis.

According to the investigator, their actions were "deliberate and malicious."

exc   ▶   EXCLAMATION POINT

Avoid using exclamation points in the writing of reports, letters, memos, and e-mail messages so that you never come across as easily excited or agitated. If writing instructions, use exclamation points as necessary with cautions and warnings.

frag   ▶   FRAGMENT

A sentence fragment is a phrase or a clause punctuated as though it were a complete sentence. This error is usually fixed by connecting the fragment to the preceding sentence.

WRONG: The findings were exactly as expected. Although we were hoping for better news.
RIGHT: The findings were exactly as expected, although we were hoping for better news.
WRONG: The report came straight from the investigating committee. Which included two forensic scientists and the city's medical examiner.

RIGHT: The report came straight from the investigating committee, which included two forensic scientists and the city's medical examiner.

WRONG: The city council voted to change the policy. Surprising all of us at the meeting.

RIGHT: The city council voted to change the policy, surprising all of us at the meeting.

hyphen ▶ HYPHEN

Use a hyphen with the following suffixes and prefixes:

- -elect: president-elect
- -in-law: brother-in-law
- all-: all-around team player
- ex-: ex-employee
- quasi-: quasi-empirical study
- self-: self-starter
- well-: well-connected

Also use hyphens with prefixes preceding capitalized words (e.g., pre-Olympics competition), prefixes preceding numbers (e.g., post-9/11 security), and prefixes preceding acronyms and abbreviations (e.g., anti-HIV medication).

In addition, use a hyphen between words joined together to modify a word:

- It was a labor-intensive process.
- The waiting room has black-and-white-striped chairs.
- She makes six-, eight-, and twelve-string guitars.

ital ▶ ITALICIZATION

Italicize titles of books, journals, magazines, plays, films, radio and television programs, sculptures and paintings, ships, aircraft, and spacecraft.

Italicize words that are considered foreign to the English language.

Italicize Latin words for genus and species (e.g., The zoological designation for the American toad is *Bufo americanus*.)

Italicize words, letters, and numbers identified as words, letters, and numbers.

The words *compose* and *comprise* have opposite meanings.
His middle initial is *A*.
She said it scored a *5* on the grading scale.

Italicize letters used as statistical symbols:

- *M* (i.e., mean)
- *N* (i.e., number of in the studied population studied)

- *p* (i.e., probability)
- *SD* (i.e., standard deviation)

mm ▶ MISPLACED MODIFIER

A misplaced modifier is a word, phrase, or clause put in the wrong position in the sentence and thus modifying a word the writer never intended to be modified.

> WRONG: This machine was repaired almost for $100.
> RIGHT: This machine was repaired for almost $100. (*or* This machine was almost repaired for $100.)
> WRONG: He was trying to find a job for two years.
> RIGHT: He was trying for two years to find a job. (*or* He was trying to find a two-year job.)
> WRONG: The computer was available at a new store that he tried a week ago.
> RIGHT: The computer that he tried a week ago was available at a new store.
> (*or* The computer was available at a new store that he visited a week ago.)

np/ag ▶ NOUN-PRONOUN AGREEMENT

In all formal communication, collective nouns such as *each, everyone, either, neither, anybody, somebody, everybody,* and *no one* use singular pronouns and singular verbs:

> FORMAL: Each has his or her machine.
> FORMAL: Everybody was given his or her ticket.

For informal communications, the plural pronoun is widely used:

> INFORMAL: Each has their own machine.
> INFORMAL: Everybody was given their ticket.

A better solution is to revise the wording:

- All have their machines.
- Each has a machine.
- All were given their tickets.
- Everybody was given a ticket.

The same issue arises with nouns used in a generic sense, such as the word *employee* in the following:

> FORMAL: The employee must complete his or her training within one week of being hired.
> INFORMAL: The employee must complete their training within one week of being hired.

Again a better solution is to revise the wording:

- All employees must complete their training within one week of being hired.
- The employee must complete the training within one week of being hired.

With collective nouns such as *team, group, class, committee,* use the singular pronouns *it/its* if you are referring to the unit and the plural pronouns *they/their/them* if you are referring to the constituents.

- The usability team will conduct its tests according to the schedule that it posted on its website.
- The usability team will pick up their passports before they leave on this trip.

num ▶ NUMBERS

Ordinarily, use words for numbers from zero to nine and numerals for numbers 10 and higher.

In a series of numbers, if any one of the numbers is 10 or higher, use all numerals:

- The experiment involved eight vehicles and four drivers.
- The experiment involved 8 vehicles, 4 drivers, and 16 passengers

Never start a sentence with a numeral: either use words for the number or revise the sentence to shift the number from the opening position.

- Twenty-five people were involved in the experiment.
- The experiment involved 25 people.

With two adjacent numbers, use words for one and numerals for the other in order to avoid confusion.

- He ordered twelve 100-item boxes.
- The list includes 15 ten-digit numbers.

Always use numerals for dates, addresses, exact time, exact sums of money, measurements, and cross references.

- 1 February 2009 or February 1, 2009
- 4307 55th Street
- 2:00 P.M. (but two o'clock)
- $7,988.97 (but about eight thousand dollars)
- 17 km
- 35 g
- see page 86
- see Table 4

paral ▶ PARALLELISM

Use the same grammatical structure for items in a series:

> WRONG: This job candidate is proficient at writing proposals, publication management, usability tests, and designing websites.
> RIGHT: This job candidate is proficient at writing proposals, managing publications, running usability tests, and designing websites.
> RIGHT: This job candidate is proficient at proposal writing, publication management, usability testing, and website design.

paren ▶ PARENTHESES

Use parentheses to separate a tangential or explanatory comment.

Never put any mark of punctuation before an opening parenthesis, but put any required marks of punctuation inside the parentheses and after the closing parenthesis:

- Use parentheses to separate a tangential or explanatory comment (including definitions, clarifications, examples, quotations, or statistics) from the remainder of a sentence.
- Latin words are used to designate genus and species in zoological classification (e.g., *Bufo americanus* for the American toad). (Note that these scientific names are always displayed in italics).

pron ▶ PRONOUN

Use the subjective case of a pronoun (*I, he, she, we, they*) if it serves as the subject of a clause:

- She and I will work on this project.
- He visited the manufacturing facility yesterday, even though she and I made the same trip a week ago.

Use the objective case of a pronoun (*me, him, her, us, them*) if it is the object of a verb or the object of a preposition:

- The manager congratulated them and us for fixing the problem.
- The investigating committee interviewed him and her at the same time.
- The manager distributed copies of the report to them and me.
- This project will be difficult for him and me to complete on time.

quot ▶ QUOTATION MARKS

Use quotation marks for brief quotations:

- As Clarence Weisman has noted, "The intelligent solution would be to limit the population of this species."

- According to Gloria Moore, "Almost 250 billion pounds of nurdles are manufactured annually. This growing continent of plastic pellets is a looming disaster for the world's environment, especially its oceans."

For quotations of four or more lines, skip the quotation marks and indent and single space the quotation.

Use quotation marks around titles of articles from journals and magazines:

- The article "Polymers are Eternal" was originally published by Marco Quesada in 1986.
- Andrea Kolosov's "The Geologic Heritage in Dispute" claims that investment in crop diversity is dwindling.

Always put commas and periods inside the quotation marks

- According to Andrea Kolosov's "The Geologic Heritage in Dispute," investment in crop diversity is dwindling.
- Marco Quesada is the author of "Polymers are Eternal."

Put all other marks of punctuation outside the quotation marks unless they are part of the quotation.

- In 1986, Marco Quesada published his article "Polymers are Eternal": it was greeted with derision by the plastics industry.
- Andrea Kolosov's "The Geologic Heritage in Dispute" asked the question, "What are the avoidable contributors to this growing environmental crisis?"

run-on ▶ RUN-ON SENTENCE

A run-on sentence is two independent clauses joined with only a comma or with no punctuation at all.

Two independent clauses may be punctuated as two separate sentences (each with a period) or may be joined with a semi-colon, a colon, or a comma and a conjunction (*and, but, for, nor,* or *yet*):

WRONG: A corporate code of conduct has legal and ethical implications, it must address multiple audiences both inside and outside the organization.
RIGHT: A corporate code of conduct has legal and ethical implications. It must address multiple audiences both inside and outside the organization.
RIGHT: A corporate code of conduct has legal and ethical implications; as a consequence, it must address multiple audiences both inside and outside the organization.
RIGHT: A corporate code of conduct has legal and ethical implications, and thus it must address multiple audiences both inside and outside the organization.

A run-on sentence may also be repaired by changing one or the other of the independent clauses to a dependent clause or phrase

> RIGHT: Because a corporate code of conduct has legal and ethical implications, it must address multiple audiences both inside and outside the organization.
> RIGHT: A corporate code of conduct has legal and ethical implications, making it necessary to address multiple audiences both inside and outside the organization.

semi ▶ SEMICOLON

Use a semicolon to join related independent clauses (e.g., The mysterious illness shared symptoms of pneumonia; however, unlike typical pneumonia, this illness was viral and unresponsive to antibiotics.)

Use a semicolon to separate items in a series if the items are internally punctuated with commas (e.g., The equipment order included security cameras for all exits; fire extinguishers, smoke detectors, and carbon monoxide detectors for both floors; projectors, computers, and screens for all twelve classrooms; and computers and telephones for thirty-five offices.)

av/ag ▶ SUBJECT-VERB AGREEMENT

Note that the words *each, either, and neither,* take a singular verb regardless of intervening words:

- Each is qualified.
- Each of the job candidates for the two supervisor positions is qualified.
- Either is qualified.
- Either of the job candidates that we interviewed yesterday is qualified.
- Neither is qualified.
- Neither of the job candidates who interviewed yesterday with us is qualified.

In a coordinated subject joined by *or* or *nor,* make the verb agree with the closer noun or pronoun:

- The original letter or my copies are available for examination.
- My copies or the original letter is available for examination.
- Neither the original letter nor my copies are available for examination.
- Neither my copies nor the original letter is available for examination.

In a coordinated subject joined by *and,* the verb is always plural:

- The original letter and my copies are available for examination.
- My copies and the original letter are available for examination.

With collective nouns such as *team, group, class, committee,* use a singular verb if you are referring to the unit and a plural verb if you are referring to the constituents.

The usability team is in the conference room.
The usability team are in line for big raises this year.

WW ▶ WRONG WORD

The following words are often confused and misused. Here are examples of correct usage:

We **accept** your explanation.
The portfolio included everything **except** his résumé.

The price of gasoline **affected** [influenced] the company's profits.
The product failure **effected** [caused] the company's bankruptcy.

The reports were **already** written.
We were **all ready** to write the reports.

The supervisors were **all together** [united] in their opposition to the proposal.
The supervisors were **altogether** [completely] opposed to the proposal.

We don't purchase office supplies from that company **anymore**.
We don't need **any more** office supplies.

We talked **awhile** but came to no agreement.
We talked for **a while** but came to no agreement.

The designers think that **canvas** will be a durable material for this product.
The managers will **canvass** their employees for opinions about the new policy.

He failed to **cite** sources in his report.
The **site** of the accident was inaccessible to emergency vehicles.

The illustrations **complemented** the step-by-step instructions.
The supervisor **complimented** the writers on their efforts.

Six employees and one supervisor **compose** the grievance committee.
The grievance committee **comprises** six employees and one supervisor.

The boiler is **continually** [repeatedly] overheating.
The technicians worked **continuously** [without interruption] all afternoon to fix the boiler.

The **council** [committee] of advisors was in agreement.
The president was grateful for their **counsel** [advice].

She was always **discreet** [prudent] in discussing confidential issues.
Each item on the agenda is **discrete** [separate].

She is considered a truly **eminent** authority on homolytic fission.
The arrival of the safety investigators is **imminent**.

Their **everyday** routine includes a period of stretching exercises.
She bicycles to the office **every day**.

He realized the refinery was five miles **farther** [distance].
The committee decided to investigate **further** [degree].

We tallied **fewer** [number] accidents this month.
We noticed **less** attention [amount] to safety.

The company is moving **forward** with new technologies.
This report will include a **foreword** of two pages.

The report **implied** [suggested] that the engineer was incompetent.
The manager **inferred** [concluded] that closer supervision of the project was necessary.

It's [it is] no longer under warranty.
Its warranty has expired.

He ordered testing for **lead** contamination.
The manager **led** the team through a difficult project.

We rejected the **principal** recommendation of the report.
The **principal** of the mortgage is slowly shrinking.
We rejected the recommendation on **principle.**

This **quotation** will reinforce the urgency of the report's recommendations.
We will probably **quote** the president in this report.

The judge talked **respectfully** to the members of the jury.
The offices in Portland and Salem were closed on July 1 and July 15, **respectively**.

She bought **stationary** bicycles for the exercise room.
She bought white paper for the company's **stationery.**

I know that **they're** flying to the district office later today.
She was aware of **their** departure.
He was also going **there** in the morning.

The **weather** this year has been unusual.
The profits for the industry hinge on **whether** the price of gasoline rises.

Whose division reported the highest sales?
Who's joining the company?

I appreciate that **you're** working on the report.
I am grateful for **your** work on the report.

Appendix B

Documentation Systems: MLA, CMS, and APA

The MLA System

In the MLA (Modern Language Association) system of documentation, cite sources parenthetically by author's last name (or by authoring organization or by title if no author is identified). If you cite a specific passage or quote from a source, include specific pages:

> Publishing the instructions in a picture-intensive but unconventional medium (e.g., playing cards, wall calendars) could offer "unexpected solutions to such problems as delivering information to remote populations or communicating with inattentive or resistant audiences" (Malone 59).

In a list titled Works Cited, detail your sources in alphabetical order by the author's last name (or by authoring organization or by title if no author is identified):

Book:
Sethi, Priti. *Setting International Standards: Guidelines for Multinational Corporations.* New York: Dolphin, 2009. Print.

Collection:
Van Pelt, Carolyn, ed. *Visual Communication in a Digital World.* Boston: Beacon Hill, 2005. Print.

Essay or article in a book:
Handa, William, and Alice Felmier. "Computer-Mediated Classrooms: Bridging Academic and Industry Environments." *Collaborative Writing: Investigations in Theory and Practice.* Ed. Mary M. Karis and William M. Lay. Chicago: Radius, 1991. 170–205. Print.

Article in a professional journal:
Malone, Edward A. "The Use of Playing Cards to Communicate Technical and Scientific Information." *Technical Communication* 55.1 (2008): 49-60. Print.

Article in a monthly publication:
Raffael, Pauline. "Living with Gorillas." *Natural Life,* Oct. 2009: 48–59. Print.

Article in a daily newspaper:
"Cancer Patient Gets New Therapy." *Los Angeles Tribune* 14 Jan. 1999: A13. Print.

Government publication:
United States Department of the Interior, Minerals Management Service. *Investigation of Fall and Fatality, Main Pass Block 140, May 19, 2000.* MMS 2001–042. Washington: GPO, 2001. Print.

Article in an online journal:
Rice, Kevin. "A New Media Approach to Teaching Classical Rhetoric." *Writing Studies* 11.3 (2007). Web. 3 Mar. 2008.

Article in an online news source:
Ramirez, Juanita. "Bird Flu Strikes Nicaragua." *INN.org.* International News Network. 17 Dec. 2007. Web. 19 Dec. 2007.

Page of a website:
"History of WHO." World Health Organization. 2007. Web. 12 May 2007.

Online multimedia source:
Ramirez, Juanita. "What is Bird Flu?" Video. *INN.com.* International News Network. 17 Dec. 2007. Web. 19 Dec. 2007.

Online posting to e-mail distribution list or bulletin board:
Cooper, Geoffrey. "Ethics and Professionalism." Message to ATTC Distribution List. 9 Oct. 2008. E-mail. http://lyris.tu.edu/read/messages?id=406780

THE CHICAGO SYSTEM

The Chicago (*Chicago Manual of Style*) notes system of documentation includes a numerical list of citations (i.e., Notes) in the order cited as well as a list of sources (i.e., Bibliography) in alphabetical order by author's last name (or by authoring organization or by title if no author is identified).

For each source cited, insert a superscript number in the text corresponding to the appropriate source in the numerical list:

> Publishing the instructions in a picture-intensive but unconventional medium (e.g., playing cards, wall calendars) could offer "unexpected solutions to such problems as delivering information to remote populations or communicating with inattentive or resistant audiences."[2]

Notes:
1. Priti Sethi, *Setting International Standards: Guidelines for Multinational Corporations* (New York: Dolphin, 2009), 117.

2. Edward A. Malone, "The Use of Playing Cards to Communicate Technical and Scientific Information." *Technical Communication* 55 (2008), 59.

3. Sethi, *Setting International Standards*, 89.

4. Malone, "The Use of Playing Cards," 53.

Following are a variety of sources as each would be displayed in numerical Notes and in the alphabetical Bibliography:

Book:

1. Priti Sethi, *Setting International Standards: Guidelines for Multinational Corporations* (New York: Dolphin, 2009), 117.

Sethi, Priti. *Setting International Standards: Guidelines for Multinational Corporations*. New York: Dolphin, 2009.

Collection:

2. Carolyn Van Pelt, ed., *Visual Communication in a Digital World* (Boston: Beacon Hill, 2005), iii-iv.

Van Pelt, Carolyn, ed. *Visual Communication in a Digital World*. Boston: Beacon Hill, 2005.

Essay or article in a book:

3. William Handa and Alice Felmier, "Computer-Mediated Classrooms: Bridging Academic and Industry Environments," in *Collaborative Writing: Investigations in Theory and Practice*, ed. Mary M. Karis and William M. Lay (Chicago: Radius, 1991), 181.

Handa, William, and Alice Felmier. "Computer-Mediated Classrooms: Bridging Academic and Industry Environments." In *Collaborative Writing: Investigations in Theory and Practice*, edited by Mary M. Karis and William M. Lay, 170–205. Chicago: Radius, 1991.

Article in a professional journal:

4. Edward A. Malone, "The Use of Playing Cards to Communicate Technical and Scientific Information." *Technical Communication* 55 (2008): 59.

Malone, Edward A. "The Use of Playing Cards to Communicate Technical and Scientific Information." *Technical Communication* 55 (2008): 49-60.

Article in a monthly publication:

5. Pauline Raffael, "Living with Gorillas," *Natural Life*, October 2009, 51.

Raffael, Pauline. "Living with Gorillas." *Natural Life*, October 2009, 48–59.

Article in a daily newspaper, anonymous:

6. "Cancer Patient Gets New Therapy," *Los Angeles Tribune*, January 14, 1999, A13.

"Cancer Patient Gets New Therapy." *Los Angeles Tribune*, January 14, 1999, A13.

Government publication:

7. U.S. Department of the Interior, Minerals Management Service, *Investigation of Fall and Fatality, Main Pass Block 140, May 19, 2000.* MMS 2001–042 (Washington, DC: U.S. Government Printing Office, 2001), 12.

U.S. Department of the Interior, Minerals Management Service. *Investigation of Fall and Fatality, Main Pass Block 140, May 19, 2000.* MMS 2001–042. Washington, DC: U.S. Government Printing Office, 2001.

Article in an online journal:

8. Kevin Rice, "A New Media Approach to Teaching Classical Rhetoric," *Writing Studies* 11, no. 3 (2007), http://kairos.technorhetoric.net/11.3/binder (accessed March 3, 2008).

Rice, Kevin. "A New Media Approach to Teaching Classical Rhetoric." *Writing Studies* 11, no. 3 (2007). http://kairos.technorhetoric.net/11.3/binder (accessed March 3, 2008).

Article in an online news source:

9. Juanita Ramirez, "Bird Flu Strikes Nicaragua" *INN.com*, December 17, 2007, http://www.inn.com/2007/HEALTH/conditions/12/17/hm.flu/index.html (accessed December 19, 2007).

Ramirez, Juanita. "Bird Flu Strikes Nicaragua" *INN.com*, December 17, 2007. http://www.inn.com/2007/HEALTH/conditions/12/17/hm.flu/index.html (accessed December 19, 2007).

Page of a website:

10. "History of WHO," *World Health Organization*, http://www.who.int/about/history/en/index.html (accessed May 12, 2007).

"History of WHO." *World Health Organization*. http://www.who.int/about/history/en/index.html (accessed May 12, 2007).

Online multimedia source:

11. Juanita Ramirez, "What is Bird Flu?" Video, *INN.com*, December 17, 2007, http://www.inn.com/2007/HEALTH/conditions/12/17/hm.flu/index.html#innSTCVideo (accessed December 19, 2007).

Ramirez, Juanita. "What is Bird Flu?" Video. *INN.com*. December 17, 2007. http://www.inn.com/2007/HEALTH/conditions/12/17/hm.flu/index.html#innSTCVideo (accessed December 19, 2007).

Online posting to e-mail distribution list or bulletin board:

12. Geoffrey Cooper, "Ethics and Professionalism, " ATTC E-mail Distribution List, online posting, September 4, 2007, http://lyris.tu.edu/read/messages?id=406780 (accessed February 18, 2008).

Cooper, Geoffrey. "Ethics and Professionalism." ATTC E-mail Distribution List, online posting, September 4, 2007. http://lyris.tu.edu/read/messages?id=406780 (accessed February 18, 2008).

THE APA SYSTEM

The APA (American Psychological Association) system of documentation cites sources parenthetically using the author's last name (or authoring organization or title if no author is identified) and the year of publication, separated by a comma. If emphasizing or quoting a specific passage, also cite specific pages using the abbreviation *p.* or *pp.* as necessary:

> Publishing the instructions in a picture-intensive but unconventional medium (e.g., playing cards, wall calendars) could offer "unexpected solutions to such problems as delivering information to remote populations or communicating with inattentive or resistant audiences" (Malone, 2008, p. 59).

In a list titled "References" and organized alphabetically by author's last name (or by authoring organization or by title if no author is identified), detail your sources. If available, include the Digital Object Identifier (DOI), a unique alphanumeric designator of the source's fixed location on the Internet. If the source is available online only but has no DOI, include the URL. If the online source is transitory (e.g., wiki, website), include the date of retrieval.

Book:
Sethi, P. (2009). *Setting international standards: Guidelines for multinational corporations*. New York: Dolphin.

Collection:
Van Pelt, C. (Ed.). (2005). *Visual communication in a digital world*. Boston: Beacon Hill.

Essay or article in a book:
Handa, W., & Felmier, A. (1991). Computer-mediated classrooms: Bridging academic and industry environments. In M. M. Karis & W. M. Lay (Eds.), *Collaborative writing: Investigations in theory and practice* (pp. 170–205). Chicago: Radius.

Article in a professional journal:
Malone, E.A. (2008). The use of playing cards to communicate technical and scientific information. *Technical Communication, 55*, 49-60. doi: 10.4321/TC012345678

Article in a monthly publication:
Raffael, P. (2009, October). Living with gorillas. *Natural Life, 38*, 48–59.

Article in a daily newspaper, anonymous:
Cancer patient gets new therapy. (1999, January 14). *The Los Angeles Tribune*, p. A13.

Government publication:
U.S. Department of the Interior, Minerals Management Service. (2001). *Investigation of fall and fatality, Main Pass Block 140, May 19, 2000* (MMS 2001–042). Washington, DC: GPO.

Article in an online journal:
Rice, K. (2007). A new media approach to teaching classical rhetoric. *Writing Studies, 11* (3). doi: 10.1234/WS9876543210

Article in an online news source:
Ramirez, J. (2007, December 17). Bird flu strikes Nicaragua." *INN.com.* Retrieved from http://www.inn.com/2007/HEALTH/conditions/12/17/hm.flu/index.html

Page of a website:
History of WHO. (2007). World Health Organization. Retrieved May 12, 2007, from http://www.who.int/about/history/en/index.html

Online multimedia source:
Ramirez, J. (2007, December 17). What is bird flu? [Video]. *INN.com.* Retrieved from http://www.inn.com/2007/HEALTH/conditions/12/17/hm.flu/index.html #innSTCVideo

Online posting to e-mail distribution list or bulletin board:
Cooper, G. (2008, October 9). Ethics and professionalism. Message posted to ATTC electronic mailing list, archived at http://lyris.tu.edu/read/messages?id=406780

Appendix C

Annotated Report for Study

The following report was prepared by a member of the Texas A&M Premedical Honor Society. The advisor, Dr. Anderson, had invited students to develop reports on topics of concern to future physicians. Kendra Wheeler, a senior pre-medical student, proposed this report on malpractice. Dr. Anderson accepted her proposal, which appears in Chapter 9.

Her report illustrates effective organization and development of the idea she proposed. Note the integration of her letter of transmittal, summary, table of contents, and discussion. Note also that she uses a casual, conversational style to present her findings.

Kendra Wheeler
400 Nagle St. Apt#200
College Station, TX 77840

April 26, 2007

Mr. Filo Maldonado
Director of Admissions
Texas A&M Health Science Center
College of Medicine

Dear Mr. Maldonado:

As a member of Alpha Epsilon Delta who benefited greatly from this organization during my application process to medical school, I would like to offer the following report to other members of AED. As an interviewer, you know the importance of being familiar with current events in medicine for medical school applicants. I chose the areas of defensive medicine, malpractice, and malpractice insurance as my topics for the report. I believe that these topics will be applicable to other members both for interview purposes and to gain knowledge of issues in the field they hope to enter.

> Opening paragraph states the purpose of the letter and justifies the topic.

Defensive medicine has received an inherently negative connotation. Several definitions of defensive medicine, used simultaneously, confuse the issues. After establishing a definition of defensive medicine, the report examines some of the fears motivating defensive medicine and some of the outcomes of employing it

Malpractice insurance is a major financial burden for physicians. Premiums vary widely between specialties and geographic regions. The recent spike in premium costs has raised a cry for reform but has also revealed the complications faced in determining what factors are driving this spike. The report covers some of the major suspected factors and what can be done to control premium costs in the future.

> Paragraphs 2–4 offer highlights of the main divisions of the report.

Malpractice is a topic that seems to make people in the medical field shiver. Understanding the legal issues, such as negligence and the tort system, is important to understanding new reforms and developments in this area. However, these topics are not necessarily something that undergraduate students are familiar with. These issues are discussed in the report as well as some alternatives to the current tort system.

When I was inducted into AED, I had no idea what the process of applying to medical school looked like. Over the course of my membership, this organization was one of my greatest supports in persevering through the process. When I did not like my classes, the doctors that came to speak reminded me why I was in those classes to begin with. When I was deciding when to take the MCAT and how best to study, the experience of members who had gone through the process before me greatly aided me in choosing the best course of action for me. In honor of these benefits that I have received, I would like to contribute this report to the students coming after me as a resource to better understanding these current issues in the field of medicine.

> Concluding paragraph generates good will.

Thank you for your support as well over these last few years.

Sincerely,

Kendra Wheeler

Medical Malpractice:
Planning for the Worst, Hoping for the Best

Submitted to

Alpha Epsilon Delta

Kendra Wheeler

April 26, 2007

Abstract

Descriptive abstract tells
readers the main content of
the report.

As a future physician, AED students must be aware of current issues in the
medical field. This report is designed to take the complicated issues of defensive
medicine, malpractice insurance, and legal aspects of malpractice and present
essential information in a digestible portion. The report takes information and
interpretations of data from several different sources in an effort to present as
much of the full story as possible. AED students may wish to study more closely
many of the sources used in this report.

Table of Contents

Summary reflects the organization of the paper and discusses the main points presented in the paper.

Summary

Subject and Purpose

Undergraduate students are often so focused on keeping up with their complicated schedules that it is difficult to sort through all of the information on the issues relevant to their future profession. The following report makes an attempt to wade through the statistics and media coverage to aid these future physicians in becoming aware of current issues in the areas of defensive medicine, malpractice insurance, and the ways malpractice is handled in the legal system.

The majority of the information in this report was gathered through a search of the database Academic Search Premier. The sources vary from legal articles to articles from medical journals to news paper articles. Information from interest groups is cited to a limited extent since the information is pertinent, but the objectivity is questionable.

Section 1, as noted in table of contents.

Defensive Medicine

The primary obstacle I faced in interpreting information on defensive medicine was the wide variety of definitions in use. Some definitions, such as the one I used, seem to lend themselves more to allowing researchers to better define their sample populations and the parameters of their research. The government, however, choses a narrower definition that limits defensive medicine to procedures prescribed solely for the purpose of protection from malpractice suits. This definition seemed more difficult to apply conclusively, so I chose the broader definition cited in the report.

Other subtopics discussed were the types of defensive medicine, where it is applicable and/or useful, and other measures that can improve protection against lawsuits. Additionally, some seemingly common misconceptions about malpractice suits are discussed.

Section 2, as noted in table of contents.

Malpractice Insurance

The first issue to be addressed in understanding malpractice is to be comfortable with the legal vocabulary. This is followed by a discussion of the need for malpractice insurance. The most plausible sources of the recent drastic increase in premiums are the stock market recession and subsequent dip in the insurance economic cycle, and an increase in payouts for malpractice suits. I found more detailed sources stating evidence of the economic cycle theory and therefore more heavily emphasized it.

The report also discusses the concept of an insurance crisis, how Texas is handling the situation, and further suggestions on how to control premium prices in the future.

Section 3, as noted in table of contents.

Malpractice and the justice system

The majority of sources that I found discussing the current tort system agreed that it is not accomplishing its goals. After explaining its downfalls, the report offers a few alternatives or additions to the current system that may be able to increase efficiency and effectiveness.

It can be concluded that there is a long road ahead in finding an effective method to handle malpractice cases. The negotiation between doctors, patients, and the legal system is fraught with financial issues and political interests. The surprising contradictions in opinion that I found during research even from reliable sources made me realize that statistics is not an exact science. That is a highly important thing to keep in mind when continuing to observe media reports on these issues.

The best thing for a physician to do in negotiating these topics is to keep and eye out for what works and what does not. The current system does not work- it neither reliably compensates victims of malpractice nor does it offer any real incentive for physicians to provide a high quality of care. The tort reforms being enacted in states like Texas seem to currently be reducing insurance premiums. Other reforms and methods of handling claims have also achieved some amount of success. Defensive medicine itself has a place in protecting the patient, but should be monitored by any practicing physician to ensure that these practices are bringing about the best possible outcome for the patient.

Each section provides the main ideas as these occur in the body of the paper.

iv

Medical Malpractice:
Planning for the Worst, Hoping for the Best

Introduction

"Surgeon leaves sponge in patient—50 billion dollars awarded!" How much is hype, how much is an issue you should be concerned about? Am I going to make it all the way through ten years of medical school and residency only to ruin my career with one wayward sponge? Of course doctors make mistakes. It is called malpractice. They pay hefty insurance premiums to make sure that the repercussions of malpractice do not financially destroy them. Still, there are many things that they can do to protect themselves. The following report makes an attempt to wade through the statistics and media coverage to tell you, as a future physician, what to be aware of current issues in the areas of defensive medicine, malpractice insurance, and ways malpractice is handled in the legal system.

Perspectives on Medical Malpractice

Defensive medicine

Even the name itself seems to have a negative connotation. "Defensive medicine." It sounds like the doctor is putting the goal to protect him or herself first in their practice of medicine. Most of the information I have encountered over the course of my undergraduate career spoke down on defensive medicine for increasing cost with no real benefit to the patient. It seems contradictory then that defensive medicine is reportedly so widely practiced. There are many good physicians out there—why would they be engaging in this practice? One of the primary problems in understanding the use and abuse of defensive medicine is settling on a definition.

A Definition

For the purposes of this paper, the following definition will be used.

> *"Defensive medicine occurs when doctors order tests, procedures, or visits, or avoid high risk patients or procedures, primarily (but not solely) to reduce their exposure to malpractice liability. When physicians do extra tests or procedures primarily to reduce malpractice liability, they are practicing positive defensive medicine. When they avoid certain patients or procedures, they are practicing negative defensive medicine.*[1]*"*

Is defensive medicine really that selfish?

Defensive medicine itself is a fairly neutral concept. The doctor is really the deciding factor. There are several forces driving a doctor's motivation that contribute to the black, white, and shades of gray you will find in trying to discern the intent behind defensive practices. As a future physician, being aware of these factors can help you to be more aware of your own motivations in your practice. As an Aggie and as a future heath care provider, I'll assume you have a sincere desire to serve the needs of your patient to the best of your ability as I tackle this subject.

Black, white, grey, and gray

When evaluating a defensive procedure, it can be categorized in one of four categories. Depending on its impact on cost and how it affects the quality of patient care, it may be classified as:

1. cost reducing/quality raising
2. cost raising/quality raising
3. cost reducing/quality reducing
4. cost raising/quality reducing.[1]

All but the last category have responsible motives outside of protection from malpractice. Type 1 has the most obvious benefit. Often type 2 procedures are necessary to diagnose disease. Type 3 is less desirable but often necessary in situations such as free clinics. In some situations, defensive medicine is a beneficial option:

- when the suspected disease or condition is life threatening or disabling
- when time plays an imminent role in how the disease is treated or the success of the treatment
- when a change in therapy could make a significant difference in the patient's state of health
- when the treatment is readily available at low-risk[1]

In many such situations, the defensive procedure is so ingrained into medical custom that physicians do not even realize the procedure is defensive. When you finally do enter medical school and clinical training, such procedures will probably be passed on to you as the normal protocol. That's ok in many cases. As a patient, if there is a possibility that my ankle is fractured, I would rather get the X-ray than to have a life time of soreness when it does not heal correctly.

Be not afraid

The scariest drivers I have ever ridden with are the ones who drive in constant fear of having a wreck. They hesitate often, frustrate drivers around them, and take precautions that are so unexpected that they make the situation more dangerous. A fearful physician is also dangerous. Fortunately, the media has made the situation look much worse than reality. Most physicians greatly over-estimate their likelihood of being sued. The media has also made the financial to the doctor seem much more significant than they really are. In a following section I will discuss the prevalence of high dollar malpractice suits, but for now let's just say that the media tends to highlight the unusual and more dramatic cases.

Not only are expensive malpractice suits relatively rare, but the physician pays very little during the litigation process. Most of their expenses come from days lost at work. The real cost to a physician comes while paying for their insurance premiums (that will be discussed later as well). In cases where gross negligence is found, regional boards review the case for further action. Then number of physicians who receive additional disciplinary actions is actually rather low[1]. As I said before, I assume that you have a sincere desire to serve your patients to the best of your ability. In that case, there really is no reason to live in fear of a malpractice suit. The following tips should help any well meaning doctor to manage their risks.

---

[1] U.S. Congress, Office of Technology Assessment, *Defensive Medicine and Medical Malpractice,* OTA-H--6O2 (Washington, DC: U.S. Government Printing Office, July 1994). 27–43. 20 Apr. 2007. http://www.wws.princeton.edu/ota/disk1/1994/9405/9405.PDF.

Patients that like you and other ways to not get sued

One doctor that spoke at a past AED meeting stated that he had never been sued (and he was not a young man). He then clarified that it was not because he had never made a mistake. He had even, on one occasion, recommended to his patient that the patient sue him, but in each case his patients had a sufficient relationship with him that they chose not to sue him and continued to trust him for their medical needs. His secret, he said was his doctor-patient relationships, not his perfection as a physician.

A medical practice is a business too. As such, there is pressure to see patients quickly. Depending on who's running the show, it seems that some where between 10 and 15 minutes is an acceptable amount of time to spend with each patient. No matter how much time you spend with each patient, the point to keep in mind is to make them feel that you listened to them and that their concerns are being addressed. This can be achieved through simple interpersonal skills such as eye contact, orienting your body towards the patient, and responding to the patient's concerns with nodding or appropriate comments.

A related aspect of the routine examination is communication. A little small talk during an examination can help your patient to feel more comfortable. Involving personal information transforms the doctor's visit from a business transaction into a personal encounter. The goal is not to exchange life stories, but this additional comfort level can be useful in reaching a diagnosis. Dr. McDermott, a philosophy professor at A&M, gave this example: If a patient enters your office with a wide variety of symptoms, knowing that he is an alcoholic would be useful to your diagnosis. That is not information that comes out during a business transaction. It requires a level of trust between the patient and the doctor. With this trust, a patient is more likely to disclose information that they were either unsure was important or were too embarrassed to report.

This communication can be extended to obtaining informed consent. By taking advantage of open communication to ensure that your patient knows the possible outcomes of a treatment, they are far less likely to be dissatisfied by the outcome. Additionally, thorough documentation of medical record can protect a physician by recording the thought process leading up to treatment.

Beyond individual precautions, a physician can encourage the group or hospital they are working with to develop protocols and communication skills that minimize the possibility of medical errors. Between 44,000 and 98,000 deaths occur every year in the United States due to medical error. The majority of these are not the result of the incompetence of an individual. They are the result of bureaucracy, poor communication, and other obstacles that arise when multiple individuals and groups are joined together to treat one patient. Many of these errors could be prevented by the development of stringent protocols that could enable all involved parties to know what the other parties are doing and why.[2]

This need for defensive medicine indicates that there must be an underlying problem occurring in the medical field today. That problem is malpractice. There are two major issues involved in malpractice. Taking care of the victim of malpractice is the obvious issue. The less obvious issue is how to do this while keeping doctors in business- namely, how to control malpractice insurance premiums.

---

[2] Smith, Christopher. <u>Alternate Solutions for Rising Medical Malpractice Insurance Premiums</u>. American Medical Student Association. 2006. 23 Apr. 2007 http://www.amsa.org/hp/MedMal _AlternateSolutions.pdf.

Malpractice insurance

Lawyer speak

Medical Malpractice is "an act of professional incompetence that results in harm to a client/patient. This includes wrongful action and acts of omission." Malpractice is considered "negligence" meaning that the doctor did something a reasonable person would not do, or failed to do something a reasonable person would do. Negligence falls under the larger label of tort law. Tort is "a wrongful act, intentional or accidental, which causes injury to another.[2]" The media talks about "tort reform" when it talks about caps being put on malpractice awards.

An injured patient has to prove three points to win a malpractice suit:

1. "Show that they were under the medical care of the defending physician.
2. Prove negligence.
3. Prove that the negligence caused their injury.[2]"

> List draws reader's attention to important points about malpractice suits.

If these things are proven, then a monetary award is decided on by the jury. The award is broken down into economic and non-economic damages. Economic damages are the amount of money estimated to have been lost by the patient as a result of the injury, for example, the amount of money lost due to time away from work or required to pay additional medical bills. These awards make up the majority of the amount generally awarded. Non-economic damages include awards from pain and suffering and, possibly punitive damages, or damages specifically meant to punish the defendant.[2]

This is how a lawsuit should go down, ideally. In practice, nothing is so black and white primarily because of how difficult it is to determine medical negligence. "In one study, one-third of experts reviewing cases outside of the courtroom failed to reach consensus on whether negligence was evident." Evidence also suggests that rather than negligence being the definitive factor in a malpractice suit, the severity of patient injury is more predictive of the final price tag.[2]

In any case, the effectiveness of this tort system is being called into question as malpractice premiums dramatically increase and demand reform. The current scapegoat of choice for why premiums are so high is frivolous lawsuits.

> Writer shows good aspects of malpractice insurance before beginning discussion of the bad aspects.

Why malpractice insurance is good

This may seem painfully obvious, but let's keep the objective in mind. A review of medical malpractice insurance rates for the state of Connecticut outlined two purposes for this type of insurance:

1) To protect health care workers from the financial consequences of being found negligent in their practice
2) To compensate the people who suffer from that negligence[3]

These are important goals. Unfortunately, medical malpractice insurance has gotten a bad rap in the medical community. It's not because it isn't accomplishing these goals. It is because, for example, in Texas between 1999 and 2003, the major malpractice insurers increased their rates by an average of 110%[4]. Similar

---

[3] Connecticut. Connecticut General Assembly. The Legislative Program Review and Investigations Committee. Medical Malpractice Insurance Rates Final Report Digest. Feb. 2003. 18 Apr. 2007 http://www.cga.ct.gov/2003/pridata/Studies/Medical_Mal_Final_Report_Digest.htm.

[4] Black, Bernard S., Silver, Charles M., Hyman, David A. and Sage, William M., "Stability, Not Crisis: Medical Malpractice Claim Outcomes in Texas, 1988-2002". U of Texas Law & Economics Research Paper No. 30; Columbia Law & Econ Research Paper No. 270; U Illinois Law & Economics Research Paper No. LE05-002. Available at SSRN: http://ssrn.com/abstract=678601.

drastic increases took place across the country. Malpractice insurance is one of the largest expenses a physician has. Using Ohio as an example, in 2004, it consumed 18% of a physician's income, and averaged $40,385 per doctor per year in premiums[5]. (A premium is the amount paid for insurance coverage.)

What's to blame: frivolous lawsuits or just a moody economic cycle?

Frivolous lawsuits draw a lot of press about frivolous law suits. They sell. Who doesn't remember the woman who spilled her coffee and took McDonald's to the cleaners. Malpractice suits are getting similar coverage. Less than 5% of malpractice suits in Texas between 1988 and 2002 ended in payouts of $1 million or more[4]. Not a huge percentage over 14 years, but they do spice up a headline.

In Texas, we handled this issue by putting a cap on pain and suffering awards. When the media discusses a "cap" on awards for malpractice suits, they are talking about pain and suffering. Awards for quantifiable damages, like economic damages, are not capped. The idea is that insurance companies can make estimates on future expenses by knowing how much it costs to lose time at work or to pay for a hospital stay. Insurers point out that how much a jury will award for "pain and suffering" is not objective enough to foresee. These caps are intended to pay patients for their monetary loss and reduce "frivolousness" of pain and suffering awards for insurers. Texas heralds their cap as a success now that insurance rates in the states have stabilized, insurers are entering the market, and a flood of doctors is applying for licensure from out of state. Are rising payouts really the only factor in drastic premium increases?

Not as much as the media has led us to believe. If increasing payouts for malpractice suit awards are the culprit, then we would expect to see an increase in those payouts that coincides with rising premiums. The following figure, Figure 1, tracks premiums and awards. "DPW" stands for Direct Premiums Written, the amount of money insurers received as premiums that year. "Paid losses" refers to what insurance companies paid in settlements and claims in addition to what they paid in legal fees.

Figure 1

> Note that figure is clear in its relationship to the content. Also, source of the graphics appears below the figure.

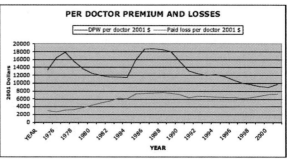

Sources:
A.M. Best and Co. special data compilation for AIR, reporting data for as many years as separately available; U.S. Bureau of the Census, 1975 (2001 Estimated)[2]; Inflation Index: Bureau of Labor Statistics, 1975 (1985 estimated).

---

[5] Denise, Trowbridge. "Malpractice Insurance Rates Decline." <u>The Columbus Dispatch, Ohio</u> 11 Nov. 2006. 18 Apr. 2007 http://web.lexis-nexis.com.ezproxy.tamu.edu:2048/universe/document?_m=b7a22b7166849c73eee69e369406bd14&_docnum=2&wchp=dGLbVtz-zSkVA&_md5=af09555038176070d6c522cf3a74b488.

Rather than rise drastically, malpractice payouts have been rising at roughly the rate of inflation.[6] Where then do the peaks and valleys of premium costs come from?

Insurers have another source of income other than premiums. The insurance cycle, or how well insurance companies are profiting, is heavily dependent on the stock market. As I said before, they invest the money received as premiums. When interest rates on their stocks are high and the market is booming, investment income increases and this is called a "soft market". Insurers may even lower rates during these periods because whatever they lose in premiums can be more than recovered in investments. This also increases competition between insurance providers and further lowers the rates. This happened through most of the 90's, with a small dip around 1992 after Hurricane Andrew. Insurance companies lost money in payouts, but the over all economy was fairly stable, so there was no subsequent spike in premiums.

When the stock market busts and interest rates on stocks drop, insurers suddenly find themselves with decreased investment income and premium rates that are too low to compensate[6]. This is called a "hard market." Insurers may even leave the malpractice market due to loses, reducing competition for market share and, therefore, competitiveness of rates.

The following figure, Figure 2, is a depiction of the insurance cycle from a slightly narrower time frame than Figure 1.

Figure 2

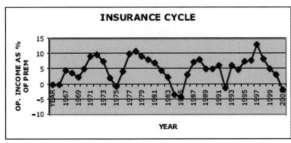

Source:
Medical Malpractice Insurance: Stable Losses/Unstable Rates. Americans for Insurance Reform. 2002. 18 Apr. 2007 http://www.insurance-reform.org/StableLosses.pdf.

It looks suspicious doesn't it? On Figure 2 in 1975, the insurance cycle crashes. On Figure 1 in 1976, the first peak in premiums begins. Nineteen eighty-five marks another huge dip in the insurance cycle. By 1986, the corresponding peak in premiums is undeniable. The figures stop just after 2000, but I think we all remember 9/11 and the subsequent frenzy about a stock market bust. Insurers paid out 40 billion dollars following 9/11[7], making the previously noted 110% premium increase for Texas in 2003 make a little more sense—the insurance cycle was plummeting.

But for every source that preaches the gospel of the insurance cycle, another relates evidence that the amount of money insurers are losing in payouts really

---

[6] Medical Malpractice Insurance: Stable Losses/Unstable Rates. Americans for Insurance Reform. 2002. 18 Apr. 2007 http://www.insurance-reform.org/StableLosses.pdf.

[7] Treaster, Joseph B., and Joel Brinkley. "Behind Those Medical Malpractice Rates." The New York Times 22 Feb. 2005. 18 Apr. 2007 http://proquest.umi.com/pqdlink?did=796017261& Fmt=3&clientId =2945&RQT=309&VName=PQD.

is pushing insurers out of the malpractice market. The issue becomes even more complicated when reserve fund mismanagement, reinsurance costs, and medical care inflation are taken into account[2]. During soft market periods, revenue is put into reserve funds to be kept for times when the market is hard. If this is not done properly, premiums must rise to make up for losses. Reinsurance, insurance for insurance companies, keeps costs during a given year below a certain limit and also limits losses per year. After 9/11, insurers lost so much money in payouts, that reinsurance suffered as well.[8] According to the AMSA, once the average malpractice claim payments between 1991 and 2003 are adjusted for medical care inflation, they rose only 22% as opposed to the total increase of 110%[2]. Those are just a few of the issues that can turn your head in circles. One at a time, each issue can make a convincing argument in which ever direction the author chooses.

The moral of the story is that there is more to the monster than an increase in claim payouts. A good starting point to negotiate these issues is to just look at the current state of affairs.

How bad is it, Doc?

At the beginning of 2007, the American Medical Association classified 17 states as being in a medical liability crisis. A medical liability crisis is where liability pressures lead to decreased access to medical care. The following figure, Figure 3, illustrates the current status of each state.

Figure 3

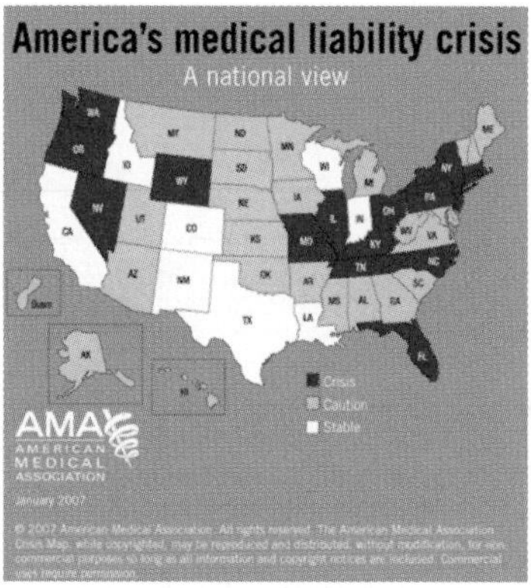

Several contributing pressures cause this decrease in care. Many physicians are choosing to retire early, relocate, or are no longer performing high risk procedures[9]. In some areas, doctors have even gone on strikes[2]. Fields of medicine that are high risk such as obstetrics and general surgery are harder hit than most. In southern Florida, the most expensive place in the country to practice medicine, these two fields paid $280,000 for malpractice insurance in 2004[7]. Dead or injured babies rightly pull on the heart strings of any jury, but a woman with a high risk pregnancy still needs a doctor. If obstetricians are avoiding high

---

[8] Henley, Eric. "Malpractice Crisis: Causes of Escalating Insurance Premiums, and Implications for You." The Journal of Family Practice 55 (2006): 703-706. 20 Apr. 2007 http://search.ebscohost .com/login.aspx?direct=true&db=aph&AN=22379896&site=ehost-live.

[9] "Medical Liability Crisis Map." 20 Dec. 2006. 20 Apr. 2007 http://www.ama-assn.org/ama/ noindex/category/print/11871.html.

risk procedures, how do you get these procedures done when they are needed? That is why this is a crisis.

"You may all go to Hell, and I will go to Texas."—Davy Crockett

This may be an applicable motto as physicians flee from rising rates in their former states and try to flood Texas as a result of the implementation of the non-economic medical malpractice cap. According to the Texas Medical Association, this tort reform creating a cap at $250,000 resulted in a 17% decrease in malpractice insurance rates for physicians[10]. A piece of legislation that's doing its job!

But are we treating the symptoms or finding the cure? "Stability, not crisis: Medical Malpractice Claim Outcomes in Texas, 1988-2002" in the *Journal of Empirical Legal Studies* presents a detailed break down of malpractice claims paid between 1988 and 2002. After summarizing their findings in the introduction, the authors state, "This evidence suggests that no crisis involving malpractice claim outcomes occurred... litigation reforms may not prevent future insurance crises." However, other sources site data that indicates that states with caps have significantly smaller premium growth rates[2].

So yes, as yearly insurance premiums are dropping by tens of thousands of dollars, legislators may deservedly throw themselves a party and exchange a few high fives, but not over the long term. "Who cares about the long term?" you may ask. You do. As premedical students, you have at least 7 more years of school beyond the bounds of your undergraduate career. Excluding the economic boom of the 90's, the insurance cycle bottoms out roughly every 10 years. Freshmen, that would put the next "crisis" right around the time that you will be finishing your residencies and hoping to start making the money that will pay off your student loans. Current doctors are excited by these reforms and the $10,000+ per year that they are getting to keep in their wallets. This will be your issue.

Stabilizing malpractice insurance . . . forever.

If only it were that easy. There are, however, some steps that can be taken to insure future stability, if we don't rest on our laurels.

California is often heralded as a model for stability in medical malpractice insurance. It was one of the first states to cap non-economic damages[9] (1975) and made the shift from one of the most expensive places to practice medicine to one of the least. But they didn't stop with a damage cap. In 1988, they prohibited insurers "from raising rates more than 15% a year with out a public hearing."[5] During an insurance crisis, the percent increase in rates per year often far exceeds this 15% limit in states without this restriction. Limiting the percent increase of premiums is one step that can be taken.

The committee reviewing medical malpractice insurance rates in Connecticut made additional suggestions. While it supported a cap on pain and suffering damages (non-economic) it also suggested implementing an immediate premium assistance fund to aid physicians who could not otherwise get insurance in order to act quickly in alleviating the issue[3]. In the current climate where the press emphasizes frivolous suits, a cap on pain and suffering seems like an obvious choice. It leaves the option open for the patient to still financially recover from medical bills incurred through medical negligence and monetary losses from time lost at work. It does not, however, take into consideration the situations of children and the elderly. With no time lost at work, there are fewer dollar signs hanging over their heads to attract lawyers to their case.

---

[10] "Proposition 12 Produces Healthy Benefits." <u>Texas Medical Association</u>. 15 Feb. 2007. 22 Apr. 2007 http://www.texmed.org/Template.aspx?id=780.

To encourage competitive rates, the committee also suggested increased competitiveness of the malpractice insurance market. During an insurance crisis, insurers often leave the market in pursuit of more lucrative areas. By attracting new insurers to compete for a market share, rates tend to cater more to the interests of the customer.

As a long term suggestion, the committee proposed a more stringent continuing education program. Although this does not directly address insurance rates, it does help to address the over all goal of the tort system. The *Journal of Family Practice* states, "In theory, a tort system to resolve malpractice claims is supposed to serve as a negative incentive to physicians to practice high quality medicine.[8]" It goes on to point out, "Unlike auto insurance, malpractice premiums are mainly determined by the class of physician and geography, rather than by an individual's practice experience." Is a negative incentive really the most effective way to ensure a high quality of medical practice? If high quality is what we are looking for, perhaps a more developed system of continued education would better address the issue.

Malpractice and the justice system

The tort system: More effective than an English pastry?

The committee in Connecticut is not the only group questioning the effectiveness of the tort system. In fact, in an article from the American Medical Student Association they label it as a failure. Here's why: "A review of 30,000 randomly selected medical records found that only 1.5% of adverse outcomes due to negligence resulted in malpractice claims." The same article estimated that 40-60% of tort awards actually went toward administrative costs (aka lawyers) meaning the patient only gets about half. It is not effectively compensating wrongfully injured patients.

Neither is it acting as a deterrent towards malpractice itself. Although the data in this area is complicated and incomplete, it does seem to indicate that there is little correlation between a history of malpractice and deterrence. Since a system of experience based premiums was found to be too complicated to implement, individual performance has no effect on premium rates[2]. Most physicians are required by law to have malpractice insurance. If a physician is involved with a lawsuit, their insurance covers the fees and any awards leaving the physician with almost none of the financial burden[1]. The tort system, then, provides no incentive for a physician to improve, while competent physicians foot the bill through high premiums.

Not only are the right physicians not paying up, but also the system may be targeting the wrong group of people. If a doctor makes a negligent mistake, they should, by all means, receive disciplinary action through the court system. However, according to the AMSA, the majority of medical errors are the result of systematic obstacles such as the bureaucracy of a hospital or breakdowns in communication between the army of health care workers usually involved in the care of each patient. Since 44,000-98,000 patients are estimated to die every year due to medical errors, why is there not a stronger outcry for more effective patient safety?

Also disturbing is how questionable it is whether or not the outcome of a lawsuit is related to the negligence of the doctor. As stated before, establishing negligence is not an exact science. Not only that, but evidence shows that there is significantly more correlation between severity of the injury to damages received that there is between negligence and damages received[2]. No wonder doctors are shying away from high risk procedures. Perhaps it is time for a new approach. The following are some alternatives discussed by the AMSA[2].

9

No-fault insurance

One of the most immediately obvious differences between the tort system and no-fault insurance is that there is no need to determine negligence. That would be useful if in one-third of cases experts cannot come to a consensus on this issue. The idea is similar to workmen's compensation. Whenever a patient is the victim of adverse but preventable events, whether or not negligence was involved, they would go before a panel that would use a set of guidelines to compensate the victim. One major draw back of this system is that it increases the availability of financial compensation and still lacks a source of funding. Fortunately, the design does remove legal fees from the picture, meaning the money goes more towards patients.

One major hope with this system is that, without the threat of malpractice lawsuits, error reporting would become more widely adhered to. With more accurate data on how and where errors occur, it would be easier to improve patient safety. This system also could be more easily applied to enterprise liability, meaning that institutions such as hospitals are liable rather than individual doctors. If that were the case, there is greater hope for a shift towards experience-rated malpractice premiums, whereas that sort of system is too complicated when applied to individual physicians. As an added bonus, the current no-fault system in Sweden takes an average of 6 months to process, far less than a tort case. Models such as the system used in Sweden suggest positive results in improving the compensation system. The main obstacle to this sort of reform seems to be lack of political interest in such drastic reforms, although small scale no-fault insurance programs have been enacted in a few states.

Mediation

Mediation is not as widely applicable as the tort system or a no-fault system. It is primarily a method of opening the lines of communication between conflicting parties and would not cover cases with serious financial aspects. This method of dispute resolution is aimed at consoling patients who just want a thorough explanation of events, an apology, and corrective measures to prevent harm to future patients. Because mediation is based on confidentiality, there is little evidence one way or the other on its effectiveness. The primary success of this method would be expected to be higher patient satisfaction, better doctor-patient relationships, and improved communication. It requires significantly less time and money than other methods of dispute resolution, but it also does not remove the need for those other methods. It seems that mediation is widely over looked because, as a method of reducing cost, it probably would make little impact and is not a safe enough investment.

Arbitration

Arbitration is an informal trial in which there is no jury and a neutral third party makes a legally binding decision. Arbitration awards cannot generally be overturned, so arbitration would not be a good choice for cases of high importance. By agreeing to arbitration, a patient waves their right to a jury trial. There is a concern that arbitration is biased towards the physician and that the patient is at a disadvantage without a jury. Some of the advantages of arbitration are that it is faster, simpler, cheaper, and that arbitrators are informed enough to have a deeper understanding of the situation than a jury.

Screening panels

These panels examine claims prior to their entry into the litigation system. The intent is to filter out frivolous cases while encouraging valid claims. However their evaluation is non-binding. The panel generally consists of medical professionals, attorneys, judges, and possibly patient advocates. One major drawback to this process is that it adds time to an already lengthy litigation process if the case is deemed valid. Valid or invalid, the ruling of the panel is non-binding and therefore seems to have little effect on whether or not a claim proceeds to litigation. This method may even encourage frivolous cases by providing an avenue for testing to see if a case will hold up in court. If adhered to, however, panels offer the opportunity for a well informed group to filter out claims before they reach a less well informed jury. Their rulings can also be used as expert testimony.

A few viable options could modify or replace the current tort system. All have pros and cons, but the only way to improve is to try something different.

Note that if you look at only the headings and subheadings, they reveal the outline and major topics of the report.

Conclusions

Physicians will find a long road ahead as the justice system finds an effective method to handle malpractice cases. The negotiation between doctors, patients, and the legal system is fraught with financial issues and political interests. The surprising contradictions in opinion that I found during research even from reliable sources made me realize that statistics is not an exact science. That is a highly important thing to keep in mind when continuing to observe media reports on these issues.

One paragraph for each of the three main topic discussed in the report.

Defensive medicine has its place in the medical field. It can increase the quality of patient care and reduce costs if properly applied. It may also reduce the risk of malpractice suits, but must be monitored to insure that it does not become the sole motivator at the expense of quality and cost of care. There are also several other things that physicians can do beyond defensive medicine to reduce risk of lawsuits and improve patient care such as spending more time with patients, better communication, more detailed medical records, and establishing strict protocols in health care environments.

Malpractice insurance is a beast that reappears periodically. While tort reform temporarily eases the strain of skyrocketing insurance premiums, other options like government aid, limits on increases in rates per year, and encouraging competitive rates through increased competition in the insurance market should also be pursued.

To address the broader issue of how malpractice claims are handled, the tort system must be examined. The goals of the tort system have not been met, and therefore, reforms and alternative dispute resolution methods should be explored.

Recommendations

The best direction for a physician to follow in negotiating these issues is to keep and eye out for what works and what does not. The current system does not work—it neither reliably compensates victims of malpractice nor does it offer any real incentive for physicians to provide a high quality of care. The tort reforms being enacted in states like Texas seem to be working currently. Other reforms and methods of handling claims have also achieved some amount of success. Defensive medicine itself has a place in protecting the patient, but should be monitored by any practicing physician to ensure that these practices are bringing about the best possible outcome for the patient. Over all, the primary goal should be to increase patient safety.

Works Cited

Black, Bernard S., Silver, Charles M., Hyman, David A. and Sage, William M., "Stability, Not Crisis: Medical Malpractice Claim Outcomes in Texas, 1988-2002". U of Texas Law & Economics Research Paper No. 30; Columbia Law & Econ Research Paper No. 270; U Illinois Law & Economics Research Paper No. LE05-002. Available at SSRN: http://ssrn.com/abstract=678601.

Connecticut. Connecticut General Assembly. The Legislative Program Review and Investigations Committee. Medical Malpractice Insurance Rates Final Report Digest. Feb. 2003. 18 Apr. 2007 http://www.cga.ct.gov/2003/pridata/ Studies/Medical_Mal_Final_Report_Digest.htm.

Henley, Eric. "Malpractice Crisis: Causes of Escalating Insurance Premiums, and Implications for You." The Journal of Family Practice 55 (2006): 703-706. 20 Apr. 2007 http://search.ebscohost.com/login.aspx?direct =true&db=aph&AN=22379896&site=ehost-live.

"Medical Liability Crisis Map." American Medical Association. 20 Dec. 2006. 20 Apr. 2007 http://www.ama-assn.org/ama/noindex/category/print/11871.html.

Medical Malpractice Insurance: Stable Losses/Unstable Rates. Americans for Insurance Reform. 2002. 18 Apr. 2007 http://www.insurance-reform.org/ StableLosses.pdf.

"Proposition 12 Produces Healthy Benefits." Texas Medical Association. 15 Feb. 2007. 22 Apr. 2007 http://www.texmed.org/Template.aspx?id=780.

Smith, Christopher. Alternate Solutions for Rising Medical Malpractice Insurance Premiums. American Medical Student Association. 2006. 23 Apr. 2007 http://www.amsa.org/hp/MedMal_AlternateSolutions.pdf.

Treaster, Joseph B., and Joel Brinkley. "Behind Those Medical Malpractice Rates." The New York Times 22 Feb. 2005. 18 Apr. 2007 http://proquest .umi.com/pqdlink?did=796017261&Fmt=3&clientId =2945&RQT =309&VName=PQD.

Trowbridge ,Denise. "Malpractice Insurance Rates Decline." The Columbus Dispatch, Ohio 11 Nov. 2006. 18 Apr. 2007 http://web.lexis-nexis.com.ezproxy .tamu.edu:2048/universe/document?_m=b7a22b7166849c73eee69e369406 bd14&_docnum=2&wchp=dGLbVtz-zSkVA&_md5=af09555038176070 d6c522cf3a74b488.

U.S. Congress, Office of Technology Assessment, Defensive Medicine and Medical Malpractice, OTA-H--6O2 (Washington, DC: U.S. Government Printing Office, July 1994). 27–43. 20 Apr. 2007. http://www.wws.princeton.edu/ota/ disk1/1994/9405/9405.PDF.

Subject Index